A Global Agenda

Issues before the 59th General Assembly
of the United Nations

Edited by Angela Drakulich

Published by the United Nations Association
of the United States of America

New York, New York

UNITED NATIONS ASSOCIATION, USA, Inc.

Published in the United States of America
by the United Nations Association of the United States of America.
801 Second Avenue, New York, NY 10017

Copyright © 2004 by the United Nations Association of the United States of America, Inc.

ISBN 1-880632-69-1
LCCN 2004090622

Editor: Angela Drakulich.
Designer: Charlotte Staub.
Copyeditor: Dulcie Leimbach.

Contributing Editors: Barbara Crossette, Suzanne DiMaggio, Steven A. Dimoff, Anne
    Heindel, William H. Luers, Paul Underwood, John Washburn and Lawrence Woocher.

Researchers: Olivia Cobiskey, Adam Godet, Marissa Koch, Shanthi Manian, Kristine
    McNeil, Crystal Proenza, Consuelo Remmert and Jennifer Uscher.

Cover photos of the World Health Assembly in Geneva and U.N. Headquarters cour-
    tesy of WHO/P.Virot and UN/DPI.

Printed in the United States of America

Contents

Charts and Tables

Contributors

Ishtiaq Ahmad (Peacekeeping in Asia) is vice chair of the Department of International Relations at Eastern Mediterranean University, North Cyprus. A former Pakistani journalist, Dr. Ahmad worked for two English-language newspapers, *The Nation* and *The Muslim*, and served as a research fellow at the Area Study Center of Quaid-e-Azam University in Islamabad. Dr. Ahmad is the author of *Gulbuddin Hekmatyar: An Afghan Trail from Jihad to Terrorism* (2004) and co-author of *India and Pakistan: Charting a Path to Peace* (2004).

Assefaw Bariagaber (Peacekeeping in Africa) is an associate professor at the John C. Whitehead School of Diplomacy and International Relations of Seton Hall University, in New Jersey. He has written several articles on conflicts and refugee formations in Africa for publications such as the *Journal of Modern African Studies*, *International Migration* and *Ethnic and Racial Studies*. Dr. Bariagaber serves as an associate editor of the *Eritrean Studies Review*.

Simon Chesterman (Reform) is executive director of the Institute for International Law and Justice at the New York University School of Law. He is the author of, among other books, *You, the People: The United Nations, Transitional Administration and State-Building* (2004); and *Just War or Just Peace? Humanitarian Intervention and International Law* (2001).

Roger A. Coate (Development) is director of the Richard L. Walker Institute of International Studies and a professor of international organization at the University of South Carolina. The author of numerous books and articles on the U.N. and international organization, Dr. Coate directs the Transforming Global Governance for the 21st Century: Creating Effective Partnerships with Civil Society Project. This large-scale transnational collaborative research and training program is done in cooperation with the Academic Council on the U.N. System and the Office of the U.N. Secretary-General.

Olivia Cobiskey (Millennium Development Goals) is a UNA-USA intern. She has a master's degree in public-affairs reporting from Columbia College in Chicago and a certificate in Islamic Civilization: Government and Politics from Northeastern Illinois University. She has written for, among other publications, the *Chicago Tribune*, *Los Angeles Times* and *Saudi Gazette*.

Lorna Davidson (Human Rights) is a senior associate at Human Rights First (formerly the Lawyers Committee for Human Rights). Previously, she worked at Columbia Law School, the International Crisis Group and No Peace Without Justice on projects documenting war crimes and other violations of international humanitarian law committed in Kosovo. With a master's degree in law from the University of Cambridge and Columbia Law School, Ms. Davidson has also worked in the Chambers of the International Criminal Tribunal for the former Yugoslavia.

Jonathan Dean (Disarmament) is adviser on International Security Issues for the Union of Concerned Scientists (UCS), one of the largest science-based NGOs in the United States. A former ambassador, Mr. Dean's primary focus at UCS is on nuclear disarmament, including the U.S. administration's missile defense program and weaponization of space. He is chairman of the Task Force on Peace and Security of the UNA-USA/National Capital Area and co-founder of Global Action to Prevent War, a coalition-building effort of civil society and governments to stop war and armed conflict.

Jacques Fomerand (Humanitarian Assistance) served in the U.N. Secretariat's Department of Economic and Social Affairs from 1977 to 1992. From 1992 to 2003, when he retired from U.N. service, Dr. Fomerand was director of the U.N. University Office in North America. He now teaches at John Jay College of the City University of New York and Occidental College. He has been widely published on matters related to the functioning of the U.N. and is completing a Dictionary of the United Nations.

Amy Frumin (Peacekeeping in Europe) worked as a political-affairs officer in the Office of the Special-Representative of the Secretary-General in Kosovo from 2001 to 2002. She has a master's degree from the London School of Economics and Political Science, and has also worked in the Office of Emergency Operations at UNICEF. Most recently, Ms. Frumin wrote a special report on Afghanistan for the Center for Strategic and International Studies and served as an election monitor for the November 2003 elections in Georgia.

Adam Godet (Peacekeeping in the Americas / Looming Conflicts) is a UNA-USA intern and a graduate student at the John C. Whitehead School of Diplomacy and International Relations at Seton Hall University, where he is specializing in International Economics/Finance and the Middle East. Mr. Godet has studied political philosophy at St. John's College in Annapolis, and has a bachelor's degree in English and philosophy from Hartwick College, in New York.

Gordon M. Goldstein (Peacekeeping in the Middle East) is a managing director at Clark & Weinstock, a government relations and management consulting firm. A former international security adviser to the U.N. Strategic Planning Unit and a former adviser to the Global Compact Unit of the Executive Office of the U.N. Secretary-General, Dr. Goldstein served as a

Columbia University International Fellow. His articles have appeared in the *New York Times, Newsweek, Washington Post* and other publications.

Neal Higgins (International Law) is an attorney who recently joined the staff of John Kerry for President. He was previously an associate at Sullivan & Cromwell and a member of the trial team prosecuting Slobodan Milosevic for crimes committed in Kosovo in 1999. A graduate of Princeton University's Woodrow Wilson School, the Fletcher School of Law and Diplomacy and Harvard Law School, Mr. Higgins has served on the editorial staff at *Foreign Affairs* and was a Rosenthal Fellow on minority staff at the U.S. House of Representatives International Relations Committee.

Yanzhong Huang (Global Health) is an assistant professor and director of the Center for Global Health Studies at the John C. Whitehead School of Diplomacy and International Relations at Seton Hall University. His most recent publications include a monograph, "Mortal Peril: Public Health in China and its Security Implications" (2003). In May 2003, Dr. Huang testified before the Congressional-Executive Commission on China regarding the politics of SARS. Dr. Huang holds a Ph.D. in political science from the University of Chicago.

International Crisis Group Research Unit (Looming Conflicts) is an independent, not-for-profit, multinational organization with more than 100 staff members on five continents. ICG, which assisted with the research and production of the Looming Conflicts section of this book, works through field-based analysis and high-level advocacy to prevent and resolve deadly conflicts around the world.

Gail Karlsson (Sustainable Development) is a lawyer specializing in international environmental law. She is currently working as a consultant to the U.N. Development Programme, where she recently designed and facilitated a training course on environmental policy and sustainable development. She is also the New York coordinator for the Citizens Network for Sustainable Development.

Ilona Kickbusch (Global Health) is a professor of Global Health at Yale University's School of Medicine, Department of Epidemiology and Public Health. At present, she is on a leave of absence and serving as a senior adviser on Millennium Development Goals and Health Targets to the Director of the Pan American Health Organization. Before joining Yale, Dr. Kickbusch had a distinguished career with the World Health Organization (WHO), where she initiated the Ottawa Charter for Health Promotion, the WHO Healthy Cities project and other worldwide programs. She has received many awards for her publications, and is a member of a wide range of boards and advisory groups.

Ethan Kunz (Millennium Development Goals) is the Millennium Development Goals Project Coordinator for the World Federation of United Nations

Associations. As a public policy consultant, Mr. Kunz has contributed to strategic planning projects in the United States, written environmental law in Micronesia and collaborated on community development efforts for Togo, Africa.

LEE Jong-wook (Prologue) is Director-General of the U.N. World Health Organization. He took started his five-year term in July 2003. Previously, Dr. Lee worked for the WHO at the country, regional and headquarters level for 19 years, notably leading the fight against tuberculosis and vaccine preventable diseases for children. Dr. Lee holds a medical degree from Seoul National University and a master's degree from the University of Hawaii.

Edward C. Luck (U.S.-U.N. Relations) is professor of practice and director of the Center on International Organization at Columbia University's School of International and Public Affairs. From 1984 to 1994, he was president of UNA-USA. Dr. Luck has served as a senior consultant to the U.N. Department of Administration and Management and staff director of the U.N. General Assembly's working group on strengthening the U.N. system. His recent books include *Reforming the United Nations: Lessons from a History in Progress* (2003) and *Mixed Messages: American Politics and International Organization, 1919-1999* (1999).

David Lynch (Global Trade) is an associate professor of political science at Saint Mary's University, in Minnesota. With a doctorate from the University of California, Santa Barbara, Dr. Lynch's published works have focused on American trade policy, the World Trade Organization and regional trade agreements such as the North American Free Trade Agreement.

Anthony Mango (Finance and Administration) worked for the U.N. Secretariat from 1960 to 1987 and the U.N. Pension Board from 1983 to 1987. Between 1970 and 1983, he headed the Secretariat of the Advisory Committee on Administrative and Budgetary Questions. Since retiring, he has continued to consult for the U.N. and recently edited the third edition of the *Encyclopedia of the United Nations and International Agreements* (2003).

Thomas E. McNamara (Terrorism) began teaching at George Washington University's Elliott School in May 2003. A retired career diplomat, he was asked to return to the Department of State after September 11, 2001, and since then has served as a senior adviser on terrorism and homeland security to the Secretary and Under Secretary. Ambassador McNamara previously worked as Assistant Secretary of State; Special Negotiator for Panama; Ambassador-at-Large for Counter Terrorism; Special Assistant to the President; Ambassador to Colombia; NSC Director; and other senior positions. From 1998 to 2001, he was president and chief executive of the Americas Society and of the Council of the Americas.

Lea Payne (Global Health) works on a freelance basis for global health projects. Most recently, she has worked with the U.N. Development Programme

(UNDP), Pfizer Inc., Global Reporting Initiative and the World Bank's Business Partners for Development. She holds a master's degree from Yale University. Her recent articles include "21st Century Health Promotion: The Public Health Revolution Meets the Wellness Revolution" (*Health Promotion International*); "A Community of Practice for Pro-Poor Public-Private Partnerships (*UNDP*); and "Promoting a Private Sector Response to HIV/AIDS in Sub-Saharan Africa" (*AIDS Analysis Africa*, a South African-based journal).

Consuelo Remmert (Drug Trafficking) is a UNA-USA intern. She has a bachelor's degree from Columbia University and currently works for the U.N. Department of Public Information. She also writes for the *U.N. Chronicle*.

Samir Sanbar (Arab Development) is the former U.N. Assistant Secretary-General for Public Information and head of the Department of Public Information. He served under five Secretaries-General, from U Thant to Kofi Annan, over 33 years. An internationalist by commitment and journalist by profession, he initiated a series of gatherings while he was at the United Nations, bringing together creative artists, communicators and public figures from around the world to encourage dialogue among professionals and communication among cultures.

Jyoti Sanghera (Trafficking) is the adviser on trafficking at the U.N. Office of the High Commissioner for Human Rights in Geneva. Before that, she worked as an adviser on trafficking and migration with UNICEF, the U.N. Children's Fund, in South Asia and in New York. Dr. Sanghera has taught for several years in the department of Women's Studies at the University of Victoria.

Pera Wells (Millennium Development Goals) is Deputy Secretary-General of the World Federation of United Nations Associations. A writer, businesswoman and civil-society activist, Ms. Wells has served as a diplomat in Ghana, India, London (the Commonwealth Secretariat) and at the U.N. in New York.

Lawrence Woocher (U.N. Reform) is the program manager for UNA-USA's Global Policy Programs. Previously, he worked as a research associate at the Belfer Center for Science and International Affairs at Harvard University. Mr. Woocher holds a master's degree from Harvard's Kennedy School of Government.

Prologue

Health touches everyone everywhere, at any moment. The enjoyment of the highest attainable standard of health "for every human being without distinction of race, religion, political belief or economical or social condition" is a guiding principle of the United Nations World Health Organization (WHO). This was true in 1946 during the signing of WHO's constitution, after the world saw the most destructive war of the 20th century, and it is still true today.

Peace, security and justice as cornerstones of civilization and development provide the framework for establishing global health. As a result, achieving global health has become one of the driving forces for the attainment of solidarity and equity among people and societies all over the globe.

Unfortunately, unequal development in the promotion of health and control of disease contributes to discontent, and it is becoming a common danger in the fragile balance of understanding the definition of well-being and the sharing of the world's resources. Developments of the past 25 years in global health have taught us valuable lessons. We have achieved longer life spans in many countries; we have eradicated smallpox; and we are working hard to eradicate polio. On the other hand, however, we have seen emerging and re-emerging diseases like HIV/AIDS, SARS (Severe Acute Respiratory Syndrome), malaria and tuberculosis, as well as mental health problems and threats to health originating from crisis situations and environmental degradation. Countries with inadequate health systems are coping with an ever-growing demand on health services—and the gap between expectation and reality is widening.

Diseases are not restricted by borders. The experience recently gained from SARS has shown once more the value of international control and regulation mechanisms. Fast detection and swift response to outbreaks are crucially important in a world where migration is increasing and traveling is a daily business. It has become clear that sharing information and knowledge as the basis for informed decision-making has become one of the core management techniques for addressing global health problems.

As a result, in recent years, we have seen the U.N. General Assembly focus on health issues. Malaria, HIV/AIDS, SARS and most recently, road safety, have all been debated. Above all, the U.N. *Millennium Declaration* set ambitious goals for health at the beginning of the 21st century as part of a framework for human development. About half the goals, targets and indicators are directly or indirectly related to health and human well-being. As you will find in the following pages, WHO works to support national efforts for achieving each of these goals.

I would like to express our appreciation to the United Nations Association of the United States of America for its longstanding attention to global health issues, and hope you will find this edition of *Global Agenda* not only informative but also engaging and enriching.

LEE Jong-wook
Director-General, World Health Organization

Introduction

A s the United Nations heads into its 60th year—2005—it is an under-
statement to say that its member states have a full plate of issues to
contend with. The past year and upcoming year, in particular, have circled
around a whirlwind of claims, debates and, ultimately, strikes against weapons
of mass destruction, most notably in the United-States-led war against Saddam Hussein's regime. The developments leading up to the war and the
actions—and reactions—that have occurred since are covered in detail in
Chapter 5 by Ambassador Jonathan Dean. But rather than focus solely on
Iraq—as the media and as a result, the world public, have done over the past
year—this book aims to delve into the many other issues before the United
Nations, its member states and various agencies and organs.

Most pertinent among these "other" issues, as pointed out by Secretary-
General Kofi Annan at the launching of the Global AIDS Media initiative, is
HIV/AIDS, which he said "has become a devastating obstacle to development," and therefore, must remain a priority. The world must "engage
...powerful organizations as full partners in the fight to halt HIV/AIDS
through awareness, prevention and education," said the S.G. in January
2004. In addition, U.S. President George W. Bush has made combating
HIV/AIDS a U.S. priority with the establishment of his Emergency Plan for
AIDS Relief in 2003. This five-year initiative allocates $15 billion to help
treat at least 2 million HIV-infected persons with antiretroviral therapy, prevent 7 million new infections and care for 10 million persons infected with
or affected by HIV, including orphans and vulnerable children in 14 countries in Africa and the Caribbean.

For these reasons and more, we have devoted this 2004-2005 edition of
Global Agenda to health, beginning with World Health Organization (WHO)
Director-General LEE Jong-wook's prologue. Taking office in July 2003, Dr.
Lee has worked for the organization for nearly 20 years, notably leading the
fight against tuberculosis and vaccine-preventable diseases of children. Fol-
lowing this introduction, in Chapter 1, authors Ilona Kickbush and Lea
Payne take us through not only the history of U.N. efforts in health issues,
but also the current and future health challenges before the world body.
From endemic diseases such as HIV/AIDS, malaria and tuberculosis to new

deadly viruses such as SARS and avian influenza to controversies over tobacco-addiction and cloning, the U.N. General Assembly clearly has a wide agenda. As demonstrated in this first chapter, U.N. agencies such as WHO, the Joint U.N. Programme on HIV/AIDS, the U.N. Children's Fund, the World Food Programme, the U.N. Educational, Scientific and Cultural Organization and various other international organizations and governments are working night and day to address these issues.

To further highlight the importance of health on the global agenda, we have paid special attention to numerous health-related issues, such as the section on ageing in Chapter 2, the section on adolescent health in Chapter 3, the section on drug demand in Chapter 5, the section on getting affordable medicines to developing countries in Chapter 7 and the section on gay and lesbian partner benefits in Chapter 8.

A second key agenda item before the U.N. General Assembly regards the Millennium Development Goals (MDGs). Established in 2000 at the Millennium Summit, these eight goals aim to reduce poverty, hunger and more by 2015 through various targets, such as halving the number of people who live on less than $1 a day, reducing by three-quarters the maternal mortality ratio, integrating the principles of sustainable development in every country and addressing the special needs of landlocked and least-developed countries. These goals and their progress—largely being implemented and tracked by the U.N. Development Programme—are reviewed in Chapter 2. Focusing on environmental calls to action—such as ratification of the *Kyoto Protocol*, special populations such as older people and women, official development assistance, the rich-poor nation and digital divides, Chapter 2 makes the case for developing a global partnership to meet the MDGs.

Chapters 3 and 4 highlight the various human rights violations and humanitarian assistance and peacekeeping efforts taken up by the U.N. in 2003 and the first half of 2004. From deploying emergency peacekeeping troops to Burundi, Haiti, and soon, Sudan, and repatriating internally displaced persons in Liberia to empowering women in Afghanistan and negotiating the Israel-Palestine conflict, the U.N. clearly has a global presence and is working to improve the lives of individuals in need every day. Involved in these tasks are the U.N. Department of Peacekeeping Operations, the U.N. Department of Political Affairs, the U.N. Office for the Coordination of Human Rights, the U.N. Office of the U.N. High Commissioner for Human Rights and the Office of the U.N. High Commissioner for Refugees and more.

In addition to discussing in detail the situation in Iraq, Chapter 5 addresses nuclear proliferation in North Korea and Pakistan as well as provides updates on the fast-growing "vertical proliferation" of weapons states and the world's stockpiles of chemical, biological and other weapons. The chapter also takes a look at global counter-terrorism efforts and how U.N. sanctions recently led Libyan leader Muammar el-Qaddafi to disband his weapons program.

Chapter 6 digs deep into the legal cases before the world's courts, including updates on the International Criminal Court, while Chapter 7 reviews the past year's regional and bilateral trade agreements, including a look at why the Cancún Doha Development Agenda negotiations ended in a walk-out in September 2003. Last but not least, Chapter 8 tackles the sticky issue of U.N. reform—the proposals, progress and debates at stake—as well as the formulation of the U.N.'s budgets and member states' arrears. In addition, special attention is given to the status of the capital master plan, that is, the renovation of U.N. Headquarters in New York.

Each chapter ends with an analytical Commentary, providing a unique perspective on the book's content from tracking the MDGs to derailing the drug trade in Afghanistan to the challenges of health security. In addition, each section provides a forward outlook at what the General Assembly is specifically expected to do or discuss in its 59th session over 2004 and 2005.

Finally, this year's edition of *Global Agenda* concludes with three pivotal essays. Former U.N. Assistant Secretary-General for Public Information Samir Sanbar takes a look at Arab Human Development, while Director of the Center on International Organization at Columbia University's School of International and Public Affairs Edward C. Luck capitalizes on the real issues at stake in the upcoming U.S. presidential election in relation to the United Nations. Director of the Center for Global Health Studies at Seton Hall University Yanzhong Huang brings the book's focus back to health in his proposal for a local-level solution to fighting HIV/AIDS.

There is no doubt that the work of the United Nations and its various agencies is vital and relevant, as it impacts the lives of individuals world-wide everyday. To continue making progress, the U.N. requires support from all its member states, including the United States. For that reason, we at the United Nations Association of the USA are constantly working to strength-en the commitment of the U.S. government, Americans and people around the world to the United Nations so that it can become even more effective.

—*UNA-USA President William H. Luers*
and UNA-USA Managing Editor Angela Drakulich, June 2004.

Chapter 1

Ensuring Health Security in an Interdependent World

Ilona Kickbusch and Lea Payne

When you are working to combat a disastrous and growing emergency, you should use every tool at your disposal. HIV/AIDS is the worst epidemic humanity has ever faced. It has spread farther, faster and with more catastrophic long-term effects than any other disease. Its impact has become a devastating obstacle to development...We must seek to engage...powerful organizations as full partners in the fight to halt HIV/AIDS through awareness, prevention and education.
—Secretary-General Kofi Annan,
Global Media AIDS Initiative Launch, January 2004.

Health is at the very core of the global agenda. Not only does disease engender poverty, but it also negatively affects growth and security in both developing and developed countries. All social and economic development efforts manifest themselves in health outcomes, most importantly in better health and life expectancy. Increasingly, it is understood that health, in itself, is an important development factor.[1] Disease stands in the way of productivity; when sick farmers cannot work in the field, workers cannot maintain jobs and parents cannot care for their children. The global AIDS epidemic confirms this. Societies that are losing their most productive adult population are also in danger of losing their stability and social cohesion. Health must not only be viewed through the lens of development, but also through the reality of interdependence. No longer is the danger of infectious diseases confined to poor countries, as the SARS, or Severe Acute Respiratory Syndrome, epidemic clearly demonstrated; nor is the developing world safe from the health threats of modern lifestyles, as illustrated by the global tobacco and obesity pandemics. Concerning health, the world can no longer be divided into "us" and "them." Health must be increasingly recognized as a global public good that is central to an interdependent world.[2]

In light of this growing concern, health issues have increased on agendas at all levels, from the foreign policy of nation states to deliberations within the United Nations Security Council and General Assembly. The World Health Organization (WHO), a specialized U.N. agency on health, has served the global community since 1948 by setting standards, ensuring

1

health norms, dealing with outbreaks and fighting new and old diseases. WHO is an intergovernmental organization with 192 member states, and it works from a central office in Geneva as well as six regional offices and more than 100 country offices. Increasingly, other U.N. agencies, including UNICEF, or the U.N. Children's Fund, have been dealing with health issues as they converge with their respective mandates. In addition, new organizations, such as the Joint U.N. Programme on HIV/AIDS (UNAIDS) and The Global Fund to Fight AIDS, Tuberculosis and Malaria (the Global Fund) have been created to take on health matters.

As a result, the field of global health is currently characterized by a multitude of institutions, partnerships and alliances, and in the spirit of the U.N. Global Compact, which aims to ensure respect for human rights through the integration of such rights in business operations, it has spearheaded new ways for the public and private sector to work together. Thousands of NGOs, or nongovernmental organizations, are active in health and participate forcefully in setting global agendas, most prominently in recent years regarding access to antiretroviral drugs (ARVs) for AIDS patients in poor countries. Furthermore, U.N. agencies are increasingly involved in health initiatives that are conducted in partnership with many players and organizations. A health program run only by one organization is becoming the exception rather than the norm.

Despite this energy and activity, the world is not as far advanced in health as it could and should be. A recent analysis by the Global Governance Initiative of the World Economic Forum, which brought together leading experts on crucial global governance issues and asked them to focus on the goals of the U.N. *Millennium Declaration*, came to the conclusion that "...the world is failing to put forward even half of the effort needed to meet the world's basic goals."[3]

The Initiative gives the world a score of 4 out of 10 (clearly less than 50 percent) for the direct health-related Millennium Development Goals, which want to accomplish the following by 2015:

- Halt and begin to reverse the spread/incidence of HIV/AIDS, malaria and other major diseases;
- Reduce by two-thirds the under-age-5 mortality rate; and
- Reduce by three-quarters the maternal mortality ratio.

The global community still has far to go to achieve health security and provide the poorest people on earth access to a healthy life. This cannot be reached by focusing only on diseases, as important as many of the eradication and control initiatives are. It implies that what is desperately needed in the poorest countries is the establishment of strong public health and primary healthcare systems, as well as the development of human resources to deliver the services.

It is imperative to remember that the U.N. has recognized health as a human right and that society must, as Nobel Prize winner Amartya Sen has emphasized, look at health as a value and a resource that allows people to reach their full potential as human beings. This is why the health activities of the U.N. deserve increased attention and commitment by member states and the global community as a whole.

Strengthening International HIV/AIDS Initiatives

Background

"The level of the AIDS crisis, its potential to destroy economic achievement, undermine social stability and create more political uncertainty ... is so enormous."[4]

These words by United States Ambassador Richard Holbrooke in the face of the global HIV/AIDS crisis explain why it has been essential for the U.N. to be at the forefront of the global response to the disease. The U.N. has initiated and supported the establishment of new agencies to deal with the epidemic, as well as held or hosted several high-level meetings and initiatives that have helped to keep HIV/AIDS on the wider U.N. agenda. Some examples of this include the Joint U.N. Programme on HIV/AIDS (UNAIDS), the General Assembly Special Session on HIV/AIDS, WHO's 3 by 5 Initiative, the Global Media AIDS Initiative, and the Global Coalition on Women and AIDS.

The world has agreed that the magnitude of the destruction caused by the AIDS epidemic demands a coordinated and multisectored response on a global level. Millions have died from the epidemic since it began to permeate the globe in the early 1980s. Today, an estimated 40 million people are living with the disease, of which more than 6 percent are children under age 15. In 2003, 3 million people died from HIV/AIDS alone.[5]

In the hardest hit regions, HIV/AIDS threatens to erode the economic, political and social development gains of the past two decades. The disease wipes out individuals in their most productive years, destroying families and yielding parentless generations. National security is endangered by HIV/AIDS, as the virus spreads regardless of national borders and takes the lives of men and women who ensure stability and security as soldiers, policemen, politicians and civil servants. The high rates of HIV infection among teachers and school administrators unravel the progress made toward achieving universal primary education. Deaths among health workers from AIDS only exacerbate the problem, as the demand for health services increases.[6]

Low- and middle-income countries are disproportionately affected by the AIDS epidemic. Sub-Saharan Africa bears the brunt of the infection, accounting for about 75 percent of deaths from AIDS in 2003. The devastating impact of HIV/AIDS is particularly apparent in southern African countries. HIV prevalence in Botswana and Swaziland reaches almost 40 percent.[7] Even worse, the AIDS crisis shows no signs of abating. According to a recent U.N. report, AIDS is expected to cause 31 million additional deaths in India and 18 million additional deaths in China before 2025.[8] Efforts to curb the spread in Eastern Europe and Central Asia are hampered by the stigma and discrimination associated with IV, or intravenous, drug use.

ADULTS AND CHILDREN ESTIMATED TO BE LIVING
WITH HIV/AIDS, END 2003

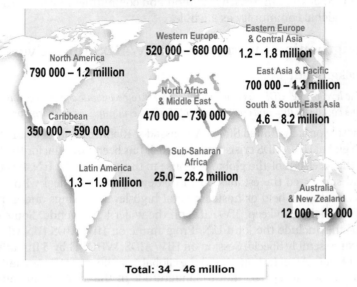

Total: 34 – 46 million

Source: UNAIDS Epidemic Update, December 2003.

Younger generations are also feeling the impact of AIDS. More than 14 million children under age 16 have lost one or both parents to the epidemic, and in six years, this number is expected to nearly double to 25 million. Almost 80 percent of these children live in sub-Saharan Africa.[9] In countries with generalized HIV epidemics, the government response to these children has been inadequate, as 39 percent lack national strategies for orphans and vulnerable children affected by HIV/AIDS.[10] These children are sometimes forced to become the head of household and work to care for their siblings. Others may be placed with foster families or relatives, thereby adding strain on the limited resources already available. Finally, in the most unfortunate cases, children are forced to live on the street. Stigma, poor nutrition and physical abuse are just a few of the hardships faced by these children on a daily basis.

Role of UNAIDS

In the early years of the AIDS epidemic, U.N. efforts to fight its spread were undertaken by the Global AIDS Program (GPA) of the World Health Organization. As the epidemic grew in magnitude, it became evident that its effects reached beyond the health sector. Additional U.N. organizations began to incorporate the disease in their programming. The U.N. Economic and Social Council (ECOSOC) formed the Joint U.N. Programme on HIV/AIDS in 1994, and the agency was formally launched in 1996. The nine cosponsoring U.N. organizations of UNAIDS include UNICEF, the World Food Programme (WFP), the U.N. Development Programme (UNDP), the U.N. Population Fund (UNFPA), the U.N. Office on Drugs and Crime (UNODC), the International Labour Organization (ILO), the U.N. Educational, Scientific and Cultural Organization (UNESCO), WHO and the World Bank. Dr. Peter Piot is the executive director of UNAIDS, which is headquartered in Geneva.

UNAIDS supports the global response to HIV/AIDS by 1) providing leadership and advocacy for effective action on the epidemic; 2) developing and distributing strategic information to guide efforts against AIDS worldwide; 3) tracking, monitoring and evaluating the epidemic and responses to it; 4) engaging civil society and developing partnerships; and 5) mobilizing resources to support an effective response. A program-coordinating board governs UNAIDS and is comprised of 22 government representatives from every region of the world. Nonvoting members include representatives of the nine UNAIDS cosponsors and five NGOs. Since its inception, the agency has been successful in reaching out to diverse groups who are impacted by HIV/AIDS, including, among others, corporations, religious groups, media, national governments, NGOs and networks of people living with HIV/AIDS. UNAIDS has also been instrumental in increasing commitment and resources for the disease as well as guiding policy. Currently, the agency's key focus is helping countries bring to scale evidence-based action on AIDS.[11]

Millennium Development Goal 6: HIV/AIDS, Malaria and Other Diseases

In September 2000, U.N. member states unanimously adopted the *Millennium Declaration*, which set forth a series of human development targets called the Millennium Development Goals (MDGs). The MDGs, which are to be achieved by 2015, "commit the international community to an expanded vision of development, one that vigorously promotes human development as the key to sustaining social and economic progress in all countries, and recognizes the importance of creating a global partnership for development."[12]

Of the eight Goals, three relate directly to health: MDG 4 to reduce child mortality, MDG 5 to improve maternal health and MDG 6 to combat AIDS, malaria and other diseases. The adoption of the *Millennium Declaration* marks the first time that heads of state identified health as a major development issue. The inclusion of HIV/AIDS in the MDGs, as outlined below, has placed the epidemic squarely on the development agenda top-priority list.

Participants at a January 2004 high-level forum on the health MDGs in Geneva agreed that in low-income countries, progress is too slow. The agreed action points of the meeting outline the need for increased financial resources in low-income countries to be invested in health systems and effective interventions; strengthening health-information systems to monitor performance; and addressing the human resources crisis in health. The participants also emphasized the importance of interacting beyond health ministries because of the multidimensionality of health and poverty.[13]

MDG 6, in particular, aims to halt and reverse the spread of HIV/AIDS, the incidence of malaria and other major diseases by 2015. The indicators used to measure progress include: HIV prevalence among pregnant women, condom-use rate, percentage of youth who have correct knowledge of HIV/AIDS and school attendance among AIDS orphans. The indicators for malaria and other diseases are the prevalence and death rates of malaria and tuberculosis (TB), proportion of people using effective malaria prevention and treatment, and the proportion of TB cases diagnosed and cured.

A February 2004 report by the Millennium Project's Task Force on HIV/AIDS (which was commissioned by Secretary-General Kofi Annan and is supported by the U.N. Development Group) has documented 10 conditions that are imperative for reaching the HIV/AIDS MDG by 2015. Some examples include ensuring equitable access to treatment, investing in health systems, integrating prevention and treatment, and empowering women and girls. Interestingly, the report also highlights the need to require more from the United Nations.

The Task Force asserts that the organization's agencies, especially UNAIDS, have taken tremendous strides in coordinating the global response to AIDS by making the epidemic a global priority as well as by forging international consensus on a comprehensive response. At the same time, however, the Task Force maintains that the U.N. must hold countries that have not fulfilled their promises in the fight against HIV/AIDS more accountable. The U.N. should, as the Task Force suggests, highlight the "failures in leadership, misguided policies and gaps in financing that continue to stymie an effective response."[14] Furthermore, the Task Force insists that the U.N. provide more technical and management assistance to countries. A key problem, especially in the most heavily impacted countries, has been insufficient presence of U.N. personnel. As of this writing, the recommendations outlined in the report were being circulated for public discussion.

General Assembly Special Session on HIV/AIDS

HIV/AIDS was elevated to the U.N. security agenda on June 25, 2001 at the General Assembly Special Session on HIV/AIDS. During this historic meeting, government representatives publicly recognized the suffering and deaths, the unraveling of development gains and the threat to the political, economic and social stability of nations from the epidemic. At the special session, member states adopted a *Declaration of Commitment*, which established a set of targets aimed at stemming the spread of the epidemic while building on the goal set forth in the *Millennium Declaration*.[15] The *Declaration of Commitment* calls for the development of partnerships, supported by the United Nations, by emphasizing increased participation in fighting the epidemic among people living with HIV/AIDS, faith-based groups, NGOs and AIDS service organizations. The *Declaration* targets for 2003 primarily focused on the establishment of national policy frameworks to enable action on HIV/AIDS, while the 2005 and 2010 targets address HIV prevention, care and impact-alleviation programs.[16]

S.G. Annan asserted in his 2003 progress report that substantial progress had been made on the goals of the *Declaration of Commitment*. Multisectored AIDS strategies and national AIDS councils are in place in nearly all the heavily affected countries, and governments are increasingly cooperating on a regional level. The report affirmed that significant financial resources have been leveraged from the global community. The $4.7 billion granted to HIV/AIDS programs in low- and middle-income countries in 2003 was a 20 percent increase from 2002 and a 500 percent increase from 1996.

At the same time, S.G. Annan also called on the international community to significantly increase its efforts to curb HIV/AIDS. According to the Secretary-General, at the current rate of progress, none of the agreed targets would be achieved by 2005.[17] Current spending on AIDS in developing countries is less than half of the $10 billion that is needed in 2005. The report highlighted the startling facts that, on the global level, fewer than 1 in 4 people are able to obtain basic information about HIV/AIDS, only 1 in 9 have access to voluntary counseling and testing, and fewer than 1 in 20 pregnant women are able to access services to prevent mother-child transmission. Furthermore, despite the fact that political commitment to AIDS has grown in recent years, leaders in countries where HIV is spreading the fastest need to take greater political action.[18] The statistics indicate that this is just the beginning. Progress toward the MDGs and *Declaration of Commitment* targets illustrate that global efforts must be considerably augmented to stem the spread of this epidemic.

Access to Antiretrovirals

"Lack of access to antiretroviral treatment is a global health emergency....To deliver antiretroviral treatment to the millions who need it, we must change the way we think and change the way we act."
　　　　　　　　　　　　　—WHO Director-General LEE Jong-wook.[19]

Currently, the global coverage of antiretroviral (ARV) treatment is extremely low. Of the 6 million people in need of ARVs in developing countries, fewer than 8 percent actually have access to them. In Western Pacific countries, ARV coverage reaches only 6 percent of people who need them, and in Africa, coverage hovers at 2 percent.[20] The primary culprit is the cost of drugs. At a conference, U.N. Special Envoy for HIV/AIDS in Africa Stephen Lewis questioned, "How can this be happening, in the year 2003, when we can find over $200 billion to fight a war on terrorism but we can't find the money to prevent children from living in terror?"[21]

In addition to prolonging lives and reducing death rates, the availability of ARVs creates an environment in which people are more likely to get tested, obtain counseling and care, and become more knowledgeable about the disease. As people begin treatment, the stigma, fear and discrimination that surround AIDS can begin to diminish.[22] Simply put, accessibility of treatment will help prevent new infections from occurring.

Recent developments have given hope to many people who thought they would never gain access to treatment. Thanks to the advocacy, education and lobbying efforts of NGOs and networks of those living with HIV/AIDS—who have proven that access to treatment is a human right—the prices of ARVs have significantly declined recently, and the distribution of the medicines has proven feasible.[23] And in August 2003, the World Trade Organization (WTO) ruled to allow poorer nations without manufacturing capacity to import generic versions of ARVs. (See Chapter 7 for more details.)

Even better news appeared in early April 2004 when four organizations (the William J. Clinton Presidential Foundation, The Global Fund, the World Bank and UNICEF) announced they were working together to help more than 100 countries obtain access to generic AIDS drugs and inexpensive AIDS tests. This new development is particularly interesting because former U.S. President Bill Clinton's support for generic drugs is positioned against the actions of the current Bush Administration. To date, President George W. Bush has not permitted U.S. funding for such generics.[24] Critics accuse the current administration of protecting the patents of U.S. pharmaceutical companies at the expense of human lives.

3 by 5 Initiative

In September 2003, the leaders of the World Health Organization declared the antiretroviral treatment gap a "global-health emergency."[25] In response to this crisis, UNAIDS and WHO launched the 3 by 5 Initiative, which aims to provide ARVs to 3 million people living with AIDS in developing countries by the end of 2005. WHO will not provide the ARVs or subsidize their cost. Instead, the agency will implement the 3 by 5 strategy with UNAIDS and its cosponsors: the Global Fund, the U.S. President's Emergency Plan for AIDS Relief, national governments and NGOs who are working in-country.

As outlined in WHO's 2003 World Health Report, the 3 by 5 plan includes:
• Emergency-response teams to assess barriers and opportunities in reaching the 3 by 5 goal;

- An AIDS medicines and diagnostics facility to improve access for ARV treatment;
- Simplified treatment guidelines for ARV provision;
- Uniform standards and tools to track the progress and impact of ARV treatment programs;
- Emergency expansion of training and capacity development for health professionals; and
- Advocacy for funding.

The 3 by 5 campaign will also collaborate with TB control programs of the World Health Organization. The WHO-backed plan, "Interim Policy on Collaborative TB/HIV Activities," will expand collaboration between HIV/AIDS and TB programs, particularly in Africa. In Africa, nearly 80 percent of tuberculosis patients are co-infected with the virus. A key component of the interim policy is to rapidly expand voluntary HIV testing and counseling in TB programs. By the end of 2005, the policy aims to refer more than 500,000 co-infected people to ARV treatment.[26] The policy does not call for the establishment of new TB and HIV programs but instead builds on existing strategies for TB control and prevention and HIV/AIDS treatment.

At present, funding is desperately needed to sustain the 3 by 5 Initiative. WHO is short $165 million of the $218 million that is needed to operate the program over the next two years. In March 2004, the agency squeezed money from its budget to fund an emergency deployment. During this deployment, 40 experts traveled to 32 developing countries to assist in the development of plans to combat AIDS, including proposals for the Global Fund in its fourth round of funding. Sixty percent of all proposals were rejected in the first three rounds because they were technically deficient. AIDS campaigners are concerned that without increased commitment of funds to the 3 by 5 Initiative, the activities of the Global Fund will also suffer.[27]

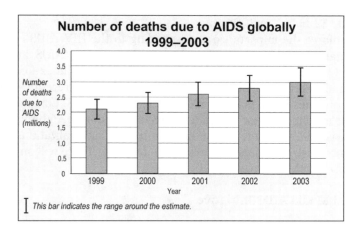

Source: UNAIDS Epidemic Update, December 2003.

The Global Fund to Fight AIDS, Tuberculosis and Malaria

The Global Fund to Fight AIDS, Tuberculosis and Malaria plays an integral role in the international response to HIV/AIDS. As countries began acting on the MDGs and *Declaration of Commitment* targets, it became apparent that substantial financial resources needed to be leveraged globally to stop the AIDS epidemic. In early 2001, S.G. Annan began to call for the creation of a global health fund. By January 2002, the Global Fund formed with the establishment of a permanent Secretariat. Supported by but not formally part of the U.N. system, the Global Fund provides the most severely affected countries with grants for their AIDS, TB and malaria efforts, paying particular attention to those that incorporate partnerships.

Accepting donations from foundations, companies, governments, individuals and others, the Global Fund has committed $2.1 billion to 121 countries to date.[28] The largest pledges have come from (in descending order) the United States, France, the European Commission, Italy, Germany, the United Kingdom and Japan. The Bill & Melinda Gates Foundation pledged $100 million, the highest donation for a foundation or not-for-profit organization; Winterthur insurance ($1 million) and Eni ($500,000) have been the largest corporate donors. The highest donations from individuals, groups and events are the People of Taiwan ($1 million) and Real Madrid Soccer Match ($112,487).[29] As a key advocate for the Global Fund and as a demonstration of his commitment, S.G. Annan made a personal donation of $100,000.

In February 2004, the Global Fund announced that it would distribute at least $900 million in its fourth round of grants in June 2004. This news came after receiving confirmation of a U.S. pledge of $547 million for 2004,[30] which constitutes part of the U.S. President's Emergency Plan for AIDS Relief's $1 billion allocation to the fund over five years. Although the pledge significantly increased the Global Fund's resources, more funds are needed. S.G. Annan called for the United States, Europe and other donors to contribute $1 billion in 2004.[31]

To reinforce the importance of responding to the HIV/AIDS epidemic, S.G. Annan recently appointed Special Envoys on HIV/AIDS including: Stephen Lewis for Africa, Nafis Sadik for Asia, Lars Kallings for Eastern Europe and George Alleyne for the Caribbean. Mr. Lewis recently deplored the lack of funds being made available to fight HIV/AIDS. Comparing this gap to the expenditures for the wars and reconstruction in Afghanistan and Iraq, Lewis said: "... there are no excuses left, no rationalizations to hide behind, no murky slanders to justify indifference. ... There will only be the mass graves of the betrayed."[32]

Global Media AIDS Initiative

Research on the effectiveness of AIDS advocacy has revealed the central role of the media in curbing the HIV/AIDS epidemic. More than 60 percent of young women in 21 countries in Africa do not know what HIV is or have at least one misconception about its methods of transmission.[33] However, in countries where the epidemic is emerging or intensifying, advocacy fosters increased public awareness and concern,[34] thereby averting many of the global HIV infections that are projected to occur.

The new Global Media AIDS Initiative, convened by UNAIDS and the U.S.-based Kaiser Family Foundation, answers the call to the media community to increase action on AIDS. In January 2004, executives from more than 20 media companies pledged to take action on HIV/AIDS by educating the public on AIDS prevention and combating stigma and discrimination. The participants represented a wide range, including, among others, the BBC, Time Warner, China Central Television, South African Broadcasting Corporation, Prasar Bharati Broadcasting Corporation and Viacom.[35]

At the meeting, the media executives discussed how to draw attention to the epidemic and create long-lasting public education campaigns. A UNAIDS report, released in conjunction with the launch of the media initiative, explored how the media can contribute in the fight against AIDS. According to the report, titled "The Media and HIV/AIDS: Making a Difference," media companies can do such things as foster discussion about HIV and interpersonal relationships, and ensure that AIDS is kept at the top of the news agenda.

Women & AIDS

The new Global Coalition on Women and AIDS, launched in February 2004, was convened by UNAIDS to energize and raise support for programs that mitigate the impact of AIDS on women and girls. Statistics show that females are increasingly vulnerable to the spread of HIV/AIDS as they now account for half of global HIV infections (in sub-Saharan Africa, women account for 58 percent).[36] The Coalition exists to strengthen advocacy efforts for women and girls affected by AIDS at national and global levels by urging the development of female-controlled HIV prevention methods, promoting access to ARVs and addressing legal inequities. The Coalition aims to build the capacity and resilience of women, and to fortify their position in their families and societies.[37]

March 8, 2004 marked the first time that HIV/AIDS was the focus of International Women's Day. During an event at U.N. headquarters in New York, numerous experts, including S.G. Kofi Annan and WHO D.G. Dr. Lee, discussed the impact of HIV/AIDS on women, strategies to increase access to ARVs, the implications of migration and trafficking, the importance of community support and the role of men and boys in preventing violence against women and the spread of the epidemic.[38]

Managing New Deadly Viruses

WHO on SARS

Severe Acute Respiratory Syndrome, or SARS, is a prime example of the effects of globalization on health security. While the first cases reportedly occurred in November 2002, in February 2003, a doctor infected with SARS from the Guangdong Province of China checked into a hotel in Hong Kong. According to the World Health Organization, this hotel became the source of the international spread of SARS, particularly the earliest and most severe outbreaks.[39] In all, the disease infected 8,422 people in 29 countries and killed approximately 11 percent of those infected, but China, Canada, Singapore and Vietnam were those hardest hit. It is estimated that the toll of SARS has already cost the economy $30 billion, largely from canceled travel (thus impacting the service industry and airlines) and decreased investments in Asia.[40]

The global efforts to contain SARS were hailed a success when, on July 5, 2003, just five months after the first reported case in February 2003,[41] WHO announced that the efforts had stopped the transmission of SARS. This was a significant achievement, given the challenges posed by the disease. For starters, there was no vaccine, treatment or valid diagnostic test to use against SARS. The virus was easily transmitted between people, spread around the world at an alarming rate and produced symptoms similar to other diseases. It also spread regardless of geography and took its heaviest toll on hospital staff.[42] Yet by employing centuries-old public-health practices, the SARS outbreak was brought under control. This was a great victory for the public-health establishment.

WHO officials acted rapidly and effectively in containing the spread of SARS. With assistance from national and local governments, scientists and clinicians, they tracked the chains of transmission, detected and isolated cases rapidly, quarantined contacts and issued travel restrictions. Mass media amplified the U.N. agency's daily updates and global alerts to encourage people to check for fever throughout the day. Once WHO issued travel recommendations on March 27, 2003, there were no additional cases associated with in-flight exposure.[43]

Two successful mechanisms that enhanced WHO's response to SARS were the Global Outbreak Alert and Response Network (GOARN) and the Global Public Health Intelligence Network (GPHIN). Developed in 2000, GOARN links experts and institutes electronically to track the evolution of SARS, verify outbreaks and respond when necessary. GPHIN, a computer application that scans global communications on the Internet for keywords in articles that might signal an outbreak, also helped to identify early SARS outbreaks.[44] These mechanisms were instrumental in stopping the spread of the virus.

Lessons learned from SARS, taken directly from WHO's 2003 World Health Report, include, among other things:

- The need to report, promptly and openly, cases of any disease with potential for international spreading;
- Travel recommendations, including screening measures at airports, help to contain the international spread of an emerging infection;
- Weaknesses in health systems play a key role in permitting emerging infections to spread; and
- An outbreak can be contained even without a curative drug or a vaccine if existing interventions are tailored to the circumstances and backed by political commitment.

At the SARS Conference in Malaysia in June 2003, participants emphasized the importance of global surveillance and response capacity to emerging diseases via timely reporting, rapid communication and evidence-based action. They also pointed to the need for international collaboration, coordinated by WHO and affirmed by strong political leadership.[45]

In response to the SARS outbreak, WHO accelerated its efforts to revise the outdated International Health Regulations (IHR), which set forth measures for effective monitoring and controlling of the international spread of diseases. The current IHR, updated in 1981, addresses only cholera, plague and yellow fever.[46] If approved, the revised IHR will give WHO more authority during outbreaks and will address syndromes as well as new and re-emerging diseases that constitute international public health risks, such as SARS, ebola or symptoms resulting from a bioterrorist attack. On the basis of extensive consultations with internal and external partners, WHO prepared a first draft of the IHR revisions and revised it at regional consultations during early 2004. The final draft, which will incorporate feedback from regional consultations, will be presented to WHO's 192-member World Health Assembly (WHA) in 2005. [47]

As an immediate measure in the revision of IHR, WHO member states adopted a resolution at the 56th WHA meeting in May 2003 that gave WHO greater authority in controlling emerging diseases. Member states voted to allow WHO to act on reports from sources other than official notifications, to alert the world about public-health threats and perform on-the-spot studies in affected countries to ensure the application of proper control measures.[48] WHO is also planning to build an operations room for a more effective, coordinated response to future deadly outbreaks. The organization is attempting to become more action-oriented and respond more rapidly to emerging diseases.[49] It will be essential that all U.N. member states cooperate fully in global outbreak control and ensure the financial basis for rapid-response action.

Meanwhile, WHO and other public-health experts are continuing to work to ensure that future outbreaks of SARS are controlled. For example, clinical research will focus on diagnostic tests, treatment and vaccines. A new SARS Scientific Research Advisory Committee is developing internationally agreed protocols for clinical trials of medicines to treat SARS as well as discussing laboratory biosafety.[50] And WHO is strengthening the GOARN network, and has enrolled the FAO to study potential animal reservoirs of the virus.

Avian Influenza

Avian influenza, an infectious disease that affects birds, has recently re-emerged as a serious threat to humans. Although the viruses are usually restricted to its avian hosts, in rare occurrences humans have acquired the disease from affected poultry. In January 2004, human cases of avian influenza (H5N1 subtype) were reported in northern Vietnam.[51] As of March 17, 2004, there were 34 human cases of avian influenza in Vietnam and Thailand, which, to date, resulted in 23 deaths.[52] According to WHO, there is no evidence that the virus has been transmitted between humans. However, when a human is infected with both human and avian influenza strains, a new subtype can be produced that is easily transmitted among humans. If this or a random mutation of the virus occurs, it can signify the beginning of an influenza pandemic. Although recent control efforts of avian influenza have exhibited success, continued outbreaks signify that the factors necessary for a pandemic still exist.[53]

The lessons learned from controlling the SARS outbreak have prepared WHO experts in their response to avian influenza. From March 16-18, 2004, WHO convened a meeting on priority public-health interventions before and during an influenza pandemic. More than 100 experts discussed practical-response measures, the use of limited vaccines and antivirals, surveillance techniques, the current risk situation, travel recommendations and early detection of changes in subtypes.[54] WHO's website also lists guidelines for infection control at hospitals, clinical management of human infection and laboratory tests for the virus. The agency provides advice to international travelers about the risks of the disease.

These recent outbreaks have shown clearly both the need for a global health organization and the capacity for WHO to act forcefully and efficiently with the support of member states and the international community as a whole.

Other World Health Initiatives

Tuberculosis

Every year, approximately 2 million people die from tuberculosis. Facilitated by increased travel and trade, the global TB situation is only getting worse. One-third of the world's population is now infected with the TB bacillus, and 8 million develop the active disease each year. After 40 years of decline, the increasing incidence rate of TB in Eastern Europe and sub-Saharan Africa is particularly discouraging. Southeast Asia, with the greatest burden of TB throughout the world, accounts for 3 million cases a year. The development of multidrug-resistant TB (MDR-TB), from poorly supervised or incomplete treatment of TB, is complicating efforts to stop the disease.[55] Rates of MDR-TB in Eastern Europe and Central Asia are 10 times higher than the rest of the world.[56]

The Global Partnership to Stop TB, launched in 2001, aims to detect 70

Tuberculosis Prevalence[a] and Death Rates, 2001

REGIONS	TUBERCULOSIS PREVALENCE RATE PER 100,000 POPULATION	TUBERCULOSIS MORTALITY RATE (DEATHS PER 100,000 POPULATION)
Developed countries	23	5
Developing countries	144	31
Northern Africa	27	5
Sub-Saharan Africa	197	46
Latin America/Caribbean	41	9
Eastern Asia	108	21
South-central Asia	184	40
South-eastern Asia	218	47
Western Asia	40	9
Oceania	215	36
Transition countries in Europe and Asia	66	16

[a] Prevalence of sputum smear positive TB excluding TB attributable to HIV/AIDS, mortality due to all forms of TB; excluding TB attributable to HIV/AIDS.

Source: U.N. Statistics Division, based on country data provided by the World Health Organization, December 2003.

percent of all new global infections of TB and successfully treat 85 percent of such cases by 2005. The Partnership also aims to reduce the global burden of TB by 50 percent by 2010. WHO plays a key role in the Global Partnership by housing the Stop TB Partnership Secretariat, which manages information and communication efforts, mobilizes resources and coordinates partners. The Partnership, made up of more than 200 organizations, operates within the framework of the Global Plan to Stop TB, which includes the internationally recommended strategy called DOTS.[57] The DOTS strategy contains five main elements: government commitment, diagnosis of TB through microscopy services, adequate drug supplies, directly observed therapy (DOT) of patients taking anti-TB drugs, and the surveillance and monitoring systems of every diagnosed patient.[58]

Continued progress toward the Stop TB goals will help countries reach the Millennium Development Goal of halting the spread of major diseases by 2015. A recent WHO report claims that the number of people diagnosed with TB is increasing faster than at any time since the DOTS launch in 1995. This growth is most predominant in India, which represents 28 percent of additional DOTS cases treated. Other countries with high rates of TB that have experienced an increase in case detection include South Africa, Indonesia, Pakistan, Bangladesh and the Philippines. The report asserts that the treatment success rate in 2001 was 82 percent, which is close to the Stop TB goal of 85 percent by 2005. Although the case detection rate in 2002 was only 37 percent, it is increasing rapidly.[59]

Tuberculosis remains one of the most challenging global health emergencies, particularly because of the great potential of multidrug resistance. It is clearly a major disease of poverty, linked closely to unhealthy living conditions and workplaces, insufficient nutrition and overall vulnerability to disease. It illustrates the close links between the various MDGs and demonstrates how good health is both an outcome of poverty reduction strategies and an important precondition for a socially and economically productive life.

Polio

Once endemic on five continents, poliomyelitis (polio) is currently limited to parts of Africa and South Asia. Since 1988, the number of polio cases has decreased by 99 percent.[60] The Global Polio Eradication Initiative, which was launched by the World Health Assembly in 1988, is chiefly responsible for the progress against the disease. As the world moves closer to global eradication, however, the polio cases in the remaining countries have been difficult to quell. In northern Nigeria, for instance, rumors that the polio vaccination was unsafe for girls and young women hampered vaccination efforts in the second half of 2003. Since then, 45 cases in previously polio-free countries have been linked to northern Nigeria.[61] The six remaining polio-endemic countries are India, Nigeria, Egypt, Pakistan, Afghanistan and Niger. Three countries, India, Nigeria and Pakistan, account for 96 percent of all cases.[62]

The Global Polio Eradication Initiative is a stellar example of a global health partnership as well as how the contribution of civil-society leaders, in close cooperation with the United Nations, can improve health. The efforts of the Global Polio Eradication Initiative have been led by WHO, Rotary International, the U.S. Centers for Disease Control and Prevention (CDC) and UNICEF. An integral element to the global polio efforts has been the role of volunteers. Rotary International, with more than 1.2 million members in 160 countries, has mobilized millions of volunteers to commit their time during National Immunization Days (NIDs).[63] Rotary also has committed a tremendous amount of resources; by the end of 2005, the organization will have given more than $600 million to polio eradication efforts.[64]

WHO provides technical direction and strategic planning for the Polio Eradication Initiative, including monitoring and evaluation, coordinating basic science research, resource mobilization and advocacy for political commitment. CDC funds large supplies of oral polio vaccine (OPV) and provides technical expertise and laboratory support (such as disease surveillance and investigating outbreaks). UNICEF contributes by supplying vaccines, forecasting vaccine needs and building in-country capacity to strengthen immunization programs. Many other organizations have been instrumental in the initiative's success as well, including governments of affected countries, private foundations, donor governments, NGOs and corporate partners.[65]

The strategy employed by the Global Polio Eradication Initiative can be divided into 2 phases: 1988-2004 and 2004-2008. Until 2004, the strategy consisted of routine immunization with OPV among infants, supplementary doses of OPV during NIDs, targeted "mop-up" campaigns, and surveillance of wild poliovirus via reporting and laboratory testing of children under 15 with acute flaccid paralysis (an indicator of polio infection).[66] During polio immunization activities in 2002, 42 countries also administered Vitamin A. A recent study suggests that since 1988, 1 million childhood deaths have been prevented from the administration of Vitamin A during NIDs.[67]

As the world progresses toward global certification, WHO is making tactical revisions to its strategies. From 2004-2008, the new strategic plan includes 1) interrupt wild poliovirus transmission; 2) achieve global certification; 3) implement policies in a post-certification era; and 4) mainstream polio eradication infrastructure. Once polio is eradicated globally, policies will have to be put in place that prohibit the use of the OPV. Outbreaks caused by vaccine-derived polioviruses have illustrated the danger that OPV can cause post-certification. From 2004 on, WHO and its partners will consult with countries that use OPV to inform them of the risks associated with its cessation and to facilitate decisions on post-OPV vaccination policies. WHO has developed a strategy for the cessation of routine immunization with OPV, including polio vaccine stockpile management and evolution, detection and notification of circulating polioviruses, and long-term containment of poliovirus stockpiles.[68]

The greatest hurdle facing the Global Polio Eradication Initiative has been lack of funding. WHO reported that in 2003, for the first time in the initiative's history, the need for funding necessitated the postponement or cancellation of activities, thereby compromising surveillance and supplementary immunization. At the end of 2002, the funding gap was $275 million; it is projected that for 2004-2005 that gap will be reduced to $130 million.[69] Still, if polio is to be eradicated, more financial resources must be committed from the international community.

Global leaders have begun to respond to the call for increased commitment during the final push in polio eradication. At a G8 Summit in June 2003, leaders recognized the importance of polio eradication and pledged an additional $500 million.[70] At the African Union Summit and the Organization of the Islamic Conference in 2003, leaders expressed their commitment to regional cooperation.[71] In January 2004, Ministers of Health and representatives of the six remaining polio-endemic countries revealed a plan to immunize 250 children multiple times during 2004 and recognized that the success of the Global Polio Eradication Initiative was now up to them.[72]

Government representatives of several West African nations launched a synchronized polio immunization effort in February 2004 intended to reach 63 million children in four days. "After eight years of incredible collaboration and investment, Africa is standing on the verge of a well-deserved triumph in public health," said WHO'S Africa Regional Director Ebrahim Samba. "But the disease is now threatening to make a comeback and the whole continent is on the brink of re-infection unless these campaigns stop the further spread of the virus. Africa has proved it can stop polio—now is the time to finish the job."[73]

It is essential that the U.N. and member states not miss this window of opportunity—not just for Africa but for the world. Otherwise, a major historic success in public health will not reach its completion, and ongoing action to defeat polio will be required in all regions of the globe for years to come.

Malaria

Along with tuberculosis and HIV/AIDS, malaria is a disease that plagues the poorest countries in the world and threatens to undermine development. Malaria kills 1 million people each year and causes illness in more than 300 million. The disease disproportionately affects pregnant women and young children and is endemic in tropical and subtropical countries. Nearly one-fifth of all deaths in young children are from the disease, and 90 percent of deaths from malaria occur in sub-Saharan Africa.[74]

In 1998, WHO, UNDP, UNICEF and the World Bank founded Roll Back Malaria (RBM), a global partnership with the goal of halving the burden of malaria by 2010. Partners of RBM include national governments, NGOs, research institutes, professional associations, U.N. and development agencies, development banks, the private sector and media.[75] The four-pronged strategy of RBM consists of 1) prompt access to effective treatment; 2) insecticide-treated nets; 3) prevention and control of malaria in pregnant women; and 4) malaria epidemic and emergency response. RBM has helped to create early warning systems for malaria in southern African countries to enhance the detection and response to outbreaks.[76]

RBM promotes the use of low-cost strategies for treatment and prevention of malaria. Insecticide-treated nets (ITNs) can thwart transmission from the Anopheles mosquito, and effective medicines and ITNs can prevent deaths. Studies have shown that the number of under-age-5 deaths can be reduced by one-fifth when ITNs are used. High demand, competition between producers and decrease in taxes and trade obstacles have reduced prices of ITNs, thereby increasing access to them in African countries. In treating malaria, WHO now recommends the use of artemisinin-based combination therapy (ACT), since the two common antimalarial drugs, chloroquine and sulfadoxine-pyrimethamine, have become parasite-resistant. However, ACT presents its own challenges; it is more expensive, and African countries have limited operational experience with it.[77] Challenging debates over the drugs used in malaria treatment—as well as whether or not RBM efforts should be combined with other fighting other diseases such as lymphatic filariasis—have recently raised questions with regard to the success and progress of the RBM strategy. The debates need to be resolved in order to make the progress that is needed in regions highly affected by malaria.

Tobacco

Tobacco is responsible for about 5 million deaths each year, particularly among poor populations and countries. Half of all smokers today will die from a tobacco-related disease. To make matters worse, the total number of people who smoke is increasing. The promulgation of tobacco use has been propelled by a combination of factors, many of which are related to globalization, such as trade liberalization, global marketing, transnational tobacco advertising and the international movement of counterfeit cigarettes.[78] Tobacco manufacturers have located a ripe marketing opportunity in low-income countries as the markets in high-income countries begin to contract.

In response to the spread of the tobacco epidemic, WHA adopted the Framework Convention on Tobacco Control (FCTC) in May 2003. After years of Working Group meetings and regional and subregional consultations, the FCTC became the first legal instrument of its kind to be negotiated by the World Health Organization. As a new global treaty on health, the FCTC "signals a new era in global and national tobacco control activities. It represents a paradigm shift in developing a regulatory strategy for addictive substances: in contrast to previous drug control treaties, the FCTC asserts the importance of demand reduction strategies as well as supply issues."[79]

Within its first week of being open for signature in June 2003, 40 countries plus the European Community signed the FCTC,[80] and by March 2004 that number increased to 100 plus the European Community.[81] Signing the treaty indicates a country's intention toward ratification. Formal ratification of FCTC, which legally binds a country to implement it, was available on June 30, 2004.[82] The FCTC takes a comprehensive approach in curbing tobacco use by promoting a mix of interventions that address government regulation, supportive environments for health and health education. Some examples of the commitments contained in the FCTC are to:

- Implement tax and pricing policies to reduce tobacco consumption;
- Protect from exposure to tobacco smoke in public places;
- Promote and strengthen public awareness of tobacco-control measures;
- Prohibit misleading tobacco labeling;
- Ban tobacco advertising, promotion and sponsorship (unless a country's constitution prohibits it); and
- Promote viable alternatives to tobacco growers and workers.

Implementation of the FCTC poses a new set of challenges for everyone involved in efforts to control tobacco. The convention requires multisectored action between ministers of health and those in trade, finance, labor, agriculture and social affairs. Such collaboration may be difficult in countries where the health ministry is overwhelmed by more powerful ministries. The role of NGOs and grassroots groups is critical in promoting the ratification and implementation of the FCTC, the introduction of tobacco control legislation and acting against tobacco companies. However, in many countries, these groups have not yet mobilized around the issue. Moreover, many governments need to strengthen their capacity for effective tobacco control (i.e., building infrastructure and human resources for basic tobacco-control programs and monitoring the tobacco industry's moves).[83]

Road Safety

The theme of World Health Day 2004 was global road safety. Global road safety is a major, yet neglected, public health challenge facing the world today. Every year, there are an estimated 1.2 million fatalities from road traffic crashes. Low- and middle-income countries account for 90 percent of these deaths. Moreover, 20 to 50 million people suffer injuries or disabilities from road traffic crashes each year. Poor populations are particularly susceptible to road traffic injuries because they are the most vulnerable road users (pedestrians, cyclists and passengers on public transport). Southeast Asia and the Western Pacific region are responsible for more than 50 percent of the global mortality related to road traffic injuries. Men have almost three times the traffic injury mortality rate than women, and more than 50 percent of road crash deaths are among individuals 15 to 44 years old. Current trends suggest that the problem is becoming worse.[84] In addition to lives lost, road traffic crashes impose social and economic difficulties.

In Paris on April 7, 2004, WHO and other U.N. agencies and organizations commemorated World Health Day by raising public awareness on the consequences of road traffic injuries and encouraging joint action to implement solutions. Regional and national road safety events, such as conferences and charity sports events, held by NGOs, local governments and others, also took place around the world. In addition, the World Health Organization and the World Bank announced a new global report on road traffic injury prevention that outlines the current knowledge of road traffic injuries, the role of the public health community, key risk factors, strategies for intervention and recommendations for prevention.[85]

Prevention of Noncommunicable Diseases

The U.N. has recognized the importance of improved nutrition in promoting health and preventing noncommunicable diseases (NCDs) for decades. The 1948 Constitution of the World Health Organization, for instance, affirmed that nutrition is a key element in promoting the highest level of health, and the 1976 *International Covenant on Economic, Social and Cultural Rights* identified food as a right of each individual. The 1996 *Rome Declaration on World Food Security* took a further step by asserting that all humans are entitled to have access to safe and nutritious food.[86]

Over the past several years, the U.N. has become more actively involved in promoting strategies to curb NCDs. It is quite fitting, given that the rise in NCDs is related, in part, to physical inactivity, that the year 2005 has been named the International Year of Sport and Physical Education. In 2001, NCDs accounted for almost 60 percent of the 56.5 million deaths and 47 percent of the global disease burden. Cardiovascular disease, Type 2 Diabetes and certain types of cancer can all be traced back to these risk factors.[87]

A second example of increased U.N. action on NCDs is WHO's "Global Strategy on Diet, Physical Activity and Health." In 2002, the agency began to formulate the global strategy upon recommendation of the member states of the World Health Assembly. Its four main objectives include 1) to reduce the risk factors for chronic NCDs; 2) to increase awareness and understanding of the role of diet and physical activity in determining public health; 3) to encourage the development, strengthening and implementation of global, regional, national and community policies and action plans to improve diets and increase physical activity that engage all sectors; and 4) to monitor scientific data and key influences on diet and physical activity.[88] An extensive series of expert and stakeholder consultations among member states, U.N. organizations, civil society representatives and the private sector over a period of one-and-a-half years culminated in the final drafting of the strategy document, which was presented to WHA in May 2004.[89]

During the negotiations on the strategy document, a report of the joint WHO/FAO Expert Consultation caused some turbulence. The document, upon which the global strategy was based, set forth recommendations on nutrition intake and physical activity goals for NCD prevention based on current evidence.[90] In particular, the report recommended that sugar not represent more than 10 percent of a person's daily energy intake. The U.S.-based Sugar Association claimed that the report was scientifically flawed and, as a result, threatened to lobby the U.S. Congress to cut off the American contribution to WHO. Despite the accusations, WHO experts were steadfast in their recommendations.[91] At the WHO Executive Board meeting on January 22, 2004, U.S. Secretary of Health and Human Services Tommy Thompson declared U.S. support for the global strategy. At the same time, he asserted that the guidelines to implement the resolution must be based on scientifically based evidence.[92]

In response to the growing threat of diabetes, WHO and the International Diabetes Federation recently created "Diabetes Action Now." The spread of this NCD is facilitated by increased sedentary lifestyles, unhealthy diets, aging, obesity and population growth.[93] Approximately 177 million people are currently living with diabetes, and the number of people with the disease is projected to more than double by 2030, especially in developing nations.[94] Diabetes Action Now is a program that targets effective surveillance, prevention and control measures for diabetes in low- and middle-income countries.[95] WHO Assistant Director-General of NCDs and Mental Health Catherine Le Galès-Camus said, "Diabetes is part of the growing epidemic of NCDs that are beginning to impose a double burden of disease on the world's poorest communities."[96] Effective approaches to prevent diabetes exist, and the Diabetes Action Now program aims to elucidate how to implement them on a global scale.

Maternal and Child Health

Maternal and child health have been largely supported by the agenda adopted in 1994 at the U.N. International Conference on Population and Development (ICPD) in Cairo. The Programme of Action of the ICPD and a subsequent special session (ICPD+5) set forth goals relating to education and literacy, reproductive healthcare and unmet need for contraception, maternal mortality reduction and HIV/AIDS.[97] In recognition of the 10th anniversary of ICPD, U.N. organizations have convened reviews in different regions of the world during 2004 to reignite countries' commitment to the Cairo agenda. At a conference in Geneva in January 2004, European population and reproductive health experts called on European countries to keep their commitment to the Cairo agenda and increase funding to population and reproductive health.[98] During a meeting in Chile in March 2004, countries of Latin America and the Caribbean expressed their commitment to a declaration that supports the Cairo health action plan. The declaration encourages countries to, among other things, provide basic services and reproductive healthcare to reduce maternal and infant deaths and illnesses.[99] Support for the Cairo program is integral to achieving the goals of the *Millennium Declaration*, even though reproductive health is not mentioned specifically in the MDGs.

Millennium Development Goals 4, 5: Maternal and Child Health

MDG 4: Reduce child mortality. Millennium Development Goal 4 aims to reduce by two-thirds, between 1990 and 2015, the under-5 mortality rate. To measure progress, countries report their under-5 mortality rate, infant mortality rate and proportion of one-year-old children immunized against measles.

MDG 5: Improve maternal health. Millennium Development Goal 5 aims to reduce by three-quarters, between 1990 and 2015, the maternal mortality ratio. Countries supply their maternal mortality ratio and proportion of births attended by skilled health personnel.

The World Bank asserts that only 16 percent of all developing countries are likely to reach the child mortality MDG, and no country in sub-Saharan Africa is on track to meet this target. For the maternal health MDG, only 17 percent of developing countries are on track. The situation in Latin America and the Caribbean is particularly problematic, with only 4.2 percent likely to meet the maternal health MDG.[100]

Child Health

Despite the substantial drop in child mortality over the past two decades, the progress in reducing child mortality slowed in the 1990s. The global under-5 mortality rate declined by 11 percent from 93 deaths/1,000 live births in the early 1990s to 83 deaths/1,000 live births in 2000. In certain

Under-five Mortality Rate, 1990-2001

REGION	DEATHS PER 1,000 LIVE BIRTHS		
	1990	2001	CHANGE (%)
Developed regions	13	9	-31
Developing regions	102	90	-12
Northern Africa	88	43	-51
Sub-Saharan Africa	176	172	-2
Latin America/Caribbean	54	36	-33
Eastern Asia	44	36	-18
South-central Asia	125	95	-24
South-eastern Asia	77	51	-34
Western Asia	70	62	-11
Oceania	85	76	-11

Source: U.N. Statistics Division, "World and regional trends," Millennium Indicators Database, December 2003.

regions, however, the situation is regressing. Children in sub-Saharan Africa, where more than 50 percent of under-5 deaths are projected to occur by 2010, are particularly vulnerable because of the AIDS epidemic and low immunization coverage, which results from a weak health infrastructure. In 2000, almost 11 million children who died were under the age of 5, and most of these deaths occurred in sub-Saharan Africa and South Asia.[101]

In addressing child health needs, efforts must focus on complimentary interventions that respond to the many causes of child mortality. Malnutrition, acute respiratory infections, diarrhea, malaria and measles account for 70 percent of under-5 deaths; these conditions are preventable and treatable.[102] The Bellagio Child Survival Study Group published a paper in *The Lancet* in 2003 that asserted that low-cost interventions, such as oral rehydration therapy, insecticide-treated materials and the promotion of breastfeeding, are not employed as often as they should and have tremendous potential to save the lives of children. These strategies are integral to meeting the child health MDG.[103] A strategy created by UNICEF and WHO called Integrated Management of Childhood Illness (IMCI) also aims to improve child health. IMCI addresses the whole child by incorporating prevention and treatment of common causes of child morbidity and mortality in the family, community and health facility settings.

Maternal Health

The leading cause of disability and mortality among women of reproductive age in developing countries is complications during pregnancy and childbirth. Every year, approximately 515,000 women die from such causes and at least 15 million more suffer injuries. In sub-Saharan Africa, a woman has a 1 in 13 chance of dying during childbirth, while in industrialized countries, that risk is 1 in 4,100.[104] In developing countries, a skilled health worker is present for only 58 percent of births, and in South Asia between 1996 and 2001, fewer than 40 percent of births were attended by a doctor or midwife. To promote maternal health, women need increased access to family planning services and a broad range of health services—including emergency obstetrical care, access to a midwife or doctor during delivery and lifesaving interventions (e.g., antibiotics, surgery, transportation to a medical center).[105] According to a recent report by the U.N. Population Fund (UNFPA) and The Alan Guttmacher Institute, current approaches undervalue the nonmedical effects of maternal healthcare. Maternal healthcare can help families remain together, promote increased savings and enhance productivity.[106]

In February 2004, the Pan American Health Organization (PAHO), a regional office of WHO, announced a new strategy to promote maternal health. A consortium of organizations, in addition to PAHO, have committed to the strategy, including UNFPA, UNICEF, the U.S. Agency for International Development, Family Care International, the Population Council, the Inter-American Development Bank and the World Bank. In Latin America and the Caribbean, the maternal mortality ratio (MMR) is 190 deaths/100,000 live births, more than 10 times the MMR of the United States. The strategy, which features the slogan "Safe Motherhood: Every Woman's Right," emphasizes:[107]

· Supporting national and municipal efforts to promote maternal health;
· Providing comprehensive maternal healthcare and services;
· Increasing public demand for services via education;
· Building partnerships; and
· Financing maternal health services.

The Cloning Debate

The U.N. is progressively beginning to address ethical issues in medical research. UNESCO, for instance, has taken up the issue of ethics of science and technology as one of its top five priorities.[108] Additionally, in December 2001, U.N. delegates voted to examine the issue of human cloning in the Sixth Legal Committee. At the committee's first meeting in early 2002, the main dividing issue that emerged was whether to mandate a ban on human reproductive cloning or all human cloning, which would also include cloning for therapeutic, experimental and research purposes.[109]

In nonreproductive human cloning, human embryos are cloned and the stem cells are removed. Once this occurs, the embryo is destroyed. Individuals who are opposed to all human cloning, including for therapeutic purposes, argue that using human embryos, even those only a few minutes old, is destroying a life. Furthermore, the techniques for both types of cloning are identical, which raises the concern of "rogue doctors" producing a cloned baby. The proponents of nonreproductive cloning argue that the method can help replace cells that are damaged by diseases such as Alzheimer's, Parkinson's and diabetes. The tissue and cells that are created from a patient's stem cells also may be less likely to be rejected during transplantation than those coming from a donor.

This division on human cloning is reflected in two competing resolutions that have been produced by members of the Sixth Legal Committee. At a meeting in November 2003, a vote of 80 to 79, with 15 abstentions, resolved to defer the debate between the competing resolutions until 2005.[110] Yet one month later, in December 2003, the General Assembly disagreed with the Committee's recommendation to postpone discussions and instead placed the issue on the 59th Assembly Agenda.[111]

Recent cloning developments in South Korea have brought the human cloning issue back to center stage. Scientists there successfully cloned human embryos and then extracted the stem cells for therapeutic purposes.[112] This marks the first time that this technique has succeeded and proves that advancements in this realm are not limited to Western nations.

Looking Forward

In the 59th General Assembly meeting, member states will follow up on the outcomes of the Millennium Summit, which includes the health-related MDGs noted in this chapter. There will also be an update on the implementation of the Declaration of Commitment on HIV/AIDS from the U.N. General Assembly Special Session in 2001, and delegates will most likely discuss the global efforts underway to Roll Back Malaria from 2001 to 2010, with a special focus on African nations. Since global road safety is the focus of 2004 World Health Day, and 2005 is the International Year of Sport and Physical Education, both issues will be reported on in the 59th Session. Delegates are expected to discuss the two resolutions that ban human cloning as well. Regarding maternal and child health, delegates will discuss the promotion and protection of rights of children. Finally, the U.N. High-Level Panel on Threats, Challenges and Change, a member of whom is Director-General Emeritus Gro Harlem Brundtland, will report its findings.

Given the close links among health, poverty and development, many other agenda items of the 59th Assembly will directly and indirectly impact on health. Health has finally become an integral part of the global agenda of governments. The next step is to ensure that the commitments, particularly those related to the Millennium Development Goals, are taken forward to concrete action at the country level. Currently, at midpoint for the Goals, the world is falling short. It will be crucial that the 59th Assembly support a new and energetic move toward 2015.

Commentary:
Health as a Security Challenge
Ilona Kickbusch

The challenges to health at a global level are significant. To ensure global health security, two interrelated strategies are required: substantial strengthening of public health within both developed and developing societies, and the establishment of a resilient, well-financed system of global governance for health. If these strategies are not put into place, we—meaning the U.N. and nations around the world—will face dire consequences in terms of human, social and economic development. At present, it is the poorest countries that are paying the price for this negligence, but there are mounting signals that a new "health divide" is in the making in the developed world. Indeed, it is becoming more and more difficult to define the rich and the poor of the world at the level of the nation state, as a large global underclass spreads across the globe and defies the old definitions of vulnerable groups. HIV/AIDS is the most visible of the diseases of poverty that undermine the life chances of the poor.

Increasingly in the health community there is the expression of the need for a new global social contract on health. The drive for such a contract can only be established politically and developed through an ethical and political debate throughout society. And outspoken public health professionals, responsible politicians and a concerned civil society at national and global levels of governance must initiate it. All countries are challenged: rich countries need to contribute more to the plight of the poor as expressed in Goal 8 of the Millennium Development Goals, and poor countries need to invest and engage in the health of their populations.

There are serious ethical questions at stake that have been taken up by the NGO community in recognition of the *Millennium Declaration* and health as a human right: is it acceptable that rich countries share less than 1 percent of their GNP (gross national product) with the world's poor? Why should the life of a citizen in the developed world be worth more than that of an indigenous mother in Bolivia or a young AIDS patient in Zimbabwe? The developing world faces a stark reality:

- A falling life expectancy in many African countries;
- A lack of access to even the most basic services;
- An excess of personal expenditures for health of the poorest;
- Health as a neglected arena of national and development politics; and
- Health as a matter of survival.

U.N. member states can no longer accept a 49 year difference between the average woman's life expectancy in Sierra Leone and Japan. We need to frame this neglect in new terms and, in some cases, it might well qualify as a crime against humanity.

We have reached a point where we need to make a choice of what type of global public health model we want to promote. It needs to be firmly grounded in a notion of global justice. Five action areas drive global public health:

- Health as a global public good;
- Health as a key component of global security;
- Health a key factor of global governance of interdependence;
- Health as responsible business practice; and
- Health as global citizenship.

The present international drive for access to AIDS medicine for developing nations is not just about health, it is the spearhead of a global citizenship movement that has recognized that global health needs to move into the realm of rights, citizenship and a global contract. The field of women's health and reproductive rights is an exemplary area of the interface between health rights and civil, political and social rights.

The political issue is, of course, more difficult. What social, political and financial price will we be willing to pay for better health both individually and as a community, at the local and the global level? Some calculations show that it would cost $100 a year for the next 15 years per each adult citizen of high-income countries to finance the achievement of the Millennium Development Goals. There are many ideas for financing, including a proposal to create a new International Finance Facility. Other ideas include a form of taxation on global consumer goods (such as airline travel and global tourism); for example, $1 from each international ticket would go to a global health security fund or a new form of taxation at the national level where a separate budget is established for the production of global public goods.

We have no choice but to build a global social contract for health to share the cost and the risk of global health.

Endnotes

1. *Macroeconomics and Health: Investing in Health for Economic Development*, WHO Commission on Macroeconomics and Health, December 2001.
2. Kaul, I., Grunberg, I. and Stern, M. (eds.). Global Public Goods: International Cooperation in the 21st Century. UNDP, 1999.
3. *Global Governance Initiative: Executive Summary 2004*, World Economic Forum, January 2004.
4. Richard Holbrooke, Interview on The News Hour With Jim Lehrer, July 13, 2000.
5. UNAIDS/03.39E (*AIDS Epidemic Update*, UNAIDS/WHO, December 2003).
6. ESA/P/WP.185 (*The Impact of AIDS*, DESA, September 2003).
7. Ibid, 5.
8. Ibid, 6.
9. A/58/184 (*Progress Towards Implementation of the Declaration of Commitment on HIV/AIDS: Report of the Secretary-General*, U.N. General Assembly, July 25, 2003).
10. UNAIDS/03.37E (*Progress Report on the Global Response to the HIV/AIDS Epidemic: Follow-up to the 2001 United Nations General Assembly Special Session on HIV/AIDS*, UNAIDS, September 2003.)
11. "About UNAIDS: What Is UNAIDS?," *UNAIDS website*, 2004.

12. "About the Goals," *MDG website*, 2004.
13. *High-Level Forum on the Health MDGs: Summary of Discussions and Agreed Action Points*, WHO, January 2004.
14. *Interim Report of Task Force 5 Working Group on HIV/AIDS*, Millennium Project, February 2004.
15. U.N. Press Release GA/10153, September 22, 2003 ("Opening High-Level General Assembly Meeting on HIV/AIDS, Secretary-General Calls for Drastic Action to Combat Disease").
16. "Intensifying the War on HIV/AIDS," *NGLS Roundup 108*, November 2003.
17. Ibid, 15.
18. Ibid, 9.
19. *Treating 3 Million by 2005: Making It Happen*, WHO, 2003.
20. Ibid.
21. Ibid, 16.
22. *The World Health Report 2003*, WHO, 2003.
23. Ibid, 19.
24. "Plan to Bring Generic AIDS Drugs to Poor Nations," *New York Times*, April 6, 2004.
25. Ibid, 22.
26. WHO Press Release, January 21, 2004 ("WHO Pushing to Rapidly Scale-Up Measures to Fight TB and HIV").
27. "Lack of Funds Hits WHO Anti-AIDS Project," *World Bank Press Review*, March 18, 2004.
28. Global Fund Press Release, February 26, 2004 ("Confirmation of U.S. Pledge for 2004 Boosts Global Fund Resources for Fourth Proposal Round to $900 Million").
29. "The Global Fund to Fight AIDS, Tuberculosis and Malaria: Pledges," Global Fund website, 2004.
30. Ibid, 28.
31. "Meeting the Need," *The InterDependent*, Spring 2004.
32. "Envoy Seeks AIDS Cash," *Toronto Star*, March 4, 2004.
33. UNAIDS/03.58E (*The Media and HIV/AIDS: Making a Difference*, UNAIDS, January 2004).
34. Ibid, 10.
35. "Global Media AIDS Initiative: Media Participants," UNAIDS, 2004.
36. "World AIDS Campaign 2004: Women, Girls, HIV and AIDS Strategic Overview and Background Note," *UNAIDS Strategy Note*, February 2004.
37. "The Global Coalition on Women and AIDS," *UNAIDS Information Note*, January 27, 2004.
38. "International Women's Day 2004 Focuses on Impact of HIV/AIDS Pandemic on Women," *Kaisernetwork.org Daily HIV/AIDS Report*, March 8, 2004.
39. "SARS: Breaking the Chains of Transmission," *WHO website*, 2003.
40. EB113/33 Rev.1 ("Severe Acute Respiratory Syndrome (SARS), Report by the Secretariat," *U.N. Secretariat Report*, January 23, 2004).
41. Ibid, 22.
42. Ibid, 41.
43. Ibid.
44. *Severe Acute Respiratory Syndrome (SARS): Status of the Outbreak and Lessons for the Immediate Future*, WHO, May 2003.
45. "WHO Global Conference on Severe Acute Respiratory Syndrome: Where Do We Go From Here?" *WHO website*, Conference in Malaysia, June 17-18, 2003.
46. "Current International Health Regulations," *WHO website*, 2004.
47. EB113/3 Rev.1 ("Revision of the International Health Regulations: Report by the Secretariat," *WHO Executive Board*, January 15, 2004).

48. WHA56.28 ("Revision of the International Health Regulations," *WHA*, May 28, 2003).
49. "Anatomy of a Global Strategy: The U.N. Responds to SARS," *InterDependent*, Fall 2003.
50. Ibid, 40.
51. "Avian Influenza: Avian Influenza ('bird flu') and the Significance of Its Transmission to Humans," *WHO Fact Sheet No. 277*, January 15, 2004.
52. "Confirmed Human Cases of Avian Influenza A (H5N1)," *WHO website*, March 17, 2004.
53. "World Health Organization to Host Influenza Pandemic Preparedness Meeting," *WHO Notes for the Press*, March 12, 2004.
54. Ibid.
55. "Tuberculosis," *WHO Fact Sheet No. 104*, Revised August 2002.
56. WHO Press Release, March 16, 2004 ("Drug Resistant Tuberculosis Levels Ten Times Higher in Eastern Europe and Central Asia").
57. "What Is Stop TB?" *Stop Tuberculosis website*, 2004.
58. WHO/CDS/CPC/TB/99.270 (*What Is DOTS?* WHO, 1999).
59. WHO/HTM/TB/2004.331 (*Global Tuberculosis Control*, WHO, 2004).
60. "Poliomyelitis," *WHO Fact Sheet No. 114*, Revised April 2003.
61. "Polio Case in Côte d'Ivoire Could Signal Re-infection From Nigeria, U.N. Reports" *U.N. News Centre*, February 25, 2004.
62. EB113/35 ("Eradication of Poliomyelitis: Report by the Secretariat," *WHO*, November 2003).
63. "Global Polio Eradication Initiative: Spearheading Partners," *Polio Eradication website*, 2004.
64. "Polio Eradication Fundraising Campaign Information," *Rotary International website*, 2004.
65. Ibid, 64.
66. "Global Polio Eradication Initiative: Background, Eradication Strategies," *Polio Eradication website*, 2004.
67. "Poliomyelitis," *WHO Fact Sheet No. 114*, Revised April 2003.
68. "Importance of Polio Policies for Post-Certification Era," *Global Polio Eradication: Polio News*, Issue 20, October 2003.
69. Ibid, 63.
70. "Health: A G8 Action Plan," *2003 G8 Summit website*, 2004.
71. Ibid, 63.
72. WHO/Rotary International/CDC/UNICEF Joint Press Release, January 15, 2004 ("Unique Opportunity for Eradication Success Now Rests With Key Governments").
73. "West Africa Gears Up to Eradicate Polio by End of 2004, UNICEF Says," *U.N. News Centre*, February 23, 2004.
74. WHO/CDS/MAL/2003.1093 (*Africa Malaria Report 2003*, WHO/UNICEF, 2003).
75. "RBM Initiative," *RBM website*, 2004.
76. Ibid, 75.
77. Ibid, 75.
78. Ibid, 22.
79. Ibid, 22.
80. "Tobacco Treaty Draws 41 Signatures in First Week," *WHO Notes for the Press No. 16*, June 24, 2003.
81. WHO Press Release, March 25, 2004 ("WHO Framework Convention on Tobacco Control Now Signed by 100 Countries").
82. Ibid, 22.
83. Ibid, 22.
84. *World Report on Road Traffic Injury Prevention*, WHO, April 2004.

85. "Road Safety Is No Accident," *WHO Newsletter on Road Safety: Newsletter 1*, November 2003.

86. "Nutrition: Aim and Objectives," *WHO website*, 2004.

87. EB113/44 Add.1 ("Integrated Prevention of Noncommunicable Diseases: Draft Global Strategy on Diet, Physical Activity and Health," *WHO Executive Board*, November 27, 2003).

88. Ibid.

89. "WHO Executive Board Agrees to Forward Global Strategy on Diet, Physical Activity and Health to May World Health Assembly," *WHO Notes for the Press*, January 22, 2004.

90. WHO Technical Report Series 916 ("Diet, Nutrition and the Prevention of Chronic Diseases," *WHO/FAO Expert Consultation*, 2003).

91. "Nutritionists Unimpressed by Sugar Lobby's Outcry," *Bulletin of the World Health Organization*, 81(6), 2003.

92. U.S. Mission Press Release, January 22, 2004 ("Opening Statement by Tommy Thompson, U.S. Secretary of Health and Human Services, at the Press Briefing Held at World Health Organization Headquarters").

93. "Diabetes Mellitus," *WHO Fact Sheet No. 138*, Revised April 2002.

94. Ibid.

95. "Diabetes Action Now: Consultation on a New WHO-IDF Programme," *WHO*.

96. WHO Press Release WHO/86, November 14, 2003 ("Diabetes Cases Could Double in Developing Countries in the Next 30 Years").

97. "Key Actions for the Further Implementation of the Programme of Action of the ICPD – ICPD+5," *UNFPA website*, 2004.

98. "U.N.-Organized Forum Call for Recommitment to Cairo Population Summit Goals," *U.N. News Centre*, January 14, 2004.

99. UNFPA Press Release, March 11, 2004 ("The Americas Reaffirm Reproductive Health Consensus").

100. WHO Press Release, January 8, 2004 ("Many Countries Not on Target to Reach Health-Related Millennium Development Goals").

101. "Progress Since the World Summit for Children: A Statistical Review," *UNICEF*, September 2001.

102. "Reduce Child Mortality," *Millennium Development Goals website*, 2004.

103. "Child Survival Series: How Many Child Deaths Can We Prevent This Year?" *Lancet*, 2003.

104. Ibid, 101.

105. "Improve Maternal Health," *Millennium Development Goals website*, 2004.

106. *Adding It Up: The Benefits of Investing in Sexual and Reproductive Health Care*, Alan Guttmacher Institute and UNFPA, 2004.

107. PAHO Press Release, February 20, 2004 ("Agencies Pledge to Cut Maternal Deaths").

108. "U.N. Panel Studies Medical Ethics in the Age of Genetic Engineering," *U.N. News Centre*, May 12, 2003.

109. "U.N. Panel on Possible Cloning Ban Wraps Up First Session on 'Troubling' Issue," *U.N. News Centre*, March 1, 2002.

110. A/58/520 ("International Convention Against the Reproductive Cloning of Human Beings," *U.N. General Assembly*, November 11, 2003).

111. U.N. Press Release GA/10218, December 9, 2003 ("General Assembly Decides to Include Item on Reproductive Cloning").

112. "Scientists Take Step Toward Therapeutic Cloning," *Science*, February 13, 2004.

Chapter 2

Managing Global Resources and Sustainable Development

Roger Coate, Gail Karlsson and
Pera Wells with Ethan Kunz

The idea is to try in this age of the expansion of democracy across the developing world to harness it to this agenda of social reform and reducing poverty. To harness it around a framework which everybody from the poorest voter to the richest, most sophisticated foundation or policymaker can understand–halving poverty, getting every kid into school–goals which provide benchmarkable, with a stretch, achievable outcomes but ones which we can all organise our different interventions and actions around, to give a sense of a world which is coherent and is on the move together to achieve these goals and, in that sense, I see what we are doing as essentially providing the social contract to underpin globalisation.
—U.N. Development Programme Administrator Mark Malloch Brown,
Opening Plenary of the 14th European Foundation Center's Annual General Assembly and Conference, June 2003.

While the 1990s witnessed the evolution of a more or less coherent framework for development that became manifest in the United Nations Millennium Declaration, international attention in the first decade of the 2000s, thus far, has focused on implementation of that vision. The new development framework took concrete form in 2000 as world leaders at the U.N. Millennium Summit committed themselves to a global social contract aimed at achieving demonstrable progress toward reducing poverty and promoting sustainable human development by 2015. This consensual development framework is structured around eight major goals called the Millennium Development Goals (MDGs). They focus collective attention on reducing poverty and hunger, achieving universal primary education, promoting gender equality and the empowerment of women, reducing child mortality, improving maternal health, combating endemic diseases, ensuring environmental sustainability and developing a global partnership for development. These MDGs and their associated specific targets and indicators provide the context within which U.N. agencies and member states approach development issues.

The Millennium Development Goals

Goal 1: Eradicate extreme poverty and hunger.
Goal 2: Achieve universal primary education.
Goal 3: Promote gender equality and empower women.
Goal 4: Reduce child mortality.
Goal 5: Improve maternal health.
Goal 6: Combat HIV/AIDS, malaria and other diseases.
Goal 7: Ensure environmental sustainability.
Goal 8: Develop a global partnership for development.

Chapter 1 of this book has already touched on three of these primary goals: reducing child mortality, improving maternal healthcare and combating HIV/AIDS, malaria and other diseases, while the third chapter pays special attention to the goal on gender equality. This chapter, therefore, focuses primarily on the first and seventh MDGs, eradicating extreme poverty and hunger and ensuring environmental sustainability, as well as on the eighth goal, developing a global partnership for development. It also touches upon the need for all individuals to receive a primary education.

The first Millennium Development Goal concentrates on what is arguably the foremost among the MDGs in that it represents the end product toward which the others are focused on attaining—that is overall poverty eradication. All the goals, however, are interrelated and reinforcing. In this respect, the seventh goal focuses on an essential element for attaining and supporting human development: environmental sustainability. The eighth MDG deals with creating the capacity for achieving these and the other five substantive goals in an effort to ultimately eliminate poverty and other maladies of underdevelopment. The seven specific targets associated with MDG 8 are wide ranging and include the following: restructuring global trading and financial systems; promoting good governance; addressing the special needs of least-developed and landlocked countries; dealing with debt problems; creating sustainable livelihoods; providing affordable access to essential drugs; and building effective cooperation with the private sector in order to make the benefits of new technologies available to developing societies.

In the next section, we begin by exploring issues, challenges and activities related to sustaining the human environment. In this regard, 2003-2004 has been rich in events and activities focusing on critical environmental concerns, including issues related to the oceans, forests, climate, ozone, biological diversity, water and sustainable development.

Sustaining the Global Environment: The Good News and The Challenges Ahead

Gail Karlsson

Addressing the ministers and other stakeholders attending the April 2004 meeting of the Commission on Sustainable Development, United Nations Secretary-General Kofi Annan warned that high-level political attention has been diverted from sustainable development "by the recent emphasis given to terrorism, weapons of mass destruction and the war in Iraq. However understandable that focus might be, we cannot lose any more time, or ground, in the wider struggle for human well-being."[1]

Certainly the sense of optimism that led the U.N. General Assembly to adopt the MDGs in 2000 has become somewhat frayed, despite reaffirmation of countries' commitment to those goals at the 2002 World Summit on Sustainable Development (WSSD). The S.G. pointed to some positive developments–new, legally binding international conventions to slow the spread of persistent organic pollutants, pesticides and other hazardous chemicals, as well as an increase in official development assistance (after a long decline), new partnerships and corporate social responsibility initiatives. Moreover, the S.G. concluded that overall awareness of what sustainable development means has deepened, in particular, the fact that it involves not just environmental protection but also social progress and economic development.

Nevertheless, S.G. Annan observed that key challenges remain: "The natural resource base is under siege. Unsustainable patterns of consumption and production are still the norm. Progress in slowing deforestation and biodiversity loss has been glacial. The AIDS epidemic is an enormous and still growing burden. The global trading system, including economically and environmentally harmful subsidies, remains biased against developing countries, hampering their efforts to rise out of poverty. Vulnerable small island states face enormous threats; some may not survive at all. Unless the United States or the Russian Federation ratifies the *Kyoto Protocol*, we cannot fully and properly address the issue of climate change."[2]

This section reviews and provides an update on some of these challenges facing U.N. member states.

Responding to Climate Change

Supporters of the *Kyoto Protocol* to the U.N. Framework Convention on Climate Change (UNFCCC) had hoped that the Russian Federation would ratify the protocol at the ninth meeting of the Conference of the Parties to the UNFCCC, which was held in Milan in December 2003. Given the U.S. government's rejection of the *Kyoto Protocol*, ratification by the Russian Federation is needed for it to enter into force. That ratification has not yet occurred because of concerns about potentially negative effects on the Russian economy. However, in May 2004, President Vladimir Putin ended months of speculation by coming out in support of the protocol.[3] It remains to be seen if the U.S. will also change its mind.

Ministers attending the December 2003 meeting agreed that "climate change remains the most important global challenge to humanity and that its adverse effects are already a reality in all parts of the world." They also noted that economic growth and climate change policies are compatible, and that if action is taken early enough, economic gains can actually be achieved. A number of countries said that every effort should be made to implement the *Kyoto Protocol* even though it has not yet entered into force.[4]

Backing up support for the protocol are clear, hard-to-ignore climate changes. The World Meteorological Organization, for example, announced that 2003 was the third warmest year on record (behind 1998 and 2002). Europe experienced unprecedented heat waves last summer, which caused unusually high death rates. The Antarctic ozone hole was as large as it has ever been, matching the record set in 2000, and the Arctic sea ice coverage matched record lows.[5]

In April 2004, British Prime Minister Tony Blair helped launch a new world organization to fight these rapidly growing concerns–the Climate Group. Prime Minister Blair said that getting support for the protocol remained a "tall order," but that the agreement represented only a first step in tackling global warming, which he said was the most serious long-term threat facing the planet.[6]

Protecting Small Islands

In preparing for the January 2005 10-year review of the Barbados Pro-gramme of Action (BPOA), the small island developing states (SIDS), stated that adaptation to climate change was a major priority for them, since the failure of most industrialized countries to reduce greenhouse gas emissions meant that the vulnerability of SIDS would be increased. They also noted that the current emphasis on security has resulted in a diversion of resources from sustainable development, and called for a multidimensional view of security that encompasses threats such as natural disasters, food and water security, HIV/AIDS, and illegal drug and arms trading.[7]

The S.G.'s report on progress in implementing BPOA recognized that global warming has brought an increase in extreme weather events affect-ing small island states, as well as coral bleaching, coastal erosion, disruption of agricultural activity and reduced resilience of land and marine ecosys-tems. As a result, the Global Environment Facility (GEF) and other donors have funded planning for adaptation to climate change and sea level rise for islands in the Caribbean and Pacific.[8]

In addition to their environmental fragility, SIDS face special challenges because of their small populations and economies, their remoteness from and dependence on international markets, their high transportation costs and the limited diversification in economic goods and services they offer. Nearly all the small island states reported high levels of economic vulnerability; these include concerns about marginalization in the global economy, and impacts of natural and environmental disasters that have hindered infrastructure development and diverted scarce resources to rehabilitation and reconstruction expenditures.[9]

Reducing Risks From Natural Disasters

In December 2003, the U.N. General Assembly approved the organization of a World Conference on Disaster Reduction, to be held in Japan in January 2005.[10] The conference is expected to review implementation of the 1994 Yokohama Strategy and Plan of Action on disaster risk reduction and set a framework for the next century, taking into account provisions of the plan of implementation adopted at the WSSD concerning vulnerability risk assessments and disaster management. Conference participants will propose ways to strengthen political commitments on identifying and monitoring risks, and to implement environmental, social and economic development measures to reduce those risks. Each country is expected to set objectives and targets according to its own priorities, placing special emphasis on vulnerable urban areas.[11]

The U.N. Development Programme's Bureau for Crisis Prevention and Recovery recently issued a report titled "Reducing Disaster Risk: A Challenge for Development." The report shows how countries facing similar patterns of risks from earthquakes, hurricanes, droughts and floods can experience widely different impacts when disasters occur, depending on their differing response strategies, investments in infrastructure and regulations controlling urban development. Unplanned development can increase disaster risks, for example, through rapid growth of informal urban settlements on steep slopes and along flood plains, while integration of disaster planning with sustainable development programs can reduce countries' short- and long-term vulnerability to environmental disasters.[12]

Preserving Fisheries and Ocean Resources

The "Global Environmental Outlook Yearbook 2003," published by the U.N. Environment Programme (UNEP), warned that some types of fish are being harvested faster than they can reproduce, and that major changes in the use and management of marine habitats are needed to prevent many fisheries from becoming commercially extinct. The total quantity of fish catches has been declining since the late 1980s and initiatives to take control of certain widely and often consumed fish, such as tuna and cod, have not been effective in protecting these species. Fishing fleets are moving farther out to sea and into deeper water, beyond the 200-mile limit of national jurisdiction. These "high seas" areas are currently not protected by international mechanisms regulating the amounts and types of fish that can be taken. Some of the species now being caught are long-lived fish like the Patagonian toothfish (aka Chilean sea bass) and the orange roughy. These species take a long time to mature sexually, and if all the older fish are harvested, it will be difficult for the species to continue.[13]

To help ensure sustainability of such marine resources, in November 2003, the G.A. established a voluntary fund to assist developing countries in implementing the 1995 Fish Stocks Agreement on managing and conserving migratory fish and species that straddle national jurisdiction zones.[14]

Some loss of fish species is attributable to invasive marine life carried from place to place by ships carrying water in their holds as ballast. When ships enter a port to take on cargo and empty out the water in their holds, alien species from other ecosystems are released. Bio-invasions by species such as Zebra mussels and comb jellyfish reproduce rapidly, displacing native stocks and causing pollution. In February 2004, after more than a decade of work, the International Maritime Organization (IMO) adopted a new *International Convention for the Control and Management of Ships' Ballast Water and Sediments* to help prevent the spread of damaging aquatic organisms.[15]

Maintaining Biological Diversity

In February 2004, parties to the *Convention on Biological Diversity* (CBD) met in Kuala Lumpur, Malaysia, to consider plans for achieving the WSSD target on significantly reducing biodiversity loss by 2010. They agreed on subtargets for conserving at least 10 percent of each type of ecosystem, establishing protected areas in places of particular importance for biodiversity, stabilizing populations of species now in decline and preventing threats to species from international trade. Examples of indicators for measuring achievement of biodiversity protection targets include numbers and costs of invasive alien species; the acreage of forests under sustainable management; the degree of fragmentation of related ecosystems; and water quality in aquatic ecosystems. Also on the agenda was discussion of how to create an international regime on granting companies or other organizations access to genetic resources, such as plants for pharmaceuticals or fragrances, and ensuring that countries and local communities share in the profits from their use.[16]

Immediately following the CBD session was the first meeting of the parties to the *Cartagena Protocol on Biosafety*, which entered into force on September 11, 2003. This protocol addresses safe handling of living modified organisms (LMOs), which may have an adverse effect on biodiversity, and calls for a decision by September 2005 on detailed requirements for the identification of LMOs shipped across borders and intended for direct use as food or feed.[17]

At the end of March 2004, the U.N. Food and Agriculture Organization (FAO) announced that the International Treaty on Plant Genetic Resources for Food and Agriculture would enter into force in June 2004, having been recently ratified by the countries in the European Community. The treaty is intended to ensure the conservation and sustainable use of plants for food or agriculture and to promote enhanced access to genetic biodiversity. At the same time, FAO warned that there has been an alarming worldwide loss of diversity in domestic animal breeds, which creates concerns about food security because genetic diversity allows farmers to select stock or develop new breeds to respond to environmental changes and spread of diseases.[18]

Managing Forests

The U.N. Forum on Forests (UNFF) met in May 2004 in Geneva to discuss aspects of sustainable forest management, including the social and cultural aspects of forests, and application of traditional forest-related knowledge. Established in 2000 by the U.N. Economic and Social Council (ECOSOC), UNFF promotes the implementation of proposals for action agreed upon in earlier years during dialogue sessions facilitated by the International Panel on Forests and the International Forum on Forests. ECOSOC also called for a review after five years to assess the institutional framework for forest protection and the effectiveness of international forest protection programs. There is currently no international treaty on forests, but a working group is considering the possibility of developing a legal framework for all types of forests and will present its recommendations at the fifth meeting of the UNFF next year.[19]

Unsustainable harvesting of tropical timber has contributed to the depletion of some types of valuable trees. In November 2003, trade regulations under the *Convention on International Trade in Endangered Species* (CITES) took effect to protect big-leaf mahogany, which is reported to be commercially extinct in parts of Latin America and South America. Exports of this wood now must be accompanied by CITES permits to ensure that shipments include only legally and sustainably harvested timber.[20] Meanwhile, negotiators worked to clarify the elements of a successor agreement to the 1994 International Tropical Timber Agreement for consideration at a July 2004 conference in Geneva.[21]

Controlling the Use of Chemicals

The 2001 *Stockholm Convention on Persistent Organic Chemicals* (POPs) entered into force in May 2004. The convention is designed to eliminate the release of certain toxic chemicals that remain in the environment for long periods of time and accumulate in the fatty tissues of people and animals throughout the world. UNEP Executive Director Klaus Toepfer stressed the importance of the agreement in the overall scope of international environmental law: "Of all the pollutants released into the environment every year by human activity, POPs are the most dangerous. For decades, these highly toxic chemicals have killed and injured people and wildlife by inducing cancer and damaging the nervous, reproductive and immune systems. They have also caused uncounted birth defects."[22]

The first meeting of the parties to the POPs convention will be held in Uruguay in early 2005. Most of the chemicals on the initial list, including polychlorinated biphenols (PCBs), dioxins and pesticides, are to be banned immediately. DDT, however, can still be used in developing countries to kill the mosquitoes that cause malaria, while more effective and less toxic methods are researched. The convention also calls for efforts to clean up stockpiles of banned or obsolete pesticides and toxic chemicals that are leaking and contaminating water resources.

In February 2004, another international treaty entered into effect, the 1998 *Rotterdam Convention on the Prior Informed Consent (PIC) Procedure for Certain Hazardous Chemicals and Pesticides in International Trade*. Jointly supported by FAO and UNEP, the convention gives importing countries tools and information for identifying potentially hazardous chemicals and excluding those they cannot handle safely. It is particularly meant to protect developing countries that have limited capacity to monitor and manage the large number of dangerous chemicals that are traded internationally. Moreover, some chemicals banned in industrialized countries are still marketed in developing countries. When chemicals are approved for import, protections are provided by means of labeling requirements and provision of information on possible health and environmental problems related to the use (or misuse) of the particular chemicals.[23]

Conserving Freshwater Resources

In many parts of the world, people do not have adequate access to clean water for drinking, washing and sanitation. Since water is so essential for human life and livelihoods, one of the targets agreed on under the MDG 7 on ensuring environmental sustainability is to reduce by half the proportion of people who do not have access to safe drinking water by 2015.

Representatives at the April 2004 meeting of the U.N. Commission on Sustainable Development (CSD) focused on issues related to water, sanitation and human settlements. The participants were not negotiating a decision or a policy document, but rather sharing information about national implementation activities, successes and challenges. This was the first CSD meeting that followed the multiyear program of work for the period 2004-2017, adopted by the Commission in 2003. The plan calls for a series of two-year cycles, with the first year serving as a review session on specified topics and the second year devoted to setting policy on those issues. Discussions this year concerned constraints and obstacles related to access to water and sanitation, including lack of adequate financing, technology and capacity, as well as suggestions for responding to those challenges.[24] Those suggestions will form the basis for next year's policy negotiations.

The S.G.'s report to the CSD on freshwater management highlighted growing concerns over a "global water crisis" resulting from increased demand for finite water resources, contamination of water supplies and degradation of ecosystems from mismanagement. In many cases this crisis results from institutional problems in managing water resources and providing water services, rather than an actual lack of water.[25]

Although many countries are likely to meet the MDG target of halving the number of people without access to safe drinking water by 2015, in some regions, most countries are not on track. Overall, meeting the MDG target will require providing access to approximately 1.6 billion people by 2015, which could require a doubling of spending on drinking water supplies. In many areas, preventing contamination of water sources by human or animal waste or industrial pollution would protect available drinking water supplies, while in urban supply systems, fixing leaks would save large amounts of water that would be otherwise lost. Integrated water resource management, involving decentralization of some management responsibilities and greater participation of local users, can also lead to improved water allocations, greater efficiency and better recovery of service costs.

Food Emergencies: A Setback in the War Against Hunger

Roger Coate

In the State of Food Insecurity in the World 2003 (SOFI 2003), released in November 2003, FAO reported that the "latest estimates signal a setback in the war against hunger." The number of undernourished and hungry people in the developing world is again on the rise after having declined during the first half of the 1990s. For the latest period in which data are available (1999-2001), 842 million people worldwide are estimated to be undernourished. Of these, 798 million, or 95 percent, live in developing countries, with most of the remainder located in transitional societies.

Only in 19 countries did the situation show continuous progress between 1990-1992 and 1999-2001. Whereas the number of "chronically hungry" people decreased by 37 million during the first half of the 1990s, the number has increased by more than 18 million since 1995-1997.[26] In terms of regions, Latin America, the Caribbean and Asia and the Pacific recorded a decline in the number of hungry, while sub-Saharan Africa and the Near East and North Africa registered increases. At the country level within and across regions, however, findings were mixed. In China, for example, there were 58 million fewer undernourished people in 1999-2001 than in 1990-1992. India, on the other hand, experienced an increase of 19 million hungry people between 1995-1997 and 1999-2001, after having had a decline of 20 million between 1990-1992 and 1995-1997.

There are, of course, many causes of chronic hunger and undernourishment. Among the most important are drought, civil conflict, endemic disease and poor economic growth. In countries most severely affected by HIV/AIDS, such as those in southern Africa, the pandemic has dramatically impacted food security as well. It reduces and diverts assets and other resources needed for agricultural investment. The agricultural labor force in southern Africa, for example, has been significantly reduced, and it is estimated that by 2020, 20 percent or more of the agricultural labor force in most southern African countries will succumb to the disease. Conversely, hunger intensifies and fuels HIV/AIDS as hungry people become engaged in risky behavior and become more susceptible to opportunistic infections.[27]

In mid-2003, FAO classified 36 countries as experiencing serious food emergencies. Most of these were in sub-Saharan Africa, but others were in northern Africa, central America and western Asia, including Mongolia. Natural causes, especially drought, accounted for well over half of the cases in the 1992-2003 period. In the case of Mongolia, however, it was not drought but excessive snowfall that devastated agricultural production and killed millions of farm animals. Floods also caused crop damage in five southern African countries. At the same time, more than 35 percent of the food emergencies in the 1992-2003 period resulted from conflict, economic problems and other human-induced causes. When viewed in the long-term context, the persistent and chronic nature of international food emergencies becomes apparent. Over the 17 years from 1986 to 2003, 33 countries experienced food emergencies during more than half that period. Of those, nearly one-quarter suffered emergencies during 15 or more years. In these cases, civil strife and war were the dominant reasons.[28]

In April 2004, 24 African countries continued to face food emergencies. The situation had improved marginally since 2003 because of improved agricultural outputs in Ethiopia and Sudan. Yet 7 million people in Ethiopia continued to require food assistance, and civil strife in Darfur, Sudan, has left close to 1 million displaced people in need of food.[29] Spring 2004 brought appeals for food aid to relieve massive suffering in Somalia, Swaziland, Lesotho, Angola, Ethiopia, Eritrea, Rwanda, the African Great Lakes region, the Central African Republic, Tanzania, Kenya and Sudan.

As part of an effort to build an international alliance against hunger, the Inter-Agency Working Group on Food Insecurity and Vulnerability Information and Mapping Systems (IAWG-FIVIMS) has been established to monitor and map the world hunger situation and to coordinate and share information. IAWG-FIVIMS is a broad-based consortium comprised of bilateral aid agencies, U.N. and Bretton Woods agencies and programs, international agricultural research organizations and regional organizations. Also, FAO has initiated the global Anti-Hunger Programme. This initiative focuses on five priority areas: improving agricultural productivity in poor rural areas; conserving natural resources; improving rural infrastructure and access to markets; capacity-building for developing and disseminating knowledge and awareness; and providing food to those most in need.[30]

The Molecular Divide

Despite efforts to construct an international alliance to fight hunger, "the gap between rich and poor farmers, between research priorities and needs, and between technology development and the actual technology transfer is widening."[31] FAO has dubbed this condition the "molecular divide" as biotechnology research has tended to ignore the needs of poor countries and their farmers. Agricultural research and development are overwhelmingly based in private multinational firms located in rich societies. Most of this new biotechnology, therefore, has focused on producing large-scale transgenetic crops that are insect- and drought-resistant; they also reduce labor and other production costs. On the other hand, very little biotechnology investment has been used to produce the types of crops that are predominant in semi-arid tropical locals.[32] Bridging this "molecular divide" is critical to redressing the problems of agricultural production and hunger in developing societies. This will require much greater investment in public-sector programs and public-private partnerships.

Population and Poverty

Roger Coate

In its biennial Report on the World Social Situation 2003, the U.N. Department of Economic and Social Affairs (DESA) focused on the sources and challenges of dealing with socially generated group-specific vulnerabilities within societies.[33] The interrelationships between poverty and social vulnerability are complex and, in many ways, mutually reinforcing in a negative way. In other words, poor people are more subject to social and economic vulnerabilities, and those who are vulnerable are more prone to the negative consequences associated with poverty. The forces of globalization have only intensified the insecurities associated with poverty and vulnerability.

The 2003 DESA report focused on children and youth, indigenous peoples, migrants, older persons, persons with disabilities, persons in conflict areas and women. While each of these groups is important in its own right, two—older persons and women—will be highlighted here as they relate to poverty reduction, human development and the attainment of the MDGs.

The Ageing

Demographic shifts and, in particular, the acceleration of ageing people in developing countries have brought the issue of ageing onto center stage at the United Nations. This became clear at the Second World Assembly on Ageing in April 2002 and was reinforced in the Madrid International Plan of Action on Ageing that was adopted at the conference. The Plan of Action was based on two interrelated approaches: a developmental approach focusing on mainstreaming older persons into development policies and programs; and a "life-course intergenerational approach" that factors in equity and all-age inclusive considerations for all policy areas. The main thrust of the plan is to integrate mainstreaming of ageing into international and national policy frameworks and development plans.[34] It outlines three thematic directions: older persons and development; advancing health and well-being in old age; and promoting and sustaining enabling environments.[35]

Historical, cultural and social practices and differences lie at the heart of the debate over the perceived appropriate and acceptable roles of older persons in society.[36] Older persons, regardless of gender, are frequently seen as being unproductive. In many, if not most, developing societies, a welfare approach has been predominant. The many potential contributions of older persons to social and economic development often become lost or obscured because of negative self-image or public misperceptions about their capabilities and potentials. For older persons, vulnerability tends to increase with advanced ageing as a lack of social security, discrimination, social marginalization and exclusion become more profound. Yet, as reflected in the DESA 2003 report and in the Secretary-General's follow-up report to the Madrid Conference, neither international agencies nor national governments have aggressively acted to build the capacity required to effectively integrate ageing into development strategies. As stated bluntly by the Secretary-General, experience has demonstrated that "without capacity-building, mainstreaming is unlikely to happen following the adoption of a plan of action."[37]

Women

The Secretary-General's report was also, in part, a response to G.A. Resolution 57/177, focusing on the situation of older women in development. Since men and women progress through life stages at different rates and in distinct ways, and since women normally outlive their male counterparts in significant numbers, the gender dimension of ageing is an important consideration for development.[38]

For some years now, mainstreaming a gender perspective into development policies and programs of U.N. agencies has been an important concern. The empowerment of women and gender equality have become widely viewed as essential components of sustainable human development and requisites for attaining the MDGs. Thirty-nine women's human rights activists, however, have argued that the MDGs fail to account adequately for critical linkages between women's empowerment and other human rights principles. "Economic empowerment without reproductive rights or education without the elimination of sexual harassment and violence against women does not allow for the full exercise of human rights or women's full citizenship."[40]

Institutionalizing a gender perspective through specific measures reaching into the field, however, has been a challenge. Frequently, resistance persists at the national and local levels as well as within the agencies themselves for cultural and other reasons. In January 2004, S.G. Annan highlighted this problem in relation to the establishment of the new government in Afghanistan, stating that, despite U.N. efforts to the contrary, Afghan women still face "gross violations" of human rights. He called for the new Afghan government to adopt a zero-tolerance policy in this regard and to undertake measures to ensure that women would be adequately represented in governance arrangements at all levels.[41] U.N. officials are coming to realize that a key to reducing gender-based violence and discrimination lies in educating men and boys about the value to themselves and society of promoting women's equality, empowerment and economic and political participation.[42] Moreover, like ageing, women's empowerment and gender equality need to be linked to other frameworks of social and economic development. *(See Chapter 3's special section on MDG 3 for more details.)*

Developing Global Partnerships:
From Education to Debt Relief

Roger Coate

At the core of Millennium Development Goal 8 is building sustainable partnerships for development to bridge rich and poor countries. Couched in the context of the liberal capitalist world economy and the associated trade and financial regimes, it specifies targets for integrating poor countries and regions more fully and effectively into those orders.

Least-developed countries (LDCs) represent the poorest of the international community's poor. Eighty percent of people living in the 50 member states of the U.N. that are classified as LDCs live on incomes of less than $2 a day. The vast majority of LDCs are located in Africa, and in these African LDCs, the percentage of people living on less than $1 a day is nearly two-thirds.[43] It is clear that LDCs represent one of the most substantial challenges for reducing poverty and attaining the MDGs.

In response to this challenge, the third U.N. Conference on the Least-Developed Countries, held in Brussels in May 2001, set out a program of action for the 2001-2010 decade. It specified the following commitments, centered on fostering a people-centered policy framework: good governance; human and institutional capacity-building; making globalization work for LDCs; enhancing the role of trade in development; environmental protection; and mobilizing financial resources for development.

Another group of developing states that provide a special challenge is landlocked developing countries (LLDCs). This group of countries shares several specific goals: securing unfettered access to the sea; reducing transportation costs; improving services to increase competitiveness; reducing delivery costs of imports; clearing trade routes of delays; lessening deterioration and loss of goods during transit; and providing mechanisms for expanding trade.[44]

In recent years, LLDCs have received increased attention, with the 56th Session of the G.A. deciding to convene an International Ministerial Meeting of Landlocked and Transit Developing Countries.[45] The Government of Kazakhstan hosted this special conference in Almaty in late August 2003. It was the first U.N. conference of its kind. The main outcome was a decision to forge a nonbinding agreement on specific actions to be undertaken by LLDCs and partner states to address the concerns and objectives identified above. These actions were encompassed in the Almaty Programme of Action, which focused on five priority areas: fundamental transit policy issues; infrastructure development and maintenance; international trade and trade facilitation; international support measures; and implementation and review.[46] Like LDCs, however, LLDCs are also confronted with a series of other constraints that hinder their ability to achieve the MDGs. The following sections explore these in some detail.

The Gender Dimension of Education and Health Access

Promoting education for all is not simply an end in itself but a means toward poverty eradication, sustainable human development and ensured human security. Yet, approximately 20 percent of children in the developing world are not enrolled in primary school, and nearly 20 percent of the world's adult population remains illiterate. Seventy percent of these are concentrated in three regions: North Africa and the Arab countries, sub-Saharan Africa and southern and western Asia.[47]

Directly tied to education, of course, is illiteracy, which is becoming a gendered phenomenon. Three-fifths of children not receiving a primary education are girls, and two-thirds of illiterate adults are women.[48] In this context, a critical issue for sustainable development and poverty reduction is dealing with gender disparities. Educated girls tend to make life choices and live lives that impact positively on other development goals. This is true for universal secondary as well as primary education. As argued succinctly in the 2003 Human Development Report, gender equality is central to creating the synergies needed to promote better health, increase productivity, reduce fertility rates and create other conditions necessary to promote sustainable development.[49]

Gendered illiteracy differences have their foundations in inequalities in access to education. Over one-third of the world's primary-school-aged children live in countries that do not provide equal access to primary education for boys and girls. Gender inequities are even more pronounced in secondary education, with about 50 percent of children residing in countries that do not provide equal access to lower secondary education and 80 percent living in countries with disparities at the upper secondary level. While gender disparities in low-income countries favor boys, disparities in high-income countries tend to favor girls. The greatest disadvantages for girls in secondary education persist in Africa and Asia.[50]

A main issue confronting the international community is what to do about this situation. The United Nations Children's Fund (UNICEF) has made the issue a priority for 2004. In its State of the World's Children 2004 report, UNICEF argues that achievements toward attaining the MDGs cannot be accomplished without first realizing gender equality in education.[51] Accordingly, educating girls stands as the most pressing issue on the global development agenda. It is a foundation for promoting women's empowerment, which is, in turn, a critical foundation for reducing poverty and sustaining development.

In the face of this acknowledged need, governments and international agencies have pledged to increase assistance for basic education. This was most clearly demonstrated in 2002 in Monterrey at the International Conference on Financing for Development. Yet the international community has, so far, not been forthcoming in terms of providing the needed investment in education for women.

In this context, UNICEF has called on governments to undertake seven specific initiatives: 1) incorporate girls' education as an essential part of development strategies; 2) undertake civic education campaigns to promote awareness of the importance of girls' education; 3) make primary education free, compulsory and universal; 4) integrate education policies into poverty-reduction strategies; 5) make schools centers for community development; 6) integrate country education development strategies to incorporate three dimensions—investments, policies and institutions; service delivery; and economic and human rights approaches; and 7) increase international assistance for education. The question now is whether donor governments, international agencies and developing states will act on these initiatives and the pledges they made at Monterrey.

As inferred above, gender inequality in developing countries is equally problematic in regard to healthcare access. One of the clearest indicators of such inequality is differential mortality rates and life expectancy between men and women. In sub-Saharan Africa, women's life expectancies are dramatically lower than in developed countries. A major factor propelling such dire statistics is lack of access to adequate medical treatment and healthcare.[52] Moreover, funding for women's health care is substantially—25 percent—lower than that for their male counterparts.[53]

Still, gender is not the only important issue regarding health access. Perhaps even more problematic, as shown in Chapter 1, is the lack of access to affordable drugs and treatments that are essential for fighting disease and protecting human health and well-being. The issue of access to such essential drugs has been a major point of North-South contention in international trade negotiations being conducted in the World Trade Organization (WTO). At the center of this controversy has been the 1995 Agreement on Trade-Related Aspects of Intellectual Property Rights (TRIPS) which provides for, among other things, minimum standards of protection and obligations for each member country. The TRIPS formulation represents an attempt to strike a balance between protecting the property rights of the inventor and providing access to the consumer.

In the context of international health, TRIPS has been trying to find a balance between the interests of pharmaceutical companies and their home states on the one hand and nontechnologically advanced countries who desire greater access to drugs that are essential for public health reasons on the other. Under Article 37 of the TRIPS agreement, members are allowed to exercise "non-voluntary licensing" without the authorization of the property right holder under certain conditions, such as public health necessities. However, the nature of this right was left rather ambiguous and became subject to dispute. Moreover, many developing countries do not have adequate manufacturing capabilities in pharmaceuticals to enable them to even make effective use of compulsory licensing.

At the WTO Ministerial Conference in Doha in November 2001, this issue came to a head. Developing-country governments, seeking greater access to drugs for treating HIV/AIDS, tuberculosis and other endemic diseases, were able to get member states to agree on a compromise that no longer prevents countries from undertaking measures to protect public health. A separate declaration adopted by the conference members specified that LDCs would be given until January 1, 2016, before being required to implement or enforce the TRIPS agreement with regard to pharmaceutical products. The declaration, however, still left unresolved the issue of how to deal with those countries that do not have sufficient manufacturing capabilities in pharmaceuticals to enable them to even make effective use of compulsory licensing.

In August 2003, WTO announced that a new agreement had been reached between rich pharmaceutical producing states and developing countries on how to deal with the controversial TRIPS implementation issue. The agreement releases states from the restrictive obligation to produce generic drugs solely for the domestic market. *(See Chapter 7 for further details.)* The new waiver, at least potentially, opens up market access to a broader set of developing country consumers.[54]

Official Development Assistance

Speaking to members of the G.A. at the High-Level Dialogue on Financing for Development in October 2003, S.G. Annan warned that efforts to increase Official Development Assistance (ODA) to developing countries had been relatively ineffective. A large gap remains between projected need and actual assistance flows. In fact, there exists a huge negative flow of money from developing to developed countries. It is on the rise and has reached new levels. Moreover, while there has been a slight increase in ODA since the Monterrey conference in 2002, other elements of the "consensus," including debt burden, market access and further deteriorating terms of trade, have not shown significant improvement. At the same time, in developing countries, corruption and other governance issues linger, frustrating resource mobilization and capacity-building.[55]

In recent years, significant steps have been taken to diminish the impact of the debt burdens of heavily indebted countries. The overall goal is to resolve the problem of unsustainable debt in low-income countries—that is, to bring debt levels into better balance with the repayment capacities of debtor states. The most noteworthy of these steps has been the Heavily Indebted Poor Countries Initiative (HIPC), undertaken by the World Bank and International Monetary Fund (IMF). In 1999, an enhanced HIPC framework was launched that aimed to provide deeper and broader relief by lowering external debt thresholds, provide faster relief by speeding up the HIPC decision process, and link debt relief to increased financial commitments to poverty reduction programs.

As of spring 2004, 27 of the 42 HIPC countries had reached their decision points under the program and were receiving some degree of debt relief. Of these, 11 had reached their completion points and were entitled to irrevocable debt relief from bilateral and multilateral creditors.[56]

The IMF issued a working paper in September 2003 that cautioned that the HIPC debt-reduction program might not be working well for some of Africa's poorest countries.[57] It found that, given current fiscal policies, these countries could be expected to continue to have unsustainable debt burdens even after they graduate from the HIPC program. Moreover, the study raised questions regarding the logic of HIPC: "By the very requirements of the HIPC Initiative, these countries are expected to increase significantly their poverty-reducing expenditure—possibly resulting in weaker fiscal primary balances and worsening debt sustainability outlook."[58]

Nicaragua, on the other hand, saw the overwhelming majority of its $6.5 billion debt wiped away by the IMF and the World Bank in January under HIPC. World Bank President James Wolfensohn praised the country, which now owes only $1.4 billion in external debt.[59]

While very important, debt relief by itself is not sufficient to launch low-income countries on the road to sustainable growth. Among various additional actions is a new UNDP initiative to expand sovereign risk credit ratings to poor African countries. In 2003, three sub-Saharan African governments—Benin, Cameroon and Ghana—received such ratings, and five more are scheduled to come on line in 2004. This experiment aims to enhance Africa as a magnet for foreign direct investment, thus reducing dependence on ODA and other forms of assistance.[60]

The New Partnership for Africa's Development

The list of commitments and promises made to Africa in global conferences over the past decade-and-a-half is impressive. Follow-through, however, has been equally unimpressive.[61]

The New Partnership for Africa's Development (NEPAD) represents, therefore, a self-initiated framework by African leaders to eradicate poverty and promote sustainable human development. NEPAD addresses social, economic, gender, medical and educational issues in Africa. The long-term NEPAD goals include the following: eradication of poverty; conflict prevention; promotion of sustainable growth and development; integration of African economies into regional and global economic processes; and empowerment of women.[62] Toward such ends, the program focuses on broad policy reforms and improvement of policy development and resources mobilization in African context. NEPAD also focuses on enhancing African leadership, promoting African ownership of its development programs, gaining greater access to developed world trade and markets, and building partnerships across all sectors of society. It calls for the creation of partnerships both among African countries and between African countries and the broader international community.

Originally initiated by five African states—Algeria, Egypt, Nigeria, Senegal and South Africa—the basic NEPAD framework was adopted in July 2001 at the Organization of African Unity (OAU) Summit. The program is sponsored by OAU's successor organization, the African Union, and has been endorsed by the European Union. The Group of 8 (G-8) committed themselves in June 2002 to join African governments in building such a partnership. In doing so, they created the African Action Plan based on these areas of engagement: 1) promoting peace and security; 2) strengthening institutions and governance; 3) fostering trade, investment, economic growth and sustainable development; 4) implementing debt relief; 5) expanding knowledge by improving and promoting education and expanding digital opportunities; 6) improving health and confronting HIV/AIDS; 7) increasing agricultural productivity; and 8) improving water-resource management.[63]

In more concrete terms, the G-8 Africa Plan of Action committed member states to mobilize additional resources for African development. This included a commitment to allocate to Africa at least 50 percent of the G-8 share of the $12 billion increase in ODA agreed on at Monterrey. They pledged to increase the use of grants rather than loans for the most vulnerable debt-ridden countries and to provide an additional $1 billion for the HIPC program. In the area of trade, G-8 members agreed to work toward opening their markets to duty-free access to LDCs.

Pledges were also made to strengthen peace and security within the region by moving to consolidate peace agreements already achieved, acting to limit the international activities of arms brokers and traffickers, and taking steps to ensure greater accountability of trade in Africa's natural resources in conflict areas. Promoting good governance was also part of the package. This was to be accomplished through capacity-building in a variety of governance areas. Finally, pledges were made to increase support for human-resource development, including education; to work to make life-saving drugs more readily available and affordable; and to provide resources necessary to deal with endemic diseases, such as HIV/AIDS, malaria and tuberculosis.[64] Each of these commitments was reinforced and others added at the WSSD in Johannesburg in August-September 2002.[65]

The foundations of these commitments to the world's poorest region had been building over the previous decade, intensifying in the preceding five years. These efforts are listed here in reverse chronological order. The World Food Summit in Rome in June 2002 specified agriculture and food security as an important development component and set the goal of halving the number of hungry through sustained growth of agricultural production. The Monterrey Consensus growing out of the International Conference on Financing for Development in March 2002 called for the immediate support of NEPAD and similar efforts. The G.A. Special Session on HIV/AIDS in June 2001 brought forth the declaration of commitment on HIV/AIDS, "Global Crisis—Global Action," and laid the groundwork for combating the pandemic in its most overwhelming manifestation in Africa. The third U.N. Conference on the LDCs in May 2001 produced the Programme of Action for the least-developed countries for the decade 2001-2010 and called for expanding systematic and sustained assistance to cover African LDCs. A year earlier, the G.A. Special Session on the World Summit for Social Development and Beyond (Social Summit+5) committed member states and the world organization to "accelerate the economic, social and human resource development of Africa and the least developed countries."[66] Finally, Chapter VII of the 2000 U.N. *Millennium Declaration* called on the international community to concentrate on meeting the special needs of Africa.

Most recently, African leaders have identified infrastructure development and food security as the top NEPAD priorities.[67] To deal with food problems and revitalize agricultural production, NEPAD has established the Comprehensive Africa Agriculture Development Program (CAADP). This initiative is organized around four "pillars": 1) extending sustainable land management and reliable water control systems; 2) infrastructure development in rural areas to enhance market access and trade; 3) increasing food supplies and access; and 4) enhancing agricultural research and technology development and dissemination.[68] Meeting these objectives, of course, requires outside assistance, and that is what both NEPAD and MDG 8 are all about.

The Digital Divide

The digital revolution has given rise to a digital divide as new ways to create and disseminate knowledge and information have privileged some and left others behind. Perhaps more than any other single force, the influence of information and communications technologies (ICTs)—the digital revolution—is driving globalization processes. Although affected in important ways, the vast majority of the world's population, however, has remained relatively powerless. The situation is slowly changing, but the fact remains that the overwhelming proportion of Internet host computers reside in the highest-income countries, while Africa and other regions remain dependent and marginalized. In addition to this digital divide, there is also a "content divide" with regard to access to ICTs.[69] This evolving asymmetric condition has profound implications for managing global resources and attaining sustainable development because access to information and knowledge is a prerequisite to achieving the MDGs.[70]

On one hand, ICTs lie at the core of human progress and development. They possess the potential to hasten efforts to deal with poverty, hunger, environmental degradation, illiteracy and poor health. They even hold the potential of enabling backward areas to leapfrog over wide gaps in social and economic inequalities. On the other hand, their very high-tech nature makes them highly allusive and, for most, seemingly beyond reach. The digital divide poses tremendous obstacles for many who remain unconnected and outside the "networked economy."

The critical question regarding the digital divide is how to make the information revolution work for all peoples in all regions of the world. This question was the focus of the World Summit on the Information

Society (WSIS) that began its first phase in Geneva in December 2003 and is scheduled to continue in Tunis in 2005. The objective is to create a common vision of the information society and develop a plan of action for using ICTs to bridge the digital divide.

This first phase of the WSIS ended with the issuance of the normal *Declaration of Principles* and Plan of Action. The declaration outlined a "common vision of the Information Society," specified a series of 11 key principles on "an Information Society for All," and stated a few nonbinding and rather ambiguous commitments. The plan specified objectives, goals and targets and outlined 11 action lines corresponding to the key principles. It also presented a "Digital Solidarity Agenda" with a statement of priorities and strategies and a discussion about mobilizing resources.[71]

Perhaps more noteworthy is the fact that, because of disagreement, the plan did not include two issues: who should govern the Internet and how to pay for bridging the digital divide. The first issue paired off the U.S. with other rich countries against Brazil, China, India, Russia and Saudi Arabia. The U.S. wanted to keep governance in the hands of the private-sector Internet Corporation for Assigned Names and Numbers. The opposing states wanted to turn governance over to the U.N. International Telecommunications Union (ITU). The African proposal to create a Digital Solidarity Fund to provide the financial resources needed to bridge the digital divide met with opposition from the European Union, the U.S. and Japan. The compromise position agreed upon for both issues was to request studies and refer the proposals to the phase two gathering in Tunis in 2005.[72]

Looking Forward

Roger Coate, Gail Karlsson

At the end of 2003, U.N. Secretary-General Kofi Annan pointed out that while the attention of the world was focused on Iraq, there were many other pressing challenges that continue to affect the daily lives of billions of people: "In 2004, the world needs to focus on these challenges with renewed determination. Above all, we have to rebuild momentum towards meeting the Millennium Development Goals," he said.[73]

With that, there are a number of important human security issues looming on the horizon. These include poverty—creating enabling environments for integrating poor countries more fully and effectively into the world economy on a more equitable basis; hunger—reversing the setback on the war against hunger and providing sustainable support to the more than 800 million people struggling to survive; and water and the environment—creating and institutionalizing more effective resource management systems.

In addition to these core issues related to the MDGs are health—stepping up the war on HIV/AIDS, malaria, tuberculosis and other devastating diseases and extracting greater commitments from donor governments; education—providing basic education to all (2003-2012 is the United Nations Literacy Decade); women—mainstreaming a gender perspective into development policies and programs and promoting empowerment, access and gender equality; development assistance—finding effective mechanisms to provide meaningful financial and technical resources, including aid and debt relief, to those countries identified by the Millennium Development Compact as top and highest priority countries (2005 is the International Year of Microcredit); and digital divide—overcoming obstacles to providing the financial and technological resources needed to bridge the divide and building an international consensus on appropriate arrangements for governing cyberspace (WSIS Phase 2 is scheduled for 2005 in Tunis).

Specifically, with regard to Goal 7, the 59th General Assembly will review the implementation plans adopted at the World Summit on Sustainable Development. Meanwhile, the 10-year review of the Barbados Programme of Action on Small Island Developing States, to take place in Mauritius in early 2005, will focus international attention on the increasingly felt impacts of climate change, and on other economic and environmental challenges currently facing developing countries. Similar issues will also be raised at the January 2005 World Conference on Disaster Reduction.

Overall, the *Millenium Compact* has been designed so that U.N. member states and agencies can focus on all these issues and work to build effective partnerships, especially private-public partnerships, for dealing with them. The 59th Assembly will no doubt review progress on each, as an overall five-year review of progress on achieving the MDGs is scheduled for 2005.

Commentary A:
Millennium Development Goal Progress:
The Relevance of Tracking Measures

Pera Wells with Ethan Kunz

At the United Nations Millennium Summit in September 2000, world leaders placed development at the heart of the global agenda by adopting the *Millennium Declaration*, which contained the Millennium Development Goals. As described in this chapter, these eight goals set clear targets for reducing poverty, hunger, disease, illiteracy, environmental degradation and discrimination against women by 2015. Tracking progress toward achieving the MDGs is an essential aspect of the global effort to improve conditions in developing countries. Fortunately, the MDGs have encouraged unprecedented systemwide collaboration among U.N. bodies and regional commissions and groups.

The U.N. Development Programme is coordinating the MDGs in the U.N. system, helping to make them an integral part of the worldwide work, particularly at the country level. All developing countries are being encouraged to produce Country Reports on the status of their national development efforts. As of May 2004, reports for approximately 50 countries were posted on the UNDP website. Through these reports, it is apparent that countries have many strategies and priorities. For example, in the Philippines, there is a strong community focus on how budgets are decided. In Kenya, a distinction is made between those targets that require policy changes (e.g., achieving gender parity in education) and those that require a change in public attitudes (e.g., using contraception).

The U.N. Statistics Division is working to maintain Millennium Country Profiles that note specific indicators of the goals and their progress. Data collected is based on 18 targets and 48 specific indicators. The first goal's target is halving the poverty gap ratio.

Every year, Secretary-General Kofi Annan submits a progress report on the goals to the General Assembly. His 2003 report stated that the "prospects for meeting the Millennium Development Goals, given current trends, are decidedly mixed, with marked differences between and within regions." While progress in East Asia and parts of South Asia holds out hope for meeting many or all of the goals, the report showed that progress in parts of Latin America is slow, and much of sub-Saharan Africa and large parts of central Asia are hardly advancing at all—or even worse, are falling back dramatically. It is expected that the S.G.'s 2004 report will make a similar assessment.

One perceived weakness of tracking the MDGs is that there are no indicators for measuring the compliance of governments and no requirement for them to produce reports. The Nordic governments took the initiative to support the drawing up of an international framework for reporting on Goal 8, and are now producing their own reports. The United States has established a Millennium Challenge Account. To qualify for funds, countries must demonstrate that they are "ruling justly, investing in their people and establishing economic freedom" via the goals. In February 2004, more than 60 countries were declared eligible for the first round of funds. The three-year contract to be signed with recipient governments, which, at the time of this writing, were to be chosen in May 2004, would make provisions based on the results of their efforts.

Despite these and other efforts to track the steps being made toward the MDGs, a lack of political will at the power centers to allocate funds for actually achieving the goals is emerging as a major obstacle. "Every year, the most powerful nations of the world spend over $1 trillion in weapons, $350 billion in subsidies for agriculture, but only $57 billion in development aid," World Bank President James Wolfensohn told the annual conference of the Bank's Parliamentary Network in February 2004. "At this pace, we are not going to meet the millennium goals by the year 2015."

Columbia University Professor Jeffrey Sachs agrees. His U.N. Millennium Research Project team—a group of scholars from developing and developed countries—has been working to identify what is needed realistically in terms of policy, expanded capacity and required investments and financing to meet the goals. In March 2004, Dr. Sachs stated that $75 billion a year is needed to do just that.

To some degree, the very credibility of the U.N. hinges upon success in achieving the MDGs. Community involvement is vital for progress toward the global goals, but should not necessarily be focused on monitoring and tracking. Of equal if not more value now is the effort to encourage people to feel ownership of the goals and to become directly involved in achieving them.

To mobilize public engagement with the MDGs, a Global Millennium Campaign is moving forward under the leadership of U.N. Executive Coordinator for the MDG Campaign Eveline Herfkens. In developed countries, the primary focus of the campaign is to galvanize public opinion to boost development assistance, trade, debt relief, technology and other support. In the developing world, the aim is to build coalitions for action, to help governments set policy as well as project and budgetary priorities and to use resources effectively.

In addition, the World Federation of United Nations Associations (WFUNA), a peoples' movement to support the United Nations, has been at the forefront of civil-society efforts to promote awareness of the MDGs. Working in close collaboration with the North-South Institute, WFUNA conducts global online surveys of civil-society engagement with the MDGs, and produces an annual We the Peoples report in time for the Assembly.

To review the progress that has been made and the remaining obstacles in achieving the goals by 2015, S.G. Annan has called for a Summit meeting of the G.A. next year. Civil-society groups involved in the Global Millennium Campaign are planning to hold their own review in 2005 as well, with a view to making an impact on the Summit and to shaping the U.N.'s agenda to give higher priority to the goal of alleviating the suffering of people living in extreme poverty on the planet.

Commentary B:
The Rich Nation-Poor Nation Divide
Roger Coate

It is faddish to speak of the world being structured in terms of gaps and great divides, such as the "digital divide," the "molecular divide" and the "rich-poor divide." But it is also helpful in terms of getting people to visualize social space in certain policy-relevant ways. Politically speaking, for example, the concept of the rich-poor divide helps people understand the recent political dynamics and stalemates that occurred at the World Trade Organization Ministerial Meeting in Cancún and at the World Summit on the Information Society in Geneva. In both cases, political debate and conflict broke largely along rich-poor lines.

On the other hand, such framings can be misleading as they tend to greatly oversimplify and even polarize things. This is especially true outside the context of conference diplomacy, such as in respect to the United Nations' human development work. In this regard, the rich-poor dichotomy does not seem to be helpful today, if it ever was. For that matter, neither does the developed-developing dichotomy. For example, the landscape of the so-called "digital divide" seems to be shifting, and the gap between developed countries and more affluent developing countries is shrinking. At the same time, however, the least-developed countries, especially those in Africa, are languishing in the dust.

Accordingly, over the past decade, there has been a narrowing of focus in development discourse and practice to concentrate heavily on least-developed and low-income countries. The U.N. Development Programme's 2003 Human Development Report, for example, identified 59 countries as "top priority" and "high priority" in respect to development work. This categorization makes a great deal of policy sense.

This narrowing of priority and movement away from a rich-poor, North-South, or developed-developing dichotomization by the UNDP was part of a more general process of international consensus-building that culminated in the Millennium Development Goals. The process was one that endeavored to bring rich and poor countries alike into a global partnership.

That said, it is hard to imagine the poorest countries achieving the first seven MDGs without the policy changes required in rich countries to achieve Goal 8, as we discussed in this chapter.. Poor countries alone cannot tackle the structural constraints that keep them in poverty traps, including rich country tariffs, subsidies that restrict market access and patents that close access to technology. High levels of commitment are required on all sides. Indeed, rich countries have made many commitments, including increasing development assistance and debt and HIV/AIDS relief. In relation to need, however, even in these areas, the situation might best be characterized as doing "too little, too late."

Moreover, some of those countries—especially the United States—in the best position to provide the policy changes and level of support needed to make a significant difference, are often distracted from doing so by things such as terrorism. These narrow preoccupations devert them not only from promoting human development, but also from the real security concerns of most of the world's people: poverty and related factors. Paradoxically, this situation tends to intensify, both materially and politically, the rich-poor divide.

Endnotes

1. U.N. Press Release, April 28, 2004.
2. Ibid.
3. "Moscow Refuses to Ratify Treaty on Climate Change," *Guardian*, December 5, 2003. / *BBC News*, May 21, 2004. Note: According to reports, President Putin's support for Kyoto was part of a deal struck with European Union officials that would also see the E.U. back Russia's entry into the World Trade Organization.
4. UNFCCC Secretariat Press Release, December 12, 2003.
5. WMO Press Release, December 16, 2003.
6. "New Front Opened in Fight Against Climate Change," *Guardian*, April 28, 2004.
7. AOSIS *Strategy for the Further Implementation of the BPOA*, Inter-Regional Prepatory Meeting of SIDS, Bahamas, January 2004.
8. E/CN.17/2004/8, March 11, 2004.
9. Ibid.
10. A/Res/58/214.
11. A/CONF.206/PC(I)/4, April 23, 2004.
12. *Reducing Disaster Risk: A Challenge for Development*, UNDP, 2004.
13. *Global Environmental Outlook Yearbook 2003*, UNEP.
14. A/58/L.18.
15. "Alien Invaders in Ballast Water—New Convention Adopted at IMO," *IMO Press Briefing*, January 29, 2004.
16. UNEP/CBD/COP/7/21/PART1 (CBD Press Release, *UNEP*, February 20, 2004).
17. Statement by CBD Executive Secretary Hamdallah Zedan, February 22, 2004.
18. U.N. Press Release SAG/244, March 31, 2004.
19. E/CN.18/2004/12, March 2, 2004.
20. UNEP Press Release, November 11, 2003.
21. *Earth Negotiations Bulletin*, May 3, 2004.
22. UNEP Press Release, February 18, 2004.
23. UNEP Press Release, November 27, 2003.
24. *Earth Negotiations Bulletin*, May 3, 2004.
25. E/CN.17/2004/4.
26. FAO, *The State of Food Insecurity in the World 2003*.
27. Ibid.
28. Ibid, 26. / *Food Supply Situation and Crop Prospects in Sub-Saharan Africa*, FAO, April 2004.
29. Ibid.
30. *The State of Food Insecurity in the World 2003*, FAO.
31. "FAO Warns of 'Molecular Divide' Between North and South," *FAO News Room*, February 18, 2003.
32. Ibid.
33. A/58/153/Rev.1. / ST/ESA/284.
34. *Interregional Consultative Meeting on National Implementation of the Madrid International Plan of Action on Ageing*, Report of the Meeting, U.N. Department of Economic and Social Affairs, December 9-11, 2003.
35. A/58/160.
36. Ibid, 33.

37. Ibid, 35.
38. Ibid.
39. "Women's Advancement Said Key to Reducing Poverty," *U.N. Wire*, March 2, 2004.
40. "Women and the Millennium Development Goals," *Women's Human Rights website*, November 2003.
41. "Annan Urges Afghan Government to Protect Women's Rights," *U.N. Wire*, January 27, 2004.
42. Ibid, 38.
43. *The Least Developed Countries Report 2002*, UNCTAD.
44. A/57/340 (August 23, 2002).
45. A/RES/56/180.
46. A/58/388.
47. Ibid. / *Global Education Digest 2004: Beyond Universal Primary Education*, UNESCO, 2004.
48. *Global Education Digest 2004: Beyond Universal Primary Education*, UNESCO, 2004. / *Human Development Report 2003*, UNDP. / *UNESCO website*.
49. *Human Development Report 2003*, UNDP.
50. *Global Education Digest 2004: Beyond Universal Primary Education*, UNESCO, 2004.
51. *The State of the World's Children 2004*, UNICEF.
52. *The World Health Report 2003: Shaping the Future*, WHO's Geneva Office, 2003.
53. "Report Outlines Gender Inequality in Access to Health Care," *U.N. Wire*, September 3, 2003.
54. WTO Press Release, August 30, 2003.
55. "U.N. Sees Mixed Results in Development Goals," *U.N. Wire*, October 30, 2003.
56. IMF Press Release, April 8, 2004. Note: The World Bank lists 38 primary HIPC countries; the remaining four are considered "potentially sustainable cases," for a total of 42.
57. *Fiscal Sustainability in African HIPC Countries: A Policy Dilemma?*, IMF Working Paper, September 2003.
58. Ibid.
59. "World Bank, IMF Slash $5.1 Billion of Nicaragua's Debt," *U.N. Wire*, January 26, 2004.
60. "UNDP Urges Expanding Credit Ratings for African Countries," *U.N. Wire*, February 27, 2004.
61. *Compendium of Commitments Made to Africa at the Global Conferences and Summits Since 1990*, Office of the Special Adviser on Africa website.
62. A/CONF.199/20.
63. *G8 Africa Action Plan*, Canada, June 27, 2002.
64. *G8 Africa Action Plan Highlights*, Canada, June 27, 2002.
65. Ibid, 62.
66. A/RES/S-24/2.
67. "Infrastructure and Food Security to Top NEPAD Priorities," *NEPAD website*, 2004.
68. "FEWS Rwanda Food Security Update 24 May 2004: Recent Dry Spell Threatens Crops," *ReliefWeb website*, 2004.
69. Interview with Kofi Annan, *International Herald Tribune*, December 9, 2003. / "Report Ahead of Information Summit Explores Digital Divide," *U.N. Wire*, December 9, 2003.
70. A/Res/56/183.
71. *Declaration of Principles* and *Plan of Action*, Reports of the World Summit on the Information Society, December 12, 2004.
72. "Nations Put Off Decision on Funds to Bridge Digital Divide," *U.N. Wire*, December 9, 2003.
73. S.G. Press Conference, December 18, 2003.

Chapter 3

Protecting Human Rights, Advancing Society

Lorna Davidson, Jacques Fomerand
and Jyoti Sanghera with Olivia Cobiskey

Such prescriptions—the strengthening of national protection systems, the enhanced implementation of human rights treaties and cooperation with United Nations special procedures—may seem ambitious when, in fact, they should be the very minimum to be expected of all countries. This basic but essential commitment to human rights is also a solid foundation for countries to step up their fight against persistent and emerging ills plaguing our modern society. Trafficking of women, racial discrimination, anti-Semitism, discrimination against minorities such as the Roma, and terrorism—these are threats to human security that require a response grounded in human rights.
—Acting High Commissioner for Human Rights Bertrand Ramcharan,
   Organization for Security and Cooperation in Europe Meeting, October 2003.

Human Rights and the United Nations

Lorna Davidson

After almost six decades of struggle and progress, the global human rights movement today faces the most serious challenge in its history. Hard-won gains, such as the creation of a broad swathe of international human rights standards and a network of institutions and mechanisms to enforce those standards, are being undermined. Civil-society activists who work to promote and protect basic rights in their societies are being branded as "unpatriotic," or threatening national security, and the very concept of respect for human rights as a central pillar of our international society is in jeopardy. Indeed, governments with abusive tendencies are exploiting the current climate of fear over terrorism to justify their past and continuing repressive measures, thus avoiding international censure and weakening the force of human rights discourse.

It is therefore incumbent upon human rights advocates to respond to this challenge. Local activists, regional bodies and all of the various human rights mechanisms within the United Nations must make increased efforts to demonstrate that respect for human rights is not only a moral and legal imperative, but also a crucial part of the eradication of terrorism and the creation of a more secure world. This has, indeed, become a central message of U.N. Secretary-General Kofi Annan and other U.N. officials, even as the U.N. itself became a victim of terrorism with the attack upon its headquarters in Iraq in August 2003. In a speech given in New York last September, S.G. Annan stated, "Upholding human rights is not at odds with battling terrorism: on the contrary, the moral vision of human rights–the deep respect for the dignity of each person–is among our most powerful weapons against it."[1] In addition, the various human rights arms of the U.N. have been at the forefront of calls upon states to ensure that counter-terrorism measures implemented in pursuit of their obligations under Security Council Resolution 1373 do not themselves violate human rights standards. *(See below for more details.)*

This section provides an overview of the U.N. human rights machinery that has been steadily built up since the creation of the organization in 1945. It examines the particular human rights challenges faced by the U.N. in 2003 and 2004, both on a thematic and a country-specific level. In addition to the increased global emphasis on security and related undermining of the primacy of human rights, the ongoing struggle for global resources and continuing challenges to multilateralism by the United States and other countries, the U.N. faces a tough road in dealing with serious conflicts and crises around the world that threaten the lives and the dignity of millions of people—fortunately, its efforts are steadfast.

The U.N.'s Human Rights Machinery

One of the tremendous gains of the human rights movement since the middle of the 20th century has been widespread acceptance that international scrutiny and censure can apply to how a state treats its citizens. A wealth of institutions has been created to examine whether states are abusing their populations, and to put pressure upon them to end such practices. Historically, the question of what fell within the "domestic jurisdiction" of states was a matter of dispute in the United Nations; it was not envisaged that the organization would be empowered to criticize or condemn human rights violations. While the U.N. Charter does state that one of the U.N.'s purposes is "to achieve international co-operation in...promoting and encouraging respect for human rights and for fundamental freedoms for all without distinction as to race, sex, language, or religion," this purpose was considered secondary to the primary function of maintaining international peace and security. In the Charter, the General Assembly and the Economic and Social Council (ECOSOC) were given responsibility for the human rights functions of the organization, which were initially limited to the creation of the *Universal Declaration of Human Rights* in 1948 and subsequent human rights treaties. As the idea of universal rights spread and states signed up to the various human rights instruments crafted at the United Nations, calls increased for the organization to have a more vigorous role in enforcement.

Commission on Human Rights

The U.N. Charter envisaged that ECOSOC, which was made up of 54 of the U.N. member states, would set up functional commissions for, among other things, the promotion of human rights. Thus, in 1946, the Commission on Human Rights was created, with nine members elected by ECOSOC to represent their states. The task of the Commission when it first convened in 1947 was to draft a *Universal Declaration of Human Rights*, which was completed and adopted on December 10, 1948. The Commission then set about formulating the rights enunciated in the declaration as binding obligations on states contained in international treaties. As a result of this work, the *International Covenant on Civil and Political Rights* and the *International Covenant on Economic, Social and Cultural Rights* were adopted by the General Assembly in 1966 and opened to signature and ratification by member states. The two covenants, along with the *International Convention on the Elimination of All Forms of Racial Discrimination*, the *Convention on the Elimination of All Forms of Discrimination Against Women*, the *Convention Against Torture and Other Cruel, Inhuman or Degrading Treatment or Punishment*, and the *Convention on the Rights of the Child*, remain the central legal texts of today's U.N. human rights system.

Although, in 1947, the members of the Commission considered that it had "no power to take any action in regard to any complaints concerning human rights," by the 1960s, this thinking began to change. Impelled by increasing international outrage about colonialism and racist regimes in southern Africa, in 1967, ECOSOC passed Resolution 1235, authorizing the Commission to "make a thorough study of situations which reveal a consistent pattern of violations of human rights." This mandate was further developed in 1970 with the adoption of ECOSOC Resolution 1503, which created a confidential procedure in which states and other bodies could submit human rights abuses to the Commission. Through these resolutions, the Commission gained the authority to engage in public debate about serious human rights violations in particular countries, and to have private discussions with states accused of such violations.

Despite the adoption of Resolutions 1235 and 1503, the nature of the Commission as a political body made up of state representatives meant that many states managed to avoid censure through political lobbying before and during its annual sessions. For example, despite the evidence of mass killings and other serious human rights abuses, the Commission failed to publicly condemn the situations in Cambodia and Uganda in the mid-1970s. Indeed, one of the main criticisms leveled against the Commission today is its failure to address serious human rights violations in certain countries where the leaders have managed to garner sufficient support among Commission members to ensure that alleged violations are not discussed at meetings or in resolutions.

A significant development in the work of the Commission took place in the 1980s, with the creation of new "special procedures." The first of these procedures was the Working Group on Enforced or Involuntary Disappearances, created largely in response to the persistence of reports of disappearances in Argentina and other Latin American states. Soon after, other working groups were established, along with special rapporteurs and experts, each with a different thematic mandate. Today, there are a total of 27 "special procedures" with thematic mandates. Each one plays a crucial role in investigating human rights violations by receiving and analyzing information from individuals and nongovernmental organizations (NGOs), carrying out urgent communications with states and going on fact-finding missions in individual countries. Each of the different mandate holders reports annually to the Commission and the General Assembly.

In addition to the thematic mechanisms, another significant development at the Commission, coming out of Resolution 1235, was the designation of country-specific experts and rapporteurs. Considered to be a crucial element of the U.N. human rights system today, these rapporteurs and experts monitor the human rights situation in numerous countries. In 2003, more than 20 reports were submitted to the G.A. by the various special procedures, while 650 urgent appeals involving 164 counties were submitted by the experts and rapporteurs.[2]

Despite some criticisms, the annual six-week meeting of the Commission remains an important event in which states, NGOs and U.N. officials engage in discussion with one another about the most pressing human rights issues of the day. The Commission now consists of 53 member states elected by ECOSOC for three-year terms, and is attended by hundreds of state officials and thousands of NGO representatives. Its agenda each year is divided into items, including the countries to be discussed pursuant to Resolution 1235; the right to self-determination; economic, social and cultural rights; and civil and political rights. In addition to assistance from the Office of the High Commissioner for Human Rights (OHCHR), the Commission is aided by the work of the Sub-Commission on the Promotion and Protection of Human Rights. This Sub-Commission is made up of 26 independent experts, who meet annually to formulate recommendations for the larger commission.

Office of the High Commissioner for Human Rights

The Office of the High Commissioner for Human Rights has emerged as another key element of the U.N. human rights system. Although not originally envisaged by the U.N. Charter, proposals for an Attorney-General for Human Rights had been put forward in the early days of the organization. In the following decades, these proposals continued to surface, but were viewed with suspicion by many states that still rejected the idea of the world scrutinizing and condemning domestic violations of basic rights. A significant push for a High Commissioner, mounted by NGOs and key governments, culminated at the 1993 World Conference on Human Rights in Vienna. The matter was referred to the Assembly and by December of that year, member states agreed to create the position.[3] The first High Commissioner, José Ayala-Lasso, was appointed in February 1994, with the authority to act as "the

United Nations official with principal responsibility for United Nations human rights activities, under the direction and authority of the Secretary-General." In 1997, OHCHR's functions were merged with the Centre for Human Rights—the U.N. human rights secretariat in Geneva—making it the primary permanent human rights organ of the United Nations.

During 2003, OHCHR went through a process of restructuring and is now divided into five branches: research and right to development, treaties and commissions, special procedures, capacity-building and field operations, and external relations. There is also an executive office. OHCHR has more than 500 staff worldwide as well as field offices in countries with serious human rights crises, such as Colombia, Cambodia and the Democratic Republic of Congo. However, each year it faces a significant funding shortage. In 2004, OHCHR appealed for $54.8 million in voluntary contributions as well as an allocation of $27.1 million from the regular U.N. budget to meet its needs.[4]

In September 2002, Sergio Vieira de Mello took office as the third High Commissioner for Human Rights. In May 2003, he was appointed Special Representative of the U.N. Secretary-General in Iraq, leaving his deputy, Bertrand Ramcharan, to take over. Sadly, Mr. De Mello was killed on August 19, 2003 with 21 others in the bombing of the U.N. headquarters in Iraq.

Louise Arbour, a Canadian Supreme Court justice and former chief prosecutor of the International Criminal Tribunals for the former Yugoslavia and for Rwanda, was appointed and approved in February 2004 to officially take over for Mr. De Mello as the fourth High Commissioner. She will take up office in the summer of 2004.

Human Rights Treaty Bodies

In addition to the so-called Charter-based human rights bodies, the implementation of each major international human rights treaty is monitored by committees of independent experts, known collectively as the "treaty bodies." Each body reviews periodic reports submitted by states, formulates questions for the relevant states, and then engages in an oral discussion with the states' representatives. At the end of this dialogue, the committees issue concluding observations, pointing out areas of concern and making recommendations for improvement. Several of the treaty bodies are also empowered to receive treaty violation complaints from individuals or states parties to the treaty.

The Committee on the Protection of the Rights of All Migrant Workers and Members of Their Families is the newest of the treaty bodies, holding its first session in March 2004. Currently, the Committee has 10 members, but this number will rise to 14 when the total number of state ratifications of the convention reaches 41. Under the terms of this convention, the Committee is empowered to review reports submitted by its states parties every five years, and to consider communications submitted by states or by individuals alleging violations of the convention, so long as the respondent state has accepted the competence of the Committee to receive and consider such communications.

The treaty bodies have long suffered criticism that they are slow, cumbersome and ineffective. Critics point to the fact that the Human Rights Committee can take several years to complete the examination of an individual complaint and issue an opinion, and as a result, is building up an ever-increasing backlog of cases. In addition, the majority of states reporting to the various committees submit their reports months or years behind schedule, and some states simply do not submit reports at all. Proposals to address these problems continue to be discussed; in May 2003, OHCHR organized a meeting in Liechtenstein, bringing together state representatives, experts and NGOs to brainstorm various ideas. Some commentators argue that some or all of the treaty bodies should sit permanently throughout the year, rather than holding periodic sessions for two or three weeks at a time. Other suggestions include the consolidation of reporting requirements, so that states do not have to submit numerous reports to the various committees, but rather can prepare and submit one report for all committees.

In his report to the 60th session of the Commission on Human Rights in 2004, Mr. Ramcharan stated that "there is an emerging consensus that the emphasis should be placed on the coordination of reporting systems," and laid out certain precepts to provide the framework for a new reporting system.[5] Of course, at the heart of the problems facing the treaty bodies–and most of the U.N. human rights system—is the chronic shortage of resources. In addition, a lack of political will on the part of states to strengthen the treaty bodies has undermined the committees' work.

Nonetheless, like the Commission on Human Rights, the work of the treaty-monitoring bodies is an important part of international efforts to ensure respect for human rights. The committee sessions provide a forum around which local and international NGOs can organize their advocacy and shine a spotlight on human rights abuses in particular countries. For example, some NGOs often submit "shadow reports" to the treaty bodies to challenge or support the information provided by states in their periodic reports. NGOs also send representatives to the sessions of the treaty bodies to give informal briefings. Last but not least, the complaints mechanisms remain an important avenue for individuals who have had their rights violated and been unable to get redress at the domestic level.

60th Session of the Commission on Human Rights

The 60th session of the Commission on Human Rights was held in Geneva from March 15 to April 23, 2004. Among the new states elected to the body for the next three years were Egypt, Eritrea, Ethiopia and Indonesia. These countries join other rights-abusing states already represented at the Commission, including Zimbabwe, Cuba, China, the Russian Federation and Saudi Arabia. The chair of the Commission rotates each year among the geographical groups within the United Nations. In 2004, Australian

Ambassador Mike Smith served as the chairman, stating that he would make great efforts to ensure that the Commission session was rigorous and effective; participants felt that he performed this task admirably.

One of the most serious challenges faced by the Commission at its 60th session was the continued effort by a coalition of mainly African, Arab and Islamic countries to end the practice of condemning individual countries for their human rights abuses (agenda item 9). These groups argued that rather than adopt such a confrontational and often politically motivated approach, the Commission should instead consider countries under agenda item 19, on advisory services and technical cooperation. Other states, and numerous human rights NGOs, argued strongly that this was simply another attempt by rights-abusing governments to avoid international censure.

Terrorism, as it related to human rights, was again on the Commission's agenda this year and continued to provoke controversy. Since the adoption of S.C. Resolution 1373 and the establishment of the Counter-Terrorism Committee, there has been a growing debate within the U.N. over the most appropriate way to ensure that respect for human rights is not sacrificed in the course of implementing counter-terrorism measures around the world.

Throughout 2003, increasing recognition of the need to ensure respect for human rights while implementing measures to combat terrorism has resulted in a range of statements and resolutions from the U.N. bodies. In April 2003, the 59th session of the Commission on Human Rights passed a resolution on "Human Rights and Terrorism," which asked the High Commissioner to respond to requests by states for assistance and advice on ensuring full compliance with international human rights standards when undertaking measures to combat terrorism.[6] And in June, the various special procedures issued a joint statement expressing alarm over the "multiplication of policies, legislations and practices increasingly being adopted by many countries in the name of the fight against terrorism, which affect negatively the enjoyment of virtually all human rights."[7]

The General Assembly also passed a resolution on the "Protection of Human Rights and Fundamental Freedoms While Countering Terrorism" at its 58th session in December 2003.[8] In this resolution, the G.A. encouraged the S.C. and its Counter-Terrorism Committee to continue developing cooperation with relevant human rights bodies, such as the OHCHR. It also requested all of the special procedures of the Commission, as well as the treaty bodies, to consider the issue of protecting human rights while combating terrorism, as it fell within their respective mandates. It finally asked the Acting High Commissioner to report back on whether the existing special procedures and treaty monitoring bodies "are able, within their existing mandates, to address the compatibility of national counter-terrorism measures with international human rights obligations." On March 12, 2004, the Acting High Commissioner submitted his interim report on the issue to the 60th session of the Commission, suggesting that the Commission consider appointing an expert to study the issue of terrorism and human rights in more detail, or that it consider appointing a new special procedure mandate.[9]

As a result of each of these acts and continued lobbying by some states and NGOs, the 60th session Commission adopted by consensus a resolution on the protection of human rights while countering terrorism.[10] The most debated part of the resolution was the provision for the appointment of an independent expert for a period of one year. According to the Mexican delegation, which put forward the resolution, this expert would not function as a new special procedure in the traditional manner, but would assist OHCHR in fulfilling its mandate. The sponsors wished to ensure that there was no loss of momentum on the urgent issue of human rights and counter-terrorism and therefore proposed that the independent expert contribute to the report being prepared by the Acting High Commissioner for the G.A. and then engage in follow-up to that report by making recommendations to the Commission's 61st session in 2005.

A further controversial discussion at the Commission session concerned human rights and sexual orientation. This issue was raised at the 59th session when Brazil tabled a resolution calling upon states to promote and protect the human rights of all persons, regardless of their sexual orientation. States opposed to the resolution managed to ensure that voting was postponed until the 60th session. However, during that session, Brazil again succumbed to pressure from the Islamic group and some other states and announced that it would request that the Commission again postpone its consideration of the resolution.

Last but not least, the 10th anniversary of the Rwandan genocide was remembered on April 7, 2004 with S.G. Annan addressing the Commission and setting out a five-point plan to prevent future genocide.[11] As part of this plan, the S.G. announced the creation of the post of Special Adviser on the Prevention of Genocide, who would collect information on potential or existing situations or threats of genocide and report through him to the Security Council, the G.A. and the Commission itself. S.G. Annan also noted with grave concern reports of serious human rights abuses and ethnic cleansing in the Darfur region of Sudan and proposed sending a high-level team to the region to investigate and seek improved access to those in need of assistance. *(A team was sent in April; see below for details.)*

Country-Specific Human Rights Actions

Lorna Davidson

The following section looks at specific calls to action made to—and taken on by—the United Nations and the aforementioned human rights bodies in those countries most affected by human rights violations in 2003 and early 2004.

Afghanistan

Under the terms of the 2001 Bonn Agreement, presidential and parliamentary elections were to be held in Afghanistan in June 2004. However, on March 28, 2004, interim President Hamid Karzai announced that both elections would be pushed back until September. The postponement indicates the recognition in Afghanistan and among the international community that the lack of security throughout the country is a major problem and barrier to transition. The prevailing absence of security also inhibits the implementation of basic human rights in Afghanistan.

At its 59th session, the Commission on Human Rights asked the S.G. to appoint an Independent Expert, for a period of one year, to develop a program of human rights advisory services for Afghanistan. Soon after, in December 2003, S.G. Annan reported to the S.C. on Afghanistan, describing the implementation of the 2001 Bonn Agreement.[12] He noted that the human rights situation had not improved and that it was unlikely to do so until a more secure environment was created.

The U.N. Special Rapporteur on Adequate Housing went to Afghanistan in late August/early September 2003 and reported to the 60th session of the Commission that a number of issues were inhibiting the enjoyment of Afghani citizens of their right to an adequate standard of living.[13] The Rapporteur specifically expressed concern about the level of destruction of houses, sanitation facilities, water sources and infrastructure, because of armed conflict over the previous two and a half decades. He also highlighted the problem of land occupations and forced evictions as well as the need to address corruption and judicial inefficiency.

Following the ousting of the Taliban regime in December 2001, and the creation of a transitional government, a U.N.-mandated International Security Assistance Force (ISAF) was sent to Afghanistan, now under NATO command. The reach of ISAF, mandated to support the central Afghan government, remains limited. Regional warlords use violence and intimidation to control the population and human rights organizations report that armed groups under the control of the warlords commit rape, killings, kidnapping, robbery and extortion. The situation for women and girls is particularly dire, and many are forced out of fear to remain indoors and thus forego education, healthcare and employment. Human rights groups have also accused the United States and the U.N. of working with and supporting the warlords; some also report that U.S. forces in Afghanistan have arbitrarily detained civilians and mistreated detainees.[15]

In December 2003, a special constitutional *Loya Jirga*, or grand council, was convened to formulate a new constitution for Afghanistan. Approved on January 4, 2004 by 502 delegates, the constitution contains new provisions on human rights and guarantees a substantial number of seats in the National Assembly to women. It also provides for equality between men and women. Critics, however, argue that the constitution does not adequately address the relationship between Islamic law and human rights protections and they state that it grants insufficient enforcement powers to institutions for the protection of human rights, such as the Afghan Independent Human Rights Commission.[16]

Despite the serious problems remaining in Afghanistan with respect to human rights, a declaration was adopted by conference participants discussing reconstruction and development in Berlin on March 31 and April 1, 2004. The participants of this donor's conference, who jointly pledged $8.2 billion to Afghanistan for the period of March 2004 through March 2007, noted "with satisfaction the substantial progress achieved under the Bonn Agreement," and agreed that the international community would assist further in the stabilization of the security situation.[17]

At the Commission's 60th session, the discussion of Afghanistan was again held under item 19 of the agenda, on technical cooperation and advisory services. However, by January 2004, no independent expert had been appointed by the S.G. and, therefore, the Commission did not receive a report to review or discuss. On April 7, 2004, OHCHR announced that Professor Cherif Bassiouni had been appointed to the position.

Millennium Development Goal 3: Alleviating Gender Disparity and Empowering Women

Olivia Cobiskey

Millennium Development Goal 3 aims to eliminate gender disparity in primary and secondary education, preferably by 2005, and in all education levels by 2015. Research confirms that basic education is an effective investment to improve the economy and create literate, self-reliant and healthy societies. A survey by the U.N. Educational, Scientific and Cultural Organization (UNESCO) showed that while countries with 40 percent adult literacy rates had an average GNP per capita of $210, countries with twice that literacy rate have five times the average GNP per capita.[18] A separate study found that a single year of primary education provided to all women farmers—a primary means of employment among the world's poorest women—in Kenya would boost maize yields 24 percent.[19] By using both their training courses and agricultural skills, many women with a little help have created successful businesses. Unfortunately, in cultures where girls are expected to stay home, education takes second place and in turn, hinders women's development and future equality with men in the economic and social realm.

Wealthy nations and international organizations have provided billions of dollars for microcredit programs, such as the Bangladesh Rural Action Committee (BRAC), to help such women. However, advocates are beginning to fear that this money is not making it to the poorest people; they are mobilizing elected officials from the United States, U.K. and Japan to petition the World Bank, the largest provider of microfinance funding, to adopt the new U.S. Congress ruling that half of American aid for microfinancing loans go to people living on less than $1 a day.[20]

As globalization has spread and manufacturing jobs have moved from the developed to the developing world, women's share of nonagricultural-wage employment has increased. However, evidence suggests that gender gaps still persist in pay and conditions.[21] The poorest countries tend to have the lowest achievement in education, literacy and nonagricultural-wage employment. The empowerment of adult women requires that women have more say in decisions that affect their lives, including in the household, community, marketplace, workplace and in levels of public assemblies and offices.[22]

For that reason, MDG 3 goes beyond education. During the U.N.'s Division for Advancement of Women's five-year review of the Beijing Platform for Action (PFA) in 2000, the Women's Environment and Development Organization launched its 50/50 campaign. The campaign's goal is to reach beyond the PFA target of placing women in 30 percent of the world's parliamentary seats to a 50/50 representation between men and women.

As of December 2002, only 11 countries had achieved the PFA benchmark: Sweden, Denmark, Germany, Finland, Norway, Iceland, The Netherlands, South Africa, Costa Rica, Argentina and Mozambique. In each of these countries, quotas were legislated or adopted on a voluntary basis. In 22 countries, the number of women's seats in parliament decreased. In two cases, a return to democracy came with a reduction of women representatives.[23]

Clearly, there is still a lot of work to do to eliminate gender disparity from the classroom to the workplace. During the 48th Session of the Commission on the Status of Women, held in March 2004, it was decided that the Beijing + 10 review to be held in 2005 would focus on implementation of the PFA and emphasized the "need to integrate a gender perspective in the implementation and review of the *Millennium Declaration* and Millennium Development Goals."[24]

China

At the 60th session of the Commission on Human Rights, the U.S. resumed its practice of introducing a resolution condemning human rights abuses in China. The draft resolution said that the country's human rights record has deteriorated since 2002 and cited reports of "severe sentences for those seeking to exercise their fundamental rights" and "legal processes that continue to fall short of international norms of due process and transparency." The resolution urged China to permit investigations into its alleged human rights abuses. In turn, China resumed its practice of introducing a procedural no-action motion and successfully lobbied for support from other Commission members. In this manner, the U.S. resolution was defeated. Acknowledging the likelihood of defeat of the proposed resolution, the head of the U.S. delegation stated at the beginning of the Commission session that there had been a "backsliding" in China with regard to human rights and that the bilateral discussion between the two countries had not been as productive as expected.[25]

Although China angrily refuted these allegations, the U.S position is supported by numerous NGO reports. NGOs documented several cases of forced evictions, arbitrary detentions, restrictions on freedom of expression and association, and crackdowns on Tibetans as well as on practitioners of Falun Gong and ethnic Uighurs living in the northwestern Xinjiang province. In addition, increased concern about the high incidence of HIV/AIDS in China and discrimination against people with the virus has been expressed.[26]

Independent trade union and labor activists have continued to be arrested and imprisoned since 2002, including Yao Fuxin and Xiao Yunliang, who were sentenced to seven and four years respectively, for their role in organizing protests in the Liaoning Province. Others, including lawyers seeking to uphold basic rights, received similar treatment. In October 2003, lawyer Zheng Enchong was sentenced to three years' imprisonment on charges of leaking state secrets. His trial was not open to the public, and the charges against him were based on his communications with the U.S.-based NGO Human Rights in China. Mr. Zheng's family reported that he was being kept in solitary confinement and subjected to physical mistreatment.

Human rights groups also reported an increase in Internet censorship in the country while Amnesty International stated that, by January 2004, there were 54 imprisoned Internet activists.[27]

During the World Summit on the Information Society, held in Geneva in December 2003, China sought to limit references to the *Universal Declaration of Human Rights* and the right to freedom of expression in the final summit documents. China also continued to use the threat of international terrorism to justify repressive measures taken against ethnic Uighurs. The government failed to distinguish between groups promoting violent separatism and those advocating peaceful dissent, and on December 15, 2003, issued a list of 11 individuals and four groups in the region named as threats to national security. Many considered this another move to suppress dissent and free speech among the Uighur population.

At the Commission, Amnesty International released a report alleging that China was responsible for nearly two-thirds of the world's known executions in 2003. According to the report, China carried out at least 726 known executions. Amnesty also noted that some of those executed were sentenced to death after holding trials that failed to meet international standards.[28]

Democratic Republic of Congo

In December 2002, following several years of brutal conflict in the Democratic Republic of Congo (DRC) that have involved a range of armed groups and forces from six foreign countries, a comprehensive power-sharing agreement was concluded in South Africa. The agreement provided for a two-year transition period, the establishment of "institutions of transition" as well as an interim government, a truth and reconciliation commission and a national observatory on human rights. On April 4, 2003, a new constitution was promulgated and in June 2003, a Government of National Unity was installed, followed by the establishment of a transitional parliament. Rwanda and Uganda finally withdrew their troops from the country, where they had played an active role in the conflict for many years.

Despite this progress toward peace, the government has yet to control all areas of the country or various rebel groups, particularly in the east. In those areas, reports of serious human rights abuses, including massacres, rapes, forced recruitment of child soldiers, sexual slavery, disappearances and torture, continue to be widespread. In addition, the government itself is responsible for unlawful killings and denies basic rights to freedom of expression and association, privacy, a fair trial and humane conditions of detention.

In June 2003, following massive violence, looting and the killing and raping of civilians in the Ituri district, a French-led multinational force, known as Artemis, was deployed with a U.N. mandate to maintain peace between government and rebel forces and to protect civilians in the town of Bunia and surrounding area.[29] While the arrival of Artemis put an end to clashes in the town itself, in other parts of Ituri fighting and attacks on civilians continued. On September 1, 2003, Artemis was replaced by a unit of the U.N. Organization Mission in the DRC (MONUC) with a broader mandate to enforce the peace throughout the district. Nonetheless, in October, MONUC reported the massacre of about 65 civilians in Kachele, a town northeast of Bunia. In January 2004, another massacre in Ituri, this time of about 100 civilians aboard a boat, was investigated by MONUC.

One of the largest human rights issues exercising the government of the DRC and the international community is the need to end the pervasive impunity that has served to perpetuate serious abuses in the country. The domestic judicial system remains extremely weak and corrupt, and is incapable of addressing ongoing, as well as past criminal violence. After the S.G. issued a May 2003 special report to the Security Council, stating that MONUC and OHCHR would strengthen their capacity to support such infrastructure and transitional justice arrangements, the S.C. sent a mission to the region to further review the situation. The team deplored the reign of impunity accompanying human rights violations in the DRC and stated that it would no longer be tolerated.[30] Shortly afterward, the Chief Prosecutor of the International Criminal Court (ICC), Luis Moreno Ocampo, announced that he had decided to "follow closely the situation in Congo and especially in Ituri." Since then, DRC President Joseph Kabila has officially referred the country situation to the ICC; only the implementing legislation awaits. *(See Chapter 6 for further details.)*

The U.N Special Rapporteur on the situation of human rights in the DRC presented a report to the 58th session of the Assembly in October 2003, stating that massive human rights violations were being committed in the country.[31] She noted that many of these violations reflected the constituent elements of genocide, crimes against humanity and war crimes as defined in the Rome Statute of the ICC. In her report to the 60th session of the Commission in April 2004, the Special Rapporteur noted that political progress had been made in 2003, but that substantial institutional reforms were still required and that serious human rights violations were ongoing. In this regard, she estimated that 1.3 million people in the DRC were infected with HIV/AIDS and that 17 million people were malnourished.

The Commission condemned these persistent violations of human rights and called for the appointment of an independent expert to provide human rights assistance to the DRC government and to study the country's evolving situation.[33]

Haiti

The small Caribbean country of Haiti celebrated its 200th year of independence in early 2004. Celebrations were marred, however, by pervasive rights violations, which escalated in February as pro- and anti-government gangs competed for control of various parts of the country and President Jean-Bertrand Aristide was forced to flee. To assist in the situation, the S.C. adopted Resolution 1529, authorizing the deployment of a Multinational Interim Force in Haiti.[34] In addition, the Council demanded the cessation of violence by all parties to the conflict in Haiti and respect for human rights, stating that there would be individual accountability for those who committed violations. France, Canada and the U.S. contributed troops to the force, which handed over power to a U.N. peacekeeping force in May. *(See Chapter 4 for further details.)* Haiti's interim president, Boniface Alexandre, established a new government on March 17, to govern the country until elections are held in 2005.

While the violence in Haiti has indeed diminished, Amnesty International reported in April 2004 that security remains a serious problem and that a number of armed pro- and anti-government groups are still active.[35] The U.N. Independent Expert on the situation of human rights in Haiti, who had submitted a report to the 60th session of the Commission on Human Rights before the upsurge in violence, made a visit to the country in April 2004. He reported back to the Commission on April 19, recommending that an office of the OHCHR be opened in Haiti as soon as possible; at the time of this writing, some actions to get the office going had begun.

Iraq

During the 59th session of the Commission on Human Rights, U.S. and allied forces overthrew the Ba'thist regime of Saddam Hussein in Iraq. The attack on Iraq by coalition forces and the removal of Hussein from power ignited a heated international debate about the legality of the operation in the absence of a Security Council resolution. On May 22, 2003, the S.C. adopted Resolution 1483, which did not explicitly approve the coalition invasion of Iraq, but determined that the situation in the country still constituted a threat to international peace and security.[36] The resolution called for the appointment of a Special Representative for Iraq with responsibilities relating primarily to coordinating humanitarian and reconstruction activities, promoting the return of refugees, economic reconstruction and the protection of human rights, as well as working with the occupying powers to establish the necessary institutions for representative governance in Iraq. This position was taken up at that time by aforementioned High Commissioner for Human Rights Sergio Vieira de Mello.

Since the installation of an interim administration in Iraq, made up of the Coalition Provisional Authority (CPA) and an Iraqi Governing Council, the most urgent and difficult issue has been human security. In April 2004, the level of violence escalated further and both Shia and Sunni uprisings against the CPA intensified and Coalition forces lost control of several areas of the country. During a six-hour assault on the town of Falluja, the U.S. fired a rocket at an area near a mosque, reportedly killing as many as 40 Iraqis inside the mosque compound and further inflaming local sentiment against them. Numerous foreign civilians were taken hostage by various groups, including citizens of countries that had not supported the U.S.-led war.

Despite being liberated from the repression and rights-abuses of Hussein and his government, the situation for the people of Iraq still remains uncertain. Power cuts, shortages of clean water, and lack of medical services threatened the health of millions of people. In addition, the power vacuum created by the destruction of the Ba'th party and its systems of control resulted in a generalized climate of insecurity, and CPA forces proved unable to perform necessary basic law enforcement. Violent crime, looting and the sexual assault of women continue to be widespread in many parts of the country and international human rights NGOs such as Human Rights Watch have criticized the CPA for failing to protect the population.[37] Moreover, rights groups accused the occupying forces of using excessive force in their response to demonstrations and during operations to track down and arrest former Ba'thists and militants. Revelations of abuse of Iraqi prisoners by U.S. soldiers in Iraq continue to be investigated and have served to increase hostility to the Coalition forces.

The question of how to combat impunity for past human rights violations in Iraq was discussed by the international community right from the takeover of power by the interim administration. With the arrest of Hussein and numerous top officials from the Ba'th party, this issue became even more pressing. Resolution 1483 itself referred to "the need for accountability for crimes and atrocities committed by the previous Iraqi regime," but no formal proposal was put forward until December 2003, when the Governing Council adopted the statute for an Iraqi Special Tribunal drafted by a Judicial Commission. Human rights groups have, however, criticized the statute and called for greater international involvement.[38] These groups also expressed concern over the country's interim constitution, adopted in March 2004, which they state does not provide sufficient protection to women's rights.[39]

Long before the 2003 Iraqi war and the current situation, in 1991, the Commission on Human Rights appointed a Special Rapporteur to Iraq to "make a thorough study of the violations of human rights by the Government of Iraq."[40] Since 1991, the Commission has annually extended the mandate of the Rapporteur for a further year, and at its 59th session in 2003, requested that he focus "on newly available information about violations of human rights and international law." A proposed trip to Iraq by the Rapporteur in September 2003 was canceled following the August bombing of the U.N. headquarters; at the time of writing, he still had not been able to visit the country. In his report to the 60th session of the Commission, however, the Rapporteur stated that this lack of access to Iraq was one of several factors inhibiting his ability to fulfill his mandate. He had, nonetheless, gathered evidence pointing to a pattern of gross and systematic human rights violations committed by Hussein's regime, including mass killings, torture, sexual assault and rape, particularly targeted at the Kurdish population. Although he did not address current human rights conditions in the country, the Rapporteur did emphasize that the deteriorating security situation in Iraq was an issue of great concern. While several NGOs had pressed for the Rapporteur's mandate to be directed to ongoing as well as past human rights violations in Iraq, because of strong pressure from the United States, no resolution was introduced or discussed at the 60th session.

Israeli-Occupied Territories

In November 2003, the U.N. Security Council endorsed the Quartet Performance-based Road Map to a Permanent Two-State Solution to the Israeli-Palestinian Conflict, which had been announced by the United States, United Nations, European Union and Russian Federation in May 2003.[41] Human rights groups have, however, expressed concern that the Road Map contains no reference to human rights or humanitarian law standards.[42]

Within Israel, suicide bombings and other attacks on civilians committed by Palestinian militants killed at least 130 people in 2003 alone.[43] In response, the Israel Defense Forces (IDF) made use of such tactics as assassinations, destruction of homes and random firing in built-up areas. In Gaza, from January 2003 to February 2004, 95 people, mostly civilians, were killed or injured by the IDF during targeted operations to kill Palestinian militants. In addition, since 2000, a total of 1,640 Palestinian homes in Gaza have been destroyed or seriously damaged, rendering about 15,000 people homeless.[44] Severe restrictions on the freedom of movement of the Palestinian population continue to have a detrimental impact on the local economy and functioning of society.

The 2004 report to the Commission on Human Rights by the U.N. Special Rapporteur on the situation of human rights in the Palestinian territories occupied by Israel since 1967, focused attention on the so-called "separation barrier" being built by the Israeli government. While the government argued that the barrier was necessary to protect its citizens from terrorist attacks, the Rapporteur stated that it could not be justified as a legitimate or proportionate response to terrorism. He noted that the construction of the barrier (known as "the Wall") has resulted in large-scale destruction of

Palestinian homes and property. Indeed, the U.N. Office for the Coordination of Humanitarian Affairs (OCHA) has estimated that approximately 680,000 people, or approximately 30 percent of the population of the West Bank, will be directly harmed by the Wall. The Rapporteur further stated that the operation of a closed zone between the so-called Green Line, demarcating the borders between Israel and the West Bank and Gaza Strip, and the wall itself continue to cause severe hardships to the Palestinian population, who must obtain permits to travel or live within the zone. This rule does not apply to the Israeli population, who may travel freely. Palestinian children living within the zone must often cross the Wall to attend school, and Palestinians requiring medical treatment must travel significant distances, crossing several checkpoints, to reach a hospital. The Rapporteur characterized the operation of the closed zone as seriously violating the rights of the Palestinians, and stated that passage through the zone was being administered in an arbitrary manner.

Expressing grave concerns about the construction of the Wall, in December 2003, the G.A. requested an advisory opinion from the International Court of Justice on the legal consequences arising "considering the rules and principles of international law."[45] Several states made written submissions to the Court and public hearings were heard in February 2004. In its written and oral presentations, Palestine argued, among other things, that two broad groups of human rights violations were committed as a result of the construction of the wall. First, it highlighted the direct seizures of land and destruction of property for the purposes of construction and, second, it emphasized the restrictions on the movement and residence of the entire Palestinian population from enforcement of the closed zone. At the time of writing, the judges were still in private deliberations.

Following its usual practice of spending significant time examining the human rights situation in Israel and the Occupied Territories, the 60th session of the Commission on Human Rights held a special sitting on March 24, 2004 to discuss the assassination of Hamas leader Sheikh Ahmed Yassin by the IDF. During the sitting, a resolution condemning the continuing grave violations of human rights in the occupied Palestinian territories, including the assassination, was adopted.[46] In addition, the Commission adopted four other resolutions concerning Israel and the Occupied Territories, reaffirming the right of the Palestinian people to self-determination, expressing concern about human rights in the occupied Syrian Golan, criticizing the continued construction of Israeli settlements, demanding the reversal of the construction of the separation barrier and calling for the release of Lebanese prisoners held by the Israeli government.

Liberia

At its 59th session, the Commission on Human Rights resolved to appoint an independent expert to facilitate cooperation between the government of Liberia and OHCHR to provide technical assistance and advisory services. Charlotte Abaka, who had reported to the Commission as an independent expert on the human rights situation in Liberia under the confidential 1503 procedure, was appointed to the position in July 2003. However, because of the security situation in Liberia, Ms. Abaka was unable to visit the country in 2003. Indeed, the armed conflict between the government of President Charles Taylor and rebel forces that had been going on and off since late 1989 intensified in 2003. In June 2003, fighting reached the capital, Monrovia, and hundreds of civilians were killed.

In the summer of 2003, President Taylor agreed to step down, and in August, went into exile in Nigeria to evade arrest and prosecution by the Special Court for Sierra Leone.[47] On August 1, the S.C. adopted Resolution 1497, authorizing the deployment of a multinational force in Liberia to enforce a cease-fire and prepare for the introduction of a longer-term U.N. stabilization force.[48] On August 18, 2003, a Comprehensive Peace Agreement was signed by the government, the two main rebel forces—Liberians United for Reconciliation and Democracy (LURD) and Movement for Democracy in Liberia (MODEL)—and the political parties. The peace agreement also specified that human rights guaranteed in the *Universal Declaration of Human Rights* and the African Charter on Human and People's Rights would be respected, and that a truth and reconciliation commission would be established. It also recognized the need for an Independent National Commission on Human Rights.

While these political maneuvers were taking place and the conflict was intensifying, the human rights situation in Liberia worsened. In addition to killings of civilians by government and rebel forces, rape and sexual violence against women and children were widespread. Reports of the forced recruitment of child soldiers and laborers continued. The humanitarian situation also deteriorated rapidly, as aid workers were unable to reach most parts of the country because of the fighting. *(See the Humanitarian Assistance section of this chapter.)* Lack of access to food, water and healthcare had a particularly negative impact on children. Moreover, those with HIV/AIDS were unable to receive adequate medical assistance.

Following the adoption of Resolution 1497 by the Security Council, the Acting High Commissioner for Human Rights published an emergency report to the bureau of the Commission on Human Rights.[49] In this report, the Acting High Commissioner described the human rights situation in Liberia as "shocking" and asserted that crimes against humanity and grave breaches of the Geneva Conventions had been committed, requiring investigation and individual criminal accountability. He further recommended the inclusion of a strong human rights component in the planned U.N. peacekeeping mission in Liberia, including technical cooperation, capacity-building and monitoring. The stabilization force envisaged by Resolution 1497 was authorized by a further resolution on September 19, which officially established and named the U.N. Mission in Liberia (UNMIL).[50] UNMIL was put under the control of the S.G.'s Special Representative for Liberia and has both military and civilian components. It was given the mandate, among other things, to facilitate the provision of humanitarian assistance, contribute to efforts to promote and protect human rights, and carry out human rights monitoring.

While the arrival of the multinational force and the subsequent deployment of UNMIL, along with the departure of President Taylor, put an end to the immediate crisis in Liberia, rural areas of the country remained insecure at the end of 2003. U.N. member states were slow to contribute the necessary forces to UNMIL, and the mission was therefore unable to deploy in the outer regions. Serious abuses of civilians by former government militias, paramilitary groups, LURD and MODEL continued in these regions, such as rape, looting and forced recruitment of child soldiers and laborers.[51] Ensuring the safe and voluntary return of approximately 500,000 internally displaced persons (IDPs) and hundreds of thousands of refugees is an enormous task for the U.N. and humanitarian agencies, in addition to assisting the building of democratic institutions, such as a functioning police and judicial system.

In her report to the 60th session of the Commission on Human Rights, Ms. Abaka, the independent expert, emphasized the importance of the complete disarmament and demobilization of all paramilitary groups, the mobilization of resources by the international community to repatriate IDPs and refugees, the rehabilitation of former child soldiers, the establishment of a functional national capacity for the promotion and protection of human rights and the creation of a truth and reconciliation commission.

Russia (Chechnya)

Nongovernmental organizations vociferously condemned the ongoing human rights violations being committed in Chechnya by Russian forces as well as by Chechen rebels at the Commission's 60th session. Often considered a forgotten conflict, particularly since President Vladimir Putin supports the U.S.-led "war on terror," NGOs presented detailed evidence that the situation in Chechnya had deteriorated further, despite the holding of presidential elections in the republic in October 2003. A report from the Medical Foundation for the Care of Victims of Torture released during the Commission session documented numerous cases of rape and sexual violence in Chechnya, committed largely by Russian forces, concluding that such cases were widespread.[52] Extrajudicial executions, disappearances, torture and arbitrary detention also continued, spilling over into neighboring Ingushetia. Conditions for the many thousands of Chechen IDPs remained dire and those who returned to their homes were often denied promised compensation for their property.

At the Commission, E.U. states sponsored a resolution condemning ongoing, serious violations of international human rights and humanitarian law in Chechnya, calling upon the Russian government to cooperate with European human rights monitoring mechanisms and to allow free and secure access for international organizations, NGOs and the media. This resolution was defeated, however, by a vote in the Commission.

Despite the absence of Commission action, other arms of the U.N. human rights system did examine and condemn the situation in Chechnya. The representative of the Secretary-General on IDPs visited the Russian Federation in September 2003, at the invitation of the government. The Representative estimated that between 400,000 to 600,000 people were displaced as a result of the conflict in Chechnya from 1994 to 1996, and an additional 600,000 have been displaced since 1999.[53] He noted that IDPs and those remaining in their homes in Chechnya have only occasional access to humanitarian aid. He also stated that Chechen IDPs in Ingushetia have been subjected to increased security measures and pressure to return to Chechnya in light of various terrorist attacks in Moscow that have been attributed to Chechens.

During its examination of the report of Russia on its 31st session in November 2003, the Committee on Economic and Social and Cultural Rights also expressed its grave concern about the situation in Chechnya, stating that the majority of rights contained in the *International Covenant on Economic, Social and Cultural Rights* were not being respected.[54] Similarly, during its examination of the Russian Federation, the Human Rights Committee stated that the government "should ensure that operations in Chechnya are carried out in compliance with its international human rights obligations" and that "abuse and violations are not committed with impunity *de jure* or *de facto*, including violations committed by military and law enforcement personnel during counter-terrorist operations."[55]

Other Countries and Thematic Issues, Including Darfur

In addition to the situations described above, human rights violations in other parts of the world—as well as specific issues and themes—received attention at the Commission on Human Rights and by other arms of the U.N. throughout 2003 and early 2004. A new special rapporteur with a mandate focusing on the human rights aspects of trafficking in persons, especially women and children, was created. *(See this chapter's Commentary for details.)*[56] Moreover, in a move hailed as a breakthrough by some NGOs, the Commission charged OHCHR with the task of compiling a report setting out the scope of existing initiatives and standards on the responsibility of corporations with regard to human rights.[57]

A major human rights and humanitarian crisis that did not receive significant international attention until April 2004 was the conflict in the Darfur region of northwestern Sudan. In April, a senior U.N. official accused Arab militiamen aligned with the Sudanese government of conducting a "scorched earth" campaign of ethnic cleansing against Darfur's black Africans. Human Rights Watch reported that the government had recruited, paid, armed and supplied more than 20,000 militiamen, and alleged that along with government forces, they had committed human rights violations and crimes against humanity, including targeting of civilians, rape, torture, summary executions, forcible displacement, looting and destruction of homes.[58] U.N agencies estimated that approximately 750,000

Sudanese have been internally displaced within the Darfur region because of fighting between the government and two main rebel groups. Tens of thousands more refugees are also present in Chad. On April 8, OHCHR sent a fact-finding mission to Chad to interview the refugees; later in the month, the team went to Sudan itself. Following comments by S.G. Annan that military action might be required to ensure access by humanitarian and human rights workers to the population in the Darfur region, the Sudanese government reacted angrily, saying that all that was required from the international community was the provision of humanitarian aid. *(See the Humanitarian Assistance section of this chapter for further details.)*

In April, the Commission passed a resolution on the situation in Darfur, which was criticized by the U.S. and NGOs as being too weak.[59] The resolution, which was the result of a compromise reached between the E.U. and the African group,[60] stated that the Commission shared the grave concern of the S.G. about the scale of reported human rights abuses and the humanitarian situation in Darfur, and requested the appointment of a Special Rapporteur on the situation of human rights in the Sudan for a period of one year.

Once again, the Commission adopted resolutions regarding human rights violations in Belarus and Turkmenistan, stating that neither country had done anything substantial to improve its record from the previous year. The Commission did not, however, create a new country rapporteur to monitor the situation in Turkmenistan. A Commission resolution did call for the appointment of a special rapporteur to investigate human rights abuses in North Korea, however, focusing on allegations that the country is testing chemical weapons on political prisoners. In addition to the mistreatment of political prisoners, one of the most serious concerns related to North Korea is the widespread denial of access to food, as reported by the U.N. Special Rapporteur on the right to food.

Indigenous Rights: International Decade Comes to an End

In December 2004, the International Decade of the World's Indigenous People will culminate with a two-day seminar to evaluate its success. The theme for the Decade has been "Indigenous People: Partnership in Action," with the objective of strengthening international cooperation to find solutions to problems faced by indigenous people in areas such as human rights, the environment, development, education and health. One goal of the Decade aimed to have U.N. specialized agencies and other intergovernmental agencies develop activities to benefit indigenous peoples. For example, OHCHR initiated an Indigenous Fellowship program in which fellows spend five months in Geneva learning about international human rights and indigenous rights; they are then expected to apply what they have learned to their home communities. The program has been so successful that it will be continued beyond the end of the Decade.

A resolution was also adopted on the situation in Myanmar, extending the mandate of the Special Rapporteur there for a further year. Despite the ongoing violations of basic civil, political, economic and social rights by the Zimbabwean government, the Commission again failed to pass a resolution on Zimbabwe because of the successful use of the no-action procedure by the African group. A resolution on Cuba was passed by a narrow majority, deploring the arrest and imprisonment of political dissidents and independent journalists, and calling upon the Cuban government to cooperate with the Personal Representative of the High Commissioner for Human Rights for Cuba.

In addition to its public debate and resolutions, the Commission used the confidential procedure established by Resolution 1503 to examine the situation in Bolivia, Djibouti, Honduras and Uzbekistan. Following this closed-session discussion, the chairman announced that an independent expert would be appointed for Uzbekistan to report to the Commission under the confidential procedure. The Commission also decided to discontinue consideration of Bolivia, Djibouti and Honduras under the Resolution 1503 procedure.

Looking Forward

Over the summer of 2004, new High Commissioner for Human Rights Louise Arbour will take office and significantly shape United Nations action on human rights. With Ms. Arbour's appointment, it is hoped that a new spirit of cooperation will be fostered between the U.N. and its member states and that a reinvigorated OHCHR will be able to take swift, effective action to address and prevent human rights crises around the world. The new High Commissioner will face major challenges, not least of which will be to develop a close working relationship with the United States government and to encourage multilateral approaches to human rights concerns. A change in administration in the U.S. following the November 2004 presidential elections, and a consequent change in U.S. foreign policy, could have a significant impact on several of the human rights issues and regional crises described in this chapter.

There is little question that the situation in Iraq will continue to exercise the U.S. and the United Nations. The need to create a more stable and secure environment in the country remains an imperative concern, with serious repercussions for the basic rights of the Iraqi population. While the U.S. government insists that a transfer of power will take place at the end of June 2004, and the U.N. is closely involved in this process, there remain many questions about how the transfer will take place and what the consequences will be in terms of ongoing violence. Similarly, in Afghanistan, the human rights situation remains very much dependent upon the improvement of security throughout the country. Local warlords seeking to grab and cling to power may increase their activities in the run-up to the presidential and parliamentary elections scheduled for September 2004. In addition to curbing the influence of such warlords through effective disarmament and providing a more robust international presence, it is crucial that the international community ensure that an independent, fair and secure voting process is in place. In both countries, the fostering of local civil-society groups, including human rights organizations, is an essential part of ensuring greater respect for the rule of law and for basic rights.

The issue of human rights and counter-terrorism will once again be discussed by the General Assembly at its 59th session in 2004. The report currently under preparation by OHCHR on this subject will be presented to the Assembly. In addition, the new independent expert appointed by the Commission on Human Rights at its 60th session will formulate recommendations for further action to ensure that all measures taken by states to combat terrorism are in full compliance with their obligations under international human rights law.

Humanitarian Assistance: The Issues at Stake

Jacques Fomerand

Just as with human rights, the provision and coordination of worldwide humanitarian assistance—external aid provided in response to, as well as to prevent, mitigate and prepare for, humanitarian emergencies—is a longstanding activity of the United Nations. One could easily trace this activity back to the work of the International Refugee Organization and the U.N. Children's Fund (UNICEF), both of which addressed the mass social disruptions, famine and refugee flows resulting from World War II.

Today, the U.N.'s role in providing humanitarian assistance to people impacted by natural and man-made disasters is well embedded in the organization's mandate. Virtually, the entire U.N. system has been mobilized, including, in particular, the U.N. High Commissioner for Refugees (UNHCR), the World Food Programme (WFP) and the Office for the Coordination of Humanitarian Affairs (OCHA). Other U.N. organs, such as the U.N. Office for Project Services (UNOPS) through its Rehabilitation and Social Sustainability Division, and the U.N. Development Programme (UNDP) with its Emergency Response Division, have acquired a significant humanitarian function. Several U.N. specialized agencies, such as the Food and Agricultural Organization (FAO), the World Health Organization (WHO) and the U.N. Educational, Scientific and Cultural Organization (UNESCO), have joined the effort as well.

The total number of beneficiaries targeted by these various bodies exceeded 45 million people in 2003. Specifically, 7 million in the Democratic People's Republic of Korea, 6.5 million in southern Africa, 6.5 million in the Democratic Republic of Congo, 4 million in Zimbabwe, 3.5 million in Sudan, 2.5 million in Uganda, 2.5 million in Angola, 2.2 million in the Central African Republic, 2 million in West Africa, 1.7 million in Eritrea, 1.7 million in Liberia, 1.2 million in Somalia and 1.2 million in Chechnya. That same year, U.N. humanitarian agencies received contributions amounting to some $60 million to assist victims affected by natural disasters in 33 countries.[1]

Various issues of debate—such as whether or not the U.N. has a right to intervene in a country to provide what it calls assistance and others call development—come up when dealing in humanitarian assistance among U.N. agencies and member states. The following section takes a brief look at a few of these topics and their accompanying challenges.

Sovereignty vs. Intervention

The U.N. humanitarian edifice may be imposing in its own rights, but the world body's growing involvement in humanitarian affairs has always been and, to this day, remains a source of considerable controversy. How direct and broad the role of the U.N. should be in the coordination of natural disaster mitigation was already a bone of contention among U.N. agencies, nongovernmental organizations (NGOs) and member states when the Office of the U.N. Disaster Relief Coordinator was created in 1972. The humanitarian assistance regime that emerged from the Cold War has rekindled this longstanding debate. In Resolution 688 of April 1991, which created "safe havens" for Kurdish refugees stranded along the Iraqi-Turkish border, the Security Council established the very radical precedent that humanitarian relief operations could be undertaken without the host country's consent. The subsequent mixed record of the U.N. in other war-torn societies like Bosnia, Chechnya, Rwanda, Somalia and, perhaps more telling, Kosovo, point to the persisting clash between those who wish to expand the U.N. humanitarian role and those who wish to limit it.

Tension between the norms of sovereignty and a right to intervene is, of course, at the root of another, shorter term issue: access. The humanitarian community loudly claims a "right to access"[2] but cases abound with obstacles raised by governments to impede the delivery of humanitarian aid. From December 2003 to February 2004, only 10 percent of the population displaced by the outbreak of violence in Sudan's western region of Darfur could be reached by humanitarian agencies because of the government's restrictive policy of travel permits for aid workers. And while Colombia's drug wars have uprooted 2 million people due to limited access, WFP currently provides food to only 300,000 internally displaced persons (IDPs).[3]

Speaking on the subject at the spring 2004 session of the Commission on Human Rights, the acting High Commissioner bemoaned the fact that none of the illegal armed groups operating in the country had responded to urgent appeals that they respect civilians' human rights. He also criticized the Colombian government's "democratic security" policy for running counter to the protection and promotion of human rights.[4] The armed conflict in Chechnya, now in its fifth year, has taken a disastrous toll on the civilian population. Yet, as a despondent observer noted, "the international community has...chosen the path of self-deception, choosing to believe Russia's claims that the situation...is stabilizing, and so be spared of making tough decisions about what actions are necessary to stop flagrant abuses and secure the well-being of the people of the region."[5]

Clearly, governments have yet to accept the notion—revolutionary in a state-based international society—that sovereignty not only means equality and territorial control, but also entails a responsibility to protect.[6]

The North-South Ideological Divide

The question of access is only one facet of the profound political divisions that split the international community. For better or worse, the humanitarian enterprise has become a sensitive North-South issue. Developing countries, led by India, Mexico and China, highlight the contrast between the humanitarian principles of humanity, neutrality and impartiality enshrined in General Assembly Resolution 182 of December 1991, and the inconsistent and haphazard interventionist record of developed countries. Indeed, there is no dearth of instances of double standards raising suspicions that the provision of humanitarian assistance is driven by political and security agendas. For example, spending per capita varies sharply from $8 in the Democratic Republic of Congo to $16 in Sierra Leone to $207 in Kosovo.[7]

From 1995 to 2000, the former Yugoslavia (now Serbia and Montenegro) was the largest recipient of humanitarian aid, receiving up to one-fifth of all donations during that period. In 2003, Afghanistan absorbed a major share of humanitarian assistance, in no minor way a consequence of the United States' interest in the region. The top two crises of the day—Afghanistan and Iraq—received more funding than all humanitarian crises combined in 2003, and most likely will again in 2004 and 2005. At the March 2004 Berlin conference, donor countries pledged $8.2 billion in aid and low-cost loans to help rebuild Afghanistan.[8] In contrast to these high-profile missions, donor nations have been reluctant to fund missions in which they have no immediate national or strategic interest. This has led to "forgotten tragedies," which receive little to none of the funds requested for them during the process of annual donor appeals. Only 44.6 percent of the funding requested last year by OCHA for Africa was received through its Consolidated Appeals Process (CAP).[9] Created in 1991, CAP is a mechanism used by aid organizations to plan, implement and monitor their activities; they use this data to produce a Common Humanitarian Action Plan and appeal and then present it to the international community every year. In March 2004, WFP and UNICEF launched an emergency appeal asking for $5.8 million to help 600,000 children and women in Namibia; two months later, they had received nothing.[10]

Against this background of inconsistencies, donor states' talk of sovereignty less as a right under international law than as a responsibility sounds hollow to developing countries. From their vantage point, humanitarian intervention under U.N. auspices in response to man-made or natural disasters is simply a smoke-screen for intrusions in what they consider to be internal affairs. The fact that, in the past decade, humanitarian aid has increased seemingly at the expense of development finance confirms their fears. Humanitarian aid accounts for roughly 10 percent of all official assistance, up from close to 6 percent some 10 years earlier. At the same time, humanitarian assistance provided through bilateral channels has become much more important relative to multilateral aid, with only a third of the $10 billion spent on humanitarian assistance going through multilateral U.N. channels.[11] The inferences to be drawn from these data may need to be qualified in light of the fact that funding that would have been earmarked for "peacekeeping" activities now often falls under the "humanitarian" rubric. But, by and large, developing countries are correct in their observations regarding bilateral aid and its strategic targeting. The other fact of the matter is that, within the U.N. itself, humanitarian assistance is still minuscule compared to development spending. OCHA's 2004 regular budget is a mere $10 million. The office's extra-budgetary funding requests for headquarters, field operations and projects amount to $74.6 million, a figure that pales in comparison to the overall $1.5 billion biennial development budget of the entire United Nations.

With regard to resources, or lack thereof, it is important to note the perennial problems of under- and late-funding. In its first year, OCHA responded to six international humanitarian crises and coordinated a total of $2.1 billion in multilateral aid through its appeal process. In 2004, the number of crises rose dramatically to more than 20 in various countries and regions, although the amount of funding channeled through OCHA increased only incrementally to $2.4 billion. (*See Table of 2004 Consolidated Appeals for the full list of crises*). The ratio of the amount of resources channeled through CAP relative to the funding requested by OCHA has never been satisfactory. In 1992, CAP received 76 percent of funding requested, whereas by 2002, that number had fallen to 57 percent. Total financial requirements to deal with humanitarian crises in each of these countries or regions were estimated by OCHA to be in the vicinity of $5.2 billion for the year 2003 up to April 2004. Yet U.N. agencies received only $3.3 billion, a 65 percent shortfall with wide variations among the regions affected.[12]

Delays in meeting aid pledges are a recurring staple of U.N. humanitarian officials' feverishly scrambling for funds as one crisis intersects with another. For instance, in the first half of 2004, WFP received only $35 million of a $253 million appeal aimed at resettling Angolan IDPs and refugees; the agency estimates that it will need at least $136 million to feed the nearly 1.4 million who have already returned to their homes or are scheduled to be repatriated from Zambia, Namibia and the Congo.[13] Roughly at the same time, UNHCR reported that it received $3 million of the $39.2 million it had sought for Liberia for 2004 and only $3 million of the $8.8 million needed for preparatory work in the Sudan, where a potential peace accord in the two-decades-long war between the government and southern rebels is expected to lead to a flood of more than half a million returnees.[14]

Relief vs. Development?

Traditionally, disaster relief was considered to be a short-term activity inasmuch as it was a response to onetime catastrophic events, such as earthquakes, droughts and floods. On the other hand, the understanding among U.N. agencies and member states was that development aid was long-term as it focused on basic infrastructural projects and was part of a capital accumulation process that often would take years, if not decades, to complete. The U.N. humanitarian experience of the 1990s and more recent "successes" in countries, such as Angola, Mozambique and East Timor, have increasingly pointed to the need to develop coherent strategies for restoring stability and sustainable normalcy linking concurrent measures: mine removal, the disarmament, demobilization and reintegration of combatants, peace-building, and post-crisis economic and social recovery work addressing the root causes of conflicts and disasters. Conditions of underdevelopment often trigger the occurrence of man-made disasters or worsen their impact. In addition, in responding to disasters, the seeds of development can—and need to be—planted. It is in these contexts that, every year, the Secretary-General now prepares a report known as "Humanitarian Assistance: From Relief to Development."

UNHCR's recent Convention Plus initiative is based on an understanding that it is not enough to focus solely on the humanitarian dimension of refugee problems and that to ensure more comprehensive predictable and effective responses to refugee situations, the economic, social and political dimensions also need to be considered. In a similar vein, the agency has developed a Framework for Durable Solutions in cooperation with UNDP, the World Bank and other partners. This framework focuses on the promotion of more targeted development assistance to areas with large numbers of refugees, an integrated approach to repatriation, reintegration, rehabilitation and reconstruction programs in post-conflict situations and, wherever possible, the local integration of refugees.

These initiatives have led to concrete projects in Afghanistan, Eritrea, Sierra Leone and Sri Lanka. But much remains to be done to operationalize these conceptual changes into workable field activities. As shown in the following section, the U.N. frequently finds itself propelled into internally highly unstable political and security situations with cross-border implications serious enough to make territorial boundaries virtually meaningless. Sudan's neighbors, for example, have been drawn into the country's civil wars by sheltering refugees or allowing the infiltration of rebel groups from their territories. In the Great Lakes region of Africa, Uganda and Rwanda have supported rebel groups seeking to overthrow the Congolese government. Insurgent movements have used bases in the territories of Tanzania and the Congo to launch attacks against the Burundi government.

At the same time, many intrastate conflicts have become entangled with transborder networks of state and non-state actors. As the cases of

2004 U.N. Consolidated Inter-Agency Humanitarian Assistance Appeals

Summary of Requirements and Contributions by affected country/region as of June 2004.

AFFECTED COUNTRY/ REGION	REQUIREMENTS ($U.S.)	CONTRIBUTIONS/ PLEDGES ($U.S.)	CARRY OVER ($U.S.)	TOTAL RESOURCES AVAILABLE ($U.S.)	SHORTFALL ($U.S.)	REQUIRE- MENTS COVERED	IMPLEMENTATION PERIOD
Angola	181,680, 807	67,089,552	0	67,089, 552	114,591,255	36.9%	Jan.04–Dec.04
Burundi	118,583,076	17,290,432	425,894	17,1765,326	100,866,750	14.9%	Jan.04–Dec.04
Central African Republic	16,850,037	2,7211,831	0	2,721,831	14,128,206	16.2%	Jan.04–Dec.04
Chad	64,980,751	26,590,295	1,257,050	27,847,345	37,133,406	42.9%	Mar.04–Dec.0
Chechnya and Neighbouring Republics (RF)	60,118,141	29,778,386	0	29,778,386	30,339,755	49.5%	Jan.04–Dec.04
Côte d'Ivoire +3	61,104,222	3,913,273	0	3,913,273	57,191,393	6.4%	Jan.04–Dec.04
Democratic Republic of Congo	160,042,056	57,390,628	0	57,390,628	102,651,428	35.9%	Jan.04–Dec.04
DPR of Korea	181,498,739	35,981,397	0	35,981,397	145,517,342	19.8%	Jan.04–Dec.04
Eritrea	117,636,804	30,158,648	124,385	30,283,033	87,353,771	25.7%	Jan.04–Dec.04
Great Lakes Region	83,961,588	23,914,606	0	23,914,606	60,046,982	28.5%	Jan.04–Dec.04
Guinea	36,044,512	3,694,100	0	3,694,100	32,350,412	10.2%	Jan.04–Dec.04
Haiti Flash Appeal	35,074,862	10,520,659	0	10,520,659	24,554,203	30.0%	Mar.04–Aug.0
Indonesia	4l,211,385	971,626	0	971,626	42,239,759	2.2%	Jan.04–Dec.04
Islamic Republic of Iran 2004 Flash Appeal	32,668,877	15,875,956	0	15,875,956	16,792,921	48.6&	Jan.04–Dec.04
Liberia	140,510,163	43,392,764	0	43,392,764	97,117,399	30.9%	Jan.04–Dec.04
Madagascar Flash Appeal	8,984,679	149,254	0	149,254	8,835,425	1.7%	–
Occupied Palestinian Territory	285,066,244	76,154,673	0	76,154,673	208,911,571	26.7%	Jan.04–Dec.04
Sierra Leone	60,639,200	6,028,135	0	6,028,135	54,911,065	9.9%	Jan.04–Dec.04
Somalia	119,126,299	23,762,431	4,116,254	27,878,685	91,247,614	23.4%	Jan.04–Dec.04
Sudan	756,625,112	112,043,245	762,863	112,806,108	643,819,004	14.9%	Jan.04–Dec.04
Tajikistan	39,781,718	4,189,782	0	4,189,782	35,591,936	10.5%	Jan.04–Dec.04
Tanzania (United Republic of)	38,766,187	13,566,652	88,441	13,655,093	25,111,094	35.2%	Jan.04–Dec.04
Uganda	112,380,013	25,139,644	122,243	25,261,887	87,118,126	22.5%	Jan.04–Dec.04
West Africa Sub-Regional	108,421,086	47,309,798	0	47,309,798	61,111,288	43.6%	Jan.04–Dec.04
Grand Total:	**2,864,057,002**	**677,627,767**	**6,897,130**	**684,524,897**	**2,179,532,105**	**23.9%**	–

Source: ReliefWeb websit

Afghanistan, Liberia, Sierra Leone, Kosovo and others show, military, economic, political and social networks that have focused on the illicit arms trade, natural resources exploitation, drug smuggling and human trafficking have had a "balloon effect" that has exacerbated internal conflicts.[15]

Against this background, it is not surprising that food-aid-saving interventions take priority and are comparatively better funded while other sectors that may also constitute a key bridge between relief and development, such as water, health, sanitation, agriculture education, rule of law and good governance, remain chronically under-funded. In the past year-and-a-half, 44 percent of donor contributions were channeled into food assistance and only 12 percent in economic recovery and infrastructure, 1.6 percent in education, 4.7 percent in health and 2.7 percent in agriculture.[16]

It is understood that humanitarian assistance and development are closely interrelated. But how one should dovetail the other and how the two should be made mutually reinforcing remain financial and, ultimately, politically unresolved questions. The following brief case studies illustrate some of the general observations made hitherto.

Country-Specific Humanitarian Assistance

Jacques Fomerand

The United Nations designated the 2004 Consolidated Inter-Agency Humanitarian Assistance Appeals as one of the "forgotten emergencies" of the world. As noted in the previous section, crises included in the appeal affect 45 million people in over 20 countries and regions–the high majority of which are in Africa, but they have not received the international attention, or humanitarian aid, of those crises in Iraq and Afghanistan. Whether caused by war or natural disasters, all of them, according to U.N. Development Programme Administrator Mark Malloch Brown, represent cases of extreme need.

Afghanistan

When the Taliban was forcibly eliminated from power in 2001, half of Afghanistan's people were living in absolute poverty. Virtually all of the country's institutions and much of its infrastructure had been destroyed. According to the World Bank, the cost of two decades of conflict in Afghanistan approaches $240 billion; per capita income stands at $175. While economic growth over the past two years has been buoyant, the country continues to be heavily dependent on humanitarian aid. Six governmental agencies, more than 50 NGOs and nine U.N. agencies are involved in humanitarian work in Afghanistan.

Their activities have brought tangible improvements as they are increasingly designed to complement and reinforce development efforts. Under its 2003-2005 Country Program, UNICEF is active in the fields of health, nutrition, education and child protection, as well as in the reduction of gender and regional disparities. Throughout 2003, 6 million children were immunized against polio and measles and 5 million children were given Vitamin A through UNICEF initiatives. Also, teaching and learning materials were distributed to 4.2 million school-age children and 35,000 teachers were trained through a partnership between UNICEF and the U.N. Office for Project Services. The work continued for the rehabilitation or construction of 200 schools for more than 170,000 girls and boys, many of them located in areas of high refugee return. To date, girls' enrolment has risen by 30 percent.[17]

Concurrently, nearly 2 million refugees have returned to Afghanistan since UNHCR started its voluntary repatriation program in March 2002. The agency plans to assist some 400,000 refugees back to Afghanistan in 2004 and approximately 1.8 million by the end of 2006.[18]

Yet the country faces daunting humanitarian, reconstruction and political challenges. Although Afghanistan is constantly threatened by various natural disasters—earthquakes, extreme drought or floods and mudslides—no structures exist to protect the population from such disasters, a situation that seriously hinders sustainable reconstruction. Some 5.4 million people, out of a total population of 24 million, remain dependent on food aid, according to WFP. Approximately 65 percent of the population in urban areas and 81 percent in rural areas do not have access to safe water. And there are an estimated 400,000 IDPs in the country.[19]

The political and security situation in Afghanistan—including the role of the U.N. Assistance Mission in Afghanistan (UNAMA)—cast even further doubt on the assumption that humanitarian efforts will lead to sustained recovery and development. The reach of the central government outside the capital is severely limited, leaving the real power resting in the hands of warlords. In fact, insecurity was the main reason for the government's decision to postpone national elections from June to September 2004 and voter registration has been restricted to the country's eight largest cities. Sporadic attacks against government targets and the foreign aid community are still hindering reconstruction efforts, prompting warnings by the S.G.'s Special Representative that the maintenance of law and order and the expansion of reconstruction and nation-building tasks could not continue unless more forces were made available to provincial authorities. Meanwhile, rural poverty and lack of income have fed a surging opium cultivation and trade.[20] *(See Chapter 5 for more details.)*

With such insecurities threatening to derail Afghanistan's entire political process, U.N. officials have observed that the country will require years to lift up.[21]

Angola

The humanitarian situation in Angola has improved significantly since the end of the 27-year-old civil conflict in 2002. At the height of the conflict, close to 3 million people were dependent on humanitarian aid. But the economy is in shambles, the transport infrastructure has been destroyed, and uncleared landmines continue to hinder the delivery of aid. Basic social services are non-existent and child mortality remains among the highest in the world. In 2003, some 1.9 million people were receiving humanitarian assistance. Despite a substantial increase in food production during the first year of peace, some 1.4 million Angolans still urgently require food aid.[22]

Burundi

The international community has paid only intermittent attention to this civil war, which broke out in October 1993 following the assassination of President Melchior Ndadaye by a group of Tutsi army officers. Since then, some 300,000 Burundians—mostly civilians—have perished in intense ethnic violence when varying groups drawn from the country's large Hutu majority rose up against the Tutsi-led government. Earlier attempts by the majority Hutu to win a share in power had been put down by the Tutsi, a minority of some 15 percent of the population who dominated political, economic and social life. The first peace treaty in the war, the 2000 Arusha Accords (also known as the Arusha Peace and Reconciliation Agreement), brought some opposition parties into the government. But two of the major rebel groups did not sign the agreement, the Forces for the Defense of Democracy (FDD) and the National Liberation Forces (FNL); thus, fighting continued.

Neighboring states have been drawn into the war as many FDD combatants are based in Tanzania and both the FDD and FNL had, according to Human Rights Watch, bases on Congolese territory. Burundian troops are supported by the current Rwandan army. A transitional government was inaugurated in November 2001, the first step toward holding national elections planned for October 2004. The government of Burundi signed a ceasefire agreement in December 2002 with three of the four Hutu rebel groups; it also signed an accord with the FDD in October 2003, agreeing yet again to end the civil war. The accord was followed by the deployment of the African Mission in Burundi (AMIB), the first peacekeeping operation mounted by the African Union. AMIB deployed some 2,800 troops to oversee the implementation of the peace accords. The FNL initially rejected negotiations with the government, but in April 2004, announced that it would halt attacks against government troops and their allies.

With peace prospects improving, S.G. Annan recommended in March 2004 that the S.C. establish a U.N. peacekeeping mission in Burundi to replace and expand on the existing African Force to provide security for elections, scheduled to be held in October. The S.C. authorized such a mission, the U.N. Operation in Burundi (ONUB), in May in Resolution 1545. Taking over for the African Union, ONUB has a six-month mandate to, among other things, support the process of disarming and disbanding militias as well as promoting the rule of law under the Arusha Accords. The immediate and longer tasks ahead seem daunting. Some 280,000 IDPs live in 230 permanent sites around the country. An additional 789,000 Burundians reside in Tanzanian refugee camps. Under a voluntary repatriation plan now being finalized, UNHCR aims to help 500,000 refugees return to and reintegrate into Burundi between 2004 and 2006. The agency is also planning to facilitate the return of at least 150,000 Burundian refugees from Tanzania in 2004.[23] The local economy has been destroyed and social services are in ruins. The level of vulnerability among the general population is one of the highest in the world. The under-age-5 mortality rate is one of the highest in the world. Less than half of school-age children attend schools. In rural areas, the percentage is even lower—35 percent.[24]

Côte d'Ivoire

As detailed in Chapter 4, in September 2002, an attempted coup-turned-rebellion in the northern part of the country shattered the myth of stability and prosperity that had hitherto prevailed about Côte d'Ivoire. Since then, the U.N. Mission in Côte d'Ivoire (MINUCI) has been in place to facilitate the implementation of the so-called Linas–Marcoussis Agreement and to complement the operations of the French and ECOWAS forces. In addition, the Security Council approved the establishment of a small staff in support of the S.G.'s Special Representative to work on political, legal, civil affairs, civilian police, elections, humanitarian and human rights issues.

Although the conflict "officially" ended in July 2003, little progress has been made toward peace and reconciliation. As of spring 2004, the Linas-Marcoussis peace accords were floundering, and the S.C. replaced MINUCI with a new peacekeeping force called the U.N. Operation in Côte d'Ivoire.[25] In spite of the arrival of the force in April, there is still no clear signal of a break in the political impasse.

Against this background, U.N. humanitarian agencies have focused their efforts primarily on the immediate critical and material needs of affected populations and the revitalization of social services. An interagency mechanism chaired by WFP and made up of UNICEF, UNHCR, WFP, UNDP, WHO, FAO, UNFPA and OCHA has been given the task of monitoring the crisis and coordinating the U.N. humanitarian response in the context of the CAP process. Since the start of the crisis, WFP has distributed about 1,500 metric tons of food aid worth $1,125,000 to displaced and other vulnerable people.[26]

Democratic Republic of Congo

In August 1999, after more than five years of conflict, the governments of the Democratic Republic of Congo, Angola, Namibia, Rwanda, Uganda and Zimbabwe and the main Congolese opposition groups reached a cease-fire agreement. The so-called Lusaka Accords set up a mechanism for the discussion of peace implementation and, in November 1999, the U.N. Mission in the Democratic Republic of Congo (MONUC) began monitoring the cease-fire and assisting in the disarmament, demobilization and repatriation of foreign forces. In July 2003, President Joseph Kabila promulgated a transitional constitution providing for power-sharing arrangements.

Neighboring Rwanda and Uganda withdrew most of their troops in the second half of 2003. But an upsurge in fighting by armed groups and militias has gripped the eastern and northern parts of the country, forcing the S.C. in June 2003 to deploy an Interim Emergency Multinational Force (MNF) to secure Bunia and reinforce MONUC's military presence. In November 2003, MONUC started to redeploy the bulk of its peacekeeping force from areas along the Lusaka Accord cease-fire line, where fighting has stopped to concentrate in the area between Bunia, Ituri District; Kindu, Maniema Province, Uvira and south Kivu Province. *(See Chapter 4 for further peacekeeping details).*

The Council's growing interventionist mood has not, however, stymied the fighting described by humanitarian agencies as "one of the bloodiest conflicts the world has known since World War II." In part, the conflict has been exacerbated and prolonged by the looting of the country's natural resources by both allies and opponents of the government, including military commanders and political leaders from Rwanda, Uganda and Zimbabwe, which a U.N. Panel of Experts first reported on in October 2002.[27] A March 2004 S.C. resolution repeated its earlier condemnation of the illegal activities taking place mainly in the DRC's mining areas, despite the July 2003-imposed arms embargo. The resolution again urged governments to help in ending the illegal trade of the countries' resources.[28]

In any event, in less than five years, an estimated 3.3 million people are thought to have been killed, the vast majority of them civilians. Violence in the region has caused massive displacements of populations–more than 3 million according to UNICEF –with children at high risk of becoming victims of various forms of exploitation.[29] As noted in the first section of this chapter, human rights abuses have become common currency. Not surprisingly, the International Criminal Court chose the DRC as the focus of its first case, centered on the northeastern Ituri region, where there have been reports of ethnic massacres over the last year and grave sites were found.[30] In April 2004, President Kabila formally requested the ICC prosecutor to look into alleged war crimes, genocide and crimes against humanity. *(See Chapter 6 for more details.)*

With this catastrophic humanitarian situation, the socio-economic situation is rapidly deteriorating in other parts of the Congo as well. The U.N. Human Development 2003 Report—which annually ranks countries based on numerous indicators from literacy and life-expectancy to employment and equality—put the Congo at number 167 out of 175 countries. According to the State of the World's Children 2004, per capita gross domestic product is $90. The average life expectancy is now only about 45 years. Only 25 percent of students attending school complete five years of primary education. And 40 to 70 percent of the country's approximately 50 million inhabitants have no access to basic medical and health care. Cholera, HIV/AIDS, tuberculosis, malaria, meningitis, sleeping sickness, measles and other infectious diseases are widespread. Chronic food shortages affect several regions.

The humanitarian community has an imposing presence in the country. Hampered by the tremendous distances, lack of functional transport systems and general insecurity, its operations are primarily focused on the provision of relief and the prevention of human suffering with particular attention to reinforcing the country's social structures, judicial systems, schools, health system and water and sanitation services. The largest actors involved are the European Commission, Belgium, Canada, France, Italy, Germany, the United States, UNHCR, WFP, UNICEF and the World Bank. Health is one of the largest sectors for donors, with activities ranging from basic support to health zones vaccinations, HIV/AIDS, tuberculosis, malaria and family planning programs. Government capacity building and support to civil society come next, followed by programs directed at income generation often linked to agriculture/food security.[31] Whether this work lays down the foundations for a transition from relief to sustainable development remains to be seen. The transitional government remains paralyzed. Militia atrocities against civilians go on unabated.[32] Fact-finding expert reports highlight the continuing flow of illegal weapons and the illegal exploitation of resources in the eastern Ituri region and the Kivus. More recently, clashes between Congolese forces and Rwandan rebels accused of taking a major part in the 1994 Rwandan genocide, uprooted about 25,000 people in South Kivu in the Eastern DRC.[33]

Haiti

From 1994 to 2003, the U.N. and the Organization of American States (OAS) undertook no fewer than 10 separate and joint missions in Haiti. They may have provided breathing space to the country but failed to resolve its long-standing political and socioeconomic problems. As pointed in the Human Rights section of this chapter, in February 2004, the situation deteriorated dramatically when armed rebels and criminal gangs took over several towns in the northern part of the country. In the wake of the resignation and departure of President Jean-Bertrand Aristide, violence continued while healthcare, education, human rights, justice and police institutions virtually collapsed.

In response to the worsening of the political, security and humanitarian situation, the S.C. authorized in February 2004 the deployment of a multinational force to re-establish law and order in the capital. In April 2004, the Council authorized the U.N. Stabilization Mission in Haiti (MINUSTAH).[34] The new mission will take over from the existing multinational force over the summer of 2004, with the objectives of securing a stable environment within which the constitutional and political process in Haiti could take place, assisting a transitional government in the reform of the Haitian national police, and implementing comprehensive and sustainable disarmament, demobilization and reintegration programs. The Council further demanded that all parties in Haiti provide safe and unimpeded access to humanitarian agencies to allow them to carry out their work.

The response has been swift. In March 2004, a U.N. assessment team arrived in the country. At the same time, UNICEF reported that 80 percent of the schools in the provinces and the capital had reopened.[35] WFP delivered 90 tons of food to schools in the northern part of the country and UNFPA sent medical supplies. OCHA launched an emergency Flash Appeal on March 9, 2004 for $35 million to meet the medical and nutritional needs of 3 million Haitians for a period of six months. This appeal was issued nearly a year after the launching of an $85 million consolidated appeal to cover 18 months of humanitarian and other aid for the entire country. (That drive had received pledges of only $38 million.)[36]

U.N. humanitarian agencies have by and large avoided a humanitarian catastrophe and successfully assisted Haiti in sailing through its latest emergency. But the country has neither the resources nor the infrastructure to cope with its recovery needs nor to meet its formidable developmental challenges. It is the poorest nation in the Western Hemisphere with life expectancy of only 49 years. Less than the half the population is literate. Malnutrition is rampant. Few people can afford primary healthcare and less than one-fourth of the population has access to safe water. More troublesome are the still unresolved political and social issues arising from the longstanding practices of successive predatory regimes to avoid referring to the present division of the country between supporters and opponents of President Aristide.

These are clearly longer-term issues requiring a sustained international commitment. The. S.G.'s special adviser on Haiti has called for an international presence that may last some 20 years.[37]

Iraq

When the war broke out in March 2003, Iraq was already facing a precarious humanitarian situation. The Iran-Iraq conflict, the first Gulf War and more than 12 years of economic sanctions had all contributed to a slow degradation of the Iraqi physical infrastructure. Income per capita, which had risen to more than $3,600 in the early 1980s fell to approximately $770 by 2001. The Oil-for-Food Programme (OFFP) began to operate in 1997 and improved material conditions but did not resolve the humanitarian crisis.[38] Because of lack of available data, Iraq does not feature in the key indexes published by UNDP in its 2003 Human Development Report but it is estimated that it would be around 117 in the table of 175 countries. UNICEF places Iraq last among 180 states in its figures for child survival over the last decade.[39]

On the eve of the war, almost three-quarters of the population depended on food handouts, and child mortality had rocketed from the combined effects of malnourishment, poor sanitation, a lack of clean drinking water and inadequate healthcare. Persisting and intensifying post-war security problems have compounded the woes of the Iraqi population and severely compromised the short-term possibilities of recovery. Electrical power is in short supply. Available water supplies in some governorates are estimated to have fallen by half since March 2003. A joint U.N.-World Bank study found that half the sewage-treatment plants were out of operation. The prices of basic commodities, such as fuel and cooking gas, have soared. According to

UNICEF, 80 percent of Iraqi schools need major rehabilitation. Health conditions and lack of medicines are a growing concern.

The need assessment prepared by the World Bank for the October 2003 Donor Conference estimated that the price tag of the most urgent reconstruction and rehabilitation needs to be addressed in the next three years stood at around $36 billion, excluding the security and oil sectors which required an additional $20 billion. These figures have most likely been rendered obsolete by the military situation.

Funds have been forthcoming, though. Following the launch of the Flash Appeal for Iraq on March 28, 2003 for $2.2 billion, $1.1 billion was made available from OFFP. Donors pledged $870 million within three months, and on June 23, 2003, U.N. agencies requested the remainder of $259 million, or 12 percent, for 2003. Largely confined to coordinating and humanitarian responsibilities, U.N. agencies have reduced or withdrawn their international staff from the country since the bombing of U.N. headquarters in Baghdad on August 19, 2003. Their work has focused on restoring vital food, health, water and sanitation services for civilians affected by the conflict and strengthening local capacity for the delivery of these services.

The core question now confronting the international humanitarian community is how to reverse the debilitating trends of the last two decades and place the country on a sustainable recovery and reconstruction path. This must be done in the context of a festering insurrection and in the context of the uncertainties still clouding the search for a legitimate central authority and restoration of some semblance of law and order. At the time of this writing, that question remains unanswered, and the number of viable options has been further narrowed by the tarnishing of the American moral standing following the publication of degrading pictures of U.S. troops brutalizing their Iraqi prisoners.

Democratic People's Republic of Korea

A series of disasters beginning in 1995—droughts coupled with an economic downturn over the past decade—have crippled North Korea's food security. Agricultural production declined throughout the 1990s, while the government's modernization policies aggravated disparities in access to basic foods between better-off rural populations and those in urban areas accounting for two-thirds of the country's nearly 23 million people. Security tensions on the Korean peninsula and the re-emergence of the nuclear issue (see Chapter 5) have weakened international response.

Improved agricultural production in recent years has reduced the gap and the need for external assistance. Immunization rates in North Korea, officially known as the Democratic People's Republic of Korea (DPRK), have vastly improved as better systems for finding and treating severe cases of malnutrition are in place. But the food crisis is most likely to persist because of the limited scope for higher output.

Despite substantial gains in nine years of humanitarian interventions, assistance is still needed and continues to play a vital role in safeguarding and promoting the well-being of millions of people. The humanitarian crisis triggered by natural disasters in the mid-1990s has been compounded by structural issues, such as global economic change, outdated infrastructure and inadequate government revenue that cannot be solved through emergency responses alone.[40] At least 6.5 million people are considered at risk.[41] Many North Koreans face continued health problems. Nine percent of children suffer from acute malnutrition while chronic malnutrition in some places is above 45 percent. Many people lack access to clean water. Because of a breakdown in water systems and poor electricity supply, the country also requires development assistance to overcome its severe economic difficulties.

WFP is still one of the major multilateral providers of relief and recovery assistance through food delivery and food-for-work projects in DPRK. A falloff in contributions has forced WFP to halt vital supplemental rations for long periods since mid-2002. In February 2004, the agency all but ran out of cereals, its staple commodity. Unless additional pledges are made soon, the number of core beneficiaries no longer receiving grain from WFP will rise from 1 million now to 3.8 million. Also critical is the need for international donations for Ryongchon, where an April 2004 explosion killed some 170 people, injured 1,300 and made another 8,000 homeless. Only $21 million has been mobilized so far this year out of the needed $171 million.[42]

UNICEF has also played a major role in DPRK. Throughout 2003, the U.N. agency focused on health needs, immunizing around 350,000 infants and 200,000 pregnant women. In addition, UNICEF handed out more than 9,000 medicine kits to health clinics and treated more than 10,000 severely malnourished children—twice as many as in 2002. More than 25,000 families in three vulnerable counties received increased water supplies as a result of UNICEF assistance during the year and schools received approximately 2 million new kindergarten and primary-school textbooks. The agency has continued with the development of emergency preparedness procedures in 2004, concentrating its efforts on the immediate humanitarian needs of 8 million children and women.[43]

Overall, the approximately $200 million consolidated appeal for the DPRK for 2004 called for greater investment in health, water and sanitation. While there was a relatively good response to food requirements in 2003, further response to water, sanitation and health needs remain.

Adolescent Health and Rights

Olivia Cobiskey

Every day, 24,000 people die of hunger or hunger-related causes. Seventy-five percent of them are children living in poor countries. In his report on the implementation of the *Millennium Declaration* in September 2003, S.G. Annan declared that this is "unacceptable."[44]

Approximately 1.2 billion people are between the ages of 10 and

19. Investing in their health and rights is critical to ensuring their present and future well-being.[45] The targets of the Millennium Development Goals (MDGs)—to reduce extreme poverty and hunger, slow the spread of HIV/AIDS, reduce maternal and child mortality, ensure universal primary education and improve and sustain development by 2015—address many of the issues faced by young people today.

According to the U.N. Population Fund (UNFPA), an estimated 238 million youth, almost one in four, live in extreme poverty. More than 13 million have lost one or both parents to AIDS, while many others have been forced to leave their homes as a result of conflict. As many as 250 million may be marginalized or living on the streets. These children are vulnerable to exploitation and sexual and physical abuse; some may also turn to commercial sex or crime to survive.[46]

There are unique concerns for young girls and women as well; child marriage, sexual violence and coercion, sexual trafficking and female genital mutilation are only a few. In developing countries, 82 million girls between the ages of 10 and 17 marry before their 18th birthday. More than 14 million girls between ages 15 and 19 give birth each year, jeopardizing not only their own heath, but also the health of their children.[47] Teenage mothers are twice as likely, and girls under 16 are five times more likely to die in childbirth than women are in their 20s.[48] Save the Children says pregnancy is the number one killer of girls 9 to 15 years old in developing countries.[49] And unsafe abortions account for 78,000 deaths a year.

Not having access to reliable contraceptives does not just lead to pregnancy. Every 14 seconds, a youth is infected with HIV. Young people, increasingly women, account for nearly half of the new cases of HIV infection worldwide. UNFPA estimates that the economic benefit of a single averted HIV/AIDS infection for a poor country with annual per capita earnings of $1,000 per year is $34,600. In 2003, UNFPA supported a new ad campaign, "What's Your Excuse?," aimed at 15- to 25-year-olds; the campaign represents one way UNFPA is preventing the spread of sexually transmitted infections, including HIV/AIDS. UNFPA also encourages peer education, training credible youth to talk to one another, and "youth friendly" reproductive health services.[50] Tied not only to the MDGs, adolescent health issues and problems relate directly to humanitarian assistance.

Kosovo

Although some powers have devolved into a multiethnic government comprising Albanians and a few Serbs in what is formally called the Provisional Institutions of Self-Government, since 1999, Kosovo has been effectively administered by the U.N. Interim Administration Mission in Kosovo (UNMIK) under the direction of a Special Representative of the Secretary-General. Until recently, there were hopes that talks on Kosovo's final status might start in mid-2005. That target may no longer be realistic after the inter-ethnic fighting that erupted in the week preceding the fifth anniversary of the NATO intervention that forced the withdrawal of Yugoslav troops. The violence left at least 28 people dead. Hundreds were injured. Nearly 40 churches and monasteries, 800 houses and more than 150 vehicles were destroyed or badly damaged. In separate incidents, two policemen were also killed.

UNMIK officials insist that things have improved considerably since the NATO-led 78-day air war led to the ousting of former President Slobodan Milosevic in 2000. By that time, close to 10,000 Albanians had been killed in massacres orchestrated by the Serbian police and paramilitaries. Some 800,000 who had taken refuge in neighboring Albania have returned since then with international assistance playing a key role in improving living conditions and getting the province back to near-normal conditions.

Yet the underlying cause of the conflict has not been addressed. For all intents and practical purposes, Kosovo remains ethnically segregated. Hostility between Albanians and Serbs runs deep.[51] Most Serbs living either in enclaves or in the northern part of the country that abuts Serbia proper, where UNMIK police and KFOR troops provide tenuous security. The Security Council, in Resolution 1244, called for "substantial autonomy and meaningful self-administration for Kosovo." Ethnic Albanians want outright independence. Albanian hardliners dream of a Greater Albania with a Serb minority, while the Serb minority (10 percent of the population) wishes to return to Serbian rule. In addition to its unresolved political status, Kosovo is saddled with a stalled economy afflicted by rates of unemployment as high as 70 percent. More than 50 percent of the population lives below the national poverty line.

Meeting such overwhelming challenges requires a reasonable period of time as well as commensurate resources. The shift in donor attention, reflected in the significant decrease in donor resources projected for 2003 and beyond, does not augur well for the future. As an *Economist* commentator wryly put it, "We are now in for a rough ride."[52]

Liberia

On June 17, 2003, a cease-fire agreement brought an end to Liberia's long civil war. The peace agreement marked the end of 15 years of continuous violence during which 250,000 persons died and more than one-third of the population was displaced. Throughout the war, virtually the entire country was inaccessible to humanitarian actors and Liberia now confronts major humanitarian challenges. At the end of the fighting, an estimated 350,000 Liberians were displaced to temporary camps with inadequate basic services. More than 35,000 fighters are believed to have been involved in the conflict, including 15,000 children and 2,000 women.

In September 2003, the S.C. established the U.N. Mission in Liberia (UNMIL), which replaced UNOMIL, the U.N. Observer Mission in Liberia. *(See Chapter 4.)* UNMIL has thus far helped Liberia to set up a National Transitional Government and is planning on holding elections in 2005. Also the result of the mission's work, the delivery of humanitarian assistance has become possible.[53]

In November 2003, humanitarian agencies launched a consolidated appeal for approximately $140 million to support emergency relief assistance to the interior of the country. UNICEF supported the implementation of a measles immunization campaign and renovated the Expanded Programme on Immunization office in the Ministry of Health. In 2004, UNICEF has focused on strengthening the national health service's delivery capacity and improving immunization services. Other priorities include the rehabilitation of health centers and maternal and child healthcare services, the maintenance and construction of water supplies and sanitation in IDP camps, and the provision of water and sanitation for schools and health facilities as well as for returning populations.[54]

Overall, approximately 1 million children were vaccinated against measles by UNICEF and WHO.[55] UNHCR plans to facilitate the return and reintegration of an estimated 320,000 refugees and 300,000 camp-based IDPs.[56] Meanwhile, the first phase of a three-year plan for the disarming, demobilization and reintegration of some 50,000 combatants started in April 2004.[57]

Sierra Leone

The country is still recovering from an 11-year-long civil war rooted in a mix of bad governance, denial of fundamental human rights and economic mismanagement and social exclusion all prolonged by the looting of natural resources. In his latest assessment of the post-war situation in Sierra Leone, the S.G. highlighted the fact that the presence of a strong U.N. force, the United Nations Mission in Sierra Leone (UNAMSIL), had paved the way toward significant progress in the implementation of the peace process, the stabilization of the human rights situation and the consolidation of state authority.[58] Civil administration had been extended and local elections took place on May 27, 2004 but were marred by low participation rates and some irregularities. *(See Chapter 4 for further details.)*

The transition had been aided by the work of the Truth and Reconciliation Commission (TRC) and the Special Court. The TRC is preparing its final report and the first trials of the Special Court for Sierra Leone are set to begin in June 2004. Thus far, 13 indictments have been issued. *(See Chapter 6 for further details about the Court.)* More than 1 million displaced persons returned to their homes. In addition, since the end of 2000, a total of 184,000 Sierra Leonans have returned home from Guinea, 90,000 of which had direct support from UNHCR. The U.N. agency is planning repatriation of Liberians from Sierra Leone in late 2004. Significant strides were also made in the rehabilitation of the social infrastructure, particularly schools and clinics. Health services improved from a capacity level of 5 to 10 percent during the war to 40 to 50 percent at present. The national economy continued to grow and GDP rose 6.5 percent in 2003. In the agricultural sector, rice and other food crops registered strong recoveries. Last year, the country earned about $76 million in diamond revenues, up from $10 million in 2000.

These accomplishments notwithstanding, the S.G. also emphasized that the country still faced major emergency relief and immediate recovery challenges. Key human rights issues still needed to be monitored, especially the human rights implications of the country's weak justice system.

Drawing on the S.G.'s assessment, the S.C. extended on March 30, 2004 the mandate of UNAMSIL for another six months and endorsed his proposal to scale down the size of the force to a residual presence next year to give the government time to assert its control over the country. The success of this "carefully managed transfer of authority" hinges not only on internal conditions of stability and recovery but also, in no minor way, on continuing international support. The U.N. country team prepared in November 2003 a Transitional Appeal for Sierra Leone for 2004 consisting of three joint programs, requesting $61.9 million. The first two programs address the care and maintenance needs of Liberian refugees and some 30,000 Sierra Leonans who are expected to return in 2004. The third program focuses on the needs of resettling communities in areas of high vulnerability. In a longer-term perspective, FAO and UNDP have funded a $670,000 assistance agreement with the government to promote food security. In May 2004, the World Bank approved projects in the amount of $37 million to help the government establish a functioning local government system. For the time being, things seem to be on track in Sierra Leone.

Somalia

Unlike Sierra Leone, developments in Somalia in 2003 offer little grounds for comfort and solace. The hopes arising from the 2002 Somalia National Reconciliation Conference proved illusory and the country still has no central government. Guided by their 2003 common humanitarian plan, U.N. agencies have haltingly helped sustain the lives of the most vulnerable. WFP continued its food distribution while UNICEF and WHO continued their programs of expanded immunization, reducing child mortality. A number of water systems have been improved or rehabilitated by UNICEF, UNHCR and UN-Habitat. It is forecast that the repatriation of Somali refugees from Ethiopia to northern Somalia will be completed by December 2004.

Nevertheless, volatile security conditions, chronic droughts, floodings and lack of funding erode food security and make many areas inaccessible to aid agencies. By any standards of human development (e.g. per-capita income, malnutrition or infant mortality), the country remains one of the poorest in the world. It is also saddled with the thankless task of attending to the needs of some 350,000 long-term IDPs and 460,000 returnees living in desperate conditions. No fewer than 750,000 people—12 percent of the population—require food assistance. The $100 million-plus requested by OCHA in its CAP for 2004 can hardly be expected to make a dent in the disastrous human condition of Somalia.[59]

Sudan

For the past few decades, the largest country in Africa has been the scene of a civil war pitting the Arab Islamic government against Southern animists, or Christian black Africans, which has left more than 2 million dead and displaced more than 4 million. Prodded by the United States, U.K. and Norway, peace talks gained momentum in 2002-2003 with the signing of several accords, including a cease-fire agreement. A cease-fire monitoring role is envisioned for the U.N. after the conclusion of a final agreement, which is expected to be signed by the end of 2004. The accord provides that the south will be autonomous for six years pending the organization of a referendum on the key issue of independence. In addition, it contains clauses spelling out how the revenues from the oil resources of the region will be shared, a significant development to the extent that this unsettled issue has undoubtedly prolonged the war.[60]

These major breakthroughs have been overshadowed, however, by another equally disturbingly ferocious internal conflict that flared late last year in the Western region of Darfur, this time pitting the central government against two Muslim rebel groups seeking power-sharing arrangements with Khartoum. The Sudanese government struck back by recruiting Arab militiamen and coordinating attacks on towns and villages considered sympathetic to the rebels, while rejecting any internationalization of the conflict and erecting regulations that effectively choked off humanitarian relief. Humanitarian agencies were denied all access from October 2003 through February 2004; access since has improved only marginally. As things stand now, almost 1 million people require urgent humanitarian assistance—healthcare, nutritional support, shelter, clean water and above all, protection from continuing attacks. Nearly 1 million are believed to have been displaced and 120,000 have taken refuge in neighboring Chad.

The response from the international community has been slow and parsimonious. As of May 2004, since the launch of the Greater Darfur Special Initiative in September 2003, just more than $32 million was pledged or received for relief operations in Greater Darfur in addition to $28 million for Sudanese refugees in Chad.[61]

In April 2004, the U.N. called upon donors to provide $115 million, a five-fold increase from its earlier appeal for food and healthcare aid, relief supplies and agricultural assistance.[62] At the same time, however, the Sudanese government came under mounting political pressure to take some action as the S.C. called for a cease-fire and the S.G. suggested international intervention.[63]

Called the worst humanitarian crisis since Rwanda, four human right experts toured Eastern Chad investigating claims of ethnic cleansing.[64] The Commission on Human Rights at its 2004 session failed to condemn Sudan but appointed a monitor to investigate human rights violations. Human Rights Watch issued a report charging the Sudanese military government of working with Arab militias to commit ethnic cleansing and crimes against humanity.[65]

With the assistance of the African Union and Chadian government, the Sudanese government and the two insurgency groups entered into a cease-fire agreement on April 8, 2004. Armed attacks on civilians continue to be reported and the humanitarian crisis still festers.

Timor-Leste

Following the promulgation of a constitution, the election of President Xanana Gusmao, the transformation of the Constituent Assembly into a National Parliament and the inauguration of a government, East Timor became independent in May 2002. It is now known as Timor-Leste. The U.N. Transitional Authority in East Timor, which since 1999 had led the country's reconstruction process, was replaced by the U.N. Mission of Support in East Timor (UNMISET) to provide assistance to core administrative structures, provide interim law enforcement and contribute to internal and external security.

The new nation's emergency phase is clearly over, and in many ways, the rebuilding of Timor-Leste can rightly be described as one of the U.N.'s biggest success stories. The overall security situation remains calm and stable. The basic infrastructure for immunization has been reestablished (health services were partially restored during 2000-2001). The struggle for independence did, however, take a heavy toll on the country. Timor-Leste is the poorest country in Asia today. Infant and maternal mortality as well as child morbidity rates are still high. Human capital is scarce, as more than 250,000 people were expelled during the violence.

Although there is potential for revenues from vast offshore oil and gas fields in the Timor Sea, the country cannot be expected to be self-reliant just yet; it still requires international assistance in its transition toward recovery and development. At a U.N. meeting in May 2002, donor countries pledged more than $44 million in financial aid to assist the country through 2005. Capacity-building is now the focus of U.N. agencies, with particular attention being devoted to the revival of the primary-school system along with re-emerging immunization services, the reestablishment of basic health services and the physical rehabilitation of water supply and sanitation. Food security and cropping conditions remain a concern and are closely monitored by WFP, FAO and international NGOs. In February and March 2004, WFP distributed food aid in several districts of the country.[67]

Looking Forward

Over the next few years, it is probable that the humanitarian assistance regime will change anew as the different notions of the norms of sovereignty, impartiality and humanitarianism vie for dominance in the United

Nations. The place of humanitarian aid in the continuum extending from early warning and prevention to peacekeeping, and from conflict resolution and peace-building to post-conflict reconstruction and development will continue to evolve. To date, there are 15 to 20 million refugees and some 40 million IDPs. There is no dearth of simmering ethnic, cultural, religious or political tensions that might trigger humanitarian emergencies, as evidenced by the recent flare-ups of communal violence in southern Thailand and Nigeria.

The "humanitarian enterprise" is clearly here to stay and certainly has legitimate claims of success in saving lives. The conditions of successful interventions are known. But what priority the humanitarian enterprise will be accorded by the international community, especially at a time when the war on terrorism has become an overriding concern, is a question still begging for an answer. As author and scholar Samantha Power noted not long ago, Western and U.N. leaders expressed their remorse on the occasion of the 10th anniversary of the Rwandan genocide and pledged to prevent the occurrence of future humanitarian catastrophes. So far, they have done little to bring to a halt the Sudanese government's campaign of ethnic slaughter and deportation, which, in the past year, has already left nearly 1 million Africans displaced and more than 30,000 dead in Darfur.[68]

Commentary:
Human Trafficking Definition Clouds True Crime
Jyoti Sanghera

Trafficking—and the human rights violations it encompasses—presents a most pressing challenge to the international human rights community today. Not only does the trafficking of persons deny victims' rights to liberty and security, it also denies them their right to freedom from torture, violence, cruelty or degrading treatment, freedom of movement, the right to protection of family, education and health—everything that makes for a life with dignity. Because of the many gross forms of human rights violations it embodies, trafficking has been defined rightly as a contemporary form of slavery.

However, the illegal trade continues to be addressed as a "law and order" problem, and is therefore located primarily within the crime prevention framework. Victims of cross-border trafficking are frequently criminalized and prosecuted as illegal aliens, undocumented workers or irregular migrants rather than as victims of a crime. Instead of receiving assistance, women and girls who are trafficked into the sex industry are charged with prostitution. As a result, notwithstanding the high profile and media coverage this issue has received globally, the rights of trafficked people and the human rights violations that come with it have often not been adequately or appropriately addressed.

Fortunately, over the past three years, there has been a proliferation of international instruments that deal with trafficking in people, including the *Protocol to Prevent, Suppress and Punish Trafficking in Persons, Especially Women and Children*, supplementing the *United Nations Convention Against Transnational Organized Crime*. These instruments are now in force. In addition, *the International Convention on the Protection of the Rights of All Migrant Workers and Members of Their Families*, which entered into force in July 2003, provides a useful platform for protecting the rights of trafficked persons by acknowledging the human rights of undocumented migrants, of whom trafficked persons often constitute a large percentage. These instruments, in conjunction with other human rights tools and mechanisms, do indeed create a more secure environment for the protection of the human rights of trafficked persons.

Yet, challenges ensue from both long-standing and emerging obstacles. While some conceptual and programmatic clarity has come about, as noted above, trafficking continues to be conflated with irregular migration on the one hand and prostitution on the other. This means that interventions aimed at eliminating trafficking end up trying to eliminate either prostitution or irregular migration or both. Furthermore, these crime-prevention-based responses have placed the principal focus on law enforcement, border control and punitive measures. This focus is rationalized by the fact that the convention and the protocol addressing trafficking are products of the Commission on Crime Prevention and Criminal Justice in Vienna, resulting, therefore, in a language that is more stringent on provisions related to the prosecution of traffickers and organized crime. However, it is important to note that despite the crime-prevention approach, the number of prosecutions of traffickers and successful sentencing has not risen by a noticeable degree.

Emerging issues that further complicate the matter include an overriding preoccupation with national security concerns. The aforementioned convention has been invoked to investigate and prosecute those that threaten national security, drawing no clear lines among terrorists, migrants, traffickers or even trafficked persons.

Recognizing that any successful approach to combating trafficking must meld the two perspectives (i.e. crime prevention and human rights), the Office of the High Commissioner for Human Rights launched the Recommended Principles and Guidelines on Human Rights and Human Trafficking in July 2002. This tool provides a blueprint to embed all anti-trafficking interventions, including laws and policies, within a human rights perspective. Furthermore, through its various mechanisms, and especially through the Special Rapporteurs of the Commission on Human Rights on violence against women, migrant workers and on the sale of children, child prostitution and child pornography, OHCHR prioritizes the protection of the human rights of trafficked persons. The recently concluded 60th Session of the Commission has gone a step further by establishing a new mandate for a Special Rapporteur on trafficking of human beings, especially women and children.

It is hoped that together these mandates and instruments will operationalize the understanding that efforts to combat this problem must address the entire cycle of trafficking. This involves improving the information base and ensuring an adequate legal framework and effective law enforcement. It also entails focusing on prevention as well as protection and support for those affected by trafficking. Above all, combating such a phenomenon necessitates effective international and regional cooperation and national responses that are based on a comprehensive, long-term strategy—one that gives priority to human rights.

Endnotes

Human Rights

1. Remarks made at conference "Fighting Terrorism for Humanity: A Conference on the Roots of Evil," September 22, 2003.
2. E/CN.4/2004/12/Add.1 ("Report of the U.N. High Commissioner for Human Rights and Follow-Up to the World Conference on Human Rights," February 24, 2004).
3. A/Res/48/141.
4. *Overview of Activities and Financial Requirements, Annual Appeal 2004*, OHCHR.
5. Ibid, 2.
6. Commission on Human Rights Res. 2003/37, April 23, 2003.
7. U.N. Press Release, June 30, 2003 ("U.N. Rights Experts Call for Respect of Liberties in Anti-Terror Measures").
8. A/RES/58/187 (2003).
9. E/CN.4/2004/91 ("Promotion and Protection of Human Rights: Protecting Human Rights and Fundamental Freedoms While Countering Terrorism," March 12, 2004).
10. E/CN.4/2004/L.106.
11. U.N. Press Release, April 7, 2004 ("Secretary-General to Commission on Human Rights: The Risk of Genocide Is Frighteningly Real").
12. S/2003/1212 ("Report of the Secretary-General, The Situation in Afghanistan and Its Implications for International Peace and Security," December 30, 2003).
13. E/CN.4/2004/48/Add.2 ("Report by the Special Rapporteur, Miloon Kothari, Addendum, Mission to Afghanistan," March 4, 2004).
14. This small force is entirely separate from the much more numerous U.S. and other coalition troops in Afghanistan as part of "Operation Enduring Freedom" which continues to combat the Taliban.
15. "Enduring Freedom: Abuses by U.S. Forces in Afghanistan," *Human Rights Watch*, March 2004.
16. "Afghanistan: Constitutional Process Marred by Abuses," *Human Rights Watch*, January 8, 2004.
17. *Berlin Declaration*, April 1, 2004.
18. *Fact Sheet: School Feeding*, World Food Programme, 2003.
19. *Women: The Key to Food Security*, International Food Policy Research Institute, June 2000.
20. "Debate Stirs Over Tiny Loans for World's Poorest," *New York Times*, April 29, 2004.
21. *Progress of the World's Women 2002: Gender Equality and the Millennium Development Goals 2002*, UNIFEM.
22. Ibid.
23. Ibid.
24. U.N. Press Release, March 29, 2004 (WOM/1447).
25. U.S. Press Briefing, March 26, 2004 ("Williamson Outlines U.S. Objectives at 60th Commission on Human Rights").
26. "Locked Doors: The Human Rights of People Living With HIV/AIDS in China," *Human Rights Watch*, September 2003.
27. "People's Republic of China: Controls Tighten as Internet Activism Grows," *Amnesty International*, January 28, 2004.
28. "The Death Penalty Worldwide: Developments in 2003," *Amnesty International*, April 6, 2004.
29. S/RES/1484 (2003).
30. S/2003/653 ("Report of the Security Council Mission to Central Africa," June 7-17, 2003).

31. A/58/534 (Interim Report of the Special Rapporteur on the Situation of Human Rights in the Democratic Republic of Congo, October 24, 2003).
32. E/CN.4/2004/34 ("See Report of the Special Rapporteur on the Situation in the Democratic Republic of Congo," March 10, 2004).
33. E/CN.4/2004/L.99, April 19, 2004.
34. S/RES/1529 (2004).
35. "Haiti: Armed Groups Still Active, Findings of Amnesty International Delegation," *Amnesty International*, April 8, 2004.
36. S/RES/1483 (2003).
37. "Sidelined: Human Rights in Postwar Iraq," *Human Rights Watch World Report 2004*, January 26, 2004.
38. *Human Rights First Letter to the Iraqi Governing Council*, Human Rights First website, December 22, 2003, among others.
39. "Iraq: Interim Constitution Shortchanges Women," *Human Rights Watch*, March 5, 2004.
40. Resolution 1991/74.
41. S/RES/1515 (2003).
42. "The "Roadmap: Repeating Oslo's Human Rights Mistakes," *Human Rights Watch*, May 8, 2003.
43. *Briefing to the 60th Session of the U.N. Commission on Human Rights: Israel/Occupied Territories*, Human Rights Watch, January 2004.
44. E/CN.4/2004/6/Add.1 ("Report of the Special Rapporteur of the Commission on Human Rights, John Dugard, on the Situation of Human Rights in the Palestinian Territories Occupied by Israel Since 1967," February 27, 2004).
45. A/RES/ES-10/14 ("Dossier No. 2," December 8, 2003).
46. E/CN.4/2004/L4
47. Taylor was indicted by the Special Court for Sierra Leone in 2003 for his role in crimes against humanity, violations of common Article 3 of the Geneva Conventions and other serious violations of international humanitarian law committed during the conflict in Sierra Leone.
48. S/RES/1497 (2003).
49. Emergency report of the Acting High Commissioner for Human Rights to the Commission on Human Rights, August 12, 2003, E/CN.4/2004/5.
50. S/RES/1509 (2003).
51. "The Guns Are in the Bushes: Continuing Abuses in Liberia," *Human Rights Watch Briefing Paper*, January 2004.
52. News Release, April 15, 2004 ("Medical Foundation for the Care of Victims of Torture," Medical Foundation for Care of Victims of Torture website).
53. E/CN.4/2004/77/Add.2 ("Report of the Representative of the Secretary-General on Internally Displaced Persons," February 24, 2004).
54. E/C.12/1/Add.94 ("Concluding Observations of the Committee on Economic, Social and Cultural Rights," December 12, 2003).
55. CCPR/CO/79/RUS ("Concluding Observations of the Human Rights Committee, November 6, 2003).
56. E/CN.4/2004/L.62.
57. E/CN.4/2004/L.73/Rev.1.
58. "Sudan, Darfur in Flames: Atrocities in Western Sudan," *Human Rights Watch*, April 2004.
59. E/CN.4/2004/L.36.
60. A regional grouping of African countries established for the allocation of certain functions, such as voting or making statements through a representative.

Humanitarian Assistance

1. *OCHA website*, 2004.
2. "Humanitarian Access a 'Right' Top U.N. Official Says," *U.N. Wire*, April 29, 2004.
3. "Crisis Facing Colombians Is Called Worst in Hemisphere," *New York Times*, May 11, 2004.
4. E/CN.4/2004/13.
5. "Glad to Be Deceived: The International Community and Chechnya," *Human Rights Watch website*.
6. *The Responsibility to Protect*, International Commission on Intervention and State Sovereignty, 2001.
7. "Forgotten People," *Refugees International website*.
8. "Led by U.S., Nations Pledge Billions to Revive Afghanistan," *New York Times*, April 1, 2004.
9. *2003 U.N. Consolidated Inter-Agency Humanitarian Assistance Appeals, Summary of Requirements and Contributions by Affected Country/Region*, OCHA: Activities and Extra-Budgetary Funding Requirements, 2004.
10. U.N. Press Release, May, 4, 2004 ("U.N. Agencies Repeat Earlier $5.8 Million Aid Appeal For Namibia After Being Ignored").
11. "Mirror, Tool, or Linchpin for Change? The U.N. and Development," *International Relations Studies and the United Nations Occasional Papers*, 2003.
12. Ibid, 1.
13. U.N. Press Release, April 20, 2004 ("Facing 'Acute Shortage,' U.N. Agencies Appeal for Urgent Aid to Feed Angolans").
14. U.N. Press Release, May 6, 2004 ("Funds Flow in for Emergency U.N. Refugee Work in Liberia, But More Still Needed").
15. War Economies in a Regional Context: Overcoming the Challenge of Transformation, *International Peace Academy*, March 2004.
16. Ibid, 1.
17. Food Security: Overview, *World Food Programme*. / Humanitarian Action Report 2004, *UNICEF*. / Humanitarian Action Donor Update 2004.
18. UNHCR Press Release, March 23, 2004.
19. U.N. Press Release, March 26, 2004 ("Securing Afghanistan's Future").
20. "U.N. Anti-Drugs Chief Calls for Greater Financial Help for Afghanistan," *U.N. News Service*, March 31, 2004.
21. U.N. Press Release, June 17, 2003 ("Faced With Insecurity and Drugs, Afghanistan Needs Beefed Up Help").
22. Ibid, 9. / Angola in 2004, UNICEF Humanitarian Action Report.
23. U.N. Press Release, April 6, 2004 ("U.N. Refugee Official Reviews Return of Burundians from Tanzania").
24. *OCHA in 2004*, OHCA.
25. S/Res/1528 (February 2004).
26. *World Food Programme website*, 2004.
27. S/2002/1146 (October 16, 2002).
28. U.N. Press Release, April 12, 2004 ("Security Council Elects Three Officers of Democratic Republic of Congo Sanctions Committee").
29. "At a Glance: Congo, Democratic Republic of the," *Humanitarian Action and Donor Update, UNICEF*, June 2003.
30. *Amnesty International Report 2003*, Amnesty International. / *U.N. Wire*, November 24, 2003.
31. Humanitarian Action Report 2004, *UNICEF*.
32. U.N. Press Release, March 30, 2004 ("Annan Disquieted by Rising Factionalism in Democratic Republic of Congo Government").

33. U.N. Press Release, May 5, 2004 ("25,000 Displaced as Democratic Republic of Congo Fighters Confront Rwandan Rebels").
34. S/Res/1542 (2004).
35. U.N. Press Release, March 23, 2004 ("U.N. Team in Haiti Winding Up Its Preliminary Work").
36. U.N. Press Release, March 9, 2004 ("U.N. Appeals for $35 Million in Emergency Humanitarian Funds for Haiti").
37. U.N. Press Releases, March 10 and 30, 2004 ("First Members of U.N. Humanitarian Mission Leave for Haiti" and "Annan's Adviser Recommends Long-Term U.N. Presence in Post-Conflict Haiti").
38. "Iraq Sanctions: Humanitarian Implications and Options for the Future," *Global Policy website*, 2004.
39. "Iraq—Country in Crisis," *UNICEF website*, 2004.
40. U.N. Press Release, March 3, 2004.
41. U.N. Press Release, March 11, 2004 ("In Visit to Democratic People's Republic of Korea, UNICEF Chief to Spotlight Children's Needs").
42. Ibid, 14.
43. *UNICEF Humanitarian Action Report 2004*, UNICEF.
44. *Fact Sheet: School Feeding*, World Food Programme, 2003. / A/58/323 (Implementation of the U.N. Millennium Declaration, Report of the Secretary-General, September 2, 2003).
45. "Making 1 Billion Count: Investing in Adolescents' Health and Rights," State of World Population 2003, UNFPA.
46. Ibid.
47. Ibid.
48. *Ibid, 45.*
49. "School Feeding Works for Girls' Education," *World Food Programme*, 2001.
50. Ibid.
51. "Kosovo Marks Five Years Since NATO Bombing," *U.N. Wire*, March 24, 2004.
52. "Fields of Sorrows: Renewed Violence Raises Troubling Questions Over Kosovo's Future," *Economist*, March 27, 2004.
53. S/2003/1175 ("First Progress Report of the Secretary-General on the United Nations Mission in Liberia," December 15, 2003).
54. *UNICEF Humanitarian Action Liberia in 2004*, UNICEF.
55. *U.N. Wire*, March 18, 2004.
56. Ibid, 19.
57. U.N. Press Release, April 10, 2004.
58. S/2004/228 ("Twenty-first Report of the S.G. on the United Nations Mission in Sierra Leone," March 19, 2004).
59. Consolidated Humanitarian Appeal 2004. / *Eastern and Southern Africa Region, UNICEF Humanitarian Action Report 2004*, UNICEF. / A/58/133 ("Assistance for Humanitarian Relief and the Economic and Social Rehabilitation of Somalia," Report of the Secretary-General, July 11, 2003).
60. *Sudan, Oil, and Human Rights*, Human Rights Watch, 2003.
61. *OHCA website*, 2004.
62. U.N. Press Release, April 16, 2004.
63. "Sudan: U.N. Asks for $115 Million to Help Internally Displaced Within Darfur," *U.N. Wire*, April 8, 2004.
64. "U.N. Probes Claims of 'Ethnic Cleansing' in Sudan," *U.N. Wire*, April 7, 2004.
65. *Human Rights Watch website*, 2004.
66. *WFP Emergency Report*, March 2004.
67. "Remember Rwanda, but Take Action in Sudan," *New York Times*, April 6, 2004.

Chapter 4

Negotiating Peace at the Table, Building Peace on the Ground

Assefaw Bariagaber, Ishtiaq Ahmad, Amy Frumin, Gordon Goldstein, with Adam Godet and the International Crisis Group

The success of a U.N. peacekeeping operation in any conflict region depends on several factors. First and foremost, the parties to the conflict concerned must be ready to put the fighting behind them and abide, in good faith, by the commitments that they have made....Where favourable conditions exist for U.N. peacekeeping, success can only be assured if the operations concerned are provided with all the political, financial, material and human resources required to fulfill the mandated tasks. This requires unanimity within the United Nations Security Council (UNSC) on the desired outcome of the U.N.'s involvement.

— Secretary-General Kofi Annan,
Interview in Conflict Trends Journal, 2002.

The difficulties the United Nations faced dealing with Iraq before the United States and Coalition forces decided to overthrow Saddam Hussein's regime in March 2003 have revived old debates as to whether the U.N. is relevant. In particular, the debate over the management of disarming Iraq and role the international community has played—and should play—in this endeavor has brought about an unenviable spotlight on the organization, especially its most important organ, the Security Council. There has been much talk of the "multilateralism" of the early 1990s giving way to "unilateralism," which was also present during the Cold War era. However, by early 2004, there were "signs of rebounding spirits at the U.N.," especially after U.S. President George W. Bush invited the organization to play a central role in shaping Iraq's future.1 More importantly, the world public is increasingly realizing that the world body is indispensable when it comes to managing nations in transition—from Iraq and beyond.

This chapter reviews that indispensable role by looking at the various peace missions and operations the U.N. is currently undertaking. It is important to note that the U.N. heads not only peacekeeping missions, but also various political and peace-building missions. Peacekeeping missions, in particular, are deployed with the full consent of the parties involved and only after a cease-fire has been issued; they focus on maintaining or restoring international peace and security. Peacekeeping missions do not have enforcement powers, but do involve military personnel. Political and peace-building missions, on the other hand, support peacekeeping missions through reconciliation and negotiation between parties and ensure that conflict does not reignite by implementing development activities.

Africa

Assefaw Bariagaber

The various peace operations undertaken by the U.N. over the past few decades are concrete manifestations of the management of nations in transition. Since its founding in 1945, the U.N. has approved 59 peace operations, 41 approved since 1991.[2] More recently, the U.N. has been particularly visible in security issues in Africa. Before 1991, the U.N. approved only three peace operations in Africa, out of 18 worldwide. This constituted only 17 percent of all peace operations, as Africa did not attract the kind of multilateral attention required for the U.N. to act. For example, while France has, on many occasions, intervened directly in the affairs of Francophone Africa, the U.S. and the former Soviet Union have been particularly active in the Horn of Africa. As a result, African-relevant issues, especially those that were security-based in nature, were more likely to invite unilateral interventions.

As the Cold War came to an end in the early 1990s, the S.C. became increasingly involved in African security issues. By the end of 1991, it had

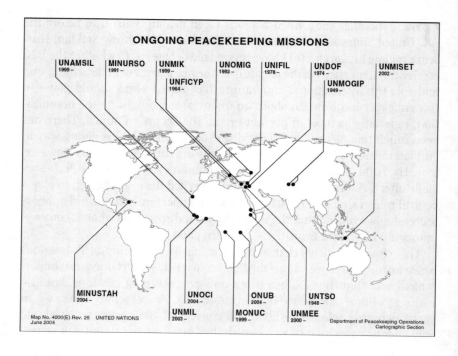

ONGOING PEACEKEEPING MISSIONS

| UNAMSIL 1999 – | MINURSO 1991 – | UNMIK 1999 – | UNOMIG 1993 – | UNIFIL 1978 – | UNDOF 1974 – | UNMISET 2002 – |

UNFICYP 1964 –

UNMOGIP 1949 –

MINUSTAH 2004 –

UNOCI 2004 –

ONUB 2004 –

UNTSO 1948 –

UNMIL 2003 –

MONUC 1999 –

UNMEE 2000 –

Map No. 4000(E) Rev. 25   UNITED NATIONS
June 2004

Department of Peacekeeping Operations
Cartographic Section

approved 39 peace operations worldwide, 18 of which (approximately 46 percent) were in Africa.[3] It is clear that, although U.N. peace operations worldwide showed dramatic increases, U.N. peace operations in Africa grew even more dramatically. Currently, there are 16 peacekeeping operations worldwide, seven of which (nearly 45 percent) are in Africa. Of those seven, two were approved this year: Burundi and Côte d'Ivoire. While this indicates increased U.N. concern and interest in Africa, it also indicates that conflicts and problems of governance continue to haunt Africa more than ever; for that matter, African countries have shown increasing readiness to welcome external assistance to help resolve internal conflicts.

At the same time, African leaders have come to understand that they cannot rely exclusively on U.N. support and, through the newly established African Union, have taken steps to find "African solutions to African problems."[4] In fact, South Africa, Ethiopia and Mozambique have sent nearly 2,500 African peacekeeping contingents to help monitor the peace process in Burundi. This, as well as endeavors by the Economic Community of West African States (ECOWAS) in Sierra Leone, Liberia and Côte d'Ivoire, heralds a new type of partnership between the U.N. and regional organizations in the search for peaceful resolutions in Africa.

International financial institutions, such as the World Bank, are assisting countries in "transitional post-conflict period" and actively supporting U.N. endeavors in the demobilization and reintegration of former combatants. For example, the World Bank has been instrumental in organizing a successful donor conference, where more than $500 million was pledged to

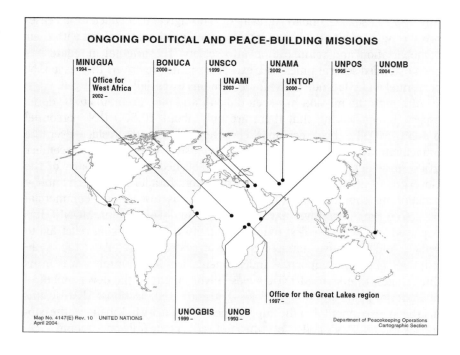

ONGOING POLITICAL AND PEACE-BUILDING MISSIONS

help post-conflict reconstruction in Liberia.[5] It has also approved a $33 million grant to support demobilization of combatants in Burundi.[6] More importantly, and to underscore the regional dimension of the conflicts in Sierra Leone, Liberia and Côte d'Ivoire, U.N. mission commanders in those countries have met to coordinate their activities to seek a regional solution to a regional problem.[7] World Bank President James Wolfensohn visited the ECOWAS subregion, underscoring the Bank's support for more integration of the area.[8]

At present, there are five fully operational U.N. missions in Africa: Liberia (UNMIL), Democratic Republic of Congo (MONUC), Sierra Leone (UNAMSIL), Ethiopia and Eritrea (UNMEE) and Western Sahara (MINURSO). Recently, a sixth and seventh mission have been established: Côte d'Ivoire (UNOCI) and Burundi (ONUB). The following section provides a look at the history of each country's conflicts and how the U.N. has played a vital role in helping to resolve them.

Democratic Republic of Congo

The peace mission in the Democratic Republic of Congo (DRC), called the U.N. Organization Mission in the Democratic Republic of Congo (MONUC), remains the most challenging and difficult of all current U.N. peace operations in Africa. This is not only because of the vastness of the conflict and the multiplicity of ethnic-based parties involved, but also because of the manifest intervention of several African countries, some of which intervened in pursuit of the Congo's riches. Established by S.C. Resolution 1279 in November 1999, MONUC's original mandate was to help implement the July 1999 Lusaka (Zambia) Agreement. This agreement called for a cease-fire, disengagement and disarmament among combatants, along with their demobilization and reintegration into society. The original mandate has been extended several times and, except for minor revisions that gave U.N. personnel wider latitude to use force, remains essentially unchanged.

Although the mission has been difficult and much remains to be done, especially considering that there are only about 10,500 U.N. personnel present, MONUC has accomplished several things. It presided over the implementation of the Global and All Inclusive Agreement of December 2002, in which parties to the conflict established the main bodies of the Government of National Unity and Transition. In addition, there is now a functioning commercial airline linking various towns, and commercial barges on the Congo River have resumed.[9] Equally important, MONUC has deployed troops for the first time to escort 36 trucks carrying relief aid to remote and previously dangerous parts of eastern DRC.[10] Also, the establishment of the all-important Independent Electoral Commission is in its final stages, thanks to MONUC's close involvement in the development of operational plans and budgets for registration and elections. MONUC has also been instrumental in the improvement of security in Kinshasa, the capital, as the country's police force has not yet become fully operational.

While MONUC was able to make a positive impact in these areas, there are outstanding issues. As S.G. Annan has noted, progress has been slow in the Congo, especially regarding the legislative agenda, military integration, demobilization and reintegration of combatants.[11] The most difficult part of MONUC's mission, however, has been maintaining peace and security in certain parts of the country. Sporadic fighting between factions continues around Bunia and its surrounding area, where a European Union-led Interim Emergency Multinational Force (IEMF) was deployed to quell violence in June 2003. IEMF was successful in stabilizing the region and withdrew its troops in September 2003. Five months after its departure, however, members of the Union of Congolese Patriots (UPC) opened fresh hostilities with MONUC and killed a Kenyan U.N. Military Observer. According to S.G. Annan, there have been about 20 attacks on U.N. forces between December 2003 and March 2004.[12] In short, progress in the restive Ituri province, where a series of massacres have occurred numerous times, has been slow, and the situation in Bunia and the surrounding area remains volatile.

The situation in other parts of DRC is likewise unstable. Katanga remains less than peaceful, with serious human rights violations against civilians by rival Mayi Mayi factions. Hundreds have been killed, tortured or raped.[13] Such incidents have also occurred in Bukova, South Kivu. MONUC was not able to do much because it still lacks the capacity to deploy troops quickly.

MONUC's mandate is set to expire July 30, 2004, and there is no doubt that it will be extended for at least another term. There is hope that the elections scheduled for mid-2005 will take place on time. Until then, talks of U.N. troops leaving toward the end of 2004 are probably overly optimistic.[14] The attempted coup d'état in March is a reminder of the fragility of the peace process.[15]

Côte d'Ivoire

Known as an island of economic prosperity and political stability in an ocean of poverty and conflicts, Côte d'Ivoire has lately succumbed to the destructive forces of ethnic and religious segmentation. This change is uncharacteristic of its reputation as a tolerant society, where immigrants from neighboring countries often flock in droves for a better life. The conflict began largely because of economic hardships faced by countries in West Africa during the 1980s. The stagnant commodity prices, stringent structural adjustment programs imposed by the International Monetary Fund (IMF) and World Bank, and the question as to what constituted an "Ivorian" all converged, dividing the country along ethnic and religious lines.

According to Dwayne Woods, an associate professor of political science at Purdue University, conflict between migrants and Ivorian natives occurred because land, given to migrant developers when it was cheap, became increasingly rare. Also, the overexploitation of tropical forests and increases in labor costs have encouraged natives to reclaim such land.[16] This started a spiral of conflicts not only between migrants and natives, many of whom were Muslim, but also between the mainly Christian south and Muslim north. Moreover, controversies over nationality laws and the question of eligibility to compete in national elections have become central issues in post-Houphouët-Boigny, Côte d'Ivoire. In this region, power-seeking elites have played the ethnic and religious card to activate and mobilize ethnic groups.

Each of these factors led the country's armed forces to seize power in December 1999, the first such instance in Ivorian history. In October 2000, the military organized national elections and handed power over to current President Laurent Gbagbo, despite disputes surrounding the election. Tension continued, and by September 2002, rebel forces seized more territory, largely in the northern half of the country. In October 2002, a cease-fire agreement was reached, thanks to the efforts of ECOWAS, which also deployed troops to monitor the cease-fire. However, many issues, especially the nationality question, remained unresolved.

There are two phases to consider when dealing with the U.N. involvement in Côte d'Ivoire. The first started on May 13, 2003, after S.C. Resolution 1479 approved the political mission, MINUCI, the U.N. Mission in Côte d'Ivoire to provide support for the full implementation of the January 2003 Lina-Marcoussis Agreement that was reached between the various Ivorian parties. This agreement required the various parties to establish a broad-based government of national reconciliation to oversee free and fair elections, restructure the armed forces and disarm and integrate the armed combatants.[17] While France and ECOWAS provided security, the U.N. merely provided political support. Nonetheless, the parties failed to form a government of national reconciliation, mainly because of disputes over both the allocation of cabinet posts and the delineation of the powers of the president and prime minister. Because of this, a climate of insecurity continued throughout the country.

A second, more expanded U.N. peace operation in Côte d'Ivoire began in early 2004 after the Security Council, with Resolution 1528, approved the U.N. Operation in Côte d'Ivoire (UNOCI). UNOCI was approved in February but it did not take over until April, when MINUCI's mandate ended. Among other things, UNOCI was mandated to observe and monitor the implementation of the comprehensive cease-fire agreement of May 3, 2003, and investigate violations of the cease-fire; assist the Government of National Reconciliation in monitoring borders, re-establishing trust between all the Ivorian forces involved; help in the disarmament, demobilization and reintegration of the combatants; and guard weapons, ammunition and other military material handed over by the former combatants. Moreover, in a remarkable departure from past peace operations in Africa and elsewhere, Resolution 1528 authorized French forces to "use all necessary means" to support UNOCI. The U.N. mission will eventually consist of 6,000 peacekeepers and is set to expire on April 4, 2005. An advance party of 35 personnel had already arrived at the end of March 2004 with the full force to follow over the summer.[18]

It is important to note here the way in which U.N. peace operations are evolving in Africa. Whereas past operations have been conducted solely by the organization, the cooperative peace mission between ECOWAS and the U.N. that first started in Liberia *(see below)* has continued with earnest in Côte d'Ivoire. The U.N. is also relying on French forces to provide necessary security. Even with the arrival of the full U.N. force over the summer of 2004, UNOCI will continue to rely on other international actors. Also noteworthy is that U.N Force Commanders from Sierra Leone, Liberia and Côte d'Ivoire are coordinating their activities. They have established liaison offices to exchange information and act in concert if and when the need arises.[19]

Many challenges lie ahead in Côte d'Ivoire, including separating the warring factions and monitoring the cease-fire as well as the return of an estimated 500,000 internally displaced persons (IDPs), and, more importantly, overseeing the disarmament and reintegration of former combatants. There is hope the peace process will stick. As Prime Minister Seydou Diarra of the Government of National Reconciliation stated, Ivorians have "started down the road to peace and will not turn back."[20] However, it is too early to say with confidence whether this mission will proceed without hiccups, as spoilers have derailed the peace process before.

Ethiopia and Eritrea

Badme, the small village that became synonymous with the 1998-2000 Ethiopian-Eritrean border conflict, continues to dominate the political discourse in the search for a peaceful end to the conflict. Initially in July 2000, with Resolution 1320, the S.C. approved the U.N. Mission in Ethiopia and Eritrea (UNMEE) to monitor the December 2000 Algiers Peace Accord. The parties had further agreed to abide by the decisions of an independent Boundary Commission based at The Hague. The Commission rendered its verdict in April 2002. While neither party got everything it requested, Badme was awarded to Eritrea. UNMEE was therefore adjusted in August 2002 to include "administrative and logistical support for the Field Offices of the Boundary Commission" authorized to demarcate the border.

Ethiopia objected to the Commission's decision, especially pertaining to Badme, and has threatened to reject the entire decision unless changes are made to place Badme within Ethiopia. Eritrea, on the other hand, has been steadfast in its rejection of possible revisions of the April 2002 decision and had initially refused to see Lloyd Axworthy, the S.G.'s Special Envoy, who was appointed to end the stalemate between the two countries. Under immense pressure, Eritrea has only recently agreed to see the Special Envoy on condition that the negotiations focus on the implementation of the Commission's decision.[21] His forthcoming trip to the region is eagerly awaited.

Meanwhile, the stalemate continues and tension has been increasing along the border. In fact, the parties have exchanged gunfire, conducted military training and, in some cases, imposed increased restrictions on UNMEE's activities.[22] In short, as S.G. Annan has stated, there has been a slow erosion of cooperation between the parties and UNMEE since late 2003.[23]

While these are some of the challenges UNMEE faces at present, there are also positive developments. For the first time, Ethiopian and Eritrean military officers have met to discuss security issues at the Mereb River Bridge, which separates the two countries in the central sector of the temporary security zone. The meeting is significant because the mistrust between the two parties has required previous meetings to be conducted in third countries.[24] Since then, a second meeting has taken place at the Humera Bridge in the western sector. In addition, UNMEE has carried out a series of quick-impact projects designed to alleviate water, health, education and sanitation problems in the temporary security zone.

UNMEE is set to expire on September 15, 2004. Although the S.C. is expected to renew the mandate, as it has periodically done since July 2000, it has also expressed its dismay at the inability of the two countries to reach a final and comprehensive peace agreement at a time of increasing demand for U.N. peace activities elsewhere.[25]

Liberia

The conflict in Liberia started because of economic hardships the country faced in the 1970s. The precipitous fall in the price of timber, the main commodity for export, coupled with price increases of imported oil and rice, created an impossible situation for the Americo-Liberian President William Tolbert.[26] As a result, Master-Sergeant Samuel Doe seized power in a coup d'état in 1980, bringing an end, albeit temporarily, to the uninterrupted rule of Americo-Liberians. However, perhaps because of shortages of trained manpower, his government included such Americo-Liberians as former President Charles Taylor. Despite this, his regime was seen as ethnic-based, where the Krahn, an ethnic group, dominated the government and the military in alliance with the Mandingo ethnic group, which dominated commerce. As a result, many people, including Mr. Taylor, left the government and started an armed rebellion in 1989 to seize control of the government. Other non-Americo-Liberians flocked to Mr. Taylor's National Patriotic Front of Liberia, especially after Alhaji Kromah, who was then the Minister of Information, made a "Mandingo call to arms to defend and finance the government."[27]

While it appears that economics were at the heart of Liberia's problem, leaders have exploited ethnicity for ulterior motives. The trajectory of this ethnic manipulation put Americo-Liberians on one side and non-Americo-Liberians on the other. During the first half of the 1990s, Mr. Taylor's forces controlled a significant part of the country, while Mr. Doe and Prince Yormie Johnson controlled parts of Monrovia, the capital. In the midst of this standoff, and to alleviate the humanitarian catastrophe that the conflict had caused, ECOWAS brokered a peace deal between the parties in August 1990 and established the Military Observer Group in Liberia (ECOMOG) to monitor the cease-fire and conduct free and fair elections. Because ECOMOG forces were not sufficiently armed to contain the conflict, the group failed to fulfill its mandate. In September 1993, with Resolution 866, the S.C. established the U.N. Observer Mission in Liberia (UNOMIL), primarily to help ECOMOG in its endeavors. As such, UNOMIL became the "first United Nations peacekeeping mission undertaken in cooperation with a peacekeeping operation already established by another organization."[28] Thanks, in part, to the newly founded cooperation between the U.N. and ECOWAS, UMOMIL ended successfully in September 1997; only a few staff members were left behind to work out of the U.N. Peace-Building Support Office in Liberia (UNOL), established in November 1997. Mr. Taylor was officially elected that year.

In addition to ECOWAS and UNOMIL's commendable efforts, the mission's success can also be attributed to the country's economic prosperity going on at the same time. After an economic slowdown in 1999, however, fighting between the government and the Liberians United for Reconciliation and Democracy (LURD) resumed in the northwestern part of the country. In 2002, another group, the Movement for Democracy in Liberia (MODEL) seized territories in the eastern and southeastern parts of the country. During 2002 and 2003, both groups controlled significant parts of the country and made threats to attack Monrovia, unless President Taylor left the country. Seeing no way out of this predicament, the President resigned and left for Nigeria on August 11, 2003. On September 19, 2003, the S.C. established the U.N. Mission in Liberia (UNMIL), consisting of about 15,000 personnel. It is the second peace mission in Liberia in less than a decade and is set to expire on September 19, 2004. UNMIL is mandated, among other things, to observe and monitor the implementation of the cease-fire agreement, assist in the development of cantonment sites and provide security at these sites, observe and monitor the disengagement and cantonment of military forces of all the parties, carry out voluntary disarmament, and provide security at key government installations.[29]

At less than a year old, UNMIL has accomplished several things. There is now "general compliance" with the cease-fire agreement; institutions of the National Transitional Government are slowly evolving; and appointments for the National Elections Commission, the Truth and Reconciliation Commission and the Independent Human Rights Commission have been completed.[30] Moreover, significant advances have been made in disarmament, demobilization, reintegration and repatriation of combatants and refugees. In fact, some 12,664 combatants had already been demobilized by December 17, 2003, and about 12,000 refugees had been repatriated. The process continues to this day, as more and more ex-combatants are turning in their weapons to return to civilian life. Also, to help maintain law and order in an environment where armaments and armed groups exist in large numbers, a training program for an interim police force has been launched. Last but not least, in April 2004, U.S. Ambassador to Liberia John W. Blaney III announced that the U.S. government, which has held a shipping registry in Liberia since 1949 that hosts more than 2,000 foreign vessels, has contributed $245 million dollars to UNMIL to assist in the mission's efforts.

Despite these developments, there is much left to accomplish. There are reports of minor cease-fire violations, and the harassment of civilians by all conflicting parties continues. Disagreements over the allocation of assistant ministerial positions are also an issue and, perhaps more unsettling, recent disagreements and fractionalization within the leadership of LURD have the potential to derail the peace process altogether. In addition, the humanitarian situation remains bleak, as there are hundreds of thousands of IDPs and refugees in neighboring countries. *(See Chapter 3 for more details.)*

Sierra Leone

After four-and-a-half tumultuous years, the U.N. Mission in Sierra Leone (UNAMSIL) is finally winding down. What at one time appeared headed for failure is irreversibly coming to a successful end. Indeed, had it not been for the United Kingdom, which provided much-needed military assistance in mid-2000 and rescued almost 100 U.N. peacekeepers kidnapped by the Revolutionary United Front of Sierra Leone (RUF), the peace process could have collapsed.

UNAMSIL began in October 1999 with S.C. Resolution 1270. The mission's mandate was to monitor the cease-fire between the government and RUF, support free and fair elections, and assist in the demobilization and reintegration of RUF combatants. The mission has been extended several times. Similarly, the size of the U.N. forces, which began at 6,000, has been progressively expanded to reach its maximum level of nearly 17,500 troops. Elections, where RUF competed and lost, were successfully conducted in May 2002; since then, Sierra Leone has been steadily moving away from its brutal past. As a result, the U.N. force was reduced to about 11,500 troops by February 2004. This number will be further reduced to 5,000 by October 2004.

Significant progress has been made in all areas. UNAMSIL and the U.K. have accelerated training of the national police force and armed forces. More than 50,000 ex-combatants, approximately 10,000 of whom were child combatants, have been reintegrated into society. State authority has been expanded with administrative agencies, magistrate courts and ministries opening offices in all districts.

The significant accomplishments over the last couple of years make the likelihood of UNAMSIL's staying beyond December 2004 slim, especially because U.N. peacekeepers are increasingly needed elsewhere in Africa. However, there is talk of a post-UNAMSIL peacekeeping presence. This may be necessary because of the still volatile situation along the border with neighboring Liberia and nearby Côte d'Ivoire. All three countries continue to face problems, whose roots may be traced to the economic slowdown of the 1970s and 1980s. Overall, UNAMSIL is expected to end in December 2004 with a post-UNAMSIL residual U.N. peacekeeping presence most likely to follow.[31]

Western Sahara

Situated in northwest Africa, Western Sahara (formerly Spanish Sahara) became a Spanish colony in 1884 and remained a colonial domain until 1975. It did not attain independence the same way most African countries did because both Morocco and Mauritania claimed the territory. Initially, the former took control of the northern two-thirds of the territory while the latter took the remaining southern third. Around the same time, the Frente Popular de Liberación de Saguía el Hamra y Río de Oro (El Frente POLISARIO) was formed to press for independence. Under intense political and military pressure, Mauritania renounced its claim and withdrew from the territory, which Morocco immediately annexed.

At present, Morocco continues to occupy the entire territory, and Frente POLISARIO continues to press its case for a full measure of self-determination. So far, the two sides have failed to find a mutually acceptable formula for a peaceful end to the conflict. According to the United Nations, therefore, Western Sahara remains a "non self-governing" territory, pending Saharawi right to self-determination through a referendum.[32] The International Court of Justice recognized this right in its 1975 ruling.[33] Pursuant to the above, the Security Council, with Resolution 690, approved the U.N. Mission for the Referendum in Western Sahara (MINURSO) in April 1991, mainly to conduct the proposed referendum in a peaceful environment. As such, it is the oldest peacekeeping mission in Africa. Although it is difficult to predict if and when the proposed referendum will take place, MINURSO has accomplished a few things.

It continues to monitor the cease-fire, which both parties are respecting. Also, the Identification Commission, set up to compile a voter registration list in 1993, has successfully completed its work, and, as a result, the civilian component of MINURSO withdrew at the end of 2003.[34] Frente POLISARIO also released about 250 Moroccan prisoners of war in September 2003, although many remain captive. These prisoners have been held since 1979 and are known as the "world's longest-serving POWs."[35] Similarly, a U.N. High Commissioner for Refugees (UNHCR)-operated telephone connection between refugee camps in Algeria and the territory has been re-established. Finally, in early March 2004, MINURSO carried out weeklong visits for families who were separated in 1975; there is hope these visits will become a weekly event.[36]

While all these events are important and point to some of MINURSO's successes, Morocco and Frente POLISARIO have yet to agree on the modalities of the proposed referendum. The U.N. has now agreed on a peace plan, which includes semiautonomy for Western Sahara for a period of up to five years, after which the proposed referendum will take place.[37] Frente POLISARIO has accepted the plan. Morocco, on the other hand, has shown no enthusiasm for it. The U.N. seems to be running out of options. The conflict in "Africa's last colony" shows no sign of ending, and one of Africa's ongoing wars may be "forgotten, but still not over."[38] The present mission expired in April but was immediately extended to October 31, 2004, by S.C. Resolution 1541. In the same resolution, the S.C. reaffirmed its support for the Peace Plan for Self-Determination of the People of Western Sahara in hopes that the two parties would find an agreement while cooperating fully with the Secretary-General and his Personal Envoy in their efforts to resolve the dispute.[39]

Looking Forward

Of the ongoing U.N. peace missions in Africa, UNMEE and MINURSO were not expected to last this long. As Secretary-General Annan has made amply clear, these missions were only created to provide conditions conducive to peace, but never to support the status quo. U.N. patience is, therefore, wearing thin, especially because it is being called upon to support other peace processes in places such as Burundi and, more recently, Sudan. In fact, as pointed out, a mission was just approved in May 2004 in Burundi. The U.N. Operation in Burundi (ONUB) will take over for the African Union with a six-month mandate to support the process of disarming and disbanding militias as well as promoting the rule of law. As for the situation in Sudan, the Darfur region in particular, the U.N. has expressed its deep concern at the massive human rights violations perpetrated against the inhabitants, including the reported "ethnic cleansing" by Arab militias. There have been calls for U.N. intervention before it is too late.

The Americas

Adam Godet

Haiti

In January 2004, violent protests against the country's president, Jean-Bertrand Aristide, interrupted Haiti's celebration of its bicentennial of independence. Elected contentiously in 2000, controversy over President Aristide began after the 2000 legislative elections, which were won by his party and deemed flawed by the opposition. In a protest against the legislative elections, the opposition party boycotted the presidential election and anti-government demonstrations have been common ever since.[1]

On February 5, 2004, rebels staged a surprise assault on the main police station, forcing the heavily armed officers to flee and torching the building.[2] The Haitian government was hardly equipped to handle the violent uprisings that followed. Since President Aristide disbanded the Haitian military in 1994, rebel gangs faced little armed resistance from the government.[3] Although the Haitian government was ill-equipped to quell the uprisings, gangs of pro-Aristide fighters supported the remaining police forces, thus escalating the level of violence.

Viewing the President as a dictator, rebels saw his resignation as the only acceptable solution. Aristide, whose presidential term was scheduled to end in 2006, refused to step down, arguing that it was the only way to strengthen Haiti's fledgling democracy. As a compromise, the U.S. drafted a power-sharing agreement that would have allowed President Aristide to remain the titular head of state while a government of national unity gained power under a neutral prime minister. The opposition forces rejected this plan and on February 29, 2004, President Aristide resigned; adhering to the Haitian constitution, Chief Justice of the Supreme Court Boniface Alexandre was sworn into office. President Aristide's resignation received explicit support from the French and implicit support from the United States.[4]

Although the constitution clearly states that Mr. Alexandre, as Chief Justice, should become president, it also states that this appointment must be ratified by the legislature, which was dissolved in January 2004.[5] This ambiguity, following President Aristide's departure, created a power vacuum, which has been filled, to some extent, by the opposition forces.[6] This has left Haiti without any clear authority.

On the day of President Aristide's resignation, the United Nations approved the immediate deployment of the Multinational Interim Force (MIF) with a 90-day mandate.[7] The force consisted largely of troops from the United States, France, Canada and Chile.[8] After fulfilling the three-month mandate, these forces were followed by a new U.N. peacekeeping mission—and the only mission currently in the Americas. Called The Multi-Dimensional U.N. Stabilization Mission in Haiti (MINUSTAH), it consists of nearly 7,000 troops, 1,600 civilian police officers and additional international and local civilian staff. MINUSTAH's initial 24-month mandate is to restore and maintain order before the end of 2005, when parliamentary elections are scheduled to take place.[9]

Asia

Ishtiaq Ahmad

Afghanistan

Following the 58th Session of the General Assembly, the United Nations continued to lead peacekeeping efforts across Asia, conducting peace work in Afghanistan, Bougainville, India-Pakistan, Tajikistan and Timor-Leste over 2003 and early 2004. While the U.N. curtailed its operations in Timor-Leste, where significant progress was achieved, its role seemed to expand in war-torn Afghanistan, where insecurity is rampant. This section reviews the U.N.'s critical work in Afghanistan before addressing the aforementioned countries and regions.

In the past year, the political timetable established in December 2001 by the Bonn Peace Agreement in Afghanistan was, for the most part, kept: the constitutional *Loya Jirga*[1] concluded successfully, giving Afghanistan its first democratic constitution. With the help of the U.N. Assistance Mission in Afghanistan (UNAMA), a political mission, and other U.N. agencies, the Afghan Transitional Administration was able to articulate a National Development Framework and a national budget. In addition, the country adopted a new national currency, laid the foundation for a national army and police force, reformed the Ministry of Defense, began the pilot phase of the disarmament, demobilization and reintegration program, and laid the groundwork for a number of key national reconstruction and development programs.

Perhaps the foremost achievement of the UNAMA-led state-building process was the adoption of a new constitution on January 4, 2004 by the 502-member *Loya Jirga*. That constitution set up a democratic presidential system, with a directly elected president and a two-chamber national assembly. U.S. Ambassador to Afghanistan Zalmay Khalilzad called it "one of the most enlightened constitutions in the Islamic world."

Under the constitution, an independent judiciary is to be organized, and 25 percent of the seats in the lower house of parliament are reserved for women. The country was renamed the Islamic Republic of Afghanistan, combining democracy and religion. There is to be a system of civil law, but no law can be contrary to the beliefs and provisions of Islam. Although Pashtun remained the language of the national anthem, the constitution recognized minority languages as being official in those areas where they are used by the local majority.

However, the process to choose delegates for the *Loya Jirga* was not flawless. Some delegates were alleged war criminals and, during the elections for the *Loya Jirga* convention, Human Rights Watch documented numerous cases of local military or intelligence commanders intimidating candidates and purchasing votes. There was also a problem with the approved constitution itself. In the Charter, several provisions enunciated basic political, civil, economic and social rights, but there was little language creating institutions to uphold them. For example, the Afghan Independent Human Rights Commission was given a mandate, but lacks many of the powers necessary for it to credibly protect basic rights.[2]

The threat that factional forces posed to the peace process was increasingly compounded by the terrorist tactics of extremists. Under the Bonn Agreement, presidential and parliamentary elections in Afghanistan's 32 provinces were scheduled to be held in June 2004. However, on March 28, President Hamid Karzai postponed these elections to September, citing rampant insecurity. As of April 21, only 1.8 million Afghan voters out of an estimated total of 10.5 million had registered to vote.[3]

Meanwhile, a series of attacks by insurgent forces confirmed that the U.N. had become a target: in November, a car bomb exploded outside U.N. offices in Kandahar; a staff member from the Office of the U.N. High Commissioner for Refugees was murdered in the Ghazni province. In March 2004, a Turkish road engineer and a member of the Red Crescent Society were killed in the Zabul province. Consequently, the U.N. implemented additional safety measures for its staff members, including the suspension of some of its operations, largely in the south, southeast and eastern parts of the country. Earlier, in October 2003, the S.C. had authorized the International Security Assistance Force (ISAF), led by the North Atlantic Treaty Organization (NATO), to deploy beyond Kabul.[4]

On January 15, in his final report to the Council, then Special Representative to Afghanistan Lakhdar Brahimi stated that the key challenges facing Afghanistan were implementing the constitution and organizing elections, broadening the popular base of the government, strengthening a governance system based on the rule of law, increasing the pace of reconstruction, stopping illicit drug production and improving security.[5]

As before, Afghanistan remained beset by rampant insecurity caused by insurgent forces of Taliban, Al Qaeda and regional warlords. Clashes in the north and west—areas generally considered more stable than others—underscored the problems facing the interim government, as it tried to extend its authority into the provinces. In March 2004, two major rebellions by powerful warlords acted against government-appointed commanders. Skirmishes between northern warlord General Rashid Dostum and government-appointed commander General Hashim Habibi erupted in northern Faryab province, for example. Moreover, in the western city of Herat, fierce factional fighting between forces loyal to governor Ismail Khan and those loyal to a government-appointed commander left more than 100 people dead.[6]

One of the main reasons for insecurity was that the pace of ISAF expansion lagged behind that of the political process. Despite its October decision to extend ISAF beyond Kabul, NATO continued to lack troop commitments from its member states to deploy additional Provincial Reconstruction Teams (PRTs) across northern Afghanistan.[7] ISAF's 5,300 peacekeepers operated separately from the U.S.-led coalition's 11,500-strong force. As for PRTs, as of March 2003, 11 of them—each consisting of 60 to 100 soldiers and civilians—were deployed nationwide, with 10 under coalition command and the first ISAF team under German command in Kunduz province.[8]

In his March 19 report to the Council, which recommended the extension of UNAMA until March 19, 2005, the S.G. stated that the deployment of PRTs had "contributed to stability in a variety of ways."[9] The progress in Afghanistan's security, however, remained slow. As of March, the Afghan National Army (ANA) had a central corps of just over 5,000 troops, while another 3,000 recruits were in training. It was expected that some 10,000 ANA troops—compared to the target strength of 70,000 to be achieved under a 10-year plan—were to be operational by the summer of 2004. As for the Afghan National Police, 4,340 police officers had completed their training by March, while 1,500 officer cadets and 500 border police were in training.[10]

The Disarmament, Demobilization and Reintegration (DDR) program also fell short of expectations. By March 6, just over 5,000 of the estimated 100,000 Afghan fighters who pledged loyalty to different warlords had surrendered their weapons. Lack of political will on the part of regional warlords was also apparent.[11]

Beyond security, another major threat to Afghanistan's long-term peace and stability over the past year was its growing drug trade. An internationally sponsored Afghan government report, which formed the basis of deliberations at the March 31-April 1, 2004 Afghan Donors Conference in Berlin,[12] stated: "The general lawlessness surrounding a pervasive drug industry could lead to the emergence of another fundamentalist government harbouring Islamic extremists." [13] *(See Commentary and Chapter 5 for more details.)*

Overall, a multitude of social-, political- and security-related challenges face Afghanistan, some of which, such as the drug problem, are worsening. Enhanced international engagement is needed to further develop the country. Certainly, the $8.2 billion three-year funding commitment made by donors in Berlin was an important indicator of the international community's sustained engagement in Afghanistan—even though it fell short of the $28 billion seven-year target set by the Afghan government.[14]

Bougainville

On December 23, 2003, the Security Council supported the recommendation of the S.G. to establish the U.N. Observer Mission in Bougainville (UNOMB). This office succeeds the U.N. Political Office in Bougainville (UNPOB), which has overseen the peace-building process on the island since 1887, but with significantly reduced strength. Since January 1, 2004, UNOMB has facilitated the efforts of the government of Papua New Guinea and the Bougainville parties in their transitional period—including chairing the Peace Process Consultative Committee, monitoring weapons disposal and ensuring the parties' compliance to it, and overseeing the constitution and its implementation process—leading to the holding of elections ideally by the end of 2004.

In December 2003, Australia sent a small police force to help Bougainville in its policing operations.[15] This force replaced the small civilian Transition Monitoring Team from Australia, New Zealand, Fiji and Vanuatu, which had provided logistical and operational support to UNPOB since the withdrawal of the Australian Peace Monitoring Group in June 2003.[16]

As for progress on the political front, in March 2004, the Bougainville Interim Provincial Government passed legislation to establish the Bougainville Constituent Assembly (BCA). This legislation was a major step forward in preparation for the autonomous Bougainville government. The General Assembly will consider the third and final draft of the country's constitution in the light of the report submitted by the Bougainville Constitutional Commission (BCC).

On April 26, BCC Chairman Joseph Kabui announced that the third draft of the constitution should be approved before elections.

India-Pakistan

During 2003 and early 2004, relations between India and Pakistan improved significantly, especially with the resumption of a "composite dialogue" covering all of their unresolved issues, including Kashmir, in February 2004. Meanwhile, the U.N. Military Observer Group in India and Pakistan (UNMOGIP), the oldest U.N. peacekeeping operation in Asia, continued to monitor the Line of Control in the disputed state of Jammu and Kashmir, and to investigate and report its findings to U.N. headquarters.[17]

India and Pakistan have fought three wars, two of them over the status of Kashmir. During 1999-2002, Kashmir could have caused yet another war between the two nuclear rivals with catastrophic consequences. The resumption of dialogue, coupled with unilateral announcement and mutual implementation of a number of Confidence Building Measures (CBMs), reflected the willingness of their respective leaderships to finally pursue bilateral peace as increasingly desired by the international community, especially the U.N. and the United States.

On October 22, 2003, India offered Pakistan a number of CBMs, including the resumption of sports, air and shipping links, and a bus service between the capitals of Indian- and Pakistani-administered Kashmirs. While Pakistan agreed in principle to these proposals, on the issue of bus service, it insisted that U.N. personnel oversee the border crossing and that Kashmiris who use the route entry carry U.N. documents.[18] For its part, on November 23, Pakistan unilaterally announced a historic cease-fire along the Line of Control.[19] India followed suit, extending the cease-fire to the Siachen glacier area to north of the Line of Control. On January 1, 2004, the two countries' airline over-flight and landing rights were restored and train and bus services across their international border-crossing point at Wahga were back in service. By March, their national cricket teams entertained the world in a cricket test series—the first such series between the two nations in 15 years.

To understand this turnaround in relations, one has to go back to January 6, 2004, when former Indian Prime Minister Atal Behari Vajpayee and Pakistani President-General Pervez Musharraf met on the sidelines of the 12th summit of the South Asian Association for Regional Cooperation (SAARC) in Islamabad. There, the two leaders decided to "commence the process of the composite dialogue in February 2004 [that would]...lead to peaceful settlement of all bilateral issues, including Jammu and Kashmir, to the satisfaction of both sides."[20]

The decision won instant international acclaim. S.G. Annan hailed the meeting as an "important step forward in the continuing bilateral efforts to improve relations and resolve outstanding issues between the two countries." He urged "both sides to continue with these efforts."[21]

On February 17, following two days of parleys, the foreign secretaries of India and Pakistan announced their agreement to approach the composite dialogue. More importantly, they issued a road map for talks on issues, such as Kashmir, terrorism and nuclear weapons, which would involve additional meetings over the summer of 2004.[22]

While the road map seemed to set the India-Pakistan relationship on a stable path toward peace, resolving the dispute over Kashmir remains an uphill task. The two countries have entrenched positions on the region that are more than a half-century old. Pakistan continues to prefer the implementation of S.C. resolutions that envisage the Kashmiri people determining in a plebiscite under U.N. auspices whether to accede to Pakistan or India. Aware that a plebiscite was unacceptable to India, Pakistan also seems to be exploring, albeit unofficially, other solutions, such as restructuring the current Line of Control in a way that would best promote Pakistan's strategic and political interests.[23]

India's bottom line on Kashmir remains unchanged. The country insists that the state of Jammu and Kashmir is an integral part of the Indian Union and that any settlement of the crisis must be effected within the confines of the Indian constitution. However, differences abound within Indian policy circles on the future shape of a possible solution, from support for incorporating into India all of Jammu and Kashmir, including territories currently under Pakistani and Chinese control, to the territorial status quo, to the increasingly apparent shift in official policy for recognition of the Line of Control as the international border.[24]

Nonetheless, Indian and Pakistani leaders showed unprecedented flexibility on Kashmir. On December 2, 2003, President Musharraf offered to pull back troops from Pakistan-administered Kashmir, if India did likewise in its part of the disputed territory.[25] On January 22, in a radical departure from the past, the Indian government also held first-ever talks with the leadership of an umbrella organisation of Muslim Kashmiri separatists, the All-Parties Hurriyat Conference.[26]

Against this backdrop, it was clear that the United Nations, along with the U.S. and European Union, could help the India-Pakistan dialogue process move forward, especially on Kashmir, by facilitating communications. UNMOGIP, in particular, could play a crucial role by overseeing a negotiated settlement of Kashmir, whether it involved overseeing border modification or supervising a plebiscite.

Tajikistan

The U.N. Tajikistan Office of Peace-Building (UNTOP) continued to work closely with the parties to the 1997 General Agreement on the Establishment of Peace and National Accord over the past year. The accord ended a five-year civil war between the Tajik government of President Emomali Rakhmonov and the United Tajik Opposition (UTO). While working closely with the U.N. resident coordinator, UNTOP focused on consolidating peace and national reconciliation in a number of ways, including promoting the rule of law, strengthening democratic institutions and building national capacity in the area of human rights. The Office also supported the social integration of ex-combatants by providing vocational training.[27]

UNTOP was established in June 2000 after the expiration of the mandate of the U.N. Mission of Observers in Tajikistan (UNMOT), which had supported the peace-building process since the 1997 accord. UNTOP will continue to support peace-building efforts in Tajikistan, which should lead to the holding of its free and fair elections in spring 2005.

Meanwhile, UNTOP has some challenges to face. The first emanated from Tajikistan's role as a frontline state in the U.S.-led war on terrorism in central Asia—a challenge underscored by the S.G. in May 2003, when he proposed extending UNTOP's mission to June 1, 2004: "A multiplicity of problems related to the civil war, including the high unemployment rate among ex-combatants, the spread of small arms among civilians, drug trafficking and the resurgence of extremist organizations, such as Hizb-ut-Tahrir, make the political equilibrium of the country fragile."[28]

Second, despite UNTOP's best efforts in partnership with the U.N. country team as well as the Organisation of Security and Cooperation in Europe (OSCE), the Tajik government continued to engage in gross violation of human rights. Citing the war against terrorism, the government frequently persecuted its opponents, subjected religious leaders to intense surveillance and handed down lengthy prison sentences to leaders and followers of radical Islamic parties like Hizb-ut-Tahrir and Islamic Renaissance Party, a key UTO member.[29]

Timor-Leste

The second and final mandate of the U.N. Mission of Support in East Timor (UNMISET), which has assisted Timor-Leste since independence from Indonesia in May 2002 by strengthening its institutions and national security, was scheduled to end in May 2004. However, after violent attacks by armed elements in January and February, and simultaneous appeals by Timorese leaders, the S.C. decided to slow the schedule for downsizing the Mission's police and military components. On February 13, the S.G. recommended that UNMISET's mandate be extended until May 20, 2005, even though in a modified form and reduced size.[30]

East Timor, renamed Timor-Leste since independence, was a Portuguese colony before Indonesia took it over in 1975 and ruled it, often brutally, for 24 years. Until independence on May 20, 2002, when UNMISET began its first mandate, the U.N. Transitional Administration in East Timor (UNTAET) had maintained peace. However, unlike UNTAET, whose mandate entailed full-scale administrative responsibilities, UNMISET has acted only as a temporary support system for the government in political and security matters. Under its new mandate, the Mission has 352 military personnel and a support team of 215—as opposed to just over 3,000 international troops and a support team of 1,900 during its previous two years.[31]

However, Timor-Leste leaders' calls to extend the U.N. Mission before S.G. Annan's February recommendation to that effect were motivated by the country's continuing security predicament.[32]

Despite such concerns, UNMISET has achieved a great deal in its three assigned programmes, including stability, democracy and justice; international security and law enforcement; and external security and border control.[33] For example, the development of the public administration of Timor-Leste has progressed considerably, and recruitment of Timorese personnel is relatively advanced. Preparation of a Civil Service Act has begun and "organic laws" for some key ministries have been adopted, while the parliament is considering draft legislation that would establish an Office of the Provedor for Human Rights and Justice. In the area of serious crime investigations, the Special Panels for Serious Crimes had, by February 2004, issued 44 judgments; while the office of the Deputy General Prosecutor for Serious Crimes had submitted 81 judgments.

UNMISET has also played an instrumental role in enabling the Policia Nacional de Timor-Leste (PNTL) to assume full responsibility for the maintenance of law and order. As of February 2003, PNTL had just over 3,000 trained police officers and 33 civilian support staff and its specialized units were sufficiently developed.

Under their current mandate, UNMISET's 58 civilian advisers are assisting the country in developing its public administration and justice system, including support for prosecutions and trials related to serious crimes. In addition, civilian police advisers are assisting in the development of the country's police; military liaison officers are monitoring security-related developments; and some 310 military personnel are overseeing border security. It is hoped that this team will generate sufficient indigenous capabilities to help the world's newest nation cope with its remaining state-building challenges before the U.N. Mission's current mandate expires in May 2005.

Looking Forward

The 59th Session of the General Assembly is likely to express satisfaction on the overall progress that has been made during the past year in the U.N. peace activities in Asia and will most likely resolve to continue the five operations, urging member states and parties concerned in each case to contribute to their success with troops or funds. Given that the G.A.'s 59th session will coincide with the holding of elections in Afghanistan scheduled for September 2004, the U.N. contribution to the country's political process and the key challenges facing it may be deliberated upon quite extensively. The delegates, especially from Afghanistan and countries engaged in its security and reconstruction, may stress the importance of expanding the U.N.-led Bonn peace process. In addition, the Assembly may decide to expand the Afghan Mission by urging donor nations to fulfil their financial commitments toward this end. The decision by India and Pakistan to pursue dialogue is expected to receive international praise; however, the two countries may stick to their respective positions regarding the role of UNMOGIP in Kashmir. As for Timor-Leste, the G.A. is most likely to express hope that UNMISET, with its modified mandate, will be able to complete its peacekeeping and state-building activities by May 2005. Like Afghanistan, Bougainville and Tajikistan are up for elections in the coming year, meaning the Assembly will take stock of UNOMB's and UNTOP's role in the political process as well as the pace of UNOMB's weapons disposal program and UNTOP's incorporation into its agenda of human rights violations in the country.

Europe

Amy Frumin

Cyprus

The divided Mediterranean island of Cyprus has been a Security Council agenda item for longer than any other peace issue on the S.C. program. In 1964, the U.N. Peacekeeping Force in Cyprus (UNFICYP) was established to prevent the resumption of fighting between Greek Cypriot and Turkish Cypriot communities on the island. In 1974, Turkey invaded Cyprus in response to a Greek military attempt to take over the island. UNFICYP's mandate was thus expanded to monitor the newly established cease-fire and buffer zone, which to this day divides the Turkish Cypriot north from the Greek Cypriot south.

In April 2004, the island came closer than ever to reuniting. The main push toward reunification was the May 1 accession to the European Union of the Greek Cypriot government, the only internationally recognized government on the island. Much to the disappointment of the international community, the historic opportunity was lost when Greek Cypriots voted 75 percent against the U.N.-brokered peace deal in the April 24 referendum. In 1999, the E.U. promised the Greek Cypriots that their accession would not be contingent upon reunification of the island. At that time, it was the Turkish Cypriots who had been obstructing a peace deal. However, five years later, it was the Turkish Cypriots who cooperated with the international community and voted 65 percent in favor of reunification.[1] As a result, on May 1, the Green Line separating the Greek Cypriots from the Turkish Cypriots became the new border of the European Union, meaning the Turkish Cypriots would not join the Union.

Over the past year, UNFICYP has continued to carry out its peacekeeping mandate to prevent resumption of fighting. In addition, the U.N. has worked toward negotiating a peace plan under the auspices of the Good Offices of the Secretary-General. As promised last year, the "Basis for an Agreement on a Comprehensive Settlement of the Cyprus Problem," which was rejected by the Turkish Cypriots in March 2003, remained on the negotiating table. Upon reassessment of the situation, the S.G. invited Greek and Turkish Cypriot leaders to New York to discuss a renewed effort to find a settlement before the May 2004 accession of Cyprus to the Union. Talks concluded on February 13, 2004, with all sides agreeing to a three-phased plan for negotiations.

The first phase sought a political and technical compromise between Greek and Turkish Cypriots. The two sides made progress on technical issues, producing more than 9,000 pages of federal laws to enter into force upon unification. However, little advancement was made at the political level, and negotiations ended on March 22, 2004. The second and third phases, held in Bürgenstock, Switzerland, were equally unsuccessful, despite the participation of the Greek and Turkish foreign ministers and, in the third phase, the participation of their prime ministers and S.G. Annan himself.

In accordance with the provision made on February 19, the S.G. used his discretion to finalize the text of a "Comprehensive Settlement of the Cyprus Problem." Known as the Annan Plan for Cyprus, the document was presented to the Greek Cypriot, Turkish Cypriot and guarantor states (Greece, Turkey and the United Kingdom) on March 31, 2004 and was subsequently put to a simultaneous public referendum in the north and south on April 24, 2004.[2]

The comprehensive settlement document contains detailed plans as to the type of state envisaged for the United Cyprus Republic, and how that state will come into being. Included in the document is the foundation agreement, which calls for the creation of a new internationally recognized and sovereign single federal state, with a single citizenship. Expressly forbidden in the Annan Plan[3] is the partition or secession of any part of the state and union of any part with another state. The cultural distinction and political equality of the Greek Cypriots and Turkish Cypriots are recognized in the document. The government envisaged in the plan is headed by a Presidential Council, made up of four Greek Cypriots, two Turkish Cypriots and three nonvoting members (two Greek Cypriots and one Turkish Cypriot). Decisions in the Council would require a simple majority, but must include at least two Greek Cypriots and one Turkish Cypriot vote. The bicameral legislature would include a Senate with an equal number of representatives from the north and south, and a Chamber of Deputies, in which representation would be based on population. The Supreme Court would break deadlocks in the federal government, with the bench consisting of equal numbers of Greek and Turkish Cypriots and, until decided otherwise by the Cypriots, three non-Cypriot judges.[4]

With regard to land claims, all dispossessed owners would be entitled under the Annan Plan to full and effective compensation for their lost property, at the least. The Plan placed limitations on the number of Greek Cypriots who could live in the north and vice versa, as well as the number of Turks and Greeks who could move to Cyprus. These limitations, enforced during a transitional period, aim to ensure that each group retains a majority in its constituent state and to address Turkish Cypriot concerns that more than 100,000 Greek Cypriots could return to the north upon reunification.[5]

Among the matters submitted to the U.N. Security Council was a detailed description of the new and expanded U.N. peacekeeping mandate, which would have created the U.N. Settlement Implementation Mission in Cyprus (UNSIMIC). The number of U.N. troops would double, while the number of international civilian police and personnel would grow more than tenfold. UNSIMIC would monitor lands to be adjusted as well as troop reduction.[6] On April 21, 2004, a draft resolution was presented to the S.C. calling for its commitment, should both sides vote to reunite. The Russian Federation felt compelled to exercise a technical veto for the first time in 10 years, saying that there had not been enough debate on the issue.[7]

Opinion polls indicated that the main issue that swayed Greek Cypriot voters was concern that the Turkish military would not fulfill its commitment to draw down its forces in the north. The veto of the U.N. resolution, designed to address these fears by strengthening the U.N.'s role in ensuring compliance with the plan, pushed the AKEL party to support the "no" campaign along with Greek Cypriot President Tassos Papadopoulos. President Papadopoulos claimed the plan would solidify the island's division, legitimize the 30-year Turkish occupation of Cyprus and violate the right of refugees to return to their homes. He told the people that the U.N. plan would always be there and that the next round of negotiations would promise more concessions by the Turkish Cypriots. His rationale was based on the fact that the Greek Cypriots' accession to the E.U. was guaranteed, and that their seat in the Union would allow them leverage over the Turkish government, itself seeking membership to the Union.[8]

In the run-up to the referendum, the Greek Cypriot population was exposed only to these types of arguments made by the ruling party against the Annan Plan. Senior U.N. and E.U. representatives were prohibited from giving interviews on Greek Cypriot television to explain the complex and lengthy agreement.[9] The international community criticized Greek Cypriot leaders for manipulating public opinion by restricting media access.

The Greek Cypriots have entered the E.U. under a shadow, according to the E.U. Commissioner for Enlargement. E.U. leaders felt that Greek Cypriots misled the Union into believing that they would support reunification even after Cyprus was invited to join.[10] The U.N. was also furious with President Papadopoulos for rejecting the plan after so much time and energy had been invested into finalizing a deal, not to mention the personal involvement of the Secretary-General.

The Turkish Cypriot "yes" vote was motivated by the possibility of joining the Union. E.U. membership would have meant an end to effective embargo, which has crippled the Turkish Cypriot economy since 1974, restricting travel and investment. These benefits outweighed the negative factors of the Annan Plan for the Turkish Cypriots, which included the loss of land and a potential security threat. It should be noted that security concerns were mitigated after the historic and successful opening of the Green Line in April 2003. Greek and Turkish Cypriots have been crossing at a rate of 13,000 daily without major incident.[11]

In addition, political impediments were reduced both in the north and in the guarantor state of Turkey. Parliamentary elections in Northern Cyprus on December 14, 2003, installed a more moderate government, which balances Turkish Cypriot President Rauf Denktash's staunch opposition to a peace deal. Turkey also softened its opposition to a peace deal. Turkish generals had been the backbone of the opposition to a peace deal, because of Cyprus's strategic location in the Mediterranean. After a reshuffling of senior positions in the military, Turkish generals have fallen in line with Turkish Prime Minister Recep Erdogan in supporting a peace deal.[12] Prime Minister Erdogan recognizes the strategic importance of Turkish Cypriots sitting with the Greek Cypriots at the E.U. table in order to fulfill his own accession aspirations.

While Turkey and Turkish Cypriots were disappointed by the referendum, both gained important political capital on April 24, 2004. For the Turkish Cypriots, they shed the image of being obstructionist.[13] In addition, the E.U. agreed to give them 259 million euros that had been set aside for the north in the case of reunification.[14] For the Turks, their support for a "yes" vote is being rewarded with improved credibility in the international community. Prime Minister Erdogan claimed, "This is the most successful event in the last 50 years of Turkish diplomacy." He hopes his newfound international prestige will pay dividends in E.U. accession discussions.[15]

Georgia-Abkhazia

After Georgia gained independence from Russia in 1991, three break-away republics within its borders began their own struggle for independence. The bloodiest revolt was in Abkhazia, where a war between 1992 and 1993 left 10,000 people dead. The U.N. Observer Mission in Georgia (UNOMIG) was established in 1993 with a mandate to negotiate a peace, monitor the most recently negotiated cease-fire agreement,[16] oversee the Commonwealth of Independent States (CIS) peacekeeping force—which is comprised of mostly Russian soldiers, and contribute to safe conditions abetting the return of refugees and internally displaced persons (IDPs).

U.N. efforts to negotiate for peace continue to be rejected by Abkhaz leaders, who refuse to receive the December 2001 paper, "Basic Principles for the Distribution of Competences between Tbilisi and Sukhumi."[17] This paper was drafted by the S.G. and his Group of Friends (the Russian Federation, the United Kingdom, the United States, France and Germany) and is considered by the international community to be the basis for a comprehensive settlement. Abkhaz leaders, claiming independence, rejected the paper because they did not feel the need to negotiate competences with Tbilisi.

There are several established mechanisms to negotiate a peace. The Geneva Peace Process, begun in 1997, continued efforts to find a peace in two meetings over the past year. The July 2003 meeting included, for the first time, representatives from both Abkhazia and Georgia, in addition to the regular participation of the Group of Friends and U.N. officials. Three issues were recognized as essential to a peace settlement: economic cooperation, return of IDPs and refugees, and political and security matters. Little concrete progress was made in any of these areas, despite numerous meetings in a variety of forums. In addition to U.N. efforts, Russia and Georgia began a bilateral dialogue on practical areas to pave the way for an eventual peace negotiation.[18]

With regard to security, several initiatives were taken to improve safety after an especially violent October, particularly along the cease-fire zone. Among them was a request for an additional 20 international civilian police officers to train, monitor and advise local law enforcement, and to facilitate cooperation between law enforcement groups on either side of the cease-fire line.[19] As of April 2004, only 11 officers had been deployed because of the Abkhaz Parliament's objection to UNOMIG civilian international police presence on what they consider their sovereign territory.[20]

UNOMIG personnel themselves fell victim to violence when, on June 5, 2003, an unidentified group of armed men took four UNOMIG personnel hostage in the Kodori Valley. After six days of negotiations, all four were freed unharmed. UNOMIG has suspended all patrols in the Kodori Valley as a result. CIS peacekeeping forces now patrol the valley.[21]

There are four main players who hold influence in the potential peace in Abkhazia: the Abkhaz, Georgians, Russians and Americans. Each group's role is discussed below.

The October 2004 presidential elections in Abkhazia have made imminent progress on the peace settlement unlikely. The election campaign has created an atmosphere that is not conducive to politicians taking risks and cooperating with the Georgians.[22] The current Abkhaz administration is staunchly uncompromising regarding independence. There is the possibility of post-election progress as the current president, Vladislav Ardzinba, is seriously ill and will not stand for re-election. Jockeying for his position are pro-Russian parties, who are most likely to take cues regarding a peace deal from Russia, and pro-Abkhazia parties, who could be persuaded to accept a peace deal on a bilateral basis if Georgia presents an amenable settlement.[23] Hopefully, the election will bring as profound a change in Abkhazia as was witnessed in Georgia, and the new leader of Abkhazia will take up Georgian President Mikhail Saakashvili's outstretched hand to find a peace deal.

No matter the leader after the October elections, the issue of returns will continue to be a crucial one for the Abkhaz. Following the 1992-1993 conflict, more than 200,000 primarily ethnic Georgians fled Abkhazia, making the Abkhaz a majority, except in the Gali district. If a peace deal allows for unrestricted numbers of ethnic Georgians to return, the Abkhaz people fear they will once again be a minority in Abkhazia.

The new Georgian President, Mikhail Saakashvili, has offered some hope for peace. He recognizes the threat of Georgian disintegration as a state and has made the resolution of internal conflicts a priority. His strategy is to entice the breakaway republics to seek association with Georgia by creating economic opportunity and establishing good governance. His holistic approach acknowledges the interconnectedness of reunification with reform.[24] The Abkhaz Foreign Minister echoed this sentiment by requiring Georgian internal economic and government reform before new relationships can be built.[25]

However, it is clear that the Abkhaz situation will not be resolved in the immediate future as President Saakashvili is focusing on Adjara, an autonomous southern province that recently flared up. In addition, he does not plan to begin negotiations in earnest until a new Abkhaz president is elected.[26]

Russia plays a vital role in finding a peace in Abkhazia. However, it may not be in Russia's interest to assist a peace negotiation. A peace settlement would mean that the legal Russian troop presence in Abkhazia, through the CIS peacekeeping forces, would most likely be made unnecessary. This troop presence and Russian direct political, economic and military support to the Abkhaz people has given Russia leverage in Georgian internal politics, which it have used to extract concessions from Georgia.[27]

Yet, the change in Georgian administration may compel improved cooperation by the Russians, as many sources of tension between Russia and Georgia have been diffused. For example, President Saakashvili does not have historical links to Russia's collapse, which embittered relations between many Russian politicians and former Georgian President Eduard Shevardnadze. In addition, President Saakashvili has agreed to the long sought joint patrols along the Russian-Georgian border. Rebuffing President Saakashvili's overtures and disregarding his call to respect Georgia's national sovereignty[28] by ending support to Abkhazia could jeopardize the improving relations. It could also undermine Russia's argument for noninterference in Chechnya.

The U.S. also has a strategic role to play in Georgian stability. The U.S. has invested more money in Georgia than any other post-Soviet state in the hopes of creating a pro-American "zone of stability" in the southern Caucasus,[29] which is, in turn, essential to creating a stable Eurasia and Middle East.[30] Georgia also provides the U.S. access to the Caspian oil reserves, some of the largest unexploited ones in the world.[31] Construction began in May 2003 on the Baku-Tbilisi-Ceyhan pipeline, which will bring Caspian oil to the Mediterranean, importantly bypassing Russia. Yet another reason the U.S. seeks stability in Abkhazia is American sensitivity to unrecognized states and their potential for collapse in the post-September 11th environment.[32] Settling the Abkhaz situation would not only bolster Georgia's stability, but it would also remove one avenue for Russian influence in Georgia and help secure a non-Russian source of Caspian oil.

Kosovo

In 1999, NATO delivered humanitarianism from the skies to Kosovo, by bombing and ending former President Slobodan Milosevic's ethnic-cleansing regime, which left some 10,000, mostly Kosovo Albanians, dead. Soon after, the U.N. Interim Administration Mission in Kosovo (UNMIK) was established with S.C. Resolution 1244, officially making Kosovo a U.N. protectorate in Serbia. Fast forward five years to the scene of the worst violence in Kosovo since the end of the NATO bombing and what has been called by some an organized attempt at cleansing Kosovo of its minority Serbian population (currently about 10 percent).

The interethnic violence broke out on March 17, 2004, following reports of the drowning of two Kosovo Albanian children in the divided town of Mitrovica. Inflammatory media reporting fanned rumors that the children were chased to their deaths by Kosovo Serbs, though later investigations could not substantiate the story. According to the United Nations, but disputed by other observers,[33] the initial spasm of violence was spontaneous in nature, but co-opted and prolonged by organized elements into two more days of hostilities. Over three days, 19 people were killed, 954 civilians were injured, 730 homes (mostly belonging to minorities) were burned or damaged, and 16 Serbian Orthodox religious and cultural sites were damaged or destroyed. In addition, 65 international police officers, 58 Kosovo police officers and 61 KFOR

(NATO's Kosovo forces) personnel were injured, and more than 100 UNMIK vehicles were damaged or burned.[34] What happened? Or, some have claimed, the more appropriate question is, what has not happened in Kosovo?

Before the violence in March, UNMIK was working with the Kosovars toward implementing a plan to establish a multiethnic, democratic and economically viable Kosovo. In 2002, UNMIK developed the "standards before status" strategy, creating an incentive structure for the Kosovo Albanian community by making the discussion of Kosovo's final status, and its potential independence from Serbia, contingent upon achieving several standards. The standards are functioning democratic institutions, respect for the rule of law throughout Kosovo, freedom of movement for all of Kosovo's inhabitants, sustainable return of displaced persons and refugees to their place of origin in Kosovo, minority rights and economic development, respect for property rights, functioning relations with Belgrade and a professional Kosovo Protection Corps. Working together, the Provisional Institutions of Self-Government (PISG) and UNMIK developed the Kosovo Standards Implementation Plan (KSIP), presented on March 31, 2004. The plan details responsible parties and timelines for each of the standards. A comprehensive general review of the plan is scheduled for mid-2005, the outcome of which will inform the S.C.'s discussion of Kosovo's final status.[35] KSIP notes that some sections of the plan will have to be adjusted, considering the recent violence.

Another incentive to achieve the benchmarks set out in the "standards before status" policy is E.U. accession. The European Commission has established a Stabilization and Association Tracking Mechanism to ensure that Kosovo's development is in line with E.U. standards with a view toward an eventual accession process.[36] The Office of the Prime Minister established a Standardization Unit to ensure that laws are compatible with E.U. law and its Constitutional Framework for Provisional Self-Government.

What has happened? While significant progress was made toward each of the eight standards during 2003 and early 2004, the events of mid-March have overshadowed and, in some cases, reversed these accomplishments, as is demonstrated by a brief review below of some of the benchmarks.

By the end of 2003, UNMIK had handed over all those responsibilities designated by the Constitutional Framework for transfer to the PISG, an important milestone. In some areas designated as competencies reserved for the S.G.'s Special Representative in the Constitutional Framework, PISG is taking an advisory role in the administrative and operational functions.[37] However, PISG's capacity and the desire of Kosovo Albanian leaders to establish a multiethnic Kosovo are dubious. On several occasions, Kosovo Albanian leaders overstepped their competencies as laid out in the Constitutional Framework, often to the detriment of the Kosovo Serb community, demonstrating significant resistance to multiethnicity.[38] While Kosovo Albanian politicians are attempting to exercise more responsibilities than delegated to the PISG, minority communities in Kosovo have failed to engage substantively in the exercise of self-government. For example, minority community political representatives in the Assembly have proposed few legislative initiatives.[39]

Kosovo Albanian leaders' ambivalent response to the March violence offered a poignant illustration of their failure to accept the multiethnic character of the province. Only with prompting from the international community did a late condemnation come from the majority population political leaders. However, several Kosovo Albanian leaders at the municipal level broke ranks within their political party leaders and expressed support for the violence,[40] indicating the strong sentiments of those perhaps less influenced by international pressure.

Upon assuming his position as the SRSG in August 2003, Harri Holkeri[41] identified the improvement of the rule of law and security, especially for minority communities, as a top priority for Kosovo. Local and international policing capacity has been enhanced. The Kosovo police service is now in command of seven police stations.[42] And the legal grounding of the law enforcement infrastructure was bolstered with the April 5, 2004, promulgation of the Provisional Criminal Code and Provisional Criminal Procedure Code.[43]

Since the March violence, the international community established measures to provide security for those minorities who have not fled. NATO immediately augmented the 18,500 soldiers with an additional 2,000 personnel. UNMIK police and KFOR have increased patrols and are securing abandoned property.[44] As of mid-April, 183 people had been arrested in connection with the violence. However, some observers have noted that the initial lack of an effective and timely response to the violence in March demonstrated a critical lack of coordination between and within elements of the security structure in Kosovo. These same critics applauded the performance of the Kosovo Police Service, many of whom (with some exceptions) came to the aid of besieged minorities.[45]

In the area of return and reintegration of refugees and IDPs, some significant progress was made over the last year. In July 2003, the Kosovo Assembly signed an open letter to the IDP and refugee community, calling on them to return to their homes in Kosovo. PISG also committed 7 million euros from the 2002 Kosovo Consolidated budget surplus for returns, covering only a small part of the huge funding gap for returns. Despite a lull in returns following the summer of 2003, which witnessed many incidents of interethnic violence, including the murder of 19 Kosovo Serbs, a total of 3,629 IDPs and refugees had returned to Kosovo by the end of 2003, of which nearly 1,500 were Kosovo Serbs. However, the March violence proved a major setback to the return process. In a few violent days in March, just over 4,100 of the nearly 5,000 Kosovo Serbs who returned to Kosovo over the course of 2000-2004 fled.[46]

The already cool relations between Kosovo's capital, Pristina, and Belgrade were frozen by the March violence. However, 2003 saw some small successes in this area as well. In June 2003, Kosovo Albanian and Serbian representatives committed themselves at the E.U.-Western Balkans Summit in Thessaloniki to a direct dialogue between Pristina and Belgrade. The initial phase of this dialogue was launched in Vienna in mid-October 2003; however, no significant engagement or contact occurred between Pristina and Belgrade delegations. Since Vienna, there has been little progress. In addition to the March 2004 violence, relations between Belgrade and Kosovo's capital Pristina continue to be strained by Belgrade's support of parallel government structures in Kosovo Serb communities.

Serbian Prime Minister Vojislav Kostunica has called for the cantonization of Kosovo. While his government has yet to present a plan, his aim is to allow Kosovo Serbs greater representation at the local level. It is significant to note that the calls for cantonization have been coming from Belgrade, which acts as the mouthpiece for the Kosovo Serbs. The Kosovo Albanians are wholeheartedly opposed to the idea, as it would allow the Kosovo Serbs political control in areas where they are a majority, and by extension would legitimize Belgrade's influence in Kosovo. The U.N. is in the very early stages of considering a program of decentralization, which, like cantonization, would bring power to the local level. Discussions will likely be based on a Council of Europe plan, presented late in 2003.

What has not happened? Critics have noted that the failure of the international community to resolve the question of Kosovo's final status has contributed to growing levels of frustration among various sectors of the population and has slowed political, social and economic development in the province. Much like the Kosovo Albanians, critics see the "standards before status" strategy as a delaying technique to stave off the painful debate within the divided international community about Kosovo's independence. Until the final status of Kosovo is addressed, it is probably unlikely that the people of Kosovo can begin normalizing relations among communities. Kosovo Albanians are likely to continue to fear coming once again under Belgrade's authority while Kosovo Serbs and Belgrade are likely to remain opposed to any move that could bring Kosovo closer to independence.[47]

Another major criticism is that UNMIK's strategy employs a weak incentive structure for lofty demands.[48] Critics claim that the March 2004 violence was a bloody demonstration of the political failure of the "standards before status" strategy. It should jolt the international community into taking a more realistic look at the lack of substantial development in Kosovo and the fact that that development has been slowed by the lack of status. Critics have recommended that UNMIK's entire disposition be altered from a peacekeeping mission to a development mission to reflect the reality in which it is now operating, nearly five years after the end of the NATO bombing.

Looking Forward

In the year ahead, the Cyprus situation faces several potential conflicts. The E.U. has now inherited the only remaining divided capital in Europe. It will do what it can to make the Green Line as flexible as possible and work toward lessening the negative impact on the cooperative Turkish Cypriot population. For its part, the U.N. closed the Good Offices of the S.G. and will not consider another renegotiation. The mandate of UNFICYP was extended in November 2003 to June 15, 2004. There is a possibility, however, that the size of the peacekeeping force will be reduced in June. With regard to Georgia, as SRSG for Georgia Heidi Tagliavini noted in 2004, "There is, nevertheless, reason for cautious optimism in the longer term." With new leadership in Georgia, there is hope of loosening the previously entrenched positions of the disputing parties. However, the new Georgian leadership awaits a similar change of administration in Abkhazia before any substantial progress will be made.

Less optimism surrounds analysis of UNMIK, which finds itself in an awkward political dilemma. A frustrated Kosovo Albanian population has seen that KFOR is no longer inviolable and that there is a more direct route to self-rule (i.e., violence) than the UNMIK's path, which may or may not lead to independence. However, the international community has expressed its determination that recent violence not be allowed to dictate policy and will continue to pursue the KSIP. Renewed international interest in Kosovo has included the appointment of an E.U. special envoy and the establishment of the Kosovo Support Group, made up of representatives from the E.U. and others, who will visit the province every six weeks. As for the United Nations, the organization must take a sober look at its own operations and how it can support the Kosovars. It must also be realistic in assessing the possibilities for creating a safe environment for Kosovo Serbs.

The Middle East

Gordon Goldstein

Iraq

On May 1, 2003, following a dramatic televised landing on the aircraft carrier U.S.S. Abraham Lincoln, United States President George W. Bush addressed the nation: "My fellow Americans, major combat operations in Iraq have ended," he said. "In the images of celebrating Iraqis, we have...seen the ageless appeal of human freedom."[1]

Exactly one year later, as U.S. forces in Iraq concluded the bloodiest month of the occupation yet, the irony of the President's remarks was widely noted. Major combat operations had, of course, not ended; they flared violently throughout the country, in Sunni cities such as Fallujah and Shia cities such as Najaf. There were no images of celebrating Iraqis.

The strategy for Iraq assumed a much different outcome. In May 2003, the Bush Administration anticipated that it would need only a minimal military presence to stabilize the country. Before the war, Deputy Secretary of Defense Paul Wolfowitz told Congress: "I am reasonably certain [the Iraqi people] will greet us as liberators; and that will help us keep requirements down."[2] When the Army Chief of Staff, General Eric Shinseki, told lawmakers that "several hundred thousand soldiers" would be required to secure Iraq, Mr. Wolfowitz rebuked him for offering an inflated estimate. The Pentagon's senior leadership disclosed plans to collapse the five U.S. military divisions in the country to fewer than two by the fall.[3]

Despite official expressions of optimism, there were some indications of concern. General Jay Garner, the first American administrator of the liberated Iraq, was quickly sacked. His replacement was L. Paul Bremer, a former senior counter-terrorism official in the Reagan Administration. Meanwhile, at the United Nations, the Secretary-General met with members of the Security Council, who complained angrily that Washington was keeping them in the dark about Iraq's future governance.[4]

In late May 2003, the S.C. passed Resolution 1483, conferring power in Iraq to the Coalition Provisional Authority (CPA) and phasing out the U.N.'s administration of the Oil-for-Food Programme (OFFP) in the following six months. The resolution, which passed by a margin of 14-0, appeared to reflect a desire to move beyond the acrimonious debate that had fractured diplomatic relationships within and beyond the Council, particularly among the United States, France and Germany.

In the summer of 2003, Iraqi citizens cheered the demise of two hated figures from the past: Saddam Hussein's sons, Uday and Qusay.[5] In July, the interim Iraqi Governing Council held its first meeting. The Council's 25 members—each appointed by Ambassador Bremer—broadly reflected Iraq's ethnic makeup of Sunnis, Shias and Kurds. While the Governing Council had the power to appoint ministers and pass a budget, ultimate control of the country rested with the U.S. administrator.[6]

Throughout the early months of the occupation, the U.N. played a marginal role in Iraq, reflecting the Bush Administration's obvious indifference to the organization. The modest U.N. operation was terminated after the devastating attack of August 19, when a car packed with explosives destroyed the organization's headquarters in Baghdad, killing 22 people, including the highly regarded mission chief, Sergio Vieira de Mello. By October, S.G. Annan had withdrawn all U.N. foreign staff members from the country. A report produced by an outside panel commissioned by S.G. Annan concluded that senior officials had been "blinded by the conviction that U.N. personnel and installations would not become a target of attack, despite the clear warnings to the contrary."[7] Under-Secretary-General Shashi Tharoor called the attack "our 9/11."[8]

Despite the loss, S.G. Annan reiterated to the G.A. in September 2003 the organization's willingness to eventually return to Iraq.[9] In October, the S.C. unanimously approved a U.S.- and United Kingdom-sponsored resolution authorizing a U.S.-led multinational force in Iraq. The measure also set a December 15 deadline for the Governing Council to announce a timetable for creating a constitution and democratic government. The resolution, however, did little more than varnish over the political cracks that still divided the

Council. The countries that had most vocally opposed the war—Russia, France and Germany—issued a joint statement qualifying their support: "We believe that the resolution should have gone further on two major issues: first, the role of the United Nations, in particular the political process, and second, the pace of the transfer of responsibilities to the Iraqi people."[10]

While progress was slow on the political track, the security situation within Iraq continued to deteriorate rapidly over the remainder of 2003 and into 2004. Twenty-seven people, including 18 Italians, were killed in a suicide bombing in Nasiriya on November 12. Lieutenant General Ricardo Sanchez, the top U.S. military commander in Iraq, disclosed that attacks on his officers had increased from six each day five months earlier to a new level of between 30 and 35 a day.[11]

Iraq's eroding stability, coupled with the rising voices of political opposition—articulated most influentially by Shia cleric Ayatollah Ali Al-Sistani—prompted the Bush Administration to accelerate its timetable for the formation of an interim government. In mid-November, the White House announced that the U.S. would end its formal occupation, but not its military presence, on June 30, 2004. The U.S. decision followed reports that the fractious Governing Council was approaching rebellion over the plan to draft a constitution first and then transfer power after national elections. Ayatollah Al-Sistani also insisted that elected representatives, not American nominees, draft the new constitution.[12] The growing clamor on the political scene was eclipsed briefly by a historic announcement the following month. U.S. Administrator Paul Bremer told a crowded press conference, "Ladies and gentlemen, we got him. Saddam Hussein was captured Saturday 13 December at about 2030 local, in a cellar in the town of al-Dawr...This is a great day in Iraq's history."[13]

The exuberance over Hussein's capture quickly dissipated in the New Year. In late January, David Kay, the departing chief U.S. arms inspector in Iraq, disclosed that the search for nuclear, chemical and biological weapons had been totally fruitless. "We were all wrong," Mr. Kay told a Senate committee. He speculated that Hussein was perhaps manipulated into financing phantom weapons programs run by scientists caught in what he called a "vortex of corruption" in the late 1990s. Mr. Kay also suggested that Hussein may have tried to play it both ways: maintain the prestige and deterrent value of his presumptive WMD capability, while hoping that international sanctions against Iraq might be lifted if there was no tangible proof of his arsenal's existence.[14] The Bush Administration was sharply criticized for the intelligence failures surrounding illicit Iraqi weapons. The charges that intelligence findings were politically manipulated to strengthen the case for invasion will likely be a central theme of the President's historical legacy.

March 2, 2004, turned out to be the deadliest day in Iraq since U.S. troops toppled the Hussein regime. In coordinated attacks on Shia Muslims gathered at mosques in Baghdad and Karbala for one of the holiest days of the religious calendar, suicide bombers detonated mortars, grenades and roadside bombs, killing 143 people. It was assumed that Hussein loyalists eager to reconstitute Sunni dominance over Iraq's post-occupation government carried out the attacks.[15] Political tensions spilled open later that month when all 25 members of the Governing Council signed an interim constitution that included a bill of rights and guarantees for women. Immediately after the signing ceremony, a spokesman for 12 of the 13 Shias on the Governing Council read a statement saying that they intended to amend those portions of the document that they considered undemocratic.[16] In a letter to Ambassador Brahimi, Ayatollah Al-Sistani warned of "dangerous consequences" if the U.N. endorsed the American-sponsored interim constitution.[17]

In April 2004, Iraq erupted in a seemingly anarchic swirl of violence. Four American contract workers were murdered and mutilated, their bodies set on fire and hung from a bridge. Street battles around the country by the middle of the month had claimed the lives of 90 coalition soldiers, making it the deadliest period for Americans since the fall of Hussein. By some estimates 500 or more Iraqis were killed in Fallujah, a Sunni Muslim stronghold with a population of 300,000. U.S. troops became mired in an extended assault on a militia led by Shia leader Moktada al-Sadr.

America's declining fortunes in Iraq infused the Bush Administration with an uncharacteristic new enthusiasm for multilateral institutions. Edward Mortimer, a senior aide to the Secretary-General, noted that the disparagement the U.N. received from the Bush Administration had been replaced in early 2004 with increasingly urgent calls for assistance. "It's quite nice when you've been generally dissed about your irrelevancy and then suddenly have people coming on bended knee and saying, 'We need you to come back,'" he said. "On the other hand, it's quite unnerving to feel you're being projected into a very violent and volatile situation where you might be regarded as an agent or unfaithful servant of a power that has incurred great hostility."[18]

In late April, Ambassador Brahimi advised the S.C. that an accelerated timetable for the selection of a caretaker government in Iraq was necessary for the transitional leaders to reach "crystal-clear understandings" of their relationship to the occupation authorities they would replace, as well as the remaining American military forces. The primary purpose of the interim government, as envisaged by Ambassador Brahimi, would be to prepare the nation for elections in 2005.[19]

As if the U.S. did not already confront profoundly difficult political and military challenges in Iraq, the Abu Ghraib prison scandal exploded, shredding any semblance of American credibility. As former U.S. Ambassador to the U.N. Richard Holbrooke observed, "This is the most serious setback for the American military since Vietnam."[20] The diplomatic front was also becoming more complex. With the June 30 handover approaching, France and Russia cautioned that a new S.C. resolution sought by the U.S. must ensure that Iraqis have genuine control over their political future.

Meanwhile, on May 17, another suicide car bombing near an entrance to the CPA headquarters killed the head of the Governing Council and six other civilians. Ezzidin Salim was the second member of the American-appointed Council to be assassinated. "The terrorists who are seeking to destroy Iraq have struck a cruel blow with this vile act today," said Ambassador Bremer. "But they will be defeated."[21]

It was unclear whether Ambassador Bremer's confidence was justified. The deteriorating situation in Iraq increasingly correlated with a progressive diminution of American objectives. Beginning with a grandiose commitment to create a stable and modern democracy that would drive geopolitical change throughout the region, the administration found itself in a frantic scramble to cobble together a viable interim government that would remain dependent for its survival on 130,000 foreign troops. With one month to go before the handover of sovereignty, Ambassador Brahimi finally announced the composition of the interim government. Sheikh Ghazi Al-Yawar, 45, a former civil engineer and member of the Governing Council, was appointed the new Iraqi President. Ayad Allawi, a neurologist and businessman, was named prime minister. Mr. Allawi served as a consultant to the U.N. Development Programme, the World Health Organization and the U.N. Children's Fund. It was also reported that he had been a CIA operative in Iraq.

The proposed sequence for Iraq's transition to democracy called for the establishment of a National Council in July 2004 and for elections in January 2005, followed by the ratification of an Iraqi constitution 10 months later. The plan faces serious obstacles. The goal of the Bush Administration is for roughly 400 U.N. civilians to organize the January elections and for their security to be protected by a new force of roughly 5,000 troops. But nearly two-dozen nations have declined to contribute to the force, suggesting that the U.N. will have to depend on overstretched Coalition troops for protection and transportation.[22]

The new foreign minister, Hoshiyar Zebari, told the S.C. that Baghdad wanted American forces to remain in his country. "I stress that any premature departure of international troops would lead to chaos and the real possibility of a civil war in Iraq," he said.[23]

Israel-Palestine

It was called the Road Map, a negotiating framework that envisioned a two-state solution to the Israeli-Palestinian conflict by 2005. The Road Map was endorsed by the Quartet, a diplomatic coalition made up of the United States, Russia, the European Union and the United Nations. In support of the Road Map, Hamas (aka the Islamic Resistance Movement) and Islamic Jihad declared a "suspension of military operations against the Zionist enemy for three months." On July 1, 2003, Israel Prime Minister Ariel Sharon and the Palestinian Prime Minister at the time, Mahmoud Abbas, made a carefully choreographed public appearance together in Jerusalem to demonstrate their commitment to the Road Map. It thus appeared in the summer of 2003 that a moment of modest possibility had finally arrived in the Middle East peace process.[24]

That moment would soon pass. Critical observers in the diplomatic world expressed skepticism about the Road Map. According to the International Crisis Group, the plan's "various elements lack definition, and each step is likely to give rise to interminable disputes between the two sides. There is no enforcement mechanism, nor an indication of what is to happen if the timetable significantly slips. Even more importantly, it fails to provide a detailed, fleshed-out definition of a permanent status agreement. As such, it is neither a detailed practical blueprint for peace nor even for a cessation of hostilities."[25]

The second factor frustrating the peace process was the Israeli "security wall" being erected in the Occupied Territories, a barrier designed to impede infiltration of Palestinian suicide bombers. Even President Bush, a staunch ally of Prime Minister Sharon, called the wall "a problem."[26] The Bush Administration did not object to the wall's completed northern section, however, which roughly follows the Israeli border that existed before it occupied the West Bank in 1967. It is the central section of the wall that has raised alarm, passing through a swath of territory encompassing a Jewish settlement called Ariel and cutting across Arab communities that the Palestinians regard as essential to any vision of a future independent state.

The Road Map was also derailed by political violence, which resumed in a familiar spiral. On August 12, 2003, two suicide bombers blew themselves up—one in a grocery store near Tel Aviv and another near a West Bank settlement—killing two Israelis. Two days later, Israeli forces killed Mohammed Seder, a leader of Islamic Jihad.[27] On August 19, a Hamas suicide bomber killed 22 Israelis on a Jerusalem bus.

Prime Minister Abbas resigned on September 6. Three hours later, Israel tried to kill Sheikh Ahmed Yassin, the founder and spiritual leader of Hamas, and other leaders of the militant Islamist movement. Three days after that, Hamas struck again, its suicide bombers killing 15 Israelis in two separate attacks in Tel Aviv and Jerusalem. Israel then attacked the home of Mahmoud Zahar, a Hamas political leader, killing his son.[28]

Political commentators noted that internecine rivalries within the Palestinian Authority, coupled with Israeli intransigence, further contributed to the Road Map's collapse. Prime Minister Abbas and Yasser Arafat, the leader of the Palestinian Authority, had a venomous relationship. Mr. Arafat opposed the effort by Prime Minister Abbas to wrest control of the Authority's security forces, as called for in the Road Map. Mr. Arafat perceived this provision of the peace plan to be part of a broader American and Israeli strategy to strip him of power. The Israelis rejected the Road Map's requirement to freeze settlement construction, consequently weakening Mr. Abbas and strengthening Mr. Arafat. Prime Minister Sharon's determination to erect his divisive security wall—swallowing large chunks of Palestinian farmland and extending the barrier into parts of occupied East Jerusalem—further compromised the Road Map's viability. Finally, the Bush Administration, which helped engineer Mr. Arafat's removal from power, never used its leverage with Israel to demonstrate that Mr. Abbas could, in fact, achieve tangible results as a peace partner to Prime Minster Sharon.

While Mr. Abbas was not perceived as a credible negotiating partner to Israel, Mr. Arafat was now perceived as a target. Following a meeting of the Israeli cabinet, a government spokesman announced a dramatic shift in policy: Israel, he said, would "remove" Mr. Arafat, the veteran Palestinian president, "in a manner, and at a time, of its choosing." The threat to exile or assassinate Mr. Arafat was met with outrage by Palestinians. Even Washington distanced itself from Israel's new policy. The S.C. voted on a Syrian-sponsored resolution condemning Israel for its threat, but the U.S. used its veto to block the measure, asserting that the resolution's language was not strong enough in condemning terrorist acts by Palestinian militant groups.[29]

Within weeks, the S.C. was confronted with yet another spectacular terrorist attack. On October 4, 2004, a 29-year-a Palestinian woman—an attorney—detonated a suicide bomb in a Haifa restaurant, killing 19 people. Israel retaliated by attacking an abandoned terrorist training camp in Syria. The air strike was launched on the eve of the 30th anniversary of the Yom Kippur war. It was Israel's first direct attack on Syria, its northern neighbor, since 1973. The message communicated with the air strikes was clear: Syria would be punished for supporting terrorist groups, such as Islamic Jihad, which Israel blamed for the Haifa attack.[30] The S.C. held an emergency session but the U.S. once again threatened to veto because the resolution, proposed by Syria, did not refer to the Haifa suicide attack. U.S. Ambassador to the U.N. John D. Negroponte said Syria was "on the wrong side in the war against terrorism."[31]

Surveying the collateral damage, S.G. Annan declared: "I have repeatedly and consistently condemned all terrorist attacks on Israel as morally wrong and counterproductive for the Palestinian cause and have stressed the obligation of the Palestinian Authority to assume full security responsibility in areas still under its control. In addition, I have urged the Government of Israel to refrain from the excessive and disproportionate use of deadly force in civilian areas and, consistent with international humanitarian law, to take steps to ensure the protection of Palestinian civilians." Mr. Annan acknowledged that "the implementation of the road map has been frozen, and some steps have actually been reversed."[32]

Although the Road Map led nowhere, another vision of a revived peace process emerged, a "virtual" peace accord hammered out by unauthorized Israeli and Palestinian negotiators, Yossi Beilin and Yasir Abed Rabbo. They launched their effort after the sraeli elections of 2001, when Ehud Barak lost to Ariel Sharon. The two men built a broad coalition of support for the virtual accord including, on the Israeli side, members of the Likud, Shinui, Labor and Meretz parties as well as retired government officials, economists and intellectuals. Palestinians supporting their accord included officials from Arafat's Fatah faction, parliamentarians and leading academics.[33]

The virtual agreement resembled the deal Mr. Arafat walked away from in the 2000 Camp David Summit. The Palestinians conceded the so-called "right of return" for several million descendants of Arabs exiled as a result of the U.N. partition plan of 1947. For the Israelis, the price of a peace plan would be the dismantling of varied settlements in the occupied territories and the willingness to make Jerusalem, which Israel claims for itself, a shared capital. While U.S. Secretary of State Colin Powell invited the architects of the peace accord to Washington for further discussions, conservative Israelis criticized the Secretary's gesture of support.[34]

It became clear that Israel favored unilateral action over negotiation. In early February 2004, Prime Minister Sharon disclosed plans to evacuate Israel's 7,500 settlers from Gaza, where they live surrounded by Israeli soldiers among a population of 1.2 million Palestinians.[35] In the West Bank, the Prime Minister would preserve Israeli control over five major settlements encompassing a large proportion of the roughly 230,000 settlers who live in the Occupied Territories. Although Israel has more than 120 settlements in the West Bank, only a handful have been cited as possible candidates for withdrawal under the Sharon plan.[36]

Mr. Sharon's plan was attacked by his own Likud party, which, in a referendum vote, rejected the proposed Gaza withdrawal by a margin of 60 to 40 percent.[37] Less than one week later, however, the Bush Administration announced that it would launch a major American diplomatic effort to persuade skeptical governments in Europe and the Middle East that the Sharon plan represented the only realistic path to peace.[38]

The senior envoys representing the Quartet also offered qualified support. Following a meeting at the United Nations, S.G. Annan, Secretary Powell and the senior envoys of Russia and the European Union said that Prime Minister Sharon's plan "should provide a rare moment of opportunity in the search for peace in the Middle East." While welcoming Israel's stated intent to withdraw from Gaza, the Quartet did not endorse Israeli positions on the future status of the West Bank and Palestinian refugees.[39]

As Prime Minister Sharon moved ahead with his unilateral solution to the Israeli-Palestinian conflict, he also continued the controversial practice of targeted assassination. On March 22, 2004, Israel Defense Forces assassinated Sheikh Ahmed Yassin, a founder of Hamas. Ahmed Qurei, the new Prime Minister of the Palestinian Authority, called the Israeli action "a crazy and very dangerous act—it opens the doors wide to chaos."[40]

In mid-April 2004, a Palestinian suicide bomber in Gaza blew himself up at an industrial park near the crossing to Israel, killing one Israeli security worker and wounding three others. Fewer than five hours later, an Israeli helicopter gunship fired on a car carrying Abdel Aziz Rantisi, the militant Hamas leader who had succeeded Sheikh Yassin. Dr. Rantisi and two others, including a bodyguard, were killed. The Hamas leader, who had given frequent interviews calling for attacks on Israelis, was one of Israel's top targets. Hamas carried out about half of the more than 100 suicide bombings in the previous three-and-half-years of fighting.[41]

On May 19, 2004, Israeli tank fire killed eight Palestinians and wounded dozens more who were protesting military operations in the Rafah refugee camp.[42] Bertrand Ramcharan, the U.N. Acting High Commissioner for Human Rights, called on Israel to "abide by its obligations as an occupying power, to respect international law and to stop immediately the disproportionate use of force in the Gaza Strip."[43] It appeared, however, that the cycle of violence between Israelis and Palestinians would continue.

Lebanon and the Golan Heights

The U.N. Interim Force in Lebanon (UNIFIL) was created in 1978 to confirm the Israeli withdrawal from Lebanon, restore the international peace and security and help the Lebanese Government resume its effective authority in the area.[44] While the mission has presided over a period of relative calm since mid-2002, a significant escalation of hostilities occurred during the summer of 2003. On August 8, Hezbollah launched missiles, mortars and small-arms fire at positions of the Israel Defense Forces (IDF). The IDF retaliated and, for the next two days, the battle escalated.

In addition, after Israel's October air-strike in Syria (see above section), sniper fire was directed from the Lebanese side of the Blue Line,[45] killing an Israeli soldier in an area south of Metulla. On December 9, 2003, the IDF shot and killed two Lebanese civilians carrying rifles who had crossed the Israel side of the Blue Line. On January 19, 2004, Hezbollah fired an anti-tank round at an IDF bulldozer that had crossed the Blue Line into Lebanon, killing one Israeli soldier and wounding another.

According to a January report of the Secretary-General, fighting concluded when an Israeli teenage boy was killed and four civilians were injured, essentially shocking both sides into halting combat.[46] He also noted that UNIFIL would continue to "contribute to the restoration of international peace and security by observing, monitoring and reporting on developments in its area of operation and maintaining liaison with the parties to preserve calm."[47] UNIFIL currently has approximately 2,000 troops and is assisted by some 50 military observers from the U.N. Truce Supervision Organization (see below).[48] At the S.G.'s request, in January 2004, the S.C. extended UNIFIL's mandate until July 31, 2004.[49]

In the Golan Heights, the U.N. Disengagement Observer Force (UNDOF), was formed in 1974 after Israeli and Syrian forces left the region. Today, UNDOF continues to supervise the implementation of the agreement and monitors the cease-fire. The mission has experienced relative calm over the years. That may change, however, if Israel expands its settlements in the Golan Heights, as it has been rumored to be considering.[50] In the past year, UNDOF has witnessed two Israeli violations—a Syrian police officer was killed and another was kidnapped. In addition, Israel carried out an attack on a peaceful Syrian village and destroyed a residential building in the region.

UNDOF has just over 1,000 troops and is assisted by some 80 military observers of the U.N. Truce Supervision Organization as well as 39 international civilian personnel and 93 local civilian staff. Its current mandate is set to expire June 30, 2004.[51]

United Nations Truce Supervision Organization Update

The United Nations Truce Supervision Organization (UNTSO) was the first peacekeeping mission established by the U.N. in 1948. Its military observers remain in the Middle East to monitor cease-fires, supervise armistice agreements, prevent isolated incidents from escalating and assist other U.N. peacekeeping operations in the region. Currently, it assists and cooperates with both UNIFIL in the Israel-Lebanon sector and the U.N. Disengagement Observer Force (UNDOF) in the Golan Heights in the Israel-Syria sector. With 157 military observers, supported by 97 international civilian personnel and 109 local civilian staff, UNTSO is also present in the Egypt-Israel sector in the Sinai and maintains offices in Beirut and Gaza.[52]

Looking Forward

Continuing turmoil and violence appear to be the inevitable prognosis in the Middle East. With regard to Iraq, while the continued presence of U.S. forces seemed assured at the time of this writing, the country's tenuous political future was not. Unless elections are accompanied by a new political compact preserving minority rights in Iraq, democracy is not likely to produce stability. In the endless Israel-Palestine conflict, it appears that Prime Minister Sharon's effort to extricate his country from Gaza will continue to be the dominant political story. In Lebanon and the Golan Heights, it appears that the UNDOF and UNTSO's presence there will almost certainly need to continue.

Looming Conflicts

Adam Godet with the International Crisis Group

Bolivia

Having endured instability for most of its history, Bolivia is once again on edge. The latest trouble began in September 2003, when then President Gonzalo Sanchez de Lozada announced the government's intention to allow multinationals to export Bolivian natural gas to the United States through a Chilean port. The country's impoverished Andean Indian community, already alienated by a sense of economic exclusion, viewed the plan as a means to enrich foreigners and the political elite. They called a general strike and set up roadblocks. The President responded with military force, and days of violent clashes killed more than 80 people. On October 17, with the capital, La Paz, surrounded by tens of thousands of protesting Indians, Mr. Sanchez de Lozada resigned.[1]

The plan to export natural gas was a catalyst for the expression of larger grievances. Bolivia's slow embrace of the free market, beginning more than two decades ago, has been anything but smooth.[2] The vast majority of Bolivians have yet to see the benefits of austerity measures that were prescribed by the United States, World Bank and International Monetary Fund.

Protesters represented a wide range of groups, from trade unionists, farmers and miners to coca growers unhappy with the government's plan to eradicate of most of their crops. Initial anger at the gas export scheme quickly broadened into general hostility toward the President and his perceived commitment to U.S.-backed free-market principles. Protesters called for the nationalization of the natural gas industry, redistribution of income and appropriation of assets from the elite.

Protesters were also angered by the government's intention to use Chilean ports to export the gas. The ports in question belonged to Bolivia before its 1879 war with Chile, and their proposed use ignited nationalist sentiments.[3]

Following President Sanchez de Lozada's resignation, Carlos Mesa, his vice president, took over.[4] But in April 2004, tensions mounted again over the gas issue. To stave off further protests, Mr. Mesa reshuffled his cabinet and announced that a referendum on a modified export plan, routing the pipeline through Peru rather than through Chile, would be held on July 18th.

Protesters, however, remain displeased with Mr. Mesa's policies and have demanded new elections. With the economy in a desperate state and the unions threatening to strike anew, Bolivia may face yet another outbreak of violence.

Nepal

Nepal has suffered political instability for many years. The most recent period followed the 1995 dissolution of the Communist government and consequent insurrection of the Communist Party of Nepal (CPN). The number of people killed in the insurgency is put at about 9,000 since it began in 1996.[5] Generally referred to as "the Maoists," the insurgents' goal is to replace the monarchy of Nepal with a Communist republic.

Successive cease-fires and attempts at talks have failed. On August 17, 2003, after Maoist insistence on a new constitution redefining the role of the king was rejected, rebel leader Comrade Prachanda, whose real name is Pushpan Kamal Dahal, pulled out of the January 2003 truce and a new period of intense violence erupted.[6] The immediate period after the cease-fire saw an average of more than 15 killings per day.[7] The Maoists' strategy moved away from mass attacks on district police and army headquarters to attacks by smaller cells and more widespread urban assassinations of army, police and party officials to tie down security forces in the cities.[8]

The Nepalese government responded by establishing the Unified Security Command. This placed the Nepalese army, whose supreme commander is King Gyanendra, in charge of counter-insurgency operations.[9] On October 31, 2003, the U.S. declared the Maoist rebels a threat to U.S. national security; freezing all of the groups' assets in the U.S. or under any U.S. jurisdiction.[10] Neither the U.S. policies nor the efforts made by the Nepalese government have been successful in ending the violence. The greatest factor galvanizing support for the Maoists and alienating the public from the government has been the Royal Nepalese Army's (RNA) widespread use of indiscriminate violence.[11]

The crisis in Nepal is mainly but not confined to the Maoist insurrection. In May 2002, parliament was dissolved amid political confrontation over extending the state of emergency installed by King Gyanendra.[12] Prime Minister Sher Bahadur Deuba was dismissed in October 2002 and replaced by a royalist[13] and a cabinet of the King's nominees. Despite mounting international pressure for the palace and the political parties to work together, King Gyanendra still appears reluctant to install a genuine all-party government or fully restore the democratic process.[14]

On March 27, 2004, the Nepalese government ruled out any immediate chance of peace talks with Maoist guerrillas and rejected calls by the rebels for U.N. mediation.[15] In April, King Gyanendra announced his intention to hold long-delayed elections by April 2005 but did not set a date. An offer from the King for talks was rejected by the alliance of the five main parties,[16] who called on the royalist government to resign and the King to make a public commitment to follow the advice of the (mainstream) parties.[17] U.N. Secretary-General Kofi Annan has appealed to both sides to take immediate steps to end the violence and has stated that the U.N. stands ready to assist in searching for a solution to the problem.

Sudan (Darfur Region)

At a time when Sudan's 20-plus-year civil war between the government and the south appears to be ending, one of the world's most horrific humanitarian crises has erupted in the western Sudan region of Darfur.

Open warfare broke out in Darfur in early 2003 when the two loosely allied rebel groups, the Sudan Liberation Movement/Army (SLM/SLA) and the Justice and Equality Movement (JEM), attacked military installations. The rebels, who seek an end to the region's chronic economic and political marginalization, also took up arms to protect their communities against a 20-year campaign by government-backed militias recruited among groups of Arab extraction in Darfur and Chad.[18] These "janjaweed" militias have, over the past year, received greatly increased government support to clear civilians from areas considered disloyal. Militia attacks and a scorched-earth government offensive have led to massive displacement and indiscriminate killings, all in breach of Common Article 3 of the 1949 *Geneva Conventions*, which prohibits attacks on civilians.

This new civil war, which risks inflicting irreparable damage on a delicate ethnic balance of millions of people who are uniformly Muslim, is actually a grouping of multiple intertwined conflicts. One is between government-aligned forces and rebels; in a second, government militia raid civilians; and yet a third involves a struggle among Darfur communities themselves. The implications of these conflicts go beyond Darfur's borders, threatening both the entire Sudan and neighboring Chad. The Janjaweed's crimes include raiding villages, killing civilians, raping women, and burning homes and fields in their wake. Human Rights Watch and the U.N. claim that more than 10,000 civilians have been killed, some 100,000 have fled to Chad and nearly 1 million have been internally displaced.

Darfur is now one of the worst humanitarian crises in the world, and the world is finally beginning to take notice. In April 2004, both U.S. President George W. Bush and S.G. Annan called on the Sudanese government to end attacks on civilians in Darfur.[19] *(See Chapter 3 for more details on recent U.N. humanitarian intervention in the Sudan.)*

The growing international outcry over the horrific crimes still taking place in Darfur may force the Sudanese government to end atrocities. Failing this, the international community appears ready to act.

Uganda

The conflict in northern Uganda is producing yet another humanitarian and political crisis for Africa and the world.[20] This crisis is largely the work of the Lords Resistance Army (LRA), a rebel group led by Joseph Kony. Claiming prophetic and spiritual powers, Mr. Kony formed the LRA after the 1986 defeat of Presidents Milton Obote and Tito Okello by forces loyal to Uganda's current leader, Yoweri Museveni.[21] Other than being opposed to President Museveni's government, the LRA insurgency lacks any clear political objective.

For the past 18 years, the LRA has committed gross acts of violence, including abducting children and forcing them to be soldiers of the rebel movement. Abducted girls are forced to be sexual slaves for the leaders of the group.[22] Accounting for an estimated 80 percent of the LRA soldiers, these children are sometimes forced to kill their parents, leaving them no place to return should they try to escape the clutches of the LRA.[23] The actions of the LRA have also forced 1.5 million people from their homes in northern Uganda.[24]

The majority of LRA's attacks have occurred in Northern Uganda, where it is estimated that the group has abducted more than 20,000 children.[25] The Ugandan government has been ineffective in preventing these attacks and, despite the atrocities, there has been no international intervention to date.

A particularly horrific attack on February 21, 2004 did, however, bring the brutality of the conflict to the attention of an international audience. That evening, LRA rebels attacked a refugee camp in northern Uganda, killing more than 300 men, women and children.[26] The attack prompted the prosecutor of the International Criminal Court (ICC) to make the situation in northern Uganda the subject of the Court's first investigation.[27] *(See Chapter 6 for more details.)* It also caused the S.C. to issue a formal condemnation of the LRA along with a statement that the crimes of the LRA "should not remain unpunished."[28] Last but not least, the attack prompted President Museveni to offer to hold peace talks with the LRA, an offer supported by S.G. Annan.[29]

The support of the international community is still needed to put an end to the disaster.

Commentary:
Drug Trade Derails Afghan Reconstruction; Requires International Assistance
Ishtiaq Ahmad

Ironically, since the defeat of the Taliban in late 2001, Afghanistan's illegal drug trade has more than significantly increased. In fact, Afghanistan is currently the world's largest producer of opium and trafficker of heroin. The 2003 Opium Poppy Survey, conducted by the United Nations Office on Drugs and Crime, estimates that the income of opium farmers and drug traffickers in 2003—totaling more than $2.3 billion—was equivalent to more than 50 percent of the country's gross domestic product. In 2004, with Afghanistan's opium production set to reach a record high, the international community must begin to treat drug trade as the country's principal challenge.

The Afghan government's plan to eliminate their production by 2013 seems unrealistic. Thus far, its efforts under United Kingdom supervision have concentrated on building the capacity of government institutions, such as the country's Counter-Narcotics Directorate and Counter-Narcotics Police. While these activities are essential to the long-term fight against drugs, they have not yet had an immediate effect on the amount of opium cultivated or trafficked. Furthermore, opium has the ability to finance not only many of the warlords currently serving in the government, but also the resurgent Taliban and even Al Qaeda. Since the biggest beneficiaries of the drug trade are both partial and total spoilers of the state-building process being led by the U.N. Assistance Mission in Afghanistan (UNAMA), it is crucial to root out the key sources of the trade.

As Ambassador Lakhdar Brahimi stated in his January briefing to the Security Council, the problem can be solved only if achievements are made in other sectors. This means that farmers in poppy-growing provinces, such as Helmand and Nangarhar, need to be provided with more viable sources of livelihood. It also means that tougher law enforcement needs to be adopted. Growing opium has been officially illegal in Afghanistan since 2002, but the current retaliatory measures are not enough to enforce the law. The enforcement of a narcotic drugs law, passed in early 2004, and the planned establishment of a Central Planning Cell for eradication constitute important steps.

Still, more is needed. The International Security Assistance Force and the U.S.-led coalition force need to expand their security agendas beyond counter-insurgency operations. Their fight against insurgent forces will not succeed without a simultaneous military campaign against drug traffickers. It is only by adopting more stringent measures to repress drug traffickers, dismantle heroin labs and destroy terrorists' and warlords' stake in the opium economy that the international community can help Afghanistan's legitimate economy grow and its constitutional processes move forward.

Endnotes

Africa

1. "After a Hard Year, Signs of Rebounding Spirits at the U.N.," *New York Times*, March 8, 2004.
2. Numbers compiled from the U.N. Department of Peacekeeping Operations website.
3. Ibid.
4. "An African Peacekeeping Force: How to Put the House in Order," *Economist*, March 13, 2004.
5. "Donors Pledge $500m Liberia Aid," *BBC News*, February 7, 2004.
6. World Bank News Release ("Burundi: The World Bank Approves Support for Reconstruction," March 18, 2004).
7. "U.N. to Hold Talks on West Africa," *BBC News*, February 12, 2004.
8. "West Africa's New Challenge: Making Peace Pay," *World Bank Group*, March 21, 2004.
9. S/2003/1098 (November 17, 2003).
10. "Armed Convoy to Aid Congolese," *BBC News*, January 28, 2004.
11. S/2004/251, March 25, 2004.
12. Ibid.
13. Ibid, 11.
14. "DR Congo Peacekeepers 'Can Leave,'" *BBC News*, February 9, 2004.
15. "'Coup Attempt' in DR Congo Capital," *BBC News*, March 28, 2004.
16. "The Tragedy of the Cocoa Pod: Rent-Seeking, Land and Ethnic Conflict in Ivory Coast," *Journal of Modern African Studies*, December 2003.
17. For more details on the Linas-Marcoussis Agreement, consult S/2003/374 (March 26, 2003).
18. "Advance Party of U.N. Peacekeepers Arrive in Côte d'Ivoire," *U.N. News Centre*, March 31, 2004.
19. Press Release ("Force Commanders of U.N. Missions to Côte d'Ivoire, Liberia, Sierra Leone Meet in Abidjan").
20. "U.N. Peace Force for Ivory Coast," *BBC News*, February 28, 2004.
21. "Eritrea Gives Condition for Meeting U.N. Envoy," *Sudan Tribune*, April 8, 2004.
22. S/2003/1186 (December 19, 2003) and S/2004/180 (March 5, 2004).
23. S/2004/180 (March 5, 2004).
24. "1st Sector MCC Meeting Held at Mereb Bridge," *UNMEE website*, March 3, 2004.
25. S/Res/1531/2004 (March 12, 2004).
26. "From 'Warlord' to 'Democratic' President: How Charles Taylor Won the 1997 Liberian Elections," *Journal of Modern African Studies*, September 1999.
27. Ibid.
28. S/1997/712 (September 12, 1997).
29. S/Res/1509 (September 19, 2003).
30. S/2004/229 (March 22, 2004).
31. S/2004/228 (March 19, 2004).
32. "Oil: Western Sahara's Future," *BBC News*, March 4, 2003.
33. "Profile: Western Sahara," *BBC News*, February 20, 2004.
34. S/2004/39 (January 19, 2004).
35. "Polisario Releases Moroccan POWs," *BBC News*, September 2, 2003.
36. "Western Sahara Families Reunited," *BBC News*, March 5, 2004.
37. S/Res/1495, July 31, 2003. / "U.N. Agrees Sahara Peace Deal," *BBC News*, (July 31, 2003.)

38. "Africa's Last Colony," *BBC News*, October 21, 2003.
39. U.N. Press Release, April 29, 2004.

The Americas

1. "Insurgents Take Haiti's Second City as Crisis Grows," *New York Times*, February 23, 2004.
2. "Hispaniola Adrift," *Economist*, February 14, 2004.
3. "Violence Spreads in Haiti; Toll Is Put at 41," *New York Times*, February 10, 2004.
4. "Powell, Too, Hints Haitian Should Leave," *New York Times*, February 27, 2004.
5. "The Aristide Resignation: Security Council; U.N. Panel Backs Plan to Aid Haiti With Troops," *New York Times*, March 3, 2004.
6. "After the Fall: Haiti," *Economist*, April 24, 2004.
7. S/Res/1529.
8. Ibid, 5.
9. S/Res/1542 (2004). / "Annan Recommends Proposed U.N. Mission to Haiti Begin Sending Troops," *U.N. News Service*, April 20, 2004.

Asia

1. *Loya Jirga* is a Pashtun phrase meaning "grand council." For centuries, leaders in Afghanistan have convened *Loya Jirgas* to choose new kings, adopt constitutions and decide important political matters. The most recent *Loya Jirga* process was set in motion by the Bonn Agreement of December 5, 2001, that created an interim administration which would lead Afghanistan for two years until a "fully representative government can be elected through free and fair elections."
2. "Flawed Charter for a Land Ruled by Fear," *International Herald Tribune*, January 7, 2004.
3. "Afghan Elections Put Back to September," *Guardian*, March 29, 2004.
4. U.N. Press Release SC/7894, October 13, 2003.
5. "Statement of Mr. Lakhdar Brahimi, Former Special Representative of the Secretary-General for Afghanistan on the Situation in Afghanistan," *U.N. Assistance Mission in Afghanistan*, January 15, 2003.
6. "Official Killed as Strife Grows in Afghanistan," *New York Times*, March 22, 2004.
7. "Elections and Security in Afghanistan," *Asia Briefing, International Crisis Group*, March 30, 2004. / "NATO Agrees to Widen Afghan Force," *Agence France-Press*, October 6, 2003.
8. "Afghan Officials Applaud Widening of ISAF Mandate," *Financial Times*, October 14, 2003.
9. A/58/742-S/2004/230 (March 19, 2004).
10. Ibid.
11. "U.N. Aims to Disarm Afghan Fighters," *Christian Science Monitor*, December 2, 2003. / "Militia Men Give Up Their Arms," *Institute for War and Peace Reporting*, February 18, 2004.
12. "Securing Afghanistan's Future: Accomplishments and the Strategic Path Forward," Afghan Interim Administration, March 17, 2004.
13. A/58/742-S/2004/230.
14. "Afghanistan: One Step Forward, Two Steps Back," *Foreign Policy in Focus*, April 8, 2004.
15. Minister for Foreign Affairs Joint Media Release, December 11, 2003 ("Australian Police for Bougainville," Australia).
16. "Secretary-General Annan Welcomes Dispatch of Regional Transition Team to Bougainville," *U.N. Information Service*, June 17, 2003.

17. UNMOGIP was established in 1949 to supervise the cease-fire between the two countries in the disputed state of Jammu and Kashmir.

18. "List of Pakistan's Proposed CBMs With India," *Daily Times*, October 30, 2003.

19. "Pakistan Declares Cease-fire Along LOC Unilaterally: Willingness to Reopen Khokhrapar Route, Start Srinagar Bus Service and Revive Air Links: PM's Address to the Nation," *Dawn*, November 24, 2003.

20. Ishtiaq Ahmad and Aamir Bashir. "Joint Statement of India and Pakistan, January 6, 2004," *India and Pakistan: Charting a Path to Peace*, Islamabad (Pan-Graphics, 2004).

21. U.N. Press Release SG/SM/9104, January 6, 2004.

22. Ibid.

23. "Kashmir: The View From Islamabad," Asia Report No. 68, International Crisis Group, December 4, 2003.

24. Ibid.

25. "Musharraf Offers Kashmir Pullout," *BBC News website*, December 2, 2003.

26. "India Holds First Talks With Kashmiri Separatists," *Associated Press*, January 22, 2004.

27. "Tajikistan at the Crossroads," *U.N. Integrated Regional Information Networks (IRIN)*, January 5, 2004.

28. "Tajikistan: U.N. Peace-Building Mission Extended," *IRIN*, June 6, 2003.

29. "Human Rights Overview: Tajikistan," *Human Rights Watch*, January 1, 2004.

30. S/2004/117 (2004).

31. Ibid.

32. "East Timor Wants U.N. to Retain Presence," *Reuters*, December 10, 2003.

33. S/2004/117.

Europe

1. UNFICYP Press Release, April 28, 2004 ("Under-Secretary-General Briefs Security Council on Cyprus").

2. The settlement document had been amended three times before, on November 11, 2003, December 10, 2002 and February 26, 2003.

3. The Annan Plan can be found at www.annanplan.org.

4. S/2004/302 ("Report of the Secretary-General to the Security Council," April 16, 2004). / UNFICYP Press Release, April 14, 2004.

5. "Cypriots Facing Deadline on Wednesday in Unity Talks," *New York Times*, March 31, 2004.

6. UNFICYP Press Release, April 2, 2004. / UNFICYP Press Release, April 14, 2004. / UNIFCYP Press Release, April 19, 2004.

7. "Russian Veto Defeats Security Council Draft Resolution on Cyprus," *U.N. News Centre*, April 21, 2004.

8. "Greek Cypriots Help to North," *Financial Times*, April 26, 2004. / AKEL is a Greek Cypriot party that had traditionally been moderate regarding reunification. / "So Close and Yet So Far," *Economist*, April 23, 2004. / "Both Cypriot Leaders Reject Unification Plan," *Washington Post*, April 9, 2004. / "A Chance for Peace and Unity Wasted," *Economist*, April 27, 2004.

9. "E.U. Hits at Perceived Ban From Greek Cypriot TV," *Financial Times*, April 20, 2004.

10. "Greek Cypriots Reject a U.N. Peace Plan," *New York Times*, April 25, 2004.

11. S/2003/572 ("Report of the Secretary-General to the Security Council," May 27, 2003).

12. "Country Report: Cyprus," *Economist Intelligence Unit*, March 2004.

13. "An Ominous European Debut," *Economist*, May 1, 2004.
14. "The Loser Takes All," *New Statesman*, May 3, 2004.
15. "A Chance for Peace and United Wasted," *Economist*, April 27, 2004.
16. After two failed cease-fire agreements, in July 1993 and May 1994, Abkhazia and Georgia signed the Agreement on a Cease-Fire and Separation of Forces, which established a peacekeeping force made up of Commonwealth of Independent States (CIS) soldiers.
17. Tbilisi is the capital of Georgia and Sukhumi is the capital of Abkhazia.
18. S/2003/751 (2003). Note: The three working groups established as an outcome of the bilateral meetings will focus on railways, rehabilitation of the Inguri hydroelectric plant and return of IDPs to the Gali region, from whence many of the ethnic Georgians fled following the conflict.
19. S/2003/1019 (2003).
20. S/2004/315 (2004).
21. Ibid. / S/2003/1019 (2003).
22. S/2004/315 ("Report of the Secretary-General to the Security Council," April 20, 2004).
23. Interview with Cory Welt, *Center for Strategic and International Studies*, April 21, 2004.
24. Statement by Georgian President Mikhail Saakashvili at the Council on Foreign Relations' Russell C. Leffingwell Lecture in New York City, February 26, 2004.
25. "After the Revolution," *London Review of Books*, March 4, 2004.
26. Statement by Georgian Prime Minister Zurab Zhvania at the Center for Strategic and International Studies Statement's Forum in Washington, D.C., April 26, 2004.
27. "Country Report: Georgia," *Economist Intelligence Unit*, February 2004.
28. Ibid, 24.
29. Ibid, 25.
30. "A Rose Among Thorns: Georgia Makes Good," *Foreign Affairs*, March/April 2004.
31. "Georgia: What Now?," *International Crisis Group*, December 3, 2003.
32. Ibid, 23.
33. "NATO's Kosovo Dream Is Dead," *Financial Times*, March 27-28, 2004. / According to an April 22, 2004 ICG report, the violence was not masterminded by any one group, but rather "a vortex which different radical, extremist and criminal structures poured in and out of, an impromptu marketplace of violence to which each brought their wares and found their niche."
34. SC/8056 ("Security Council Briefing," April 13, 2004).
35. S/PV.4886 ("Security Council Briefing," December 17, 2003).
36. "Thessaloniki and After III: The E.U. and Serbia, Montenegro and Kosovo," *International Crisis Group*, June 20, 2003.
37. Ibid, 33.
38. S/PV.4770 ("Security Council Briefing," June 10, 2003).
39. S/2003/675 ("Report of the Secretary-General to the Security Council," June 26, 2003).
40. "Kosovo: U.N. Lays Down Conditions," *Institute for War & Peace Reporting website*, 2004.
41. Mr. Holkeri resigned May 25, 2004.
42. S/2004/71 ("Security General's Report to the Security Council," January 26, 2004).
43. "Kosovo: New Criminal Codes Come into Force in U.N.-administered Province," UNMIK, April 6,
44. Ibid, 33. / NATO had 50,000 forces in Kosovo at the end of the war. / "U.N.

Envoy to Kosovo Holds Talks With Leader of Serbia and Montenegro," *UNMIK website*, April 2004.

45. "Collapse in Kosovo," *International Crisis Group*, April 22, 2004.
46. Ibid, 40 and 41. / S/PV.4853 ("Security Council Briefing," October 30, 2003). / S/PV.4728 ("Security Council Briefing," July 3, 2003). Note: An estimated 130,000 Kosovo Serbs fled Kosovo at the end of the NATO bombing in June 1999.
47. Ibid, 36. / "Country Profile: Serbia and Montenegro," *Economist Intelligence Unit*, 2003.
48. Pakistan has been the most vocal critic of the standards process in the Security Council, calling the standards unrealistic.

Middle East

1. President Bush's remarks on the end of major combat, *White House*, May 2, 2003.
2. "The Best Laid Plans? How Turf Battles and Mistakes in Washington Dragged Down the Reconstruction of Iraq," *Financial Times*, August 4, 2003.
3. "U.S. Plans to Reduce Forces in Iraq, With Help of Allies," *New York Times*, May 3, 2004.
4. "U.S. Set to Name Civilian to Oversee Iraq," *New York Times*, May 2, 2003.
5. "Two Gone and One to Go," *Economist*, July 24, 2003.
6. *International Crisis Group*. / Iraq Country Profile, *BBC News*.
7. "Five Penalized by U.N. Chief in Iraq Bombing," *New York Times*, March 30, 2004.
8. "After a Hard Year, Signs of Rebounding Spirits at the U.N.," *New York Times*, March 8, 2004.
9. "Annan Calls for Reform," *BBC News*, September 23, 2003.
10. "Unanimous Vote by U.N.'s Council Adopts Iraq Plan," *New York Times*, October 17, 2003.
11. "There Must Be Some Way Out," *Economist*, November 13, 2003.
12. "The Keeper of Iraq's Keys: Man in the News Ali Sistani," *Financial Times*, November 15, 2003.
13. "Bremer's Statement in Full," *BBC News*, December 14, 2003.
14. "Whodunnit?," *Economist*, January 29, 2004.
15. "At Least 143 Die in Attacks at 2 Sacred Sites in Iraq," *New York Times*, March 3, 2004.
16. "Iraq Council, With Reluctant Shiites, Sign Charter," *New York Times*, March 9, 2004.
17. "Shiite Ayatollah is Warning U.N. Against Endorsing Charter Sponsored by U.S.," *New York Times*, March 23, 2004.
18. "U.N. Is Wary of Dangers in Taking Lead Role in Iraq," *New York Times*, April 18, 2004.
19. "U.N. Envoy Seeks New Iraq Council By Close of May," *New York Times*, April 28, 2004.
20. "They've Apologized. Now What?," *New York Times*, May 9, 2004.
21. "Iraqi Council Leader is Killed in Blast Near U.S. Headquarters," *New York Times*, May 17, 2004.
22. "U.S. Faces Growing Fears of Failure," *Washington Post*, May 20, 2004.
23. "U.N. Names Group to Organize January Elections in Iraq," *Reuters*, June 4, 2004.
24. "One Step at a Time," *Economist*, July 3, 2003.
25. ICG Middle East Report No. 14, May 2, 2003.
26. "Israel's Wall Threatens to Wipe Palestinian Village Off the Map," *Financial Times*, July 29, 2003.

27. "Call This a Ceasefire?," *Economist*, August 15, 2003.
28. "Progressing to a Bloody Dead End," *Economist*, September 11, 2003.
29. "Arafat in Their Sights," *Economist*, September 17, 2003.
30. "Israeli Frustration Versus Syrian Impotence," *Economist*, October 9, 2003.
31. "Another Yom Kippur, Another Conflict," *Economist*, October 10, 2003.
32. A/58/416-S/2003/947 ("Report of the Secretary-General," October 10, 2003.
33. "An Accord to Remember," *New York Times*, December 1, 2003.
34. "Blessed Are the Peacemakers," *Economist*, December 4, 2003.
35. "Sharon's Gaza Gambit," *Economist*, February 5, 2004.
36. "Sharon Promises to Retain 5 Big Settlements in West Bank," *New York Times*, April 13, 2004.
37. "Political Setback Prompts Sharon to Alter Gaza Pullout Plan," *New York Times*, May 3, 2004.
38. "Bush Seeks World Support for Sharon Withdrawal Plan," *New York Times*, May 8, 2004.
39. "Quartet Tentatively Backs Sharon Gaza Plan," *New York Times*, May 4, 2004.
40. Has the Death of the Sheikh Really Changed Anything?," *Economist*, March 25, 2004.
41. "Leader of Hamas Killed by Israel in Missile Attack," *New York Times*. April 18, 2003.
42. "Palestinians: Israel Fired on Demo," *CBS News*, May 19, 2004.
43 U.N. Press Release ("Acting Rights Chief Deeply Disturbed by Recent Israeli Actions in Gaza," May 21, 2004).
44. *DPKO website*.
45. In May 2000, IDF dismantled and evacuated southern Lebanon, where it had retained control since the 1980s. Shortly thereafter, Hezbollah forces, Lebanese civilians and security forces flooded into the area, but stopped short of the line of withdrawal—the so-called "Blue Line."
46. S/2004/50 ("Report of the Secretary-General on the United Nations Interim Force in Lebanon," January 20, 2004.
47. Ibid.
48. Ibid, 44.
49. A/Res/58/1525.
50. E.U. Press Release, Presidency Statement on Golan Heights.
51. Ibid, 44.
52. Ibid, 44.

Looming Conflicts

1. "Five Protestors Die in Bolivia After President Calls in Troops," *New York Times*, October 13, 2003.
2. Country Report: Bolivia, *Economist Intelligence Unit*, March 2004.
3. "Fresh Anger Over Bolivia Gas Plan," *BBC News*, April 16, 2004.
4. "Bolivian Leader Resigns and His Vice President Steps In," *New York Times*, October 18, 2003.
5. *Nepal: Dangerous Plans for Village Militias, ICG Asia Briefing*, February 17, 2004.
6. Ibid.
7. "Nepal Sliding Deeper Into Violence as Maoist Clashes Escalate," *Agence France-Presse*, November 4, 2003.
8. "Nepal: Back to the Gun," *ICG Asia Briefing*, October 22, 2003.
9. Ibid, 7.

10. "U.S. Declares Nepalese Maoists a National Security Threat, Freezes Assets," *Agence France-Presse*, October 31, 2003.
11. *Nepal Backgrounder: Ceasefire – Soft Landing or Strategic Pause?*, ICG Asia Report, April 10, 2003.
12. King Gyanendra came to power after the June 1, 2001 murder of King Birendra and other close relatives by Crown Prince Dipendra, who then shot himself.
13. Lokendra Bahadur Chand, who resigned in May 2003, was replaced by another royalist, Surya Bahadur Thapa.
14. Ibid, 8.
15. "Nepal Says No Chance Soon of Peace Talks With Maoists," *Agence France-Presse*, March 27, 2004.
16. For a review of these parties, see Ibid, 7.
17. "Nepal's Main Parties Reject King's Offer of Talks," *Reuters*, April 23, 2004.
18. "Darfur Rising: Sudan's New Crisis," *International Crisis Group*, Africa Report No. 76, March 25, 2004.
19. "International Community Must be Ready to Act in Sudan," *Agence France-Presse*, April 7, 2004.
20. "Q&A: Uganda's Northern Rebellion," *BBC News*, February 23, 2004.
21. "Profile: Uganda's LRA Rebels," *BBC News*, Feburary 6, 2004.
22. "Uganda's Shell-Shocked Children," *Toronto Star*, August 10, 2003.
23. "Security Council Condemns Rebel Group's Atrocities Against Children in Uganda" *U.N. News Service*, April 14, 2004.
24. Ibid.
25. "Profile: Uganda's LRA Rebels," *BBC News*, February 6, 2004.
26. "Trying Times in Uganda," *Diplomat*, April 5, 2004.
27. Ibid.
28. Press Release SC/8057, AFR/900.
29. "Annan Welcomes Ugandan President's Offer to Hold Peace Talks With Rebel Group," *U.N. News Service*, April 16, 2004.

Tracking Weapons, Terrorism & Drug Trafficking in an Age of Proliferation

Jonathan Dean and Thomas E. McNamara
with Consuelo Remmert

We will not tolerate WMD proliferation. We will not acquiesce to it. And we certainly will not reward it. We will not put our people at risk as a result of this kind of activity. It is a matter of sad necessity that both proliferation and terrorism hold a share of the definition of our age. But we must not let these dangers dominate that definition.

— U.S. Secretary of State Colin Powell,
Princeton University, February 20, 2004.

O ver the course of latter 2003 and early 2004, the world has witnessed the capture of Saddam Hussein and the resumption of bloody conflict in Iraq, especially in the central Sunni area. Some level of armed conflict seems likely to continue for some time to come.

No weapons of mass destruction (WMD) were found in Iraq after a costly search involving thousands of military personnel and expenditure of nearly $1 billion; it seems increasingly probable that the bulk of Iraqi WMD were destroyed after the first Gulf War to avoid United Nations inspectors. Furthermore, the United States Administration has yet to resolve three key problems that have dogged the occupation of Iraq from the very outset: insufficient forces to maintain public order, Iraqi nationalist resentment of foreign military occupation and lack of broader support from the international community. The Bush Administration, unwilling to share power with others, has kept the U.N. at arm's length. Despite this, the U.N. provided vital help on preparing for Iraqi elections and on appointing a caretaker regime to succeed the ineffective Iraqi Governing Council, but the new Iraqi government will have considerable difficulty in preparing elections for January 2005.

Outside Iraq, the nonproliferation regime continued to dangerously decline during the past year. Not only were two fruitless rounds of six-power talks held on North Korea—whose nuclear threats became even more explicit—but also further revelations of Iranian activities almost certainly directed toward the production of nuclear weapons became available, along with news of scientist A.Q. Khan's nuclear black market activity in Pakistan. Last but not least, Libya admitted to its chemical, biological and nuclear weapons activities. The nonproliferation regime is in urgent need of repair. Two U.N. institutions, the Security Council and the International Atomic Energy Agency (IAEA), are deeply involved.

This chapter describes and analyzes these startling developments. It also discusses U.N. activities to combat terrorism, illicit drug demand and cultivation and tells the fascinating story of how U.N. sanctions brought Libya's Muammar el-Qadaffi to renounce his weapon programs.

Iraq – A Year of Continuing Crisis

Jonathan Dean

The year since President George W. Bush declared the end of major hostilities in Iraq on May 1, 2003 has been one of recurrent resistance by Iraqi insurgents and continuing bloodshed on both sides despite the capture of Saddam Hussein on December 13, 2003. The U.S. Administration moved toward its June 30, 2004 deadline for transfer of sovereign authority to an as yet unnamed Iraqi political authority, whose main figures were appointed in early June. Some economic progress was made: restored exports of Iraqi oil netted $7.5 billion in 2003 for the Iraqi people, although few appeared aware of it.[1] Intensive searching in Iraq for stocks of WMD failed to find any evidence that they existed. This led to heavy criticism of the Bush Administration, whose main justification for invading Iraq was the claim that Iraq was a threat to the U.S. and the entire Mideast because of its large WMD arsenal. Discussion and evaluation led to the conclusion that Western intelligence on WMD in Iraq, dominated by U.S. intelligence services, had been of extremely low quality. This outcome also led to the formation of commissions in the U.S. and United Kingdom to investigate and recommend changes in the intelligence services of both countries. Success was only modest for continuing administration efforts to broaden the base of support both internationally and within Iraq for the Coalition Provisional Authority (CPA), composed of the United States, its allies and the Iraqi Governing Council, which has 25 representatives of various Iraqi ethnic and religious groups, designated by the CPA.

The effort to gain broader international support for the occupation of Iraq led to recurrent efforts by the U.S. Administration to engage the United Nations. These were frustrated by the August 19, 2003 bombing of the U.N. compound in Iraq and its aftermath, and also by the continuing reluctance of the Administration to share its authority in Iraq. However, as the time for transfer of authority came closer, the administration appeared increasingly dependent on the success or failure of U.N. Special Adviser Lakhdar Brahimi's efforts to form a provisional Iraqi government, which would rule until nationwide elections could be held, hopefully, by the end of January 2005.

Security

Establishing security in Iraq is—and must be—the primary objective of

CPA forces. A year after President Bush declared on May 1, 2003 that major combat operations in Iraq were over, this objective had not been achieved. In April 2004, CPA forces were simultaneously faced with heavy fighting in Fallujah, a center of Sunni resistance, and in the Shia areas of southern Iraq where militia forces of Shia leader Moktada al-Sadr controlled several cities, especially Najaf. Coalition forces were also confronted with the possibility that these two hostile groups might join forces in a united front against the United States. On the other hand, if these two crises could be resolved, this might open the road to improved security throughout Iraq.

Casualties

As of May 1, 2004, 736 U.S. servicemen and servicewomen had been killed in Iraq since March 20, 2003 when hostilities began, 617 of them since the May 1, 2003 announcement of the end of hostilities. Fifty-nine U.K. and 51 Coalition soldiers have died. U.S. wounded totaled 3,466. One-hundred-fifty United Nations employees, international aide personnel and foreign contractors have been killed, plus 24 journalists. Iraqi deaths, both military and civilian, as of May 1, 2004, were estimated between 11,000 and 15,000; about two-thirds were estimated to be combat deaths. These figures will increase. Iraqi prisoners of U.S. forces in Iraq were estimated at about 8,000 in May 2004. A large number of them were held at the Abu Ghraib prison complex near Baghdad, where extensive physical abuse of prisoners by U.S. personnel was reported in the press at the end of April 2004, with highly negative impact on public opinion throughout the world.[2]

Almost at the moment that President Bush was declaring on May 1, 2003 aboard the U.S.S. Abraham Lincoln that the operational phase of fighting in Iraq was over, U.S. forces fired on a demonstration in the town of Fallujah, one of the strongholds of pro-Saddam Hussein sentiment in the area that has come to be known as the "Sunni triangle." The same city was under outright siege by U.S. forces a year later.[3] In the same period, just after the end of operations against Iraqi armed forces, al-Sadr organized a large Shia demonstration in Baghdad, demanding that the CPA surrender power to an elected Iraqi government, with election candidates to be selected by Shia clergy. A year later, al-Sadr's militia forces were besieged in Najaf and Baghdad. On May 7, 2003, the U.S. military commander in Iraq, Army Lt. General David D. McKiernan, reported that a widespread, organized insurgency of pro-regime elements in Iraq had emerged.[4] U.S. forces had moved so rapidly through Iraq in the face of token Iraqi resistance that they had not paused to capture or disarm the Iraqi armed forces, nor had they established order in Baghdad or other population centers.

In mid-May 2003, President Bush appointed L. Paul Bremer, a former foreign service assistant of Secretary of State Henry Kissinger, as Chief U.S. Civilian Administrator in Iraq. Contrary to Ambassador Bremer's intentions, his early actions compounded the security problem in Iraq: He moved rapidly to purge senior members of Hussein's Ba'th Party from leading government positions and completely dissolved the 400,000-strong Iraqi armed forces, also permitting its members to keep their weapons. Both actions were categorical; Ambassador Bremer did not place either Ba'th Party members or military personnel in categories of lesser offenders or rank-and-file members who might be useful to the 150,000-man occupation forces in governing a country of 25 million. These steps, which were substantially revised a year later, have since been strongly criticized as major errors.[5] Ambassador Bremer did initiate training of a new Iraqi army scheduled to reach 40,000 men after two years. However, initial deployment of these units in Fallujah a year later was premature and disastrous.

In mid-July 2003, U.S. forces killed Hussein's two sons, Uday and Qusay, after a fierce firefight in the city of Mosul. Also in July, the U.S. Defense Department increased U.S. forces available for service in Iraq by extending the average tour of duty from six months to one year, the deployment period used for the Vietnam War. The Pentagon's plan was based on the assumption, which was not fulfilled, that three multinational divisions could be recruited for Iraq.[6]

One of the heaviest post-war blows suffered by the Coalition was the August 19, 2003 suicide attack by a cement-mixer truck packed with explosives on the U.N. compound in Baghdad. The attack killed 22 people, including Sergio Vieira de Mello, special representative of the Secretary-General in Iraq. It was the deadliest attack on the U.N. in its history and an additional shock because it meant that Iraqi insurgents would direct their attacks not only at Coalition soldiers, but also at the United Nations, relief organizations and nongovernmental organizations (NGOs). Following the attack, the U.N. withdrew most of its staff, as did the Red Cross and other NGOs.[7] Withdrawals increased after a suicide car bombing at Red Cross headquarters in October 2003.

The August bombing again raised questions of whether the U.S. forces were numerous enough to create secure conditions in Iraq. Roadside bombings using improvised explosive charges, originally an innovation, increased in number around Baghdad and in the Sunni triangle during Fall 2003 and continued. In September, the commander of U.S. forces in the area said that he was no longer counting on foreign forces to relieve U.S. forces in Iraq and that this fact would require the U.S. to call up reserves and deploy Marines for peacekeeping duty. At the time, non-U.S. Coalition forces consisted of two light divisions, totaling about 20,000 men, one of U.K. forces and the other under Polish command. They have not increased significantly since.[8]

A positive development for the CPA government and forces finally came on December 13, 2003, when U.S. troops were led by an informant to a decrepit farmhouse about 10 miles from Saddam Hussein's home city of Tikrit. There, they captured Hussein hiding in a hole dug under the floor. President Bush promptly announced that he would be tried in Iraq.[9]

Suicide bombing attacks continued in January and February 2004, with attacks increasingly aimed at Iraqi police and also at Ambassador Bremer himself.[10] Despite these ongoing attacks, the U.S. Central Command in Qatar announced in January that 130,000 U.S. troops would be withdrawn from Iraq and replaced by 105,000 troops. The new contingent would include nearly 40,000 personnel from the U.S. National Guard and Reserves. These inexperienced forces would replace more experienced troops on occupation duty with little overlap to pass on know-how. This unwise decision was reversed within four months.

After terrorist bombs on four suburban trains in Madrid killed an estimated 200 people on March 11, 2004, President José Maria Aznar, faulted for having tried to pin the blame for the bombings on the Basque ETA instead of on the Islamic extremists who were rapidly identified as the bombers, was voted out of office and replaced by a Socialist. Leaders of the new government said they would withdraw Spanish Coalition troops (about 1,300) from Iraq. Honduras and the Dominican Republic also withdrew their small contingents.

In addition to the United States, other countries contributing troops in Iraq, as of mid-March 2004, were: United Kingdom-8,200; Italy-3,000; Poland-2,500; Ukraine-1,650; The Netherlands-1,307; Spain-1,300; Australia-850; Romania-500; Thailand-451; Denmark-410; Honduras-370, and a total of 3,722 in small contingents contributed by 25 other Coalition countries.[11] In Baghdad, the CPA began to try to compensate for inadequate troop strength by hiring private security forces to protect the Green Zone. By April 2004, these personnel, as well as representatives of foreign companies involved in reconstruction, had become targets of insurgent attacks and hostage-taking.

Suicide bombing of Shia shrines in Baghdad and Karbala on March 2, 2004 raised the specter of civil war in Iraq between majority Shia Iraqis and the Sunni minority favored by Saddam Hussein.[12] But subsequent developments brought the opposite outcome.

In early April 2004, American forces opened a heavy attack on the Sunni stronghold of Fallujah, where insurgents had killed four American contract security employees and publicly burned their bodies. At the same time, the CPA closed the Baghdad newspaper of al-Sadr, who had been baiting the American occupation from its outset, and issued a warrant for his arrest. Al-Sadr retired to the Shia city of Najaf in southern Iraq and heavy fighting broke out there as a result. This unfortunate chain of events brought spontaneous expressions of mutual support from Shias and Sunnis, uniting them in opposition to the United States, at least for the time being. To compound the problem, a battalion of the newly formed Iraqi army refused to move into support positions in Fallujah, casting serious doubt on the value of the newly formed force.

The U.S. military command announced that the already-formed Iraqi armed forces would be retrained and that former officers of Saddam Hussein's Iraqi armed forces would be recruited to command positions. Ambassador Bremer also revised his blanket exclusion of Ba'th Party members, now permitting former Party members not accused of major offenses to take positions in government departments or the new armed forces. On April 9, 2004,

General John Abizaid, chief of U.S. Central Command, said he would hold several U.S. units in Iraq beyond their planned redeployment dates. And in early May, the Pentagon announced that it planned to keep as many as 138,000 U.S. troops in Iraq through 2005 and that it was also increasing shipments of tanks and armored vehicles that had been left behind when lightly armed U.S. units carried out their blitz attack on Iraq. Shia militias in the south seized about 40 foreign workers from a dozen countries. Russia, Ukraine, France and Germany urged their citizens to leave Iraq.[13]

As the spring drew on, Iraqi negotiators were busy in both Sunni-controlled Fallujah and Shia-controlled Najaf. Decisive developments on security in Iraq appeared to be in the making. The end of April brought the first fruits of this consultation: U.S. marines withdrew to the periphery of Fallujah and their place was taken by a Sunni militia force, the Fallujah Protection Army, headed by former officers of the Iraqi Army.[14]

Governance

After taking over as Chief Administrator, reporting to the U.S. Department of Defense and heading the CPA, Ambassador Bremer presented a multi-step plan for returning sovereignty to Iraqis that was designed to maximize Iraqi participation at each stage. The steps included: (1) a national convention in July 2003 that would select an interim government; (2) elections in mid-2004 for members of a constitutional convention; and (3) a national referendum to approve the constitution, national political elections and transfer of sovereignty to an independent Iraq. Ambassador Bremer moved rapidly on July 13, 2003 to appoint a Governing Council of 25 people, most of them political refugees from the Hussein regime, to start this process.

However, it proved impossible to create sufficient agreement among the main Iraqi factions—Shias, Sunnis and Kurds. To create the impression of progress, in particular, Shia Iraqis, whose views were often voiced by a prominent cleric, Ayatollah Ali Al-Sistani, sought energetically to rapidly translate the numerical Shia majority in the Iraqi population to majority political power in the new government. They demanded immediate elections for this purpose. In February 2004, U.N. Representative Brahimi visited Iraq in order to deflect Shia pressures for immediate elections and declared that elections for a transitional government before June 30, 2004 were not feasible.

By March 2004, Ambassador Bremer's plan had been reduced to two steps, agreement by the Governing Council on an interim constitution and transfer of sovereignty to an Iraqi provisional government on June 30, 2004. The interim constitution, drafted by the Iraqi Governing Council with important inputs from the Coalition Provisional Authority, was approved on March 8, 2004. It established a transitional period in two phases. The first phase shall begin with the formation of a fully sovereign Iraqi Interim Government that takes power on June 30, 2004 (Article 2B). The new Iraqi government is to arrange elections by the end of January 2005. The National Assembly elected in those elections will be responsible for drafting a permanent constitution to be approved by popular referendum no later than October 15, 2005. Elections for a new government under this constitution are supposed to be held by the end of 2005.

It seemed unlikely that all these deadlines would be maintained. When Ayatollah Sistani vetoed Ambassador Bremer's caucus idea as an inadequate substitute for immediate elections that would reflect the true composition of the Iraqi electorate and its Shia majority, the administration once again called on the U.N. to rescue it from its difficult position. Ambassador Brahimi returned to Baghdad in April 2004 for a series of consultations with Iraqi political leaders. While there, he ruled out the idea of expanding the Governing Council because of lack of public support and instead suggested the designation by the United Nations, with advice from the CPA, the Governing Council and others, of a government of non-political experts or "technocrats" who could administer the country on an interim basis until elections could be held. This government, with limited authority, would be assisted by a council of 100 notables from all parts of the country, and by a separate eight-person Iraqi election commission, backed by a strong U.N. team, which would prepare elections. There were complaints from Sunni, Shia and Governing Council representatives. Appointment of the new transitional government made evident the failure of the Coalition-designated Governing Council to gain public support after a year of effort and replaced it with a mainly U.N.-designated body. These problems will almost certainly remain.[15]

In further developments in April 2004, the U.S. indicated that much of the interim constitution would be suspended during the period of the interim government. The U.S. also announced that John D. Negroponte, U.S. permanent representative to the United Nations, would take over as U.S. ambassador in Baghdad heading an embassy of 3,000, replacing Ambassador Bremer, with responsibility shifting from the Pentagon to the State Department. Ambassador Brahimi announced that the interim leadership of Iraq would consist of a president and two vice presidents (assuring Sunni, Shia and Kurdish representation), as well as a prime minister. In the end, the Governing Council showed surprising resilience and, in effect, successfully pushed through its candidates for president and prime minister over those backed by both Ambassador Brahimi and Bremer.[16]

The Search for WMD

While the security situation in Iraq erupted in continuing violence and the Coalition Provisional Authority plan to hand over power to the Iraqis was curtailed, the hunt for the weapons of mass destruction in Iraq continued. The first disconfirming information came early on, when the operations of the 75th Exploitation Task Force, the group directing all U.S. search efforts for WMD in Iraq, were closed down in June 2003 and the group left Iraq without finding any weapons. Highly vocal criticism of the invasion of Iraq emerged from Prime Minister Tony Blair's Labor Party and from Democratic leaders in the United States. By August, the U.S. Administration's new chief weapons hunter, David Kay, who had worked as a U.N. inspector and headed a 1,400 survey team in Iraq, reported to Congress that his team's efforts had been inconclusive. In October, Mr. Kay stated that his group had found no nuclear, chemical or biological weapons in Iraq and that while Iraq had been working to acquire chemical and biological weapons and had various missile programs, it had only a rudimentary nuclear program. He supported the administration's request for an additional $600 million to finance a further search of six to nine months.

However, in December 2003, Mr. Kay notified administration officials he planned to resign. On January 23, 2004, CIA Director George Tenet appointed Charles Duelfer, also a former U.N. weapons inspector, to succeed Mr. Kay. Freed from constraints by his resignation, Mr. Kay told *Reuters* on that same day that he did not think the Iraqi weapons stockpiles claimed by the Bush Administration existed or that there had been a large-scale Iraqi production effort in the 1990s.[17]

In an interview on January 24, 2004, Secretary of State Colin Powell defended his dramatic February 5, 2003 speech to the U.N. Security Council claiming extensive WMD in Iraq and said the speech had been based on "what our intelligence community believed was credible." However, Mr. Kay repeated his criticisms in interviews and testimony. Then, U.N. Chief Inspector Hans Blix, touring the U.S. to introduce his new book, Disarming Iraq, added to the fray, commenting that the Bush Administration had a set mind about Iraqi weapons and ignored evidence to the contrary. On January 30, members of the House and Senate intelligence committees backed Mr. Kay's criticism of U.S. intelligence on Iraq, saying that the CIA had relied too heavily on outdated intelligence. Meanwhile, Prime Minister Blair launched an official inquiry into U.K. intelligence on Iraq in February.

These developments pushed a reluctant President Bush to name a seven-member commission to investigate U.S. intelligence operations. By establishing these commissions, both the U.K. and U.S. governments in effect confirmed the claim that their prewar intelligence on Iraqi WMD activities had been inaccurate. Mr. Duelfer said he was now seeking information not on existing WMD stocks, but on whether Saddam Hussein might have been planning to develop a capacity to produce biological and chemical weapons at short notice.[18]

The Economic Side

From the outset, Ambassador Bremer has claimed that solid progress was being made in restoring Iraq's economy, that most of Iraq was peaceful and that insurgents numbered only a few thousand at most. But most of the positive news was drowned out by attacks on Coalition troops. The United Nations, World Bank and CPA estimated Iraq's reconstruction needs for 2004 would be around $55 billion. The U.S. pledged more than $17 billion from an $87 billion Congressional appropriation for Iraq and Afghanistan. A donors' conference in Madrid raised pledges of about $4 billion. However, the donors insisted that contributions be paid not to the CPA but to a separate fund administered by the U.N. and the World Bank. The CPA announced on April 13, 2004 that it had deposited $7.54 billion in proceeds from Iraqi oil export sales in its Development Fund for Iraq since the March 2003 invasion. This high figure suggests relative success in restoring the Iraqi oil industry in spite of numerous acts of sabotage.

The Iraqi Governing Council announced in September 2003 that foreigners would be permitted to buy up to 100 percent ownership in Iraqi businesses, except for oil resources, and that foreign banks would be permitted to buy into Iraqi banks. To raise revenue for the government, a 5 percent reconstruction surcharge would be levied on all goods except humanitarian goods brought into Iraq. Active negotiation by former Secretary of State James Baker succeeded in reducing or postponing Iraq's large external debt, estimated at $350 billion. The Bush Administration created considerable ill will by declaring that it would award reconstruction contracts in Iraq only to governments that had supplied forces for the Coalition army in Iraq.[19]

In terms of actual reconstruction, the U.S. Agency for International Development reported that Iraq surpassed pre-war levels of electricity by October 2003, and that it had rebuilt major bridges, reopened airports, expanded telephone service, renovated more than 2,300 schools and helped the Iraqi Central Bank carry out a currency exchange. However, in late April 2004, it was revealed by the CPA that, seven months after the U.S. Congress had appropriated more than $18 billion for reconstruction in Iraq, only $1 billion had actually been spent; the reason was the ongoing poor security situation and bureaucratic fumbling. Surprisingly, in a February 2004 poll, 57 percent of Iraqis said life was better for them now than before the war. Not surprisingly, 64 percent described regaining public security as the primary goal for Iraq in the coming year.[20]

Overall, the costs to the U.S. Treasury of the engagement in Iraq were very large. Congress approved a $79 billion bill in the spring of 2003 to pay war costs. In September 2003, President Bush asked for an additional $87 billion for Iraq and Afghanistan for fiscal year 2005. And in early May 2004, the administration requested a supplementary appropriation of $25 billion for U.S. forces in Iraq, which were at a higher level than had been originally planned. It was indicated that further supplemental appropriation of about $50 billion would be requested by February 2005. In the past year, the U.S. defense budget has increased to more than $400 billion. Many forecasts estimate that U.S. forces will continue in Iraq at least into 2006 at very high costs for personnel, family separation allowances and for munitions and equipment.

Iraq and the United Nations

According to President Bush's interviews in author Robert Woodward's book Plan of Attack, the President began specific planning for armed attack on Iraq by U.S. forces in December 2001, nearly a year before his administration appeared before the U.N. challenging the Security Council to enforce compliance with S.C. resolutions on Iraq. Turning to the U.N. clearly was not an integral part of his plan.

However, administration rejection of the U.N. lasted only a few days after President Bush's announcement aboard the U.S.S. Abraham Lincoln on May 1, 2003 of the end of the main combat phase. On May 9, 2003, the administration circulated a draft S.C. resolution ending Council sanctions on Iraq and giving the U.S. control of the Iraqi oil industry until control could be handed over to a representative Iraqi government.

The draft was passed unanimously on May 22, 2003 as Resolution 1483, with the votes of the S.C. members who had opposed the U.S.-U.K. attack on Iraq.[21] The resolution recognized the U.S. and U.K. as occupying powers in Iraq, lifted U.N. economic sanctions on Iraq and gave the U.S. and U.K. authority over Iraqi oil; each of these actions was indispensable for the U.S. occupation of Iraq. However, contrary to U.S. desires, the resolution also continued the existence of the U.N. Monitoring, Verification and Inspection Commission (UNMOVIC), the organization that had inspected Iraq in late 2002 and early 2003 before military action.

In July 2003, the U.S. again turned to the U.N. as Secretary Powell began discussion of a new S.C. mandate that could provide a basis for broadening troop contributions from states like India, Russia, Pakistan, Germany and France. These efforts were revived after the August 2003 bombing of the U.N. compound in Baghdad and continued into September, but were finally abandoned by the U.S. as unlikely to lead to a productive outcome. The underlying cause was U.S. refusal to accept significant sharing of power in Baghdad with other troop donors. As a substitute, the U.S. focused on the effort to increase troop contributions from members of the Coalition who already supported the Iraqi invasion.

The U.S. succeeded in increasing the number of troop-contributing countries from 18 in April 2003 to 33 in April 2004, but increased the total number of Coalition forces in Iraq only by a few hundred. The U.S. then moved to present a draft resolution to the S.C. with the narrower aim of acknowledging and giving status to the Iraqi Governing Council established by the U.S. and United Kingdom. The Council passed Resolution 1500 on August 14, 2003, welcoming the creation of the Iraqi Governing Council and establishing the U.N. assistance mission for Iraq. *(See Chapter 4 for more details.)*

The bombing of the U.N. compound in Baghdad took place only five days later on August 19, 2003. Six months later, in March 2004, S.G. Annan fired Tun Myat of Myanmar, the U.N.'s top security coordinator, and disciplined several other U.N. officials for their inadequate performance with regard to the bombing. In another U.N. problem area connected with Iraq, the S.G. appointed former Federal Reserve Chairman Paul Volcker in April 2004 to head a panel to probe allegations of corruption in the U.N. agency managing the Oil-for-Food Programme (OFFP) in Iraq; the agency sold Iraqi oil and turned over the proceeds to purchase necessities for Iraq's civilian population.

Reflecting on the events of the previous March leading to the U.S.-U.K.

attack on Iraq, the S.G. told the General Assembly on September 23, 2003, "we have come to a fork in the road. This may be a moment no less decisive than 1945 itself, when the United Nations was founded—the Council needs to consider how it will deal with the possibility that individual States will use force 'preemptively' against perceived threats."[22] The S.G. announced the establishment of a panel of eminent personalities to assess current security threats and the best use of collective action to respond to them.

On October 16, 2003, the Council approved Resolution 1511, which "determines that the Governing Council and its ministers are the principal bodies of the Iraqi interim administration"; invited the Governing Council to provide to the Security Council "a timetable and programme for drafting a new constitution and for the holding of democratic elections under that constitution" and requested the U.N. to lend its expertise for these processes. The resolution also authorized a multinational force under unified command for Iraq and urged member states to contribute assistance, including troops, to this force.[23] There was little enthusiasm for this resolution in the Council. Although it passed unanimously, as soon as it was adopted, French, Russian and German officials stated they would provide no money or troops.

U.S. discussion of a U.N. role in Iraq resumed in December 2003. But S.G. Annan soon stated that the security situation precluded rapid resumption of an expanded U.N. presence there. In April 2004, the U.S requested U.N. member states that were not members of the Coalition in Iraq to establish a special force of at least 1,500 troops to protect an expanded U.N. mission in Baghdad, including particularly the election commission helping Iraqis to prepare nationwide elections by the end of January 2005. The State Department also submitted a new draft S.C. resolution that would extend U.N. authorization for the forces of the military coalition in Iraq after the June 30 transition, confer status on the new Iraqi interim government and define the U.N. role there.

Meeting in Washington on April 16, 2004, President Bush and Prime Minister Blair endorsed the proposal that the U.N. should designate an Iraqi interim government to take over on July 1, 2004.

It is ironic that, following persistent efforts by the Bush Administration to minimize the role of the U.N. in Iraq and to keep all decisions for itself, the U.N. should now find itself in a key role there. But what lies ahead will not be simple. The U.N. is unlikely to want or to receive a major role in post-June 30 decisions by the U.S. military or by the 3,000-man U.S. embassy in Baghdad, which will direct economic reconstruction. But there will probably be competition between the U.N. authority and the U.S. embassy regarding advice to the new Iraqi government on political issues. Many suggestions have been made for an augmented role for the United Nations, including making Iraq a U.N. trusteeship territory for the transition and appointing an international high commissioner to supervise the transition, but these moves appear unlikely except as a last resort should Coalition forces completely lose control in Iraq.[24]

Looking Forward

Given the failure to find any WMD stocks in Iraq, the war can be characterized as a mistaken, preemptive war launched without U.N. Charter authority. But the war was also poorly carried out, with two cardinal errors: failure to gauge the temper of the Iraqi people—whose main reaction was not joy and gratitude toward their U.S.-U.K. liberators but nationalistic resentment of foreign invaders—and the failure to provide a sufficient number of military forces to provide nationwide security. Part of the problem can be ascribed to excessive reliance by U.S. senior administration officials on the views of Iraqi émigrés, prominently Ahmed Chalabi. But most of the blame for these errors goes to the low quality of Western intelligence.

At the time of this writing, the U.S. was still floundering in Iraq, with about 140,000 troops. The U.S. Administration was unwilling to strip Army and Marine force everywhere to raise the necessary manpower it needed—as many as 500,000 troops according to some. That left foreign armies, but the administration was unwilling to share its power with others in order to provide the broad S.C. mandate needed to justify foreign troop contributions. Even if there had been such contributions, in all probability, the additional confusion, increased difficulty of Coalition decision making, and the likelihood that Iraqis would be hostile to all foreign forces, means that the manpower problem would not have been easily solved.

Added to these two cardinal problems was the failure of the Iraqi Governing Council itself to gain acceptance and support from the Iraqi public. The U.S. outreach also failed to extend to Iran, whose difficult government has considerable influence with Iraqi Shias. Simultaneous military action by Coalition forces against both Sunni and Shia resistance groups in April 2004 seems to have been an avoidable, major tactical error. It is possible that both of the crises with the Sunnis in Fallujah and with Shias in Najaf will be resolved, with positive general effects.

The U.S. Administration knows what it has to do to make good in Iraq—increase the number of ground forces keeping order; help to gain the support of the Iraqi people for the new government that is to be appointed on June 30, 2004; and further reach out to the international community for troops, money and political support. Whether it can do these things depends on whether it can overcome its main shortcoming—its unilateral reliance on its own power. As for the United Nations, it will now have to focus on the details of the transition from military occupation to Iraqi authority and on preparing the elections—without taking on broader responsibility.

Beyond Iraq: Controlling Weapons of Mass Destruction Worldwide

Jonathan Dean

While the attention of the U.S. and the world public was riveted on increasingly bloody events in Iraq, the nuclear nonproliferation regime—the complex of treaties, export controls and verification inspections designed to control nuclear weapons—was being battered by a series of negative developments, including nuclear weapons activities in North Korea, Iran and Libya, as well as the discovery of a nuclear sales network run by the chief of Pakistan's nuclear weapons program and "vertical proliferation" in the U.S. and other weapon states. These developments seemed the most dangerous in the 60 years since introduction of nuclear weapons in 1945. Taken together, they appeared to threaten the collapse of the entire nonproliferation regime. The following section outlines each of these developments, beginning with a brief look at the U.N. bodies and elements that deal with global proliferation issues.

The United Nations' Role in Nonproliferation

As demonstrated in the case of Iraq, the United Nations is deeply involved in international efforts to control weapons of mass destruction. The Security Council is the final implementing instance for treaties controlling such weapons. The First Committee of the General Assembly reviews security and disarmament issues each year. The Committee's resolutions provide a guide to member state concerns regarding the security field and often mark the initiation of new efforts on some specific topic.

In addition, the 66-nation Conference on Disarmament (CD) in Geneva—which negotiated the Nonproliferation Treaty (NPT), the Comprehensive Test-Ban Treaty and the Chemical Weapons Ban—determines its own rules and agenda, but reports annually to the G.A. and deals with negotiating topics referred to it by the Assembly. Last but not least is the U.N. Disarmament Commission, whose main task over the past year was to prepare a further General Assembly Special Session on Disarmament (SSOD).

The NPT is the primary focus of international nonproliferation efforts. Every five years, 187 U.N. member states that are parties to the NPT review performance of the treaty parties; the next review conference is scheduled for 2005. Each review period is now preceded by up to four sessions of a Preparatory Committee, known as PrepCom.

Last but not least among the U.N. organs that deal with weapons and proliferation is the U.N. Department of Disarmament Affairs, now headed by Under-Secretary-General Nobuyasu Abe. This department provides support for U.N. arms control and disarmament conferences and maintains the U.N. Arms Registry.

First Committee

The annual discussion held in the U.N. First Committee on International Security and Disarmament is a worthwhile barometer of the concerns of

U.N. member states. First Committee resolutions are often a guide to member state policy. The 2003 First Committee met from October 6 to November 7, 2003 and adopted 47 resolutions and seven decisions, an average number. On December 8, 2003, the Assembly voted to confirm the Committee's draft resolutions and decisions.

The focus of the fall 2003 session was once again terrorism and the lack of progress in disarmament. First Committee members discussed procedural reforms and decided that two studies by national experts should be conducted: the first on global information and telecommunications; the other a continuation of the study of missiles by a panel of national experts initiated by Iran in 2002 and backed by a new First Committee resolution (UNGA 58/37). There were 57 abstentions in the vote on this resolution, including the United States, possibly because the text failed to mention The Hague Code of Conduct on Missile Proliferation and because of suspicions of Iranian activities in the nuclear field.

The First Committee also commissioned an open-ended working group to develop the text of an international agreement that would enable member states to identify and trace small arms and light weapons—limited but useful progress in this area.

The resolution supporting negotiation of a treaty ending the production of fissile material for weapons (UNGA 58/57) was passed by consensus in the Committee and Assembly. However, the U.S. representative indicated that, while the U.S. supported the resolution, the administration was reviewing its position on the negotiation. The U.S. also went against the stream by voting alone on budgetary grounds against the resolution on small arms and light weapons. The resolution introduced by India, "Measures to Prevent Terrorists from Acquiring Weapons of Mass Destruction" (U.N. General Assembly Resolution 58/48) was adopted without a vote.

General Assembly Resolution 58/59, "A Path to the Total Elimination of Nuclear Weapons," proposed by Japan, was agreed on with 164 votes in favor and only the U.S. and India opposed. The New Agenda Coalition sponsored Resolution 58/51, a detailed resolution on most aspects of nuclear disarmament, which describes actions designed to carry out the "Thirteen Steps" of nuclear disarmament adopted at the 2000 NPT Review Conference. The New Agenda Coalition also sponsored Resolution 58/50 on tactical nuclear weapons, emphasizing the need to reduce and eliminate these weapons, which are more portable and thus more subject to accidental and unauthorized use. Last but not least, there were resolutions supporting nuclear-weapon-free zones as well as the chemical and biological weapons conventions.[25]

NPT Preparatory Committee

Sudjadnan Parnohadiningrat of Indonesia chaired the third session of the Preparatory Committee for the 2005 review conference of the Nonproliferation Treaty, held in New York from April 26 to May 7, 2004. As usual, participants divided into two main groups. Representatives of NPT states without nuclear weapons criticized the failure of the states with nuclear weapons, mainly the United States, for not taking more decisive action to eliminate nuclear weapons. In response, the U.S. criticized the shortcomings of non-weapon states in complying with the treaty. This year, as last year, Iran was the main and frequent target of U.S. attacks for noncompliance with the treaty. The motive may be to frighten Iran into further compliance with the NPT and the IAEA or to set the stage for U.S. referral of the Iranian case to the Council with a demand for economic sanctions.

PrepCom closed on May 7, 2004, with minimal substantive agreement. The Committee did, however, endorse earlier PrepCom decisions that the 2005 Review Conference of the NPT should be held at the U.N. in New York from May 2 to May 28 and be chaired by Sergio de Queiroz Duarte of Brazil.

As in some past NPT review conferences, PrepCom was unable to agree on a substantive report of this and its past two sessions summarizing recommendations for the review conference. A main reason for the lack of outcome was acerbic debate between U.S. representatives and representatives of the nonaligned countries about whether the U.S. was maintaining its commitment "to accomplish the total elimination of their nuclear arsenals leading to nuclear disarmament to which all states parties are committed under Article VI." Representatives of the Bush Administration said they considered this commitment, as well as others undertaken at the 2000 Review Conference, no longer valid.

North Korea

In the early 1980s, North Korea ceded to Russian pressure and belatedly agreed to join the Nonproliferation Treaty. For unclear reasons, it was permitted to delay for three years signing a safeguards agreement with the IAEA, which polices compliance with the NPT. Once on the scene, IAEA inspectors detected that North Korea had begun to reprocess spent fuel rods to gain weapons-useable plutonium; IAEA inspectors impounded remaining fuel rods. North Korea then expelled the IAEA inspectors and started to withdraw from the NPT. To block North Korean development of nuclear weapons, the United States, together with South Korea, Japan and the European Union, concluded a Framework Agreement with North Korea in 1994, which provided that the "Western" partners would construct two new energy reactors and supply fuel oil while North Korea froze its nuclear developments. This agreement was suspended by the Western participants when North Korea admitted to U.S. officials in October 2002 that it was also engaging in a program of uranium enrichment, the second route to nuclear weapons, along with plutonium production.

Following the October 2002 meeting, U.S. Secretary of State Colin Powell revealed that North Korea had offered a plan to take steps in dismantling its nuclear and missile programs in exchange for economic and security benefits. A trilateral session backed by the Chinese in Beijing April 23-25,

2003, where the North Koreans reportedly told U.S. officials that they already had complete nuclear weapons, and two six-power sessions (North Korea, South Korea, U.S., China, Russia and Japan) in August 2003 and February 2004 were unable to advance agreement. After originally admitting to U.S. officials in October 2002 the existence of a North Korean uranium enrichment program, the North Koreans claimed that they had no such program. However, revelations in December 2003 of Dr. Khan's global nuclear business brought statements from Dr. Khan that he had given help to North Korea on the uranium enrichment process and had seen in North Korea what were claimed to be finished nuclear weapons.

In the February 2004 six-power session, North Korea also backed off from its earlier offer to freeze its entire nuclear industry, military and civilian, and said it wanted to keep and develop a civilian nuclear energy program. For its part, the Bush Administration, internally divided regarding policy toward North Korea, often repeated its one agreed formula, that North Korea must first formally commit itself to "Complete, Verifiable, Irreversible Dismantling" (CVID) of its entire nuclear energy program before the U.S. would begin discussion of security assurances to North Korea. In October 2003, President Bush said he was prepared to put U.S. security assurances in writing once things got to this stage. Unfortunately, the six-power sessions in August 2003 and February 2004 were unable to agree on a written communiqué despite the increasingly energetic engagement of the Chinese host government in the negotiation process. Agreement was reached in February 2004 to establish a series of working groups on different aspects of the negotiations, theoretically a good way to get some flexibility into the talks.

In late April 2004, President Kim Jong Il paid a three-day visit to Beijing while U.S. intelligence agencies stated that they were revising their estimates of nuclear weapons holdings from two or three to at least eight and that North Korea's uranium enrichment could be in full operation within three years, boosting weapons production. After the Beijing visit, the North Korean government agreed to hold a round of working group talks in mid-May. But North Korea demanded "advance payment" of economic and security assurances before it would freeze its nuclear weapons program. U.S. officials, in turn, demanded advance payment by North Korea in the form of assurances that it would totally eliminate its nuclear program before the U.S. would begin any discussion of security assurances or economic aid.[26]

It was not clear at the time of this writing whether—or when exactly—the working group meeting would take place. However, overall, North Korea seems ready to make an agreement of some kind. With a little more flexibility from the United States, it probably will be possible to obtain an adequate commitment from North Korea. The end result may be agreement to end the North Korean nuclear and missile programs, civil and military. But it may also include the possibility that President Kim Jong Il will have concealed a few warheads as insurance for survival of his regime. U.S. military action against North Korea continues to be unlikely, but the U.S. is right in its complaints that the passage of time permits the North Koreans to further develop their nuclear weapon capability. Other than IAEA involvement in verification, U.N. involvement on this issue is not direct, but the S.C. will probably be called on to guarantee the result if agreement is in fact reached—or to impose severe economic sanctions on North Korea if agreement is not reached.

Iran

Since mid-2003, more and more evidence has emerged of Iranian activities aimed at establishing a full fuel-cycle nuclear energy industry with capacity to produce fissile material for nuclear weapons. While the focus for activities concerning North Korea's nuclear activities has been the six-power meetings in Beijing, the main diplomatic forum for discussion of Iranian nuclear activities has been the 35-member Board of Governors of the IAEA, elected every two years by the General Conference of IAEA's 137 member states. Up to now, the Board's report has been finally agreed upon without reference to the Security Council, which the Iranians fear not least because of the possibility of sanctions that could cut off their exports of oil and natural gas, a main activity for a country with a weak economy and high unemployment rate, especially among younger Iranians. The problem has been, however, that each IAEA report has brought revelations of additional Iranian NPT violations and of moves toward nuclear weapons capability.

Most Iranian activities discovered by the IAEA were permissible under the NPT, but had been carried out surreptitiously. The U.S. has continued to insist that Iran was deliberately moving toward nuclear weapons capability. For its part, Iran has been in turn conciliatory and then unyielding, first committing itself to stop enriching uranium, but then insisting that it would resume the enrichment process and that it intended to sell enriched uranium reactor fuel to other countries commercially.

The June 2003 report of the IAEA Board followed this pattern. It expressed concern over several unreported Iranian nuclear activities. The September 12, 2003 report, acting on further IAEA reports in August 2003 of unreported activities, gave Iran until October 31, 2003 to clarify these issues and to prove it had no secret weapons program. Tehran continued to temporize on signing the Additional Protocol permitting broadened IAEA inspections. And as the October deadline neared, the foreign ministers of France, Germany and the United Kingdom, acting for the European Union, intervened. As a result, on October 21, Tehran agreed to suspend uranium enrichment (later stating the suspension was temporary), to give a full account of its nuclear program since its inception and to sign the Additional Protocol.

European Union foreign ministers told Iran that if it lived up to these commitments, the issue would not be referred to the Security Council. A further step whereby the E.U. would guarantee a supply of nuclear fuel in return for Iran's relinquishment of all enrichment and reprocessing activities had been discussed, but was not raised or agreed at this session. A subsequent Board resolution adopted on November 26, 2003 was even more hard-fought than before. The resolution strongly deplored Iran's past failures and breaches in disclosing its nuclear program and recorded the Board's agreement to take further steps (a euphemism for referral to the Council) if additional violations were discovered. Last December, Iran signed the Additional Protocol and pledged to comport itself as if the Protocol had already been ratified.

Through study of documents turned over by Iran, IAEA inspectors identified Pakistan as the source of much of Iran's enrichment equipment. This led to the revelation of the actions of Dr. Khan in selling centrifuges to Iran that imitate the models reportedly stolen by Dr. Khan from The Netherlands two decades earlier. In February 2004, the IAEA announced that, among the documents turned over by Iran, it had discovered undeclared blueprints for an advanced type of uranium enrichment centrifuge called the P2. On February 15, Iranian Foreign Minister Kamal Kharrazi announced that Iran intended to resume suspended enrichment activity and to sell enriched reactor fuel commercially following IAEA procedures used to record sales by others, including nuclear weapon states.

On February 24, 2004, IAEA announced that Iran had been experimenting with production of polonium, a metal used to trigger nuclear weapons but also used in some types of reactors. This matter was taken up in the March 13 report of the Board, which deplored the omission of the P2 centrifuges and polonium production from Iran's declarations and decided to defer to its June 2004 meeting consideration of how to respond to the Iranian omissions.[27] On March 13, 2004, Iran's top nuclear official suspended the entry of IAEA inspectors into Iran, but they were readmitted a month later following a visit to Tehran by Mohamed ElBaradei, director-general of the IAEA. The IAEA's June 1, 2004 report on Iran listed numerous Iranian false statements about its nuclear energy activities and concluded that Iran had pursued uranium enrichment more aggressively than it had admitted. The stage was set for vigorous debate at the Board meeting later in June.

Looking ahead, the Bush Administration has concluded from this parade of incriminating evidence that its earlier suspicions of Iranian activities were completely justified. However, the administration is effectively precluded by its problems in Iraq from undertaking a serious military campaign against Iran and will have to focus instead on the possibility of economic sanctions in the Security Council. France, the United Kingdom, Russia and China control the Council majority on this subject and prefer for the moment to use U.S. threats of S.C. action as a source of pressure on Iran, trying ultimately to gain Iran's agreement to relinquish all enrichment and reprocessing activities in return for guaranteed supply of fuel.

It is uncertain whether this combination of U.S. pressure and E.U. negotiation can bring Iran's divided political leadership, highly suspicious of the motives of all Western countries, to acquiesce. If a final agreement is in fact reached, a S.C. resolution guaranteeing the integrity and security of Iran and the surrounding region is likely to be a part of it.

Pakistan

On December 19, 2003, Libya announced its decision to relinquish its WMD program and submit to international inspection to verify the complete elimination of this program. This development, described in this chapter's Commentary, represents an important gain for the faltering nonproliferation regime. Still, revelations about the sources of Libyan and Iranian nuclear activities pointed squarely to Pakistan.

On June 24, 2003, during a visit by Pakistani President Pervez Musharraf to Camp David, President Bush announced a six-fold increase in aid to Pakistan of $3 billion, divided over five years. The increase was intended to help stabilize the shaky government of a nuclear weapons country ruled by a military autocracy whose president had already survived two assassination attempts, a country where Muslim fundamentalists had increased their representation in the national parliament. Within months of this event, a rising tide of international accusations pointed to A.Q. Khan, the "father" of the Pakistan nuclear bomb and head of its nuclear weapons complex, as the head of an international black market ring on nuclear weapons components. On December 20, 2003, it was reported from Vienna that documents provided by Iran to the IAEA had revealed the existence of a very large international network of trafficking in nuclear components based in Pakistan.[28]

A further flood of revelations led to the appearance of Dr. Khan on Pakistani television on February 4, 2004. In the broadcast, he took sole responsibility for his proliferation sales and asserted that the government of Pakistan was unaware of them. With tightly choreographed timing, the next day, February 5, President Musharraf pardoned Dr. Khan, who, the President said, would not receive further penalties because of his signal service in developing Pakistan's nuclear bomb.[29] Further information from the IAEA indicated that companies or individuals in at least seven countries formed part of the Pakistani nuclear ring, including Malaysia, South Africa, the United Arab Emirates and Germany. Among other things, Pakistan sold designs for nuclear bombs that originated in China; it also specialized in centrifuges, devices for enriching uranium for weapons. A Sri Lankan businessman named Buhary Syed Abu Tahir told Malaysian police that he operated part of the ring for Dr. Khan from Dubai in the United Arab Emirates, ordering and trans-shipping components from all over the world, and that Dr. Khan had received $3 million cash from Iran for one shipment.[30]

IAEA Director-General ElBaradei said that revelations of the Dr. Khan proliferation network were "the most dangerous thing we have seen in proliferation in many years." He went further to call for a complete reform of the export control system.[31] The fact that Dr. ElBaradei himself has stated that the IAEA had been unaware of the Pakistani ring, and of Libyan moves toward nuclear weapons, and that it had been successfully deceived by Iran for 18 years, is a chilling record that calls for urgent corrective action.

On the positive side, a potentially important development took place in early 2004. On the initiative of Indian Prime Minister Vajpayee, talks between Indian and Pakistani officials resulted in a February agreement on an agenda of talks to include the Kashmir issue and nuclear security. The first few sessions brought useful, substantive discussion.[32]

Still, Pakistan's nuclear transgressions illustrate how complex and fraught with conflicting values foreign policy decisions often are. The transgressions are clear but the U.S. can do nothing decisive to correct them because it is dependent on Pakistan for help against terrorists and it is dependent on it to survive as a government, because the alternative—an Islamist government with a nuclear bomb—is even more threatening. In April 2004, the U.S. Administration designated Pakistan as a "major, non-NATO military ally of the U.S.," a designation that lifts restrictions on arms sales.[33] However, U.S. Vice Admiral Lowell Jacoby, director of the Defense Intelligence Agency, told the U.S. Senate Armed Services Committee on February 26, 2004 that Pakistan had recently developed the capacity to produce plutonium for nuclear weapons as well as enriched uranium. This leads in the direction of the far more destructive hydrogen bomb.[34]

A Rising Problem: Vertical Proliferation

The underlying trend in these terrifying developments in North Korea, Iran and Pakistan is "horizontal proliferation," the illicit spread of nuclear weapons capability to countries previously without it, and the resulting deterioration of the nuclear nonproliferation regime. This trend has been intensified over the past year by negative developments in the nuclear weapons policy of the states that are recognized to already have nuclear weapons, particularly the United States. This area is known as vertical proliferation, in which nuclear weapon states increase or develop their weapons stockpiles, or relax restraints on the use of these weapons. Following the conclusion of the 2002 Moscow Treaty with Russia, which will reduce the total number of operationally deployed U.S. and Russian nuclear weapons, but not stored weapons, the United States—which continues to have the largest nuclear arsenal in the world—has taken no further action on nuclear reductions. In fact, the administration has asked for funds for a new plant to produce up to 900 new plutonium bomb trigger pits a year, for development of an earth-penetrating warhead from an existing U.S. weapon, and for study of the possibility of developing low-yield mini-nukes. The Bush Administration has refused to resubmit for a Senate vote the Comprehensive Nuclear Test-Ban Treaty rejected by the Senate in 1999. It has repudiated the agreement of the Clinton Administration to the Thirteen Steps of Nuclear Disarmament developed at the 2000 Review Conference of the Nuclear NPT. And it has appropriated money to cut the time needed to prepare for resumption of nuclear testing.

Russia, too, has been engaged in vertical proliferation. It is introducing a new intercontinental ballistic missile. Like the United States, it has proclaimed a policy of preemptive use of nuclear weapons, dropping an earlier no-first-use policy, and it has hung back from negotiating reduction of its large stockpile of tactical nuclear weapons, demanding without U.S. response that the U.S. agree to withdraw its small number (under 100) of tactical nuclear weapons still deployed in Western Europe. For its part, China is modernizing and increasing the total size of its own small nuclear arsenal.

Measures to Reduce Proliferation and the Risk of Nuclear War

ElBaradei Proposals

Responding to proliferation calamities in pre-Gulf War Iraq, North Korea, Iran, Libya and Pakistan, IAEA's Dr. ElBaradei has proposed international control over enrichment and reprocessing facilities throughout the world several times. Nearly 60 years ago, the Acheson-Lilienthal report advanced the same proposal, on essentially the same grounds—that is, the acute difficulty, if not impossibility, of verifying national activities in enrichment and reprocessing.

Dr. ElBaradei did not give details of his ideas but they might entail a massive enterprise involving management, perhaps ownership, of all enrichment and reprocessing plants throughout the world. A program like this would take decades to agree on and carry out. The IAEA Director-General has also asked for an immediate freeze on worldwide production of fissile material for weapons and rapid commencement of the negotiations on this subject, deadlocked for six years at the Geneva-based Conference on Disarmament.[35]

Bush Proposals and the PSI

In a February 11, 2004 speech, President Bush presented his own program of actions against proliferation. These included the suggestion that no enrichment or reprocessing plants should be built by those countries that did not already have them and that the 40-member Nuclear Suppliers Group, which seeks to limit sales of equipment that could be used to produce nuclear weapons, should refuse to sell such equipment to these states. The latter should, however, be assured reliable supply of nuclear fuel. The President did not suggest how this would be done nor did he suggest any action for those states that already have enrichment and reprocessing plants.

Other Bush proposals against proliferation were to expand the work of the Proliferation Security Initiative (PSI), which seeks to, among other things, block illicit transport of WMD materials by sea, land or air; to increase pressure for adoption of the IAEA Additional Protocol by cutting off exports of nuclear equipment to countries that had not yet signed the protocol; and to exclude countries under investigation for violating nonproliferation objectives such as Iran from service on the IAEA Board of Governors. Of these measures, the proposal to block the spread of enrichment plants is likely to have difficulty unless accompanied by some action relating to countries that already have enrichment plants.[36]

On March 24, 2004, the U.S. Administration submitted a reworked version of the draft S.C. resolution it originally submitted to the P-5 the previous December, and the resolution was passed by the Council on April 28, 2004. The measure would outlaw transfer of nuclear, chemical and biological weapons or weapons components to terrorists or mercenary organizations *(see next section on Terrorism for more details)*. This represents considerable progress for the administration in gaining the agreement of these governments, especially that of China, on a program of actions to counter proliferation.[37]

The Nunn-Lugar Cooperative Threat Reduction Program

The Cooperative Threat Reduction Program (CTR) is designed to control and destroy the huge stocks of nuclear, chemical and biological armaments left behind in the sudden collapse of the Soviet Union in order to prevent their falling into the hands of black marketers or terrorists. The program made progress over the past year, but it is still hampered by poor coordination and data collection.

U.S. Representative Duncan Hunter, chairman of the House Armed Services Committee, has sought to speed Russian cooperation by adding reporting requirements to appropriations legislation for Nunn-Lugar, requirements that Russia has not met. This circumstance has brought repeated delays and presidential waivers of the legislation and repeated suggestions that the president appoint a nonproliferation official or "czar" to oversee the program. The latest version of appropriation legislation meets Senator Richard Lugar's repeated proposals that the program be extended beyond the boundaries of the former Soviet Union. As of February 2004, under the CTR program, more than 6,000 warheads had been separated from missiles; and 529 missiles, 124 strategic bombers, 668 cruise missiles and 408 sea-launched ballistic missile launchers had been destroyed. U.S. appropriations were running at about $1 billion a year and the contributions by G-8 partners were continuing.[38]

Chemical Weapons

The October 20-24, 2003 Conference of States-Parties to the Chemical Weapons Convention, meeting in The Hague, gave Russia a three-year extension to 2007 to destroy the first 20 percent of its 40,000 tons of chemical weapons, of which only 1 percent have been destroyed thus far. The conference also gave the U.S. a three-year extension to 2007 to destroy 45 percent of its stockpile of more than 30,000 tons. The treaty calls for destruction of all stockpiles by 2007, but it is clear that deadline will have to be extended.[39]

In March 2004, Albania announced that it had chemical weapons and began their destruction. In April 2004, trade talks between the European Union and Syria broke down with the E.U. failing to gain Syrian agreement to renounce its chemical weapons program. U.S. officials have claimed that Syria has a stock of Sarin nerve gas and is actively working on a biological weapons program.[40]

Experts from the Organisation for the Prohibition of Chemical Weapons

(OPCW), the operating arm of the Chemical Weapons Convention, participated in the inspection of Libya at Libya's invitation and announced the country's advanced WMD program was in chemical weapons. However, Libya showed what was characterized as mustard gas over a decade old, unfilled bombs, dual precursor chemicals and production equipment. It was not a very impressive program.[41]

Biological Weapons

In October 2003, the U.S. General Accounting Office (GAO) reported to Congress that it had been able to buy dual-use laboratory and safety equipment for biological weapons from the U.S. Department of Defense, indicating very lax security control.[42] On October 7, 2003, the National Academy of Sciences National Research Council issued a report calling on the U.S. government to establish a screening system to reduce the possibility that terrorists could draw on U.S. biological research. The report urged the administration to establish an independent National Science Advisory Board for Biodefense to oversee this effort and urged that an International Forum on Biosecurity be established to coordinate international efforts in this field. This proposal is a key element in the administration's effort to launch a national or international code of conduct for controlling microbiology experiments and research from the high school level to professional centers.

International activity on a code of conduct is one of the few multilateral areas in which the U.S. agreed to participate after its suspension in 2001 of efforts by the *ad hoc* group of parties to the *Biological Weapons Convention* to draft a compliance protocol to the Convention. The states parties to the convention met in Geneva November 10-14, 2003 to discuss national related legislation that had been passed in recent years. In accordance with rules proposed by the U.S. and agreed by other members in order to organize any meetings of parties in which the U.S. was willing to participate, no specific recommendations were agreed. Two more meetings will take place before the next review conference in 2006.[43]

Of note, it was revealed in February 2004 that one motive for several cancellations of international flights to the U.S. in January 2004, mainly from the United Kingdom, was the fear of terrorist use of biological or chemical weapons.[44]

Missiles and Weapons in Space

Participants in the Missile Technology Control Regime's (MTCR) International Code of Conduct against ballistic missile proliferation met several times in 2003. They established July 31 as the submission date for future voluntary annual reports describing national missile and space launch policies, with information on actual ballistic missile and space launches during the preceding year. Participants are still working on a pre-launch notification system. Progress has been delayed pending agreement on details of the

U.S.-Russian launch notification agreement adopted in the year 2000, but held up since then by U.S.-Russian controversy over taxes and liability for operation of the system inside Russia. This is a problem that has also plagued the Nunn-Lugar program and that will have to be placed on the U.S. Russian summit agenda until it is resolved.

A second session of the U.N. Panel of National Experts on missiles has started. Last year's initial session did not accomplish much, but participants believe there is a better prospect for limited agreements in this year's session.

United States Missile Defense

A July 2003 report of the American Physical Society expressed doubt that destruction of attacking missiles in their initial boost phase would be possible, especially if the missiles being attacked are using solid fuel, which can increase speed.[45] Philip Coyle, former U.S. Department of Defense Assistant Secretary for test and evaluation, expressed skepticism that the missile defense system now under construction at Fort Greely, Alaska, whose deployment is scheduled to begin in September 2004, could be effective.[46] An April 23, 2004 report by the U.S. General Accounting Office also made the point that the system to be deployed in September 2004 would be "largely unproven" because of lack of testing. Despite these shortcomings, Lt. General Ronald Kadish, director of the U.S. Missile Defense Agency, insisted in late April 2004 that the antimissile system at Fort Greely near Fairbanks would become operational by the scheduled date of September 2004.[47]

Weaponization of Space

The U.S. Missile Defense Agency is continuing to fund and plan for deploying in space several kinetic kill missile interceptors for test purposes around 2008. By many standards, this will be the first deployment of weapons in space. Others will surely follow. In the U.N.-led Conference on Disarmament, which has been blocked from negotiation on any subject by confrontation between China and the United States, China has insisted on negotiating a treaty to prohibit the weaponization of space, to negotiate nuclear disarmament and to negotiate a treaty version of the existing nuclear weapon states pledge not to attack non-weapon states with nuclear weapons. (The commitment is usually referred to as "negative security assurances.")

For its part, the U.S. has wanted to negotiate a treaty prohibiting the production of fissile material for weapons, but has opposed negotiating a treaty prohibiting the weaponization of space. In an August 2003 CD discussion, China dropped its demand to negotiate a treaty prohibiting the weaponization of space and said it was willing to "discuss" this subject instead of negotiating it. If the U.S. agrees—U.S. representatives in Geneva have repeatedly stated they were willing to do so—this could mean that China would also drop its opposition to negotiating a treaty banning production of fissile material for weapons.

In October 2003, the U.S. Representative to the U.N. First Committee reported that the U.S. was reviewing its position on the negotiation of a treaty to cut off production of fissile material for weapons, indicating that the U.S. might change its position on this subject. It seemed evident that the U.S. was concerned by the series of nuclear proliferation breakouts between 2002 and 2004 and that if it, in fact, gave the signal to begin negotiation on this subject, its requirements for verification of a treaty would be stiffer than ever.

Meanwhile, the annual vote in the First Committee calling for a treaty to ban weapons in space reached its highest number: 174 for, 0 against, with the usual abstentions from the United States, Israel, Micronesia and the Marshall Islands. China indicated informally in a March 2004 NGO conference on preventing the weaponization of space that, if official discussion of this topic was not opened in the CD, China would seriously consider moving with Russia to complete and present for international discussion the full text of a treaty prohibiting the weaponization of space.

Landmines, Arms and Other Weapons

On February 27, 2004, the U.S. Administration announced that it would not join the Ottawa Treaty banning anti-personnel landmines, but that it would move to close out its stock of anti-vehicle and anti-personnel mines that do not have built-in mechanisms to automatically turn off within some fixed period after deployment. The Administration said the U.S. will not use these "dumb" mines anywhere outside of South Korea. By 2010, the mines now deployed in Korea will be replaced by self-destructing mines. The U.S. will also seek an international agreement banning dumb mines without the capacity to self-destruct. This position revokes May 1998 pledges by President Bill Clinton that the U.S. would end the deployment of all anti-personnel landmines outside of Korea by 2003 and accede to the Ottawa Convention by 2006 if suitable substitutes for anti-personnel mines were developed in time.[48]

On November 28, 2003, the U.S. refrained from objecting to a new agreement under negotiation in Geneva on clearing up abandoned and unexploded munitions (explosive remnants of war, or ERW). If ratified, the agreement would become an addition to the *Convention on Certain Conventional Weapons*. Under the new agreement, the main responsibility for cleanup of these shells, bombs and mortar rounds belongs to the government of the territory where ERW is located. The country responsible for placing the unexploded munitions on this territory is supposed to help in the cleanup.[49]

Representatives of governments and civil society met at the U.N. in July 2003 in the first biennial review to assess progress made in carrying out the Programme of Action on Small Arms and Light Weapons concluded in July 2001. Participants agreed that progress needed to be made on stockpile destruction, export and import controls, as well as on the concept of marking small arms and light weapons to assist in tracking them. A group of government experts recommended the inclusion of an international agreement on marking. It was reported that more than 90 countries now have domestic laws to govern illicit manufacture or possession of small arms and that two million pieces of an estimated stockpile of four million small arms collected over the past decade have been destroyed.[50]

In its December 2003 meeting, the Wassenaar Arrangement—a group of 33 countries that imposes voluntary restrictions on transfer of certain conventional weapons, agreed to tighten export controls on shoulder-launched anti-aircraft missiles and to also exchange information on their exports of small arms and light weapons.[51]

To date, the U.S. remains the world's top arms seller, with $13 billion in sales agreements for 2002, followed by Russia with $5.7 billion and France with $1 billion.[52] Russia led in actual deliveries in 2003. According to the U.N. Register of Conventional Arms, 120 countries reported in 2003 on their 2002 transfers. A group of government experts that reviewed the Register has recommended that its reporting categories be expanded to include light mortars, which are often used by terrorists, and shoulder-launched anti-aircraft missiles.[53]

Looking Forward

With the negative revelations of the past year in North Korea, Iran, Pakistan and Libya, the nuclear nonproliferation regime may be nearing its breaking point. The proposal of Dr. ElBaradei to establish worldwide international control over enrichment and reprocessing plants, as well as the failure of the IAEA to detect nuclear cheating in pre-Gulf War Iraq, Iran, Pakistan and Libya, provided depressing evidence of the inability of the NPT regime to control nuclear weapons developments. If an NPT collapse occurs, the result will be a proliferated world, with up to 40 weapon states and active trade in weapons to terrorists and criminals.

Libya's announcement on December 19, 2003 of its decision to give up its WMD capability was a positive development, as was the resumption of the India-Pakistan political and nuclear dialogue. Negotiated settlement of the North Korean and Iranian issues is not excluded. The U.S. may decide to resume negotiation at the Conference on Disarmament of the treaty to cut off the production of fissile material for nuclear weapons, thus opening the way to China's desire to launch a discussion of measures to block the weaponization of space. U.S. success in gaining agreement of the P-5 to its draft of a resolution prohibiting transfer of WMD means that the necessary enhancement of the Council's role in enforcing nonproliferation is possible. But securing all these positive developments is improbable unless weapons states take decisive action to eliminate their own weapons.

As for administrative issues, the 2005 First Committee of the General Assembly will be more tightly managed in accordance with the S.G.'s recommendations on reform of U.N. procedures discussed in the 2004 session. Proposals on proliferation, Iraq, terrorism and nuclear disarmament are likely to be major themes. Criticism of the United States, including pressure to disarm, to avoid unilateralism, and to ratify the Comprehensive Test Ban Treaty is likely to increase in next year's First Committee session. The S.C. will also discuss and/or take action on Iraq and WMD issues, Iran, and the U.S.-sponsored resolution prohibiting transfer of WMD to non-state actors or terrorists. If, despite many difficulties, settlements are reached on North Korea or Iran, the Council will almost certainly be called on to guarantee their fulfillment.

As this account has brought out, WMD proliferation has intensified and it is clear that the use of nuclear weapons is appreciably closer. The U.S. Administration, the U.N. Security Council and the international community know fairly well what they have to do to counter this trend–many steps are described in this chapter. The result may very well be a race between their capacity to gather the determination to act and the launching of the first nuclear or dirty bomb.

Targeting Terrorism

Thomas E. McNamara

At the opening of the U.N. General Assembly in September 2003 and two years after September 11th, Norwegian Prime Minister Kjell Magne Bondevik and Professor Elie Wiesel organized a conference to consider the most effective responses to the threat of international terrorism. Secretary-General Kofi Annan opened the meeting and Prime Minister Bondevik closed it by summarizing the apparent consensus on six points:

- No political goal or cause justifies intentionally attacking civilians;
- States must reject religious extremism and encourage dialogue;
- Along with misery, ignorance and despair, human rights abuses fuel terrorism;
- The U.N. must focus on the roots of terrorism and resolve conflicts that feed it;
- Poverty alone does not explain terrorism, but it can provide conditions that extremists can exploit; and
- Education of youth must emphasize tolerance and mutual respect.[1]

From its first modern manifestations in the late 1960s until today, international terrorism has grown more global, more bold, more violent and more deadly.[2] The attacks of September 11, 2001, marked the apex, thus far, in catastrophic terror. Nonetheless, there have been hundreds of other attacks annually in every region of the globe. Among them was the recent one in Madrid, Spain, where 191 people died and more than 1,800 were injured in commuter train bombings on March 11, 2004. Thus, as the international community struggles to confront the threat, there is no real letup in sight.

The Cold War, the Gulf War and, more recently, the war in Iraq have demonstrated that the overwhelming military dominance of the United States and its allies and partners cannot be confronted successfully by conventional armed forces. This realization seems to drive opponents to rely even more on unconventional means, including terrorism. Additionally, the motivating ideologies of these new terrorists justify attacks on any government and people that do not share their political, social or religious goals. The attempts, mostly by Islamic terrorists, to weaken and overthrow governments in Islamic nations have increased fear and instability throughout the Islamic world. Additional incidents of terror in Latin America, India and elsewhere also contribute to the uncertainty. The result is an increased threat to world peace and security that is truly global.

Before September 11th, very few international organizations had counter-terrorism programs as primary efforts were made by those states suffering the direct blows of the terrorists. Since September 2001, this passivity has changed. The U.N. has, like many international organizations, raised counter-terrorism policies and programs to a high priority. Besides its main tool, resolutions by the General Assembly and Security Council, the U.N. has turned to S.C. committees and other U.N. organs for practical, programmatic activity. As noted above, there was also an unusual special conference convened in September 2003 on the margins of the G.A. on "Fighting Terrorism for Humanity: A Conference on the Roots of Evil." This section focuses on what the U.N. and its various committees and agencies have done in the past year to advance its goals and objectives in the fight against terrorism.

The Security Council

Since early 2003, more than a half-dozen S.C. resolutions have dealt with terrorism.[3] Several were condemnations of terrorist attacks in places such as Bogota, Baghdad, Istanbul and Madrid. Apart from those, one of the most noteworthy was also one of the shortest—Resolution 1506, which lifted sanctions against Libya that were placed by the Council in 1992-1993 for the bombing of civilian Pan Am and UTA airliners. Responding to Libyan acceptance of responsibility, payment of compensation, renunciation of terrorism and commitment to further cooperation in the investigation, this resolution ended U.N. "targeted sanctions" that had lasted more than a decade. These sanctions demonstrated that international action in support of global norms and the rule of law can have beneficial results against supporters and sponsors of terrorism. *(See this chapter's Commentary for more details.)*

One S.C. resolution that has received much attention regards weapons of mass destruction (WMD) and their proliferation to non-state entities, especially terrorist groups. The five permanent members of the Council (P-5) have informally discussed this measure for months, and in April 2004, formally adopted Resolution 1540. This groundbreaking P-5 initiative requires all states to punish terrorists and other non-state actors who acquire or sell nuclear, chemical or biological weapons or related materials, and their means of delivery. It also requires states to establish export controls and other measures to prevent non-state-actor trafficking of such weapons.[4] Most importantly, this resolution addresses a longstanding "gap" in international law by specifically denying these items to non-state actors immediately, and creating a S.C. committed to monitoring implementation.

The Counter-Terrorism Committee

In March 2003, the U.N. Counter-Terrorism Committee (CTC) convened 60 international government organizations in New York. All 60 agreed to assist the S.C. and the CTC in the full implementation of S.C. Resolution 1373. Passed in the immediate aftermath of September 11th, this resolution not only established the CTC itself, but also a comprehensive legal and political framework for counter-terrorism cooperation among member states to raise each one's capabilities in a range of areas to counter terrorists and terrorism. The March meeting provided the CTC with many needed international partners in this effort, some regionally based, others technically specialized. These major intergovernmental organizations agreed to inform one another and the CTC about international best practices, relevant codes and standards, and about their activities that might help to strengthen international counter-terrorism capabilities. It is important to note that this cooperation was not required by the resolution, which was binding only on member states.

In this pivotal meeting, all entities committed to develop and maintain mechanisms to assist their members in meeting the resolution's obligations. The CTC agreed to be the central coordinator and liaison ("the switchboard") for all points of contact, and to incorporate best practices, codes and standards in its work. In October 2003, the Organization of American States, and in March 2004, the Organization for Security and Co-operation in Europe, held follow-up conferences in Washington, D.C. and Vienna to expand the relationships begun in New York in March 2003.[5]

Unfortunately, this new workload, in addition to other obligations, placed strains on the CTC's small staff, and especially on the chairmen—first, the British permanent representative to the United Nations, and later the Spanish. To strengthen the committee, its Spanish Chairman presented a report in October 2003 urging a "revitalization" of the CTC staff by placing an Executive Director at its head, enlarging the staff to a maximum of 30 and other measures.[6] After much discussion, this change was endorsed by S.C. Resolution 1535 in late March 2004.[7]

With passage of Resolution 1535, there seems to be a good prospect of developing a professional, efficient CTC staff. Unfortunately, this management reform took almost a year, and the momentum of the CTC's work program during its first 18 months was largely dissipated. Until the new organization is functioning, it will not be clear if momentum will be regained or performance improved, especially given the opposition of the Secretariat to the reforms.

The most important new position in the CTC structure is, of course, the new Executive Director. This position fixes responsibility for the quantity and quality of all staff work with one person, who reports to the plenary committee. The reform also designates a senior CTC staff liaison with the U.N. Office of the High Commissioner for Human Rights and other human rights groups. Concerns exist that member states may, in improving counter-terrorism capabilities, endanger basic human rights (e.g., through legislation that inadvertently or deliberately restricts those rights; or by false accusations of terrorism against, and oppression of, legitimate political opposition).[8]

The CTC is also charged with the coordination of international counterterrorism assistance by matching states that need and want help to increase their counter-terrorism capabilities with those that have the ability to provide assistance.

The 1267 Committee

In January 2004, a second, less noticed but important S.C. committee was restructured and strengthened by a new resolution. The "1267 Committee"—named in October 1999 and also known as the Al Qaeda and Taliban Sanctions Committee—monitors and assesses the implementation of sanctions against the Taliban faction in Afghanistan and against Al Qaeda and any other groups working with these entities.[9] Under these Chapter VII resolutions, all member states are required to freeze assets and resources, prevent transit of individuals and embargo arms to these entities. A reconstituted "monitoring group" with an expanded global mandate and new personnel is central to the reforms.

With the military defeat of the Taliban in Afghanistan and the diaspora of Al Qaeda, the listing of individuals and organizations subject to Resolution 1267 sanctions has become more complex. S.C. Resolution 1526 is the latest effort by the Council to restructure, strengthen and update the 1267 Committee.

The General Assembly

Of the 288 resolutions passed by the 58th session of the General Assembly, six were related to terrorism. In September 2003, before the end of its 57th session, the Assembly met hurriedly and passed a resolution strongly condemning the "atrocious and deliberate" August 19, 2003, terrorist bombing of the headquarters of the U.N. Assistance Mission in Iraq. That attack killed 22 people, including Sergio Vieira de Mello, the U.N. High Commissioner for Human Rights and the Special Representative of the Secretary-General for Iraq, and wounded more than 100 people.

A special panel of experts released a report on the brutal attack in March 2004, with findings pointing out serious security flaws in U.N. Iraq operations.[10] In addition, the S.G. announced that he would keep any U.N. presence in Baghdad small for the foreseeable future and underlined the requirement that there be an increase in the security of U.N. personnel working in conflict areas.[11]

In December 2003, the 58th session unanimously approved a resolution reiterating the condemnation of the Baghdad bombing and calling for the strengthening of legal protection and safety for all U.N. personnel.[12] It charged the existing *ad hoc* committee *(see below)* to meet in April 2004 to deal with the matter.

First, Third and Sixth Committees

In addition to the resolution noted above, the G.A. passed five other resolutions on terrorism during its 58th Session. These were mostly reiterations or updates of previous resolutions. The First, Third and Sixth Committees formulated and reported drafts of these resolutions to the Assembly.

Coming from the First Committee, the first of these resolutions reiterated concern expressed a year earlier that terrorist organizations may gain access to WMD. By unanimous consent, the G.A. urged member states to strengthen national measures to prevent terrorists from acquiring such weapons, to prevent their means of delivery and to prohibit the materials and technologies related to their manufacture. This action paralleled the S.C. passage of Resolution 1540, noted above.[13] This resolution was followed by a more general resolution, reported by the Sixth Committee, urging states to take "measures to eliminate international terrorism."[14]

The Third Committee reported on a draft resolution, which was also adopted unanimously, instructing the Centre for International Crime Prevention to increase its efforts against terrorists.[15] Finally, two draft resolutions from the Third Committee focused on human rights and terror. The first condemned "the acts, methods and practices of terrorism" as violations of human rights and repeated many of the requirements of Resolution 1373 in urging member states to take action against terrorism. After significant debate, this passed with 120 in favor, 42 against and 18 abstentions. The second, repeating concerns expressed the previous year, called upon states to observe international human rights laws and norms when combating terrorism. This passed with only one abstention and 181 votes in favor.[16]

Additional Conventions Against Terrorism

Since the late 1960s, the G.A. has worked on the elaboration and negotiation of draft conventions related to international terrorism. Together with those negotiated in other venues, they comprise critical elements in the still incomplete legal and political corpus of international law and "international norms" against terrorism.

The G.A. has mandated these conventions to *ad hoc* committees in recent years. In 1996, it directly tasked such a committee to work "in the framework of a working group of the Sixth Committee" to develop, among other things, "a comprehensive legal framework of conventions dealing with international terrorism."[17] The effort was designed to produce an "umbrella" convention to complement, not replace, those more particular and focused conventions already in force (now 12 in number).

The committee has been working for nearly eight years on the draft of a comprehensive terrorism convention, and for a shorter period on a nuclear terrorism convention. On the first of these two conventions, disagreements continued during 2003 and early 2004 on a definition of terrorism and the questions of "military exclusion" (i.e., how to treat "armed forces"), "foreign occupation" and "state terrorism." The preamble and four articles of the text remain unagreed, and no significant progress on resolving differences was noted in this year's *ad hoc* committee report.[18]

The discussion of the draft convention on the suppression of nuclear terrorism suffered from essentially the same disputes. As a result, no progress was reported on this text either. Since the disagreements on the comprehensive convention carry over to this draft, the point was made in the Chairman's report that resolving differences on the comprehensive convention might lead to resolution in the nuclear convention. Despite the urging of the new Chairman, both drafts remained stalled.

U.N. Office on Drugs and Crime/Terrorism Prevention Branch

The G.A. has mandated the U.N. Office on Drugs and Crime (UNODC) to prevent and combat terrorism by strengthening international cooperation and providing technical assistance, when requested by member states. Based in Vienna, the UNODC's terrorism prevention branch (TPB) has assisted the Counter Terrorism Committee in implementing Resolution 1373 in dozens of member states. TPB has promoted ratification and entry into force of the 12 international conventions against terrorism and provided technical assistance on counter-terrorism legislation that is needed to carry out the conventions. The conventions and necessary legislation are a major element in the Resolution 1373 mandate to member states. After a slow start in 2002, the TPB's vigorous efforts over most of 2003 and early 2004 have been a significant factor in the increase in new ratifications.[19]

In September 2001, only two states had ratified all 12 conventions. By December 2003, 42 states had done so. In fact, since September 2001, the efforts of the CTC, the TPB and other organizations have produced an 85 percent increase in the number of states ratifying the U.N. general conventions on terrorist bombings and financing of terrorism.[20]

Looking Forward

The intense focus and action on terrorism in the Security Council, which has characterized its work since 2001, has been lessening gradually as other crises demand attention. That trend will continue, unless there is another catastrophic terrorist attack. Nonetheless, terrorism will still be one of the most important issues on the Council's agenda. The remainder of 2004 and 2005 promise to be interesting and active for the committees focused on such issues.

The 1267 and 1373 committees will be functioning under their reformed structures and procedures. This opens the prospect of more vigorous pursuit of their mandates. Expectations for these committees, of course, will be higher because the changes were intended to improve performance. Additionally, since the Council passed the terrorism nonproliferation resolution (1540), the U.N. counter-terrorism effort will have a new committee in that area reporting directly to the Council.

The Assembly will continue to examine the August 2003 attack on the U.N. office in Baghdad, and resolutions should appear by the end of 2004 regarding personnel protection. It is also likely that the G.A. will give added attention to the matter of non-state actors gaining access to nuclear, chemical, biological or radiological weapons. At a minimum, most of the G.A. terrorism resolutions passed in the 58th session will most likely be updated and passed again this fall.

Of course, negotiations on the comprehensive and nuclear terrorism conventions will continue. Unfortunately, the outcome of this last effort appears likely to be similar to this year's (i.e., no final texts agreed upon). On a more positive note, one can expect the work of the UNODC/TPB to continue to improve and expand beyond the promotion and assistance for the 12 conventions. The TPB can expand its focus to some of the many other areas where legal help would increase member states' capacity to fight terrorism and implement the very important Resolution 1373.

The United Nations and Narcotics: An Update

Consuelo Remmert

In June 2003, the United Nations Office on Drugs and Crime (UNODC) launched a worldwide "Let's talk about drugs" campaign to inspire authority figures and families to talk to young people about drug use. UNODC produced radio spots in 10 languages, as well as various publications to support the yearlong campaign,[1] which was kicked off on June 26, 2003, the International Day Against Drug Abuse and Illicit Trafficking. This is just one example of UNODC's efforts to combat drug demand via education. The office, along with other U.N. agencies, also focuses on combating the cultivation and trafficking of illegal drugs as well as other related crimes, as outlined below.

Drug-Demand Reduction

At the 47th Session of the Commission on Narcotic Drugs (CND)—the central policy-making body dealing with drug-related matters in the United Nations—in Vienna in March 2004, member states and NGOs discussed threats and challenges in the battle against illicit drugs. The Commission welcomed further reduction in the cultivation of opium in the Golden Triangle (shared borders among Myanmar, Laos and Thailand) and coca in the Andean region while also focusing on the latest obstacles in the elimination of the world's drug crisis. Drug-demand reduction is one of the key targets that came out of the

1998 Drug Summit—a target that member states are working to accomplish by 2008. Several issues were highlighted during this year's session, including the link between drug use and HIV/AIDS and the fact that 10 percent of all those infected with the disease worldwide are injecting drug abusers.

Vietnam presents an example of this newly identified vulnerability. Although the government succeeded in eradicating large-scale opium cultivation in the northern highlands, drug demand is on the rise among the area's youth. The country's Ministry of Health estimates that more than 90 percent of HIV-positive cases in highland regions are associated with injecting drug use. Vietnam's UNODC Country Office, in partnership with the local government, formulated a Strategic Program Framework for 2003 to 2007 to address the heroin demand and its relation to HIV/AIDS transmission.[2] UNODC is also conducting consultation workshops to prepare socio-culturally sensitive drug use and HIV-prevention materials.[3]

Last but not least, the Commission noted an increase in synthetic drug production and mounting evidence of the link between drugs and the trafficking of human beings. In his closing remarks, UNODC Executive Director Antonio Maria Costa said, "As the world drug problem evolves, staying the course is not good enough: our strategy has to adjust to meet newly emerging threats."[4]

Crop Eradication

UNODC's Illicit Crop Monitoring Programme (ICMP) promotes the Drug Summit's goal of eradicating illicit drug crops and their trafficking by devising standardized practices of data collection and analysis. U.N. member states and the international community use the ICMP's methodologies to monitor and compile surveys about illicit crop cultivation. Currently, the ICMP covers seven countries with concentrated cultivation of illicit crops: Afghanistan, Laos and Myanmar for opium poppy; Colombia, Bolivia and Peru for coca; and Morocco for cannabis. Following is a brief update on each.

Afghanistan Afghanistan's drug problem has been one of the largest and most attention-grabbing issues over the last year—and for good reason. Opium harvest in 2003 was the second largest since 1999, estimated at 3,600 metric tons of opium. UNODC's most recent survey, done in collaboration with the Afghan Counter-Narcotics Directorate, predicts that opium production will rise this year. According to the analysis, 69 percent of all farmers intend to increase their opium poppy cultivation.[5]

In February 2004, Mr. Costa stated that "persistent poverty, high opium prices and loans from traffickers are the main reasons for the higher opium production expected in 2004."[6] According to the Food and Agriculture Organization (FAO), the solution to the problem requires rehabilitating the country's agriculture. This process requires extensive funding and long-term commitment to "create alternative income opportunities."[7]

It is clear that Afghanistan needs assistance from neighboring countries to eradicate opium production. The CND's International Narcotics Control Board (INCB) criticized Turkmenistan for failing to cooperate with the international community in the fight against illicit drugs; the country shares more than 700 kilometers of borders with Afghanistan, and its collaboration is essential in preventing illicit-drug smuggling from Afghanistan.[8]

It is important to note that behind this growing drug problem is a complicated and controversial political dimension. In 2001, the multinational coalition in Afghanistan relied on Afghan mujahideen, an Islamic rebel group, for assistance in eradicating Taliban and Al Qaeda holdouts. The Bonn Accord, which created an interim administration to lead Afghanistan until elections could be held, called for the dismantling of such mujahideen armies before the *Loya Jirga*, or vote, took place—a requirement not yet carried out. Among the mujahideen are key Afghan warlords who were powerful in the early 1990s and reacquired dominant ranks in Afghanistan's present government. A few among them allegedly control and fuel the opium trade from which they reap substantial economic benefits.[9]

Morocco The government of Morocco and UNODC conducted the country's first cannabis cultivation survey in 2003. The analysis shows an increase in cannabis production that could halt prospects of sustainable development in the country. The survey estimates Morocco's raw cannabis production in 2003 at 47,000 metric tons. Cannabis cultivation is concentrated in the northern region of Morocco and accelerates soil erosion. Moreover, 6.5 percent of the country's agricultural families depend on cannabis cultivation.[10] These figures highlight the potential destabilization of the social and economic structures of the Rif region in northern Morocco from the illicit crop. Mr. Costa praised Morocco for exposing information about its cannabis cultivation and called on Europe to reduce its drug consumption. Trafficking networks in Europe control most of an annual market of $12 billion, which stimulates Morocco's cannabis cultivation.[11]

Laos and Myanmar These countries had positive news to report in 2003. The beneficial trend observed in Myanmar in 2002 continued for another year, as opium production declined further in 2003. The latest UNODC opium survey reveals that opium poppy cultivation is down by 24 percent to 62,200 hectares in 2003, as opposed to 81,400 in 2002. The largest decline occurred in the Northern Shan, where farmers act in accordance with the government's requests to discontinue opium poppy plantation.[12] Opium poppy cultivation in Laos also continued its steady decline since 1998, decreasing by 15 percent in 2003 to 12,000 hectares from 14,100 in 2002. Still, according to UNODC's latest opium survey, an estimated 40,000 households will continue to derive the largest share of their income from the opium harvests, which represented 42 percent of their annual cash income last year.[13]

Additional notes According to the latest ICMP surveys, coca cultivation has remained stable in Peru and continues its beneficial decline in neighboring Colombia. These results explain the 17 percent decline in 2002 of aggregate coca cultivation in the Andean region (Colombia, Peru and Bolivia).[14]

In terms of ATS (amphetamine-type stimulants) control, UNODC issued its global survey on ecstasy and ATS in September 2003, indicating that all countries are affected by ATS, either as consumers or producers or both. Approximately 40 million people of different ages, genders, nationalities and incomes are affected by the ATS epidemic, as amphetamine production is increasing and becoming more sophisticated.[15]

Money Laundering

UNODC's Legal Advisory Programme and the Inter-American Drug Control Commission launched a "Mock Trial on Money Laundering" project in 2003. The campaign aims to equip front-line investigators, prosecutors and judges with the know-how and tools necessary to crack complex money-laundering cases. Interaction appears to be the common denominator in UNODC's other projects aimed at apprehending money-laundering offenders. For example, its Regional Centre for East Asia and the Pacific produced a CD-ROM that requires participants to learn about money laundering.[16]

Looking Forward

In the General Assembly's 59th Session, UNODC is expected to further incorporate gender perspectives into its discussions and work.[17] Women, in fact, are more and more affected by drug abuse, through various means. Some women in Islamic societies, for example, who are addicted or cohabitate with a male drug-addicted partner suffer from dire financial consequences that drive them to prostitution and drug smuggling, fueling the vicious cycle of drug-related crime. According to the Tajik State Commission for the Control of Narcotics, two thirds of the arrests for drug smuggling in the first half of 2000 were women.[18]

Controlling the production and trade of illicit drugs is a challenging task that requires long-term commitment and international collaboration. Setbacks should not discourage action, according to Mr. Costa. "If we put together income and social trends, public health factors, detection and treatment approaches, together with perceptions and the need to show results, one message emerges. . . . the greater and the wider the commitment of society to drug control, the greater the likelihood of success," he said.[19]

Commentary:
Sanctions Can Succeed in U.N. Counter-Terrorism Efforts: The Libyan Example

Thomas E. McNamara

Now that Libyan leader Muammar el-Qaddafi has acted to end the 1992-1993 United Nations Security Council sanctions, it is time to examine why one of the strongest proponents of terrorism in support of Arab nationalism changed his mind. Most importantly for the United Nations, it is a chance to understand the role that its sanctions played in this change.

We should begin with the 1988 Lockerbie bombing, which was Qaddafi's horrific criminal response to U.S. military strikes in 1986. Those strikes came after Libya's terrorist bombing of a Berlin nightclub that killed American servicemen. That bombing, in turn, was Qaddafi's reply to U.S. military confrontations contesting his exaggerated claims to the Gulf of Sidra. And those confrontations were responses to Libya's claims and its state sponsorship of terrorism. The sequence of these tit-for-tat actions escalated into the Lockerbie tragedy.

By 1991, the Lockerbie forensic investigation pointed directly to Libya, and the U.S. faced a decision: use military action or diplomacy. President George H. W. Bush chose to break the cycle of violence. He turned to the United Kingdom and France to cosponsor Security Council sanctions against Libya for bombing Pan Am flight 103 and UTA flight 772 over Africa. For the first time, the Council imposed Chapter VII sanctions for acts of terrorism. The dispute became one between Qaddafi and the United Nations—and Qaddafi's downward spiral began.

Facing effective, targeted U.N. sanctions, the pariah chose defiance and ended up trapped for a decade, unwilling to back down and unable to use terrorism without risking stronger sanctions. He reassessed in the late 1990s, and in 1999, surrendered two thugs, hoping to end his isolation and bolster his increasingly endangered regime.

This change came about largely from the sanctions and a separate, fundamental change in the Arab world. Nasserite Arab nationalism—the ideology that fueled Qaddafi's terrorism in the 1970s and 1980s—was overtaken in the mid-1990s by more virulent, pan-Islamic religious terrorism. This new terrorism brand aims to bring down both the West and secular Islamic rulers—like Qaddafi.

The Libyan sanctions were a significant refinement of the now-discarded general sanctions, and played an important role in convincing Libya to cease its support of terrorism. These first-ever U.N.-targeted sanctions (aka smart sanctions) saved lives and advanced the international community's counter-terrorism and nonproliferation goals. They have served as a model for innovative U.N. sanctions against Liberia, in Angola and, most recently, with the Taliban and Al Qaeda. Further refinements should focus on sanctioning violators, not the innocent, by focusing on such things as arms, illegal air transit, smuggled commodities and travel sanctions. Such advances will increase the value of this tool in the U.N.'s counter-terrorism toolkit.

Endnotes

Iraq and Nuclear Proliferation

1. "Iraq's Postwar Oil Exports Exceed $7.5 billion," *Reuters*, April 13, 2004.
2. "Prisoner Abuse Probe Widened," *Washington Post*, May 2, 2004.
3. "The Fallout from Fallujah," *Washington Post*, May 1, 2003.
4. "Hussein Loyalists Blamed for Chaos," *Washington Post*, May 15, 2003.
5. "Order Dissolving Iraqi Military Raises Other Worries," *Washington Post*, May 24, 2003.
6. "Hussein's 2 Sons Dead in Shootout, U.S. Says," *New York Times*, July 23, 2003. / "Pentagon Unveils Plan to Bolster Forces in Iraq," *Washington Post*, July 24, 2003.
7. "Huge Suicide Blast Demolishes U.N. Headquarters in Baghdad," *New York Times*, August 19, 2003. / "Aid Groups Reduce Operations in Iraq," *Washington Post*, August 22, 2003.
8. "Occupation Commander Does Not Expect More Foreign Troops in Iraq," *New York Times*, September 26, 2003.
9. "Bush Says Iraqis Will Try Hussein," *Washington Post*, December 16, 2003.
10. "Bremer Survived Ambush Outside Baghdad," *Washington Post*, December 20, 2003.
11. "U.S. Seeks to Bolster Coalition," *Arizona Republic*, March 17, 2004.
12. "Will the Bloodstained Shias Resist the Urge to Hit Back?," *Economist*, March 6, 2004.
13. "138,000 Troops to Stay in Iraq Through 2005," *Washington Post*, May 5, 2004.
14. " Eight U.S. Troops Killed in Shiite Uprising," *Washington Post*, April 5, 2004. / "U.S. Targeted Fiery Cleric in Risky Move," *Washington Post*, April 11, 2004. / "Fighting Continues; Troop Deployments May Be Extended," *Washington Post*, April 9, 2004, among others.
15. "U.N. Envoy Proposes Caretaker Iraqi Government," *Associated Press*, April 15, 2004.
16. "Nominee Assures Senate on Iraq," *Washington Post*, April 28, 2004. / "U.N. Warns of Delay in Iraqi Election," *Washington Post*, May 4, 2004.
17. "Ex-Arms Hunter Kay Says No WMD Stockpiles in Iraq," *Reuters*, January 23, 2004.
18. David Kay interview, "NewsHour With Jim Lehrer," PBS, January 29, 2004. / "The Inspectors Final Report," *Guardian*, March 3, 2004. / "Frustrated, U.S. Arms Team to Leave Iraq," *Washington Post*, May 11, 2003. / "Blair Takes a Beating on the Weapons of Mass Destruction," *Washington Post*, June 4, 2003. / "Missing Weapons May Become Election Issue," *Washington Post*, June 11, 2003, among others.
19. "Rebuilding Aid Unspent, Tapped to Pay Expenses," *Washington Post*, April 30, 2004.
20. USAID website, April 2004.
21. S/RES/1483 (2003)
22. Kofi Annan, Speech before the U.N. General Assembly, September 23, 2003.
23. S/RES/1511 (2003)
24. "U.S. Offers Concessions on U.N. Arms Inspectors," *Washington Post*, May 20, 2003. / "In Search of a New Resolution," *Economist*, September 13, 2003. / "U.S. Drafts Plan for U.N. to Back a Force for Iraq," *New York Times*, September 4, 2003. / "Annan Tells the General Assembly That U.N. Must Correct Its Weaknesses," *New York Times*, September 24, 2003, among others.
25. "Troubled and Troubling Times, the 2003 First Committee Considers Disarmament and Reform," *Disarmament Diplomacy*, December 2003.
26. "North Koreans Agree to Mid-Level Talks," *Washington Post*, April 30, 2004.

27. Board of Governors Resolution, March 13, 2004.
28. "From Rogue Nuclear Programs, Web of Trails Leads to Pakistan," *New York Times*, January 4, 2004.
29. "Pakistani Scientist Apologizes; Nuclear Assistance Unauthorized, He Says," *Washington Post*, February 5, 2004; "Pakistani Scientist Is Pardoned; President Won't Submit to Nuclear Inspections," *Washington Post*, February 6, 2004.
30. "Pakistani's Exploited Nuclear Network," *Washington Post*, January 28, 2004. / "Insider Tells of Nuclear Deals, Cash," *Washington Post*, February 21, 2004.
31. "U.N. Nuclear Chief Warns of Global Black Market," *Washington Post*, February 6, 2004.
32. "Pakistan and India Agree to Peace Talks," *Washington Post*, February 19, 2004.
33. "Despite Khan, Military Ties With Pakistan to Grow," *Arms Control Today*, April 2004.
34. "$27 Million Sought for Nuclear Arms Study," *Washington Post*, March 21, 2004.
35. "U.S. Reviewing FMCT Policy," *Arms Control Today*, November 2003.
36. George W. Bush, speech at the National Defense University, February 11, 2004.
37. S/RES/1540 (2004).
38. "Lugar, Hunter Lock Horns on Threat Reduction," *Arms Control Today*, April 2003. / "Eliminating the Obstacles to Nunn-Lugar," *Arms Control Today*, March 2004.
39. "New U.S., Russian Chemical Destruction Deadlines Approved," *Arms Control Today*, November 2003.
40. "Syria – E.U. Trade Deal Stalls Over Chemical Weapons Issue," *Washington Post*, April 8, 2004.
41. Libya Made Progress in Nuclear Goal," *Washington Post*, December 21, 2003.
42. "GAO Covertly Buys Bioweapons Gear from Defense Department," *Arms Control Today*, November 2003.
43. "BWC States-Parties Meeting Yields Little," *Arms Control Today*, December 2003.
44. "Flights Cut on Fear of Al Qaeda Attacks," *Washington Post*, February, 2004.
45. "Study Casts Doubt on Boot-Phase Missile Defense," *Arms Control Today*, October 2003.
46. "Is Missile Defense on Target?," *Arms Control Today*, October 2003.
47. "Missile Defense Agency Faulted on Testing and Accountability," *Washington Post*, April 24, 2004. / "General Says Missile Defense Could Be Ready Soon," *Washington Post*, April 28, 2004.
48. "U.S. Will Not Join Landmine Treaty; Position on Fissile Material Cut-off Pact Uncertain," *Arms Control Today*, March 2004.
49. "Pact on Battlefield Munitions Reached," *Arms Control Today*, January/February, 2004.
50. "Small Arms Meeting Addresses Progress, Pitfalls," *Arms Control Today*, September 2003.
51. "Wassenaar Endorses Steps to Deny Terrorists Arms," *Arms Control Today*, January/February 2004.
52. "U.S. Still Reigns as Top Global Arms Seller," *Arms Control Today*, October 2003.
53. "Russia Tops in Quantity of Arms Shipped in 2002," *Arms Control Today*, November 2003.

Terrorism

1. *Fighting Terrorism for Humanity: A Conference on the Roots of Evil*, Report, International Peace Academy, 2003.
2. Bruce Hoffman. Inside Terrorism (Columbia University Press, 1998).
3. S/Res/1455, 1456, 1502, 1506, 1516, 1526, 1530 and 1535.
4. S/Res/1540 (2004).

5. S/2004/276.
6. S/2004/124.
7. S/Res/1535 (2004).
8. A/58/266 (Report of the Secretary-General, August 8, 2003).
9. S/Res/1267 (1999) and S/Res/1526 (2004).
10. *Report of the Security in Iraq Accountability Panel (SIAP)*, U.N. General Assembly, March 3, 2004.
11. *Statement by Spokesperson for the Secretary-General*, March 29, 2004.
12. A/Res/58/82.
13. A/Res/58/48.
14. A/Res/58/81.
15. A/Res58/136.
16. A/Res/58/174 and A/Res/58/187.
17. A/Res/51/210.
18. A/58/37, Annex I A.
19. *Global Program Against Terrorism*, U.N. Office on Drugs and Crime/Terrorism Prevention Branch, August 2003.
20. Unpublished paper by Joel Sollier, expert adviser to the CTC, March 2004.

Narcotics

1. U.N. Office on Drugs and Crime "Update" Newsletter, November 2003.
2. *Vietnam 2003: Strategic Program Framework*, U.N. Office on Drugs and Crime, 2003.
3. Ibid, 2.
4. U.N. Press Release SOC/NAR/896, March 19, 2004.
5. *Afghanistan Farmers' Intentions Survey 2003/2004*, U.N. Office on Drugs and Crime, February 2004.
6. U.N. Information Service Press Release UNIS/NAR/830, February 18, 2004.
7. U.N. Information Service Press Release SOC/NAR/899, March 30, 2004.
8. U.N. Information Service Press Release UNIS/NAR/831, March 3, 2004.
9. "Afghanistan Unbound," *Foreign Affairs*, May/June 2004.
10. *Executive Summary: Morocco Cannabis Survey 2003*, U.N. Office on Drugs and Crime, December 2003.
11. Ibid, 2.
12. *Myanmar Opium Survey 2003*, U.N. Office of Drugs and Crime, June 2003.
13. *Laos Opium Survey 2003*, U.N. Office on Drugs and Crime, June 2003.
14. U.N. Information Service Press Release UNIS/NAR/796, May 15, 2003.
15. U.N. Information Service Press Release UNIS/NAR/836, March 15, 2004.
16. Ibid, 2.
17. A/59/6.
18. Ibid, 1.
19. Ibid, 17.

Chapter 6

Maintaining International Law Across All Borders

Neal Higgins

> *In the past months, we have taken a number of strategic decisions that will guide our work. . . . Some key strategic decisions include: a collaborative approach with the international community, including cooperative states, international organisations and civil society and a positive approach to complementarity. Rather than competing with national systems for jurisdiction, we will encourage national proceedings wherever possible.*
>
> —ICC Prosecutor Luis Moreno Ocampo,
> *Statement to Diplomatic Corps at The Hague,* February 2004.

International law emerges from a wide range of sources, including the acts and opinions of states as well as decisions and resolutions from within the United Nations system. There are certain U.N. bodies and institutions, however, that have a consistent impact on the codification and development of international law. These institutions fall into three categories: legislative organs under the General Assembly, tribunals that adjudicate civil claims between states, and tribunals that adjudicate criminal charges against individuals. *(See Table on Legal Institutions.)*

The latter of the three, criminal tribunals, have undoubtedly received the most attention in recent years, especially with the groundbreaking work of various *ad hoc* tribunals and the establishment of the International Criminal Court (ICC) in July 2002. The resolution of those disputes, the first experiences and cases of the ICC, and the success or failure of various new *ad hoc* tribunals will shape international criminal law for years to come. The debate over the role and form of such tribunals continued during the 58th session of the Assembly, with the June 2003 indictment of Liberia's Charles Taylor and the December 2003 arrest of Saddam Hussein. While not currently within U.N. jurisdiction, the abuse of detainees by U.S. forces in Afghanistan, Iraq and, allegedly, Cuba, has also drawn attention to the future of international criminal law.

International criminal law, however, represents only a fraction of the wider body of public international law. The legal bodies of the G.A. and the tribunals that adjudicate disputes between states make equally important contributions to the codification and progressive development of interna-

Legal Institutions Within the United Nations System

TYPE OF INSTITUTION	INSTITUTION	SOURCE OF AUTHORITY	POSITION IN THE U.N. SYSTEM
Legislative Bodies	Sixth Committee	Delegation from the General Assembly (G.A.)	Committee of the Whole of the G.A.
	International Law Commission (ILC)	Delegation from the G.A.	Commission of the G.A.
Tribunals for Civil Claims Between States	International Court of Justice (ICJ)	U.N. Charter, ICJ Statute	Major organ of the U.N. under the U.N. Charter
	International Tribunal for the Law of the Sea (ITLOS)	U.N. Convention on the Law of the Sea (UNCLOS)	Independent Treaty-Based Tribunal
Tribunals for Criminal Claims Against Individuals	International Criminal Court (ICC)	Rome Statute of the ICC	Independent Treaty-Based Tribunal
	International Criminal Tribunal for the former Yugoslavia (ICTY)	S.C. Delegation of Authority under Chapter VII of the U.N. Charter	*Ad hoc* entity reporting to the S.C. and the G.A.
	International Criminal Tribunal for Rwanda (ICTR)	S.C. Delegation of Authority under Chapter VII of the U.N. Charter	*Ad hoc* entity reporting to the S.C. and the G.A.
	Special Court for Sierra Leone (SCSL)	Treaty between the U.N. and the Sierra Leonean government	Independent Treaty-Based Tribunal
	Extraordinary Chambers (Cambodia)	Treaty between the U.N. and the Cambodian government	Independent Treaty-Based Tribunal
	Kosovo Courts under the Supervision of the U.N. Mission in Kosovo (UNMIK)	S.C. resolutions and relevant agreements establishing UNMIK	Local courts assisted by U.N. personnel
	East Timorese Courts under the Supervision of the U.N. Transitional Administration in East Timor (UNTAET)	S.C. resolutions and relevant agreements establishing UNTAET	Local courts assisted by U.N. personnel

tional law. In the Assembly itself, the Sixth Committee and the International Law Commission (ILC) prepare treaties, while the International Court of Justice (ICJ) and the International Tribunal for the Law of the Sea (ITLOS) regularly issue rulings and judgments that affect the rights and duties of states. In some cases, their judgments touch on the most hotly contested international disputes, such as the Israeli-Palestinian conflict and the use of forces without Security Council approval.

This chapter reviews the work of each of these legal institutions over 2003 and the first half of 2004.

Conventional Law-Making at the U.N.

With regard to "conventional," or treaty-based, law, Article 13 of the U.N. Charter grants the G.A. specific authority to "initiate studies and make recommendations for the purpose of...encouraging the progressive development of international law and its codification." The G.A. pursues that mandate through its Sixth Committee with the assistance of the ILC, *ad hoc* working groups of member states and the Codification Division of the U.N. Secretariat's Office of Legal Affairs.

The Process

A proposed treaty usually originates in the Assembly, which refers it to the Sixth Committee, which in turn refers it either to the ILC or to an *ad hoc* committee made up of representatives of select member states. The *ad hoc* committees and the ILC then draft the substantive articles of the proposed treaty, which they eventually return to the Sixth Committee for comment and consideration. The Sixth Committee can return the draft articles for further work, forward them to the plenary session of the G.A. for immediate adoption or forward them to the plenary session of the G.A. with a recommendation that it convene a conference of member states to negotiate a treaty. In any given G.A. session, several proposed treaties or elements of a treaty exist at any stage in this process. A similar process can occur for other legal issues: the G.A. might, for example, ask the Sixth Committee to consider the scope of an existing treaty or the status of a non-state party that wishes to observe Assembly proceedings.

As the process itself suggests, most of the substantive discussion on legal matters occurs outside the G.A.'s plenary sessions. At the beginning of each annual session, the G.A. allocates agenda items to the Sixth Committee. Once allocated, those agenda items often reappear at a plenary session only after the Sixth Committee has proposed a resolution for adoption. The Sixth Committee is itself one of several Committees of the Whole, which serve primarily as a means for the G.A. to hold meetings on multiple topics simultaneously. All 191 U.N. member states have a seat in the Sixth Committee, although most states send international-law specialists to represent them. Because all states can participate in the Sixth Committee, there may be little left to discuss in the plenary session once the Sixth Committee has recommended a draft resolution.

Such draft resolutions do not, however, guarantee immediate action. As both a legislative and a diplomatic process, the creation of conventional international law takes time, often stretching out over many G.A. sessions. In fact, many Sixth Committee draft resolutions do little more than report on progress and call for further work at future sessions.

Sixth Committee

In its 58th session, the G.A. allocated 16 agenda items to the Sixth Committee for its consideration. The following section provides an update on a select number of these items.[1]

Administration of Justice

In April 2003, the G.A. requested that the Secretary-General provide a report on alternatives for strengthening the administration of justice within the United Nations. More specifically, the G.A. asked the S.G. to perform a management review of the appeals process for legal claims made within the U.N. system; to provide a detailed report on the Panel on Discrimination and Other Grievances; and to develop a system of personal accountability by which the U.N. could recover financial losses caused by management irregularities, wrongful actions or gross negligence by U.N. officials, each case resulting in adverse judgments by the U.N. Administrative Tribunal. For its own part, the G.A. decided to amend the statute of the U.N. Administrative Tribunal to require that candidates for that tribunal possess administrative-law experience in a judicial capacity. That task fell to the Sixth Committee, which adopted such an amendment and recommended it to the Assembly as a whole.

Principles and Norms

Resuming a discussion deferred from its 55th session, the Sixth Committee turned to the legal aspects of international economic law in the fall of 2003. Those delegates who favored debate on the topic noted the need to establish a new system of international economic relations that is based on the U.N. Charter and consistent with the *Millennium Declaration*. They suggested the agenda item be revitalized and called on states to submit proposals for debate at the Committee's next session. The Sixth Committee as a whole agreed to reconsider the item.

Appreciation of International Law

Continuing an effort begun in 1965, delegates to the Sixth Committee reviewed the work of the U.N. Programme on Teaching, Study, Dissemination and Wider Appreciation of International Law, which works with educational institutions and NGOs to raise the profile and understanding of international law. Delegates emphasized the importance of making resources available online and expanding the program to reach not just legal professionals but also the public, particularly educators and the media. They also renewed the call for voluntary contributions to fund the program, suggesting that private foundations be asked to contribute.

Protecting State Property

In 1991, the G.A. decided to convene a working group of the Sixth Committee to consider the level, if any, of immunity that states and their property should be allowed foreign legal judgments. For example, should Mexican plaintiffs suing in a Mexican court be able to collect a judgment against the Candian government? That working group eventually led to an *ad hoc* committee, which concluded its work in 2003. In October, the *ad hoc* committee presented its draft articles on the jurisdictional immunities of states to the Sixth Committee.[2] The Committee acknowledged that the draft articles were an important step forward in international law, discussed whether they could form the basis for a treaty and ultimately requested that the *ad hoc* committee put the draft articles in treaty form.[3] By helping states determine their rights before foreign courts with regard to commercial activities, such a treaty could help smooth the flow of international trade.

International Trade Law

As it does every year, the Sixth Committee reviewed the work of the U.N. Commission on International Trade Law (UNCITRAL) at its 58th session. After reviewing UNCITRAL's yearly report, delegates commended the commission for its model legislative provisions on privately financed infrastructure projects, which supplemented a legislative guide on the same topic that UNCITRAL issued in 2000.[4] Looking to the future, delegates approved the Commission's proposal to focus on commercial fraud and public procurement, but expressed concern that UNCITRAL might not receive the necessary funding to fulfill its mandate.

International Law Commission

The Sixth Committee also reviewed the annual report of the ILC, which was founded by the G.A. at its second session, in 1947, with the hope that it would assist in the codification and progressive development of international law under the U.N. Charter. The ILC now has 34 members, each elected to a five-year term; the last election occurred at the G.A.'s 56th session. At its 58th Session, the Sixth Committee's discussion of the ILC's report focused on several issues, noted below.

Responsibility of International Organizations Delegates discussed the work of the ILC on two related questions: when can conduct be attributed to an international organization, and how should international organizations be held responsible when their conduct causes harm? Some of the more difficult issues included whether an international organization's own rules can allow it to avoid responsibility under international law, and at what point should an international organization overseeing a peacekeeping operation—as opposed to individual states contributing troops—bear responsibility for the conduct of peacekeepers. Offering several suggestions on specific points, the delegates asked the ILC to continue its work.

Diplomatic Protection Reviewing the work of the ILC on diplomatic protection, or a state's ability to protect its nationals and businesses, the delegates to the Sixth Committee expressed several concerns with draft articles that were proposed by the ILC. Some focused on the question of what legal remedies a state must offer a foreign national before that person's state of nationality can intervene. Others addressed the test for determining a corporation's state of nationality, debating whether that test should look only to the corporation's state of incorporation, or whether it should also require a "genuine" or "effective" link between the corporation and its state of incorporation. Requiring such a link might, for example, prevent a U.S. corporation from reincorporating in the Cayman Islands for tax purposes. The extension of diplomatic protection to ships' crews and employees of international organizations also provoked discussion, with some suggesting that international conventions adequately covered both groups already.

International Liability for Acts Not Prohibited by International Law Delegates to the Sixth Committee discussed the ILC's efforts to establish a legal regime to manage cross-border pollution. Some favored strict liability, under which a polluter and that polluter's state would be liable for all damage caused by hazardous activities, while others preferred a negligence-based approach. Delegates also expressed opinions as to the relationship between new international standards and existing regional approaches, the standard of proof for demonstrating a connection between an act and its alleged consequences, the threshold of harm to incur liability, protection of the global commons and the role of states in preventing harm in the first place.

Unilateral Acts of States Discussing how international law should treat unilateral acts of states, in particular the recognition of new states after, for example, a secession or civil war, Committee delegates expressed a wide range of views. Some supported further study of the topic, while others thought the ILC's work should be discontinued. Specific suggestions included a continuing focus on recognition of new states, excluding acts of recognition by waiver or action by an international organization and focusing on the practice of placing conditions on the modification or revocation of a unilateral act. Individual delegates believed that a continued study of state practice would further the ILC's work, and advocated the eventual adoption of international guidelines.

Reservations to Treaties As they debated ILC proposals on reservations to treaties, delegates focused primarily on two topics: objections to reservations made by other states, and the practice of extending an existing reservation to a treaty. Some focused on the question of when a state's concerns with a reservation amounted to an objection; others questioned whether noncontracting states, or those not party to a treaty, should be able to make objections to a reservation. With regard to extending the scope of an existing reservation, delegates differed as to whether such modifications should be allowed at all and, if so, whether they should be viewed simply as a late formulation of the original reservation.

Shared Natural Resources Reviewing continuing work on the topic, speakers praised the ILC's focus on groundwater but disagreed over whether the continuing work should go beyond or set stricter thresholds than the 1997 *Convention on the Non-Navigational Uses of International Watercourses.* Emphasizing the importance of groundwater for sustainable development, delegates focused on the need to protect groundwater from pollution.

Diversification and Expansion of International Law Finally, delegates to the Sixth Committee expressed their support for ILC's continuing study of the diffuse channels through which international law is made. Some noted that although the fragmentation of international law raises potential conflicts between states, it nonetheless enhances the effectiveness of international law as a whole. Others emphasized the need for coordination between the various national and international institutions that now contribute to the development of international law, including, for example, cooperation between national judiciaries.

Report of the Committee on Relations With the Host Country

The Committee on Relations With the Host Country routinely addresses some of the more practical, if at times mundane, questions facing U.N. delegates. Its report to the Sixth Committee during the 58th session focused on two issues: the Parking Programme for Diplomatic Vehicles, an effort to address parking and congestion concerns in New York City, and delays in issuing visas for entry into the United States, resulting from heightened restrictions after the terrorist attacks of September 11, 2001.

International Criminal Court

Delegates to the Sixth Committee began their discussion of the International Criminal Court by praising the significant progress it has made since its Rome Statute entered into force in July 2002. In particular, the ICC has elected its judges, prosecutor, first deputy prosecutor, registrar and board of directors of the Victims Trust Fund. Some delegates called on all U.N. member states to become party to the Rome Statute and expressed concern over efforts to seek exemptions from prosecution through Security Council resolutions introduced by the U.S. and bilateral agreements, particularly in light of the S.C.'s recent reluctance to establish new *ad hoc* tribunals. They further suggested that the ICC would soon demonstrate its ability to function as an independent and impartial institution. Other delegates noted, however, that the ICC still had the potential to be used for political purposes.

Turning to the actual operation of the court, delegates noted with satisfaction the Prosecutor's efforts to establish a transparent policy based on complementarity, the principle that states should have the right and duty to investigate and prosecute cases before the ICC seeks to exercise its jurisdiction. Some stressed the importance of the work of the Special Working Group on the Crime of Aggression, which is still working toward a definition of that crime. Others called for geographical diversity among the Court's officials, suggesting that the second deputy prosecutor be an African.

With regard to ongoing action, delegates focused on the need to grant the S.G. the authority to negotiate, on behalf of the United Nations, an agreement establishing the relationship between the U.N. and the ICC, as the ICC is not an official organ of the world body. They also encouraged an early conclusion of the Headquarters Agreement between the ICC and its host country, The Netherlands. Focusing on the role of states parties, delegates called on states to implement the Rome Statute domestically, to provide technical assistance to the Court and to pay assessed contributions on time.

Special Committee on the U.N. Charter

Reviewing the work of the Special Committee, which has existed in various forms since 1969 and now meets annually, delegates to the Sixth Committee focused on several issues of concern. First, with regard to economic sanctions, delegates called for greater attention to the effect of sanctions on civilians both in the targeted state and in third states that trade with the targeted state. With regard to the costs that sanctions impose on such third states, delegates supported recommendations that all U.N. member states assist in bearing such costs, possibly through a trust fund or economic and trade concessions. The delegates from the Russian Federation and the Libyan Arab Jamahiriya also suggested that the Special Committee and the Sixth Committee review basic principles governing the introduction and application of such sanctions.

With regard to peacekeeping operations, various delegates suggested further study of the topic. Delegates from Belarus and the Russian Federation proposed seeking an advisory opinion from the ICJ on the legality of the use of force without previous S.C. authorization. Delegates also considered the future of the Trusteeship Council, with some suggesting that its abolishment or any change in its mandate in the broader context of U.N. reform rather than occur independently.

Last but not least, the Sixth Committee discussed the *Repertory of Practice of United Nations Organs* and the *Repertoire of the Security Council*, two Secretariat publications that assist U.N. member states as they follow and study the U.N.'s work. Noting that both publications require updating and revision, delegates supported their dissemination via the Internet but also called for appropriate funding to ensure their printed publication.

International Terrorism

In the wake of September 11th, the task of developing legal responses to international terrorism acquired new urgency. At its 57th session, the Sixth Committee instructed the *ad hoc* Committee on International Terrorism to continue its work toward comprehensive international conventions on international terrorism and nuclear terrorism. The Committee also established a working group to consider recommendations by the *ad hoc* committee and to prepare for the possible adoption of the two conventions. The Working Group began meeting in October 2003, with its chairman dividing work between two coordinators for informal consultations and calling on all states to consider the possibility of convening a conference under U.N. auspices to develop an organized international response to all forms of international terrorism.

After informal consultations, and having received reports that delegates had referred to their capitals the question of convening an international conference on terrorism, the working group reported on its work to the full Sixth Committee. As noted in Chapter 5, delegates condemned recent terrorist attacks, particularly against U.N. headquarters in Baghdad, and emphasized the urgent importance of drafting conventions on international terrorism and nuclear terrorism. But several points of contention nonetheless emerged. Some speakers restated their position that any definition of terrorism must distinguish between illegal terrorist actions and those that form part of a legitimate struggle for self-determination. Others suggested that it remained unclear what relationship the *Draft Comprehensive Convention on International Terrorism* would have to existing conventions. Various delegates added that any international conference on terrorism should occur only after the adoption of a comprehensive convention.

Turning to the substance of the draft conventions, some delegates focused on the dangers of state-sponsored terrorism, and noted that not all states judge terrorism to be unacceptable in all circumstances. Others emphasized instead the need to address the root causes of terrorism, rather than responding to terrorism with the unilateral use of force or by associating terrorism with individual regions or cultures. All agreed, however, that legal responses to terrorism should remain a priority, and that the U.N.'s Counter-Terrorism Committee (CTC) should play a lead role by enforcing S.C. resolutions.

Convention on the Safety of United Nations and Associated Personnel

In 2001, at its 56th session, the Sixth Committee established an *ad hoc* committee to consider the question of protecting U.N. and associated personnel. The *ad hoc* committee held its final meetings in March 2003, but the Sixth Committee continued its work through a working group during the 58th session. With reports from that working group and from the Secretary-General, as well as the text of a relevant S.C. resolution and the 1994 *Convention on the Safety of United Nations and Associated Personnel*, delegates to the working group and the Sixth Committee as a whole discussed the topic over several meetings.

Reviewing the S.G.'s report, some delegates to the working group expressed concern that few perpetrators of violence against U.N. personnel have been brought to justice. Others doubted that expanding the scope of legal protections for U.N. personnel would better protect U.N. personnel without further measures by host states and the Secretary-General. Nonetheless, several delegates suggested that short-term measures and existing S.C. resolutions would prove insufficient unless they were coupled with broader long-term legal protections that are both universally applicable and universally ratified by states.

Taking the discussion into account, New Zealand offered a proposal, amended by the European Union, that would make the existing convention apply more universally by eliminating the need for a declaration of "exceptional risk" and by automatically applying existing legal protections to any operation under U.N. authority. Some objected that such an expansion was undesirable and, by placing a greater burden on states in which U.N. operations occur, would make the existing legal regime even less tenable. The proposal led to a discussion of what should qualify as a U.N. operation, and what U.N. operations should be considered to pose sufficient risk for legal protections to apply. Despite these outstanding questions, delegates favored the New Zealand proposal to one offered by Jordan, which would have focused on "situations" rather than operations. With regard to form, delegates reached agreement that any new legal measure should stand as either an optional protocol to the existing convention or as a stand-alone agreement.

When the Sixth Committee considered the discussion and proposals for the working group in plenary sessions, delegates reiterated many of their concerns, but agreed that the *ad hoc* committee should reconvene in 2004 with a new mandate to develop a long-term legal solution.

International Convention Against the Reproductive Cloning of Human Beings

As pointed out in Chapter 1, at its 56th session, the G.A. recommended establishment of a working group, within the context of an *ad hoc* committee of the Sixth Committee, to consider the question of reproductive human cloning. The working group met in September 2002 but differed on how best to approach the issue, and the Sixth Committee thus recommended that it continue its work in 2003. As in 2002, debate in the working group and in the Sixth Committee as a whole focused on the moral and ethical issues involved in human cloning, as well as the feasibility of banning cloning for reproductive purposes while regulating cloning for research purposes. Some delegates pointed to national efforts along those lines, which they claimed to have struck a successful balance. Others, however, said that their states could not support a partial ban regardless of safeguards and restrictions on cloning for research purposes, and called for a moratorium on all cloning pending adoption of an international convention. As it became clear that states could not agree on the issue, delegates ultimately chose to postpone the discussion until the Assembly's 60th session.

Observer Status

After some discussion, the Sixth Committee recommended granting observer status in the G.A. to the International Institute for Democracy and Electoral Assistance, the Eurasian Economic Community and the East African Community.

Looking Forward

The General Assembly has included nearly all of the Sixth Committee items discussed in the first part of this chapter in the agenda for its 59th session. In addition, it will address the nationality of persons in relation to the succession of states, the responsibility of states for internationally wrongful acts and the status of the *Protocols Additional to the Geneva Conventions* of 1949. The 59th session's agenda also includes several items related to international law but that may not be referred to the Sixth Committee. Among these are reports from and financing for the International Criminal Tribunal for the former

Yugoslavia, the International Criminal Tribunal for Rwanda, the International Court of Justice, discussion of the law of the sea and discussion of ICJ's advisory opinion on the legality of the use of nuclear weapons.

Of these topics, discussion of the International Criminal Court promises to be the liveliest. As discussed later in this chapter, the United States has continually opposed mention of the ICC in Security Council resolutions, and has occasionally fought mention of the ICC in Assembly resolutions as well. In Resolution 58/79 of December 11, 2003, despite U.S. protest, the G.A. invited the Secretary-General to "take steps to conclude a relationship agreement" between the U.S. and the ICC, and to submit the negotiated draft to the G.A. for approval. As the U.S. does not sit in the ICC's Assembly of States Parties, which must also approve the agreement, the U.S. will likely take a strong stance on the draft.

At the time of writing, the International Law Commission had adopted its own agenda for work during its 56th session in May and July 2004. Topics discussed included responsibility of international organizations, diplomatic protection, international liability for acts not prohibited by international law, unilateral acts of states, reservations to treaties, shared natural resources and the fragmentation of international law. The ILC will present its findings to the Sixth Committee during the Assembly's 59th session.

Civil Claims Between States

Just as the Sixth Committee and its subsidiary organs fill a legislative role in the drafting of treaties, the International Court of Justice (ICJ) and the International Tribunal for the Law of the Sea (ITLOS) fill a judicial role, resolving disputes between states that arise under both existing treaties and customary international law. And just as many treaties are drafted outside the United Nations, many disputes are resolved by tribunals and panels other than ITLOS and the ICJ. Within the U.N. framework, however, they remain the foremost bodies adjudicating claims between states.

International Court of Justice

Although the creation of the International Criminal Tribunal for the former Yugoslavia and the International Criminal Court have created confusion as to what legal commentators mean by "the World Court," the phrase traditionally refers to the International Court of Justice. Unlike the ICTY or ICC, the ICJ adjudicates civil disputes, as opposed to criminal charges. Furthermore, only states and authorized international agencies can petition or appear before the ICJ; it does not hear cases brought by or against individuals or private organizations.

ICJ is the successor to the Permanent Court of International Justice, which served a similar role under the League of Nations. In accordance with the U.N. Charter and the Court's own statute, ICJ consists of 15 judges nominated jointly by the Security Council and General Assembly, hears cases between states, issues nonbinding advisory opinions at the request of the Assembly or Council and hears its cases in public and with proper regard to the rights of all parties. Most importantly, ICJ's statute outlines the sources of law on which the Court must base its decisions: international conventions, international custom as evidence of a general practice accepted as law, general principles of law, judicial decisions and the teachings of the most highly qualified publicists.[5]

While ICJ once suffered from a thin docket, it has faced the opposite problem over the past several years: Congestion threatens the Court's ability to address disputes in a timely fashion.[6] ICJ has adopted measures to expedite its consideration of cases, but a backlog remains. Between May 2003 and April 2004, ICJ issued a final ruling in one case, disposed of another at the request of the parties and heard oral arguments on the merits in a third. It also added two more cases to its docket. In total, including the eight cases filed by Serbia and Montenegro against NATO member states, 21 cases are now pending before the Court.[7] The following highlights from proceedings before the ICJ between April 2003 and April 2004 provide a sense of the Court's docket and operations.

Mexican Nationals and the United States

In January 2003, Mexico asked the ICJ to rule whether the U.S. had violated international law by allowing Mexican nationals in the U.S. to be tried, convicted and sentenced to death without being adequately informed of their right to seek assistance from Mexican consular officials. At issue in Avena and Other Mexican Nationals (Mexico v. United States of America) was the U.S.'s compliance with the Vienna Convention on Consular Relations and Optional Protocols of 1963. The convention requires states that arrest a foreign national to inform that person "without delay" of his or her right to contact a consular official. If a consular official so requests, the convention also requires the host state to notify that official "without delay" of a national's arrest or detention.[8] In the cases in question, both the convicted Mexican nationals and the Mexican government claimed that the U.S. failed to fulfill its treaty obligations.

Mexico's filings at ICJ covered 52 individuals sentenced to death in nine U.S. states. Mexico claimed that 50 of those individuals were never informed of their right to consult with consular officials, and that the other two were not informed of that right "without delay." In 29 of those 52 cases, Mexican consular officials learned of the arrest and detention of a Mexican national only after the death sentence had already been imposed. In the remaining 23 cases, Mexican consular officials learned of the arrest and detention of a national through channels other than notification by U.S. officials, and, in all cases, only after considerable delay. During the course of the proceedings, Mexico learned that three of the 52 individuals had received clemency when the governor of Illinois commuted the sentences of all individuals awaiting execution in that state. Mexico also learned, however, that one of the remaining 49 individuals received notice that he would be executed in May 2004.[9] The Court began its consideration of the case by ordering the U.S. to take all necessary measures to ensure that three of the Mexican nationals in question, who had exhausted all legal options, not be executed before final disposition of the case. It then considered and dismissed four objections to the Court's jurisdiction in which the U.S. argued that the *Vienna Convention* requirements focus solely on notification and do not provide grounds to review the arrest of foreign nationals or the operation of the U.S. criminal justice system. Also dismissed were U.S. arguments that ICJ could not declare notification to be a human right nor vacate convictions in U.S. courts. The Court also rejected U.S. objections to the admissibility of Mexico's submissions, which argued that Mexico sought to make ICJ a court of criminal appeal, that the individuals in question had not yet exhausted all local remedies, that some of the individuals enjoyed dual nationality and were therefore not entitled to protection under the *Vienna Convention*, that Mexico waived its rights by not reacting sooner and, finally, that Mexico itself failed to follow *Vienna Convention* requirements.[10]

Turning to the merits, the Court first ruled that the burden of proving that individuals possess dual nationality lay with the United States, and that it had failed to do so. The Court likewise concluded that the U.S. had failed to provide sufficient evidence in six of seven cases in which it argued that an individual claimed U.S. citizenship during arrest or detention. Turning to interpretation of "without delay," ICJ ruled that the phrase did not mean immediately or necessarily before interrogation, but did suggest that an individual should be informed of his or her rights, and the consular officer informed of a national's arrest or detention, "as soon as it is realized that the person is a foreign national, or once there are grounds to think that the person is probably a foreign national." The Court further ruled that the U.S. had failed to notify detainees of their rights "without delay" in 51 cases, and had failed to notify consular officers "without delay" of the arrest or detention of a national in 48 cases. Failing to notify consular officers without delay also meant that the U.S. had violated the officers' right to communicate with and visit their detained nationals.[11]

Having decided that the U.S. failed in its treaty obligations toward both the detainees and the Mexican government, the Court discussed remedies. Mexico argued that violation of the *Vienna Convention* duties should vitiate criminal proceedings and that the convictions should be annulled in whole or in part. The Court declined to follow that reasoning, and likewise refused to accept Mexico's contention that any statement or confession attained before notifying a suspect of his consular rights should be excluded from evidence. Noting that existing law in the U.S. could limit a defendant's ability to raise *Vienna Convention* issues on appeal, and expressing concern as to the adequacy of clemency proceedings, the Court instead determined that U.S. courts should undertake proper and effective review and reconsideration of the cases in question.[12] The Court further noted the ongoing commitment of the U.S. to meet its *Vienna Convention* obligations, and ruled that continuing efforts to do so would resolve Mexican concerns about future violations.

In the wake of ICJ's ruling, and five days before his scheduled execution, Mexican national Osvaldo Torres Aguilera was granted clemency by the governor of Oklahoma after a court granted a hearing on the state's failure to notify him of his consular rights.[13] Similar proceedings will likely occur in state courts with respect to the other 50 inmates.

Lockerbie Bombing

ICJ dispensed two more cases in 2003, albeit through decisions by the parties rather than through the Court. On September 10, 2003, the governments of Libya and the United Kingdom, in the first case, and Libya and the United States, in the second, agreed to discontinue with prejudice hearings before ICJ with regard to the 1988 bombing of Pan Am flight 103 over Lockerbie, Scotland. Reflecting ICJ's role in resolving complex international disputes, the parties chose to discontinue the case as part of a broader settlement in which they resolved outstanding issues related to Libya's involvement in the bombing.

"The Wall" and Occupied Palestinian Territory

In one of the most highly publicized cases in recent memory, in February 2004, ICJ heard oral arguments on a request from the G.A. for an advisory opinion on the legal consequences of a wall constructed by Israel along, and in some cases extending across, Israel's border with Palestinian territory in the West Bank, including in and around East Jerusalem. The request brought international attention to The Hague, with protesters on both sides of the issue staging demonstrations at the Peace Palace, home of ICJ. Forty-four states, the Arab League and the Organization of the Islamic Conference offered submissions in the case, raising questions of law relating to the use of force, the forcible acquisition of territory and the interpretation of international humanitarian law. The submissions also raised important questions as to the role of ICJ: in what circumstance can the G.A. request an advisory opinion; should the Court issue such an opinion when one party does not consent to the proceedings; and to what extent, if any, should ICJ engage itself in highly politicized international disputes? At the time of writing, the Court remained in deliberations over the issue. When ICJ does rule, however, its decision could have important ramifications for both the Middle East peace process and ICJ's future role in dispute resolution.

New ICJ Cases

Between April 2003 and April 2004, ICJ added two new cases to its docket. In Certain Criminal Proceedings in France *(Republic of the Congo v. France)*, the Democratic Republic of Congo (DRC) sought the annulment of the French exercise of universal jurisdiction to investigate and prosecute alleged crimes against humanity committed by and against Congolese nationals in the DRC.[14] The Court's eventual ruling in that case could prove important for the future exercise of universal jurisdiction by national courts. And in Sovereignty over Pedra Blanca/Pulau Batu Puteh, Middle Rocks and South Ledge *(Malaysia/Singapore)*, the parties have jointly asked ICJ to determine sovereignty over the designated territory.

International Tribunal for the Law of the Sea

Like the International Court of Justice, the International Tribunal for the Law of the Sea primarily hears civil cases between states. Unlike ICJ, however, ITLOS hears only cases arising under one treaty: the *U.N. Convention on the Law of the Sea* (UNCLOS), which entered into force in 1994. UNCLOS sought to establish a comprehensive legal framework for regulating the world's oceans and use of their resources. It addresses, among other things, fisheries, the extraction of mineral resources from the continental shelf, marine research and environmental protection and rights on the high seas. Part XV of UNCLOS establishes a system for resolving disputes arising under the convention: if unable to settle disputes through such peaceful means as provided in the U.N. Charter, states parties must resort to compulsory dispute-settlement procedures. Those procedures ultimately entail bringing the dispute to ICJ, an arbitral panel or ITLOS.

ITLOS began work in Hamburg, Germany, in 1996 and currently comprises 21 independent judges, each elected to a nine-year term and who sit in five chambers: the Chamber of Summary Procedure, the Chamber for Fisheries Disputes, the Chamber for Marine Environmental Disputes, the Seabed Disputes Chamber and a special chamber convened to consider the Case Concerning the Conservation and Sustainable Exploitation of Swordfish Stocks in the South-Eastern Pacific Ocean *(Chile/European Community)*. As the chamber titles suggest, the Tribunal's docket can include everything from disputes over fishing stocks to the fate of seized vessels to the dredging of international waterways. In its seven years of operation, ITLOS has heard 12 cases, two of which were active between May 2003 and April 2004.

Straits of Johor

The first of the aforementioned cases dealt with land reclamation activities by Singapore in the straits that separate Singapore from Malaysia. On September 5, 2003, in the Case Concerning Land Reclamation by Singapore in and around the Straits of Johor *(Malaysia v. Singapore)*, Malaysia requested that ITLOS take provisional measures to prevent Singapore from continuing reclamation work until the two states could refer the case to an independent arbitral tribunal convened according to Annex VII to UNCLOS.[15] Finding the case admissible, and ruling that Malaysia need not pursue further negotiations before seeking provisional measures, a point discussed by several judges in separate declarations, the Tribunal moved directly to considering the application. Reviewing Singapore's reclamation activities in the area of Tuas, the first of two locations cited by Malaysia, the Tribunal concluded that Malaysia had not demonstrated any urgency, nor proven that irreversible damage might occur before an Annex VII tribunal reached final resolution on the merits. It therefore chose not to order provisional measures with respect to that location.

Turning to the second location, Pulau Tekong, the Tribunal noted Singapore's commitment not to take any action that would cause irreversible damage to Malaysia until receiving the findings of a study by independent experts funded by the two states.[16] Taking that commitment into account, the tribunal ordered both states to establish a panel of independent experts that would consider Singapore's reclamation activities, and proposed measures to deal with any effects on Malaysia, particularly with regard to Pulau Tekong; to exchange information and risk assessments relating to Singapore's activities on a regular basis; and to consult on and implement such temporary measures as may be necessary for Singapore to continue reclamation work without infringing on Malaysia's rights, pending a decision by the Annex VII arbitral tribunal.

The Tribunal further directed Singapore, again pending a decision by an Annex VII tribunal, not to undertake any reclamation activities that could cause irreparable harm to either Malaysia's rights or the marine environment.[17] With provisional measures in place, Malaysia must now pursue final resolution of the dispute through an independent Annex VII arbitral tribunal.

Swordfish Stocks

The second matter pending before ITLOS, labeled the Case Concerning the Conservation and Sustainable Exploitation of Swordfish Stocks in the South-Eastern Pacific Ocean *(Chile/European Community)*, is currently dormant but remains on the docket. Chile and the European Community brought the dispute before ITLOS in 2000, requesting that the Tribunal assess their mutual compliance with UNCLOS in regard to swordfish stocks in the waters bordering Chile's exclusive economic zone. Both parties requested that ITLOS establish a special chamber to consider the dispute, under Article 15 of the ITLOS Statute, and the Tribunal did so in December 2000.[18] On March 9, 2001, both parties informed the Tribunal that they had reached a provisional agreement regarding the dispute but wished to retain the special chamber should either side choose to revive the proceedings. In its Order of March 15, 2001, the Tribunal acceded to the parties' request but set a January 1, 2004, deadline for expiration of the special chamber. In December 2003, at the request of the parties, the special chamber extended the deadline until January 1, 2006. While ITLOS did not itself adjudicate the dispute, its availability to the parties most likely aided the process of peaceful settlement.

Criminal Charges Against Individuals

While the International Tribunal for the Law of the Sea and the International Court of Justice continue to resolve disputes between states, several other permanent and *ad hoc* tribunals operating in connection with the U.N. now try criminal charges against individuals. Such charges emerge from violations of international human rights and humanitarian law that are so serious as to incur individual criminal sanctions. Those violations include crimes against humanity and genocide and serious war crimes. Both the law and the institutions that enforce it have experienced dramatic changes over the last decade, culminating in the entry into force of the Rome Statute of the International Criminal Court in July 2002. The ICC has now begun operations, with the office of the prosecutor accepting referrals and investigating its first cases.

The creation of the ICC reflects rapid development in the field of international criminal law. International lawyers traditionally distinguished between human rights law and international humanitarian law by holding that the former regulated a state's conduct toward its nationals in times of peace while the latter regulated the conduct of hostilities between parties to a recognized state of civil or international armed conflict. Major milestones in modern international humanitarian law included the 1899 and 1907 *Hague Conventions*, the 1929 and 1949 *Geneva Conventions*, and the 1977 *Protocols Additional to the Geneva Conventions*. Human rights law had its own milestones, including the *Universal Declaration of Human Rights*, the *International Covenant on Civil and Political Rights*, the *Genocide Convention* and the *Convention Against Torture and Other Cruel, Inhuman or Degrading Treatment or Punishment*. In recent years, however, the two bodies of law have increasingly converged: scholars and practitioners alike now accept that minimum standards of humanity should apply during hostilities, that crimes against humanity can occur during times of peace and that individual criminal responsibility for atrocities should not require armed conflict. When serious violations of human rights such as rape or torture occur as part of an intentional and systematic or widespread attack on a civilian population, whether during war or peace, those violations constitute crimes against humanity. If such violations occur during times of armed conflict, they also constitute war crimes. And if they occur with the intention of destroying the victimized national, ethnic, racial or religious group in whole or in part, they qualify as acts of genocide.

International criminal law also addresses the crime of aggression. Unlike the other offenses, however, the crime of aggression regulates the *decision* to engage in armed conflict. Also, unlike the other offenses, there is a lack of agreement on the definition of a crime of aggression. The S.C. has historically held the power to determine when state aggression has occurred, and the Council's permanent members have resisted sharing that authority. One set of negotiations over defining the crime of aggression continues in a working group of the Court's Assembly of States Parties (ASP).

Modern efforts to prosecute violations of international criminal law began with the tribunals at Nuremberg and Tokyo following World War II, but remained largely dormant until the advent of the International Criminal

Tribunals for the former Yugoslavia and for Rwanda in the 1990s. By bring-ing skilled jurists and prosecutors together with experts in human rights and international humanitarian law, ICTY and ICTR have created a body of precedent and experience that has come to define international criminal practice and will undoubtedly influence the operations of the ICC. The ICTY and ICTR have already helped shape the development of several other *ad hoc* tribunals, including the Special Court for Sierra Leone (SCSL), the potential future court for Cambodia, courts operating under the auspices of the U.N. Mission in Kosovo (UNMIK) and the U.N. Transitional Administration in East Timor (UNTAET). The following section reviews the most recent and impor-tant developments before the ICC, ICTY, ICTR and SCSL.

International Criminal Court

After years of discussion, negotiation and preparation, the International Criminal Court has now joined the ranks of permanent international judi-cial institutions. Unlike the *ad hoc* tribunals for Rwanda and the former Yugoslavia, the ICC's jurisdiction is not tied to a specific region or conflict, nor does the Court report to the Security Council. In fact, although con-ceived and negotiated under U.N. auspices, the ICC is not part of the United Nations. It is an independent institution that derives its authority from the 1998 Rome Statute of the International Criminal Court.

Comprising 18 judges from as many different nations, the ICC was estab-lished to hear cases alleging violations of the international criminal law standards in the Rome Statute occurring after July 1, 2002, when the statute entered into force. It cannot, for example, hear allegations relating to the U.S. bombing of Cambodia, nor to the Iran-Iraq War. Cases begin with an investigation after a referral from the S.C. or a state party to the statute, or on the initiative of the prosecutor acting with approval of the Court's pre-trial chamber, in which case either the alleged perpetrator must be a nation-al of a state party, or the alleged crime must have occurred on the territory of a state party. Non-state parties can also lodge a declaration accepting the jurisdiction of the court over a particular situation. Once a case has begun, a state whose national faces charges may choose to exercise jurisdiction itself and thus effectively remove the case from ICC consideration. The ICC can regain the case only if its appeals chamber determines that the state in question is unable or unwilling to effectively investigate or prosecute the case. In many ways, the ICC thus becomes a court of last resort for cases involving the most serious violations of international criminal law.

The period from May 2003 to May 2004 effectively covers the ICC's first year of full operations: the Court's first judges took their oaths of office in March 2003, followed by the prosecutor that May, the registrar in July and the deputy prosecutor for investigations in November.[20] In July, the ICC also celebrated the first anniversary since the Rome Statute's entry into force, marked by messages from Nobel Peace Prize Laureate and former U.S. Pres-ident Jimmy Carter as well as Spanish judge Baltasar Garzón Real.

Investigations: The Congo and Uganda

Shortly after ICC's anniversary, on July 16, 2003, Prosecutor Luis Moreno Ocampo held a press conference in which he revealed that his office had received roughly 500 complaints alleging crimes within the Court's jurisdiction since the Rome Statute's entry into force. Prosecutor Moreno Ocampo further explained that many of those complaints, including all related to the Israeli-Palestinian conflict and U.S. operations in Iraq, actually fell outside the Court's jurisdiction: some referred to crimes that occurred before the Rome Statute entered into force or were not the type of crimes that the ICC tries. Others referred to incidents that did not involve nationals or the territory of a state party.[21] The Prosecutor did note that some complaints referenced crimes alleged to have been committed by nationals of a state party, particularly by non-U.S. coalition forces operating in Iraq. Noting that the Rome Statute made the ICC's jurisdiction complementary to national jurisdiction, Mr. Moreno Ocampo stated that any investigation or prosecution of such complaints would proceed only after determining that the government in question was unable or unwilling to investigate or prosecute the alleged crime. He added that future complaints should bear that standard in mind, and should detail any efforts already taken to seek redress before national authorities.[22]

Turning to specific incidents, Mr. Moreno Ocampo noted media reports that Côte d'Ivoire might request that the S.C. refer alleged crimes against civilians in that country to the ICC. The Prosecutor added, however, that the ICC had not received such a referral. Shifting focus to the Democratic Republic of Congo, which is a state party to the Rome Statute, Mr. Moreno Ocampo stated that he had identified fighting in Ituri and the ensuing loss of civilian life as a situation that required close and urgent attention. Aware of both the peace process in the DRC and international efforts to encourage that process, he said that, if necessary, he would nonetheless request authorization from the pre-trial chamber to start an investigation.[23] The DRC referred the situation in its territory to the ICC in April 2004; it has become the Court's first official case.

The Prosecutor has also received a referral from Uganda with regard to alleged crimes committed by the Lords Resistance Army (LRA), which operates in the northern part of the country. In January 2004, Ugandan President Yoweri Museveni met with Mr. Moreno Ocampo to establish a basis for cooperation between the government of Uganda and the ICC with regard to the investigation of atrocities committed by the LRA and the arrest of LRA leadership figures.[24] Such arrests would require partial rescission of an existing amnesty, which President Museveni indicated his intent to pursue, as well as the assistance of other states and international organizations.[25]

Founded in 1986, the LRA has committed gross violations of human rights and international humanitarian law in northern Uganda, including the recruitment of child soldiers, summary executions, torture and mutilation, rape, sexual abuse of children, forcible displacement, looting and the wanton destruction of civilian property. Attacks by the LRA and clashes with government forces have forced roughly 800,000 people to seek shelter in camps for displaced persons, with thousands of children fleeing their homes at night for fear of abduction and forcible conscription into the LRA.[26] On February 21, 2004, the LRA attacked the Barlonya camp in northeastern Uganda, killing more than 200 people. On March 23, 2004, in the wake of the massacre, the Prosecutor announced that his office would begin an investigation into the attack.[27] He also made it clear that he would conduct his investigations in a fair and impartial manner and receive complaints about all crimes in the North, no matter which side of the conflict.

Assembly of States Parties

While the Prosecutor began developing his investigation strategy, the ICC's Assembly of States Parties met for the second time, and its Committee on Budget and Finance for the first time, to discuss legal and financial issues related to the ICC's first year of operations. Meeting in August 2003, the Committee on Budget and Finance elected officers and adopted a working agenda and rules of procedure. Turning to the actual budget, the Committee praised ICC's efforts to match its resources to its workload on an ongoing basis, but expressed concern that budgeting too much for contingencies could undermine cost-effective management.[28] The Committee also called for further refinement of ICC's results-based budgeting and performance indicators, reviewed individual budgeting requests from ICC's different organs and noted the ASP's intention of establishing an ICC secretariat that would operate independently of the United Nations. Last but not least, the Committee discussed the ongoing funding needs for the Court, noting that 39 states had paid their contributions in full, while 11 had made only partial payment and 39 had yet to make contributions at all.[29]

In September 2003, ASP considered a host of issues related to the early and ongoing operations of the ICC. It began with procedural and logistical matters, including the election of Eastern European members to the Committee on Budget and Finance and the election of directors of the Victims Trust Fund.[30] The ASP then considered a paper prepared by the working group on the crime of aggression; although delegates have made much progress toward defining the crime of aggression and the situations in which the ICC may exercise jurisdiction over those who commit that crime, those questions remain unresolved. ASP did reach resolution on the establishment of its own permanent secretariat, deciding that it should begin functioning in The Hague as of January 1, 2004, which it did, and naming a working group to assist in the selection of the secretariat's director. With a functioning secretariat, ASP will begin meeting in The Hague, rather than in New York, and will no longer rely on the U.N. Office of Legal Affairs for secretariat support. Finally, ASP turned to other matters on its agenda, including the budget for 2004, staff rules and the future establishment of an international criminal bar.[31]

Agreement on Privileges and Immunities

Supplementary to the Rome Statute is the Agreement on Privileges and Immunities of the ICC, which lays out both the rights of ICC personnel operating in signatory states and the duties of those states to the ICC. The deadline to sign the agreement, which is open to all states, whether or not party to the ICC, was June 30, 2004. As of this writing, 53 states had signed the agreement and nine had ratified it. It will enter into force after the 10th ratification.

U.S. Opposition

Unfortunately, any update on progress at the ICC would be incomplete without at least a brief review of U.S. policy toward the Court. Having expressed its strong opposition to the ICC and nullified the U.S. signature of the Rome Statute, the current U.S. Administration has taken numerous actions to limit ICC's jurisdiction. In July 2002, the U.S. threatened to veto authorization or reauthorization of any U.N. peacekeeping operations unless the S.C. granted immunity from ICC jurisdiction to peacekeeping personnel from non-ICC state parties. That effort resulted in S.C. Resolution 1422, which granted such personnel a one-year, renewable immunity. In Resolution 1487 of June 2003, again under U.S. pressure, the Council, with three abstentions, extended that immunity for another 12 months. And in late May 2004, the U.S. proposed a draft resolution to renew Resolution 1487 for an additional 12 months. The proposal drew heated criticism and remained under discussion at the time of writing. The U.S. also used the threat of a S.C. veto to create immunity for peacekeepers from non-ICC states in Security Council Resolution 1497, adopted on August 1, 2003, which authorizes the deployment of a multinational stabilization force to Liberia. Similarly, after the bombing of U.N. headquarters in Baghdad in August 2003, the U.S. pressed for elimination of any explicit reference to the ICC in S.C. Resolution 1502, which condemned the attack and called on states to end impunity for such crimes.

Outside the Council, the U.S. has pressured state parties to the ICC to sign bilateral immunity agreements that would prevent those states from turning U.S. service members or government officials over to the ICC. Pursuant to Section 2007 of the American Servicemembers' Protection Act of 2002 (ASPA), on July 1, 2003, President Bush announced that he would begin suspending military aid to states that failed to sign such agreements. The act creates an exemption for NATO members and grants the president the power to waive suspension of military aid when he deems necessary for national security. He has done so, for example, in the case of countries providing military support to U.S. operations in Afghanistan and Iraq. Representatives of the U.S. government, however, have exerted pressure through other means, threatening to withdraw aid projects or to delay entry into alliances and international organizations. Although U.S. officials would likely portray their actions as defending U.S. interests, their tactics have stirred considerable international opposition.

International Criminal Tribunal for the Former Yugoslavia

The International Criminal Tribunal for the former Yugoslavia is in many ways the ICC's institutional predecessor. Unlike the ICC, however, ICTY derives its authority not from an international treaty but from a decision by the S.C. acting under its Chapter VII Charter authority to maintain international peace and security.

In May 1993, in Resolution 827, the Council established ICTY to adjudicate cases involving serious violations of international humanitarian law on the territory of the former Yugoslavia since 1991. As that mandate suggests, ICTY's jurisdiction is limited both temporally and geographically: it may not prosecute offenses that occurred before 1991, nor may it prosecute offenses that occurred or occur outside the territory of the former Yugoslavia. The S.C. has not yet declared a sunset for ICTY's jurisdiction, meaning the Tribunal can still investigate and prosecute *new* violations of international humanitarian law in the territory of the former Yugoslavia. The ICTY exercised its ongoing jurisdiction, for example, when it first indicted former Yugoslav President Slobodan Milosevic for crimes committed in Kosovo in 1999. ICTY's subject matter jurisdiction includes the basic components of international humanitarian law: grave breaches of the 1949 *Geneva Conventions*, violations of the laws and customs of war, crimes against humanity and acts of genocide.

For years, ICTY suffered from a limited number of captured defendants and lack of the political and military leaders most responsible for atrocities. Entering its second decade, the Tribunal now faces almost the opposite problem. As of April 28, 2004, ICTY had 62 defendants in custody at its detention facility, with four provisionally released pending trial and another 20 still at large. In its first 11 years, the Tribunal acquitted five defendants and convicted 20, of which seven have already completed their sentences. Another 35 cases ended before conviction: prosecutors withdrew 21 indictments, and 14 defendants died under indictment. In other words, ICTY has yet to pass final judgment on more than half of those indicted to date.[32] To meet those challenges, in recent years, the Tribunal has expanded its chambers to include 16 permanent judges and nine *ad litem* judges. These 25 judges are divided among three trial chambers, each of which includes three permanent judges and a maximum of six *ad litem* judges. Each of the three trial chambers can be divided into a maximum of three sections. The appeals chamber, which doubles as the appeals chamber for the ICTR, includes five permanent judges from ICTY and two permanent judges from ICTR.

Even with its new *ad litem* judges, ICTY still faces many challenges. The S.C. has called for the Tribunal to complete its work by 2008, a deadline that may slip to 2010. Such a completion strategy requires any remaining indictments to be issued by the end of 2004. Preparing indictments and trying cases, however, often requires cooperation from the states of the former Yugoslavia, which have sometimes been far from forthcoming. While many hoped that revulsion at the assassination of Serbian Prime Minister Zoran Djindic in March 2003 would lead to greater cooperation by the government of Serbia and Montenegro, domestic politics have prevented that from occurring.[33] The Tribunal's prosecutor has expressed greater optimism as to cooperation from the new Croatian government of Prime Minister Ivo Sanader, but an indicted Croatian general, Ante Gotovina, remains at large.[34] Perhaps most notably, ICTY has been unable to win the arrest of former Bosnian Serb military leader Ratko Mladic and former Bosnian Serb political leader Radovan Karadzic, who continues to elude NATO forces in Bosnia and Herzegovina.

Despite these difficulties, ICTY continues to process the defendants in its custody. The following section provides a brief analysis of the most important trial and appellate decisions from May 2003 to May 2004.

Slobodan Milosevic

Now in its third year, the trial of former Yugoslav President Slobodan Milosevic remains one of ICTY's most watched, and sometimes most difficult, proceedings. Mr. Milosevic has consistently refused to recognize the legitimacy of the Tribunal, has sought to use the trial as a forum for making political speeches and has declined to appoint counsel to represent him in court. He also suffers from hypertension and other serious ailments, limiting his ability to prepare his own defense and causing numerous delays. Unfortunately, Mr. Milosevic isn't the only participant whose health has affected the proceedings: in February 2004, shortly after the prosecution rested its case, Presiding Judge Richard May announced that, because of illness, he would leave ICTY at the end of May 2003. Judge May's leadership and courtroom demeanor steered the Milosevic trial chamber through many difficult hearings, and his departure raised the possibility of a mistrial. With the appointment of Scottish Lord Iain Bonomy to replace Judge May, however, the trial is scheduled to resume with only a slight delay. Nonetheless, coupled with the defendant's ill health and his stated intent to call past and present world leaders to testify, the challenges posed by Judge May's retirement promise to extend the Milosevic case into 2005 and possibly beyond.

The major legal challenges in the first year of the Milosevic trial revolved around prosecution efforts to introduce evidence as expeditiously as possible within ICTY's Rules of Procedure and Evidence. The prosecution chose to call the majority of its witnesses via Rule 92*bis*, which allows for the introduction of written witness statements. Although the trial chamber required all such witnesses to appear for cross-examination, the use of Rule 92*bis* nonetheless allowed the prosecution to call more witnesses in less time. The prosecution sought to expand that approach in the trial's second year by requesting that written evidence of some witnesses who attend for cross-examination be admitted under Rule 89(F), which has fewer requirements than Rule 92*bis*, and by asking that facts adjudicated in other proceedings at ICTY be admitted into evidence pending a challenge by the accused.[35]

Despite dissents from Judge David Hunt, who felt that such measures risked putting expediency above due process, the appeals chamber ruled that the trial chamber had discretion to admit evidence under both rules.[36]

Beyond legal tactics, the second year of the Milosevic trial included new witnesses and evidence relating mostly to crimes committed in Bosnia and Croatia. In April 2003, a Serb connected to the former President's inner circle testified that, in the early days of the war, Mr. Milosevic approved plans for the deportation of non-Serbs from Eastern Slavonia, in Croatia, as part of a strategy to unify Serb territories.[37] In May 2003, a Serb officer testified as to the provision of weapons by Belgrade authorities to paramilitary and Bosnian Serb forces operating in Zvornik, in eastern Bosnia, where those forces killed and deported much of the Muslim population.[38] In June, a member of the Red Berets, the armed wing of Mr. Milosevic's secret service, testified that paramilitary forces from Serbia under Mr. Milosevic's effective control committed crimes in the Mostar area in May 1992, exercising control over regular army units and armed locals.[39] Other witnesses similarly testified to the mixing of regular and paramilitary forces, and to Mr. Milosevic's ultimate control over Serbia's support for Bosnian and Croatian Serbs. Borislav Jovic, former President of Yugoslavia and once Mr. Milosevic's right-hand man, made the latter point when he told the court, "It was like this: Mr. Milosevic was the absolute authority regardless of whether he was party president or not. Not a single important decision in Serbia was taken without him nor could it have been made without him."[40]

In addition to Mr. Jovic, the prosecution called several other high-level witnesses, including Zoran Lilic, another former President of Yugoslavia, who testified that Mr. Milosevic ordered the Yugoslav army to train Bosnian Serbs, and General Wesley Clark, former NATO Supreme Allied Commander, who testified that Mr. Milosevic exercised control over the Bosnian Serb leadership, whose forces committed the Srebrenica massacre.[41] Srebrenica is central to the genocide charge against Mr. Milosevic, which trial observers believe to be the most difficult charge for the prosecution to prove: while several witnesses testified that Mr. Milosevic controlled the forces that committed the massacre, questions remain as to whether Mr. Milosevic ordered the attack or had the necessary intent to commit genocide. The prosecution sought to introduce communications intercepts in which Mr. Milosevic is heard discussing strategy with Bosnian and Croatian Serb leaders. The trial chamber has admitted some of the intercepts into evidence, and is considering the authenticity of others.[42] If admitted, the taped conversations could provide some of the most damning evidence of Mr. Milosevic's personal involvement in the ethnic cleansing that swept through the former Yugoslavia.

Stanislav Galic

Although the Milosevic case remains ICTY's highest profile proceeding, the trial of Stanislav Galic focused on a military campaign that riveted the world: the siege of Sarajevo. Mr. Galic, formerly a high-ranking general in the Bosnian Serb Army, stood accused of directing shelling and sniping attacks on the city's civilian population. The prosecution faced several challenges in the case, including proving command responsibility for sniper units and proving that the attacks in question constituted deliberate or indiscriminate attacks on civilians, rather than legitimate attacks on nearby military targets. Addressing the second issue, which was at the heart of the defense, the trial chamber concluded that "the evidence demonstrates beyond reasonable doubt that Sarajevo civilians were indeed made the object of deliberate attack by [Bosnian Serb] forces," adding that civilians "were attacked while attending funerals, while in ambulances, trams, and buses, and while cycling. They were attacked while tending gardens, or shopping in markets, or clearing rubbish in the city. Children were targeted while playing or walking in the streets."[43] Among the many crimes that the trial chamber found Bosnian Serb forces to have committed was the mortar attack on the Markale marketplace on February 5, 1994, which killed 68 civilians and stirred international outrage. The Tribunal concluded that the attacks had "no discernible significance in military terms" and were "intended primarily to terrorize the civilian population."[44]

Turning to assertions that Sarajevo's defenders may have staged attacks on its own civilian population to win international sympathy, the Tribunal expressed skepticism and concluded that, even if true, such assertions did not disprove Mr. Galic's responsibility for the sniping and shelling attacks charged at trial. Ruling that he exercised effective command and control over his forces, and that those forces deliberately targeted a civilian population, ICTY found Mr. Galic guilty on one count of violations of the laws and customs of war, namely spreading terror, and four counts of crimes against humanity. He received a sentence of 20 years, less time already served.[45]

Milomir Stakic

In late April 1992, Bosnian Serb forces under the leadership of the Serbian Democratic Party took control of the municipality of Prijedor, in northern Bosnia. Dr. Milomir Stakic quickly became Prijedor's leading political figure and one of the people most responsible for the crimes that followed. With Dr. Stakic at its helm, Prijedor's Bosnian Serb leadership engaged in a campaign of persecution designed to force out the region's non-Serb population. That campaign included the establishment of the notorious deportation camps at Omarska, Keraterm and Trnopolje, as well as an infamous massacre on Mount Vlasic and numerous killings in Bosnian Muslim towns and villages. The trial chamber found Stakic responsible for more than 1,500 killings, as well as rapes, sexual assaults, torture, beatings, destruction of cultural and religious monuments and deportation. However, it did not find that he possessed the specific intent to destroy—as opposed to displace—Prijedor's Bosnian Muslims as a group, in whole or in part, and therefore failed to convict on the charge of genocide. Dr. Stakic received a sentence of life imprisonment, with the possibility of release after

20 years.[46] While the prosecution can certainly count his conviction and sentence as victories, the Tribunal's failure to convict on genocide suggests just how high the bar for that crime has been set, and what future prosecutors must prove to establish that acts of genocide have occurred.

Bosanski Samac

On October 17, 2003, Trial Chamber II issued its judgment in *Prosecutor v. Blagoje Simic, Miroslav Tadic, Simo Zaric and others*. The trial covered events that occurred in the municipalities of Odzak and Bosanski Samac, which formed part of a narrow corridor of land connecting Serb enclaves in Croatia to Bosnian Serb territory and the Republic of Serbia. The defendants held positions in the Bosnian Serb political and military hierarchies in the two municipalities, and were accused of commanding and perpetrating a widespread and systematic attack on the area's civilian population, with the intent of bringing the municipalities under exclusive Serb control. The prosecution alleged that, together, they planned "persecution against non-Serbs, including acts of unlawful arrest and detention, cruel and inhumane treatment, including beatings, torture, forced labor assignments and confinement under inhumane conditions, deportations and forcible transfer."[47] After reviewing the litany of charges against each individual, the court sentenced them to terms ranging from six to 17 years' imprisonment.

Appeals Chamber

ICTY's Appeals Chamber hears a host of interlocutory appeals from ongoing trials as well as post-conviction appeals by both the prosecution and defendants. From May 2003 to May 2004, the Appeals Chamber reviewed trial chamber judgments and issued final rulings in several cases. In the case against Radislav Krstic, the Bosnian Serb general convicted of genocide and sentenced to 46 years' imprisonment for the attack on Srebrenica, the Appeals Chamber upheld the trial chamber's finding of genocide, but reduced Mr. Krstic's sentence to 35 years. The crime of genocide requires an intent to destroy, in whole or in part, a group as such; Mr. Krstic's defense argued on appeal that an intent to displace did not amount to an intent to destroy, and that men of military age—the majority of those killed at Srebrenica—did not constitute a sufficient "part" of Bosnian Muslims as a whole. The Appeals Chamber disagreed on both counts, concluding that the trial chamber correctly considered that the massacre of military men, and the effect their killings would have on the Bosnian Muslim population in the area, to be sufficient evidence of an intent to commit genocide.[48] Reviewing the evidence as to Mr. Krstic's involvement in the killings, however, the Appeals Chamber concluded that he was not a co-perpetrator, but rather knew of the genocidal intent of his superiors and permitted them to use forces under his command. Ruling that Mr. Krstic was guilty of aiding and abetting genocide, and taking other mitigating factors into account, the Appeals Chamber reduced his sentence accordingly.[49]

In the case of Milorad Krnojelac, who served as a prison warden in the

KP Dom detention facility in Foca and was accused of maltreatment of prisoners, both the prosecution and the defense appealed the trial chamber's decision. The Appeals Chamber ruled for the prosecution. It decided that Mr. Krnojelac was a co-perpetrator, and not merely an accomplice, in crimes committed against non-Serb civilians at the detention facility. It further decided that Mr. Krnojelac was guilty of several crimes of which he had originally been acquitted. The Appeals Chamber concluded that the trial chamber ruled incorrectly when it held that the prosecution needed to prove that Mr. Krnojelac and guards under his command, alleged to be part of a joint criminal enterprise, agreed on every alleged crime. Rather, the Appeals Chamber ruled that the joint criminal enterprise could agree on a system in which abuses would occur, and knowledge of and participation in that system could incur criminal liability.[50] Revising the trial chamber's judgment, the Appeals Chamber increased Mr. Krnojelac's sentence from seven years and six months to 15 years.

Unlike the Krstic and Krnojelac appeals, in *Prosecutor v. Mitar Vasiljevic*, the defense only appealed. Furthermore, the appeal turned solely on issues of fact, which the Appeals Chamber at ICTY may review to determine whether a trial chamber's findings of fact were unreasonable. The Appeals Chamber's judgment in *Vasiljevic* is instructive insofar as it lays out the process by which the Appeals Chamber may review findings of fact. Mr. Vasiljevic was convicted of participating in the execution of seven Muslim men in the Visegrad region following the withdrawal of the Yugoslav National Army. Finding three factual errors in the trial chamber's ruling, pertaining to Mr. Vasiljevic's knowledge of and participation in the crime, the Appeals Chamber reduced his sentence from 20 years to 15.[51]

Guilty Pleas

Almost as striking as the number of cases tried over the past year was the number of cases not tried because of guilty pleas by the accused. With both the prosecution and defendants aware of the ICTY's completion strategy and the average length of trials at the Tribunal, an increasing number of defendants have chosen to plead guilty, presumably in the hope of receiving reduced sentences. In some cases, for the same reason, defendants have also offered to testify in later hearings. Those who plead guilty over the last year include Dragan Obrenovic, Momir Nikolic, Predrag Banovic, Darko Mrdja, Miodrag Jokic, Dragan Nikolic, Miroslav Deronjic, Ranko Cesic and, perhaps most importantly, Milan Babic.[52] Mr. Babic served as president of the Republic of Serbian Krajina, a state created by Serbs living in eastern Croatia who sought to expel the local non-Serb population and declare independence from the Croatian government. In an agreement reached with the prosecution, Mr. Babic agreed to plead guilty to reduced charges of persecution in exchange for information and testimony in other ICTY cases.[53] He already testified in the Milosevic and Krajisnik cases, but the value of his information and testimony in that and other prosecutions remains to be tested.

New Indictments, New Detainees

Over the last year, ICTY issued several new indictments and took custody over several new detainees. On May 1, 2003, prosecutors publicly announced the indictment of Jovica Stanisic, former Chief of the State Security Services in the Republic of Serbia, and Franko "Frenki" Simatovic, former chief of the State Security Services' Special Operations Unit, also known as the JSO, or Red Berets. As such, both played instrumental roles in the ethnic cleansing of Bosnia and Croatia. Mr. Stanisic was transferred to The Hague on June 11, 2003, and Mr. Simatovic on May 30, 2003.[54] Another high-level indictment, publicly announced on October 20, 2003, called for the arrest of four top-ranking military and police commanders alleged to have orchestrated and conducted the attack on Kosovo's Albanian Muslim population in 1999: Nebojsa Pavkovic, Vladmir Lazarevic, Vlastimir Djordjevic and Sreten Lukic.[55] All four remain at large. Other indictees delivered into ICTY custody include Veselin Sljivancanin, Mitar Resevic, Vladimir Kovacevic and Pavle Strugar. The last, a former general in the Yugoslav National Army, is alleged to have conducted the ground campaign during the assault on Dubrovnik.[56]

Jailhouse Electioneering

The ICTY faced a novel challenge in 2003 when two of its high-profile detainees, Slobodan Milosevic and Vojislav Seselj, were listed as candidates for parliament in the Republic of Serbia. Although former President Milosevic had abused ICTY rules regarding contact with the media early in his detention, he eventually appeared to accept them. Mr. Seselj, on the other hand, appeared to be using contact with visitors from his Serbian Radical Party to pass messages and statements to the Serbian media. Determining that such communications violate ICTY Detention Unit rules and policy, in December 2003 the registrar's office chose to limit Mr. Seselj's contact with anyone other than his immediate family, defense counsel and consular and diplomatic representatives.[57]

International Criminal Tribunal for Rwanda

The International Criminal Tribunal for Rwanda shares much in common with ICTY. It too emerged from a Security Council resolution under its Chapter VII Charter authority.[58] Until this year, the two tribunals shared a prosecutor and they still share an appeals chamber in The Hague. Just as ICTY sits in The Hague, rather than in the Balkans, ICTR sits not in Rwanda but in Arusha, Tanzania. ICTR differs from ICTY, however, in several other important respects. First, ICTR's statute limits its jurisdiction to events that occurred in 1994, when members of Rwanda's majority Hutu ethnic group engaged in a genocidal slaughter that claimed the lives of nearly 800,000 Rwandans, predominantly from the minority Tutsi ethnic group. Second, ICTR took high-ranking leaders into custody at a relatively early stage; it has suffered more from a lack of resources than from a lack of suspects. Third, ICTR operates in parallel with a Rwandan justice system that itself prosecutes those who committed acts of genocide. The post-genocide, Tutsi-led Rwandan government originally opposed creation of the ICTR, largely because the Tribunal's statute did not permit the death penalty. Although the Rwandan government has since then cooperated with ICTR, the two often have a rocky relationship, stemming in part from the possibility that ICTR might investigate crimes alleged to have been committed by current government figures.

Despite such controversy, ICTR continues to prosecute successfully those most responsible for the 1994 Rwandan genocide. In fact, the Tribunal is anticipated to complete its mandate and dissolve in 2008. As of April 28, 2004, ICTR had 21 detainees on trial, 22 awaiting trial, 12 awaiting appeal and eight beginning their sentences. One detainee had died in custody, and another has been acquitted at trial. In total, 67 detainees have been arrested and 45 housed at the U.N. Detention Facility in Arusha.[59] Addressing the G.A. in October 2003, Judge Erik Mose, President of ICTR, noted that it was on schedule to render 15 judgments by early 2004, and that 41 accused would soon have their trials either completed or in progress. Bearing in mind the 2008 completion deadline, he requested that the G.A. and the S.C. consider increasing the number of *ad litem* judges from four to nine, and to allow *ad litem* judges to perform pre-trial work.[60] The Council responded to his request in Resolution 1512 of October 27, 2003, increasing the number of *ad litem* judges and permitting them to perform pre-trial work. Such measures should allow ICTR to accelerate its progress.

ICTR underwent a second institutional change in September 2003, when the S.C. appointed a new chief prosecutor for the Tribunal.[61] Until then, ICTR and ICTY had shared a chief prosecutor, most recently Carla Del Ponte of Switzerland. But with pressure on both tribunals to complete their caseload by 2008, and with tensions mounting between Ms. Del Ponte and the Rwandan government, who suspected she might indict sitting-government officials, the S.C. determined that appointing a new, separate prosecutor for ICTR would increase the pace of work at both tribunals. The new ICTR prosecutor is Hassan Bubacar Jallow of The Gambia, formerly The Gambia's attorney general and minister of justice, a judge on The Gambia's Supreme Court, and, most recently, a judge at the Special Court for Sierra Leone.[62]

With more judges and a new prosecutor, ICTR continues to work through its caseload. Among those ICTR has in custody, or has already convicted, are Rwanda's former prime minister as well as former ministers of foreign affairs, finance, health, culture, education, commerce, interior, civil service, information, transport, and family and women's affairs. Military leaders in custody included the former director of the cabinet of the ministry of defense, the former chief of staff of the Rwandan army and several former high-ranking generals. Other suspects include media, business and religious leaders who led and participated in the genocide. The following section summarizes the most important developments at ICTR over the last year.

Eliézer Niyitegeka & Laurent Semanza

On May 15, 2003, for the first time, ICTR issued decisions in two cases on the same day. In the case of Eliézer Niyitegeka, former minister of information, the trial chamber found the accused guilty of genocide, conspiracy to commit genocide, incitement to genocide and five counts of crimes against humanity. Mr. Niyitegeka both encouraged and participated in numerous genocidal attacks in Rwanda. After the Tribunal's shortest trial, lasting only 31 days, he became the first ICTR defendant to be convicted at trial of conspiracy to commit genocide. He also became the first defendant to be convicted of crimes against humanity for inhumane acts, including the decapitation and castration of a Tutsi man and the sexual mutilation of a dead Tutsi woman. Mr. Niyitegeka received a sentence of life imprisonment.[63]

In the second case decided on May 15, 2003, Laurent Semanza was convicted of complicity to commit genocide and crimes against humanity and sentenced to 25 years. In their closing arguments, prosecutors described Mr. Semanza, former mayor of Bicumbi commune in Kigali, as an "angel of death" who "rampaged through Bicumbi and Gikoro communes," coordinating killings and maimings at various sites including two churches and a mosque.[64] Although the trial chamber found flaws in the prosecution's evidence that Mr. Semanza incited or committed genocide, as well as evidence that he engaged in specific acts of sexual violence, it nonetheless sentenced him to 25 years, less six months in recognition of violations of Mr. Semanza's rights that occurred while awaiting trial.[65]

Rutaganda Appeal

On May 26, 2003, the ICTR Appeals Chamber sitting in The Hague handed down a final judgment in the case of Georges Rutaganda, formerly second vice president of the National Committee of the Interahamwe, the youth militia of the National Revolutionary Movement for Democracy and Development or MRND party (MRND) in Rwanda. He was convicted in December 1999 of arming, orchestrating and participating in attacks on the Tutsi population in and around Nyarugenge commune in Kigali. Both Mr. Rutaganda and the prosecution appealed the conviction; the defense argued that the trial chamber had committed errors of law and fact, while the prosecution argued that the trial chamber incorrectly excluded war crimes charges when it ruled that there was an inadequate nexus between Mr. Rutaganda's crimes and a state of armed conflict.[66] Although the Appeals Chamber found that there was inadequate evidence for one charge of murder as a crime against humanity on which the trial chamber convicted, it concluded that there was sufficient evidence linking Mr. Rutaganda's crimes to a state of armed conflict. Explaining the requirement, the Appeals Chamber held that, "the armed conflict need not have been causal to the commission of the crime, but the existence of an armed conflict must, at a minimum, have played a substantial part in the perpetrator's ability to commit it, his decision to commit it, the manner in which it was committed or the purpose for which it was committed."[67] Finding such a link, the Appeals Chamber found Mr. Rutaganda guilty of war crimes and affirmed his life sentence.

Juvénal Kajelijeli

As 2003 neared its end, ICTR issued convictions in two more cases. In the first, the trial chamber found Juvénal Kajelijeli, former mayor of Mukingo, guilty of genocide, incitement to commit genocide and extermination as a crime against humanity. Although found not guilty for rape and other inhumane acts as crimes against humanity, Mr. Kajelijeli was sentence to life imprisonment for his role in attacks on Tutsis in the Mukingo, Nkuli, Kinigi and Kigombe communes in Ruhengeri *Prefecture*.[68]

The Media Trial

In its second judgment of December 2003, ICTR delivered convictions against three defendants in the joint trial known as the Media Case. The proceedings involved the prosecution of Hutu media executives for their role in inciting and instigating the genocide. In 1993, Jean-Bosco Barayagwiza and Ferdinand Nahimana founded Rwanda's Radio Télévision Libre des Mille Collines (RTLM), which became known as Radio Hate during the genocide a year later. The third accused, Hassan Ngeze, edited *Kangura* magazine, which gained notoriety for anti-Tutsi diatribes that broadcasters at RTLM often read on the air. The *Kangura* articles and RTLM broadcasts encouraged Rwanda's Hutu population to come together to attack the Tutsis. The latter even served to coordinate the genocide by listing the license-plate numbers of Tutsi-owned vehicles and directing Hutu mobs to areas where the slaughter was not yet complete. Broadcasters would infamously repeat, "Graves are only half full–who will help us to fill them?"[69] With one defendant challenging the circumstances of his arrest, and another refusing to participate in the trial, the prosecution faced procedural challenges before the case even began.[70] As the first major international prosecution for hate speech since the 1946 Nuremberg prosecution of Julius Streicher, editor of *Der Stürmer*, the case drew immediate international attention. Commentators expressed concern as to how states might abuse a finding of criminal liability, but even some journalists suggested that broadcasts directing and coordinating the genocide—in effect turning RTLM into a means of military communication—should not enjoy legal protection.

Concluding that "the power of the media to create and destroy fundamental human values comes with great responsibility," and that "those who control such media are accountable for its consequences," the trial chamber found all three guilty on charges that included genocide, incitement to commit genocide, conspiracy, extermination and persecution. Citing a broadcast interview with Mr. Barayagwiza, in which he described the discrimination he had experienced as a Hutu, the trial chamber wrote that it was "critical to distinguish between the discussion of ethnic consciousness and the promotion of ethnic hatred," but concluded that other broadcasts cited by the prosecution constituted the latter.[71]

Jean de Dieu Kamuhanda

In its first judgment of 2004, ICTR passed judgment on Jean de Dieu Kamuhanda, former minister of education in Rwanda. Although cleared of crimes in his capacity as a minister, Mr. Kamuhanda was found guilty for his role in an attack on Tutsi civilians massed at the Gikomero Parish Compound. At trial, Mr. Kamuhanda admitted that genocide occurred in Rwanda, but denied playing any role. The trial chamber concluded otherwise, determining that Mr. Kamuhanda had harbored genocidal intent and that he bore responsibility for acts of genocide and crimes against humanity, including rape, in the attacks at the Gikomero Parish Compound. Although the trial chamber also concluded that there was insufficient evidence to convict Mr. Kamuhanda on other charges, including those stemming from a second attack at the Gishaka Catholic Parish, it nonetheless sentenced him to life imprisonment.[72]

Cyangugu

In its second judgment of 2004, the ICTR convicted Samuel Imanishimwe, former military commander of the Rwandan armed forces, but acquitted André Ntagerura, former minister of transport and communications, and Emmanuel Bagambiki, former prefect of Cyangugu. The case focused on the slaughter of civilians in a wave of attacks in the Cyangugu Prefecture. The trial chamber found that Mr. Imanishimwe, as local commander, ordered soldiers to arrest, detain, mistreat and execute prisoners. With regard to Mr. Ntagerura and Mr. Bagambiki, however, the trial chamber found that the prosecution had not proven beyond a reasonable doubt that, because of their positions or authority, the accused exercised supervisory roles in the killings. Both were acquitted, while Mr. Imanishimwe was sentenced to 27 years' imprisonment.[73]

New Trials

With the pace of work accelerating, ICTR began several new trials from May 2003 to May 2004. The prosecution started proceedings against Sylvestre Gacumbitsi, former mayor of Rusumo Commune; Emmanuel Ndindabahizi, former minister of finance; and Mikaeli Muhimana, former counsellor of the Kibuye Province. Two more trials with multiple defendants are also now underway. Both involve senior government officials facing prosecution for their role in organizing and orchestrating the Rwandan genocide. The first includes Edouard Karemera, former minister of the interior; André Rwamakuba, former minister of primary and secondary education; Mathieu Ngirumpatse, former director general for foreign affairs; and Joseph Nzirorera, speaker of the Rwandan parliament and former minister of industry, mines and handcraft. The second trial includes Casimir Bizimungu, former minister of health; Justin Mugenzi, former minister of trade and industries; Jerôme Bicamumpaka, former minister of foreign affairs; and Prosper Mugiraneza, former minister of the civil service.

Special Court for Sierra Leone

Although the Special Court for Sierra Leone is an *ad hoc* tribunal that prosecutes those responsible for serious violations of international human-itarian law, SCSL differs in key respects from the International Criminal Tri-bunals for the former Yugoslavia and for Rwanda. A treaty-based tribunal, it is independent of the United Nations and known as a "mixed" tribunal, meaning that representatives of the international community share power with Sierra Leonean lawyers and judges. SCSL began work with an implicit assumption that it would complete its prosecutions, if not its appeals, with-in three years.

In its first two years of operations, SCSL has issued indictments against 13 individuals representing all three of the country's former warring fac-tions. Two indictees have since died, leaving 11 active cases.[74] One of those who died was Foday Sankoh, former leader of the Revolutionary United Front (RUF), the party responsible for the majority and the worst of Sierra Leone's atrocities. The Court's highest profile indictee is former Liberian President Charles Taylor, who has sought refuge in Nigeria. The Court's prosecutor has, so far unsuccessfully, called on Nigeria to comply with its duties under international law to deliver Mr. Taylor to the Court. On May 31, 2004, SCSL's appeals chamber echoed that demand when it ruled that Mr. Taylor does not enjoy immunity from prosecution by virtue of having been a head of state when the alleged crimes occurred. That same day, the appeals chamber ruled that the forcible recruitment of child soldiers is a vio-lation of international humanitarian law, and was already a crime under international law at the time the indictments charged as much.[75] On June 3, 2004, SCSL entered a new phase as it moved from indictments and pre-liminary hearings to actual trials.[76]

While the SCSL has been making steady progress toward its goal of hold-ing accountable those responsible for the atrocities that marked Sierra Leone's brutal civil war, its first years of operation have not been without dif-ficulty. SCSL operates parallel to a truth and reconciliation commission (TRC), a relationship that has often proven complicated. SCSL established early on that it would not subpoena testimony or evidence given at the TRC, but some Sierra Leoneans now question the need for both institutions. Many of the worst offenders are dead or on the run, and those in custody receive better treatment than their victims did. By establishing its impartiality and indicting those responsible for atrocities regardless of which side they fought for, SCSL has angered some of those who suffered at the hands of Foday Sankoh's rebels. Most recently, the president of the Court, Judge Geoffrey Roberston was barred by his fellow judges from presiding over a trial of three leaders of RUF. Although such problems might plague any effort to seek jus-tice and accountability after a long and bloody civil war in an impoverished state, they are nonetheless challenges that SCSL will have to navigate as it moves forward to trials and appeals.

Commentary:
Terrorism, Iraq and the Laws of War
Neal Higgins

In a draft memo dated January 25, 2002, White House Counsel Alberto Gonzales advised President George W. Bush as to the relevance of the third *Geneva Convention*, which protects prisoners of war. He wrote that the war against Al Qaeda and the Taliban was "not the traditional clash between nations adhering to the laws of war that formed the backdrop [for the *Geneva Conventions*]." Rather, "the new war places a high premium on other factors, such as the ability to quickly obtain information from captured terrorists and their sponsors in order to avoid further atrocities." Mr. Gonzales concluded that "this new paradigm renders obsolete Geneva's strict limitations on questioning of enemy prisoners and renders quaint some of its provisions."

Although many in the U.S. government disagreed with Mr. Gonzales, his draft memo nonetheless reflected a prevailing attitude as to the relevance of international humanitarian law, especially when dealing with terrorist tactics. After massive casualty attacks on civilian targets in New York, Washington, Bali, Baghdad and Madrid, many have grappled with the idea of extracting intelligence from suspected terrorists and with measures that law-bound societies would otherwise consider unacceptable. Perhaps as a result, the Gonzales memo had a pervasive effect: investigative reporting has suggested that rules developed for terrorist suspects held in Cuba and Afghanistan were transported to Iraq, where the despicable abuse of Iraqi detainees was protected by the *Geneva Conventions*.

That abuse may taint U.S. foreign policy and the rule of law for decades to come. But there are signs of hope. U.S. policies toward detainees have come under renewed scrutiny. Investigations have begun against those who ordered or participated in such practices, at least in Iraq. Senior U.S. military lawyers have, through intermediaries, expressed sharp disagreement with the apparent abandonment of the Geneva rules, which the U.S. helped shape and which its military has long held sacred.

Regaining credibility on issues of international humanitarian law will prove crucial to at least one U.S. priority: the trials of Saddam Hussein and other Iraqi war criminals. The U.S. announced early on that it believed Iraqis should administer those trials and seems to be abiding by that claim, but it remains deeply invested and involved.

If the U.S. is to recover from the shock of Abu Ghraib, and prevent the desecration of international humanitarian law, it must prosecute all those responsible for the abuse of Iraqi detainees, regardless of rank. It must also demonstrate a commitment to international involvement in shaping Iraqi war crimes trials. With more forces deployed around the world and engaged in active military operations than any other state, the U.S. has a vested interest in the rules that govern the conduct of hostilities. Only through strong and determined leadership can it restore its reputation and revitalize international humanitarian law for future generations.

Endnotes

1. *U.N. General Assembly Sixth Committee website.*
2. A/58/22.
3. A/C.6/58/L.20.
4. A/58/17.
5. Article 38, *Statute of the International Court of Justice.*
6. ICJ Press Release 2001/31, October 31, 2001.
7. *ICJ website,* May 5, 2004.
8. *Vienna Convention on Consular Relations,* of April 24, 2004.
9. Judgment, Avena and Other Mexican Nationals *(Mexico v. United States of America),* March 31, 2004.
10. Ibid.
11. Ibid.
12. Ibid.
13. "Mexican on Oklahoma Death Row Gets Clemency," MSNBC, May 13, 2004.
14. ICJ Press Release 2003/21, July 16, 2003.
15. ITLOS/Press 84, October 8, 2003.
16. Ibid.
17. Order, Case Concerning Land Reclamation by Singapore In and Around the Straits of Johor *(Malaysia v. Singapore),* October 8, 2003.
18. ITLOS/Press 43, December 21, 2000.
19. ITLOS/Press 87, January 7, 2004.
20. *ICC website,* May 2004.
21. ICC Press Release, July 16, 2003.
22. Ibid.
23. Ibid.
24. ICC Press Release, January 29, 2004 ("President of Uganda Refers Situation Concerning the Lords Resistance Army (LRA) to the ICC)").
25. Ibid.
26. Ibid.
27. ICC Press Release, March 23, 2004, ("Statement by the Prosecutor Related to Crimes Committed in Barlonya Camp in Uganda").
28. ICC-ASP/2/7.
29. Ibid.
30. ICC-ASP/2/10.
31. Ibid.
32. "Key Figures of ICTY Cases," *ICTY website,* May 2004.
33. "Hague Complains to U.N. over Belgrade Resistance," *Reuters,* May 4, 2004.
34. "U.N. Chief Prosecutor Confident of Croatia's Cooperation With Court," *Agence France-Presse,* January 30, 2004.
35. Decision on Interlocutory Appeal on the Admissibility of Evidence-in-Chief in the Form of Written Statements, *Prosecutor v. Slobodan Milosevic,* September 30, 2003. / Decision on the Prosecution's Interlocutory Appeal against the Trial Chamber's April, 10 2003. / Decision on Prosecution Motion for Judicial Notice of Adjudicated Facts, *Prosecutor v. Slobodan Milosevic,* October 28, 2003.
36. Decision on Prosecution Motion for Admission of Witness Declaration of Tore Soldal Pursuant to Rule 89(F), *Prosecutor v. Slobodan Milosevic,* December 9, 2003. / Final Decision on Prosecution Motion for Judicial Notice of Adjudicated Facts, *Prosecutor v. Slobodan Milosevic,* December 16, 2003, among others.
37. Transcript, *Prosecutor v. Slobodan Milosevic,* April 28-29, 2003.
38. Transcript, *Prosecutor v. Slobodan Milosevic,* May 22, 2003.
39. Transcript, *Prosecutor v. Slobodan Milosevic,* June 10-11, 2003.
40. Transcript, *Prosecutor v. Slobodan Milosevic,* June 17-19, 2003 and November 18, 2003.

41. Transcript, *Prosecutor v. Slobodan Milosevic*, June 17-19, 2003 and December 15-16, 2003.
42. Second Decision on Admissibility of Intercepted Communications, *Prosecutor v. Slobodan Milosevic*, February 9, 2004.
43. Summary of Judgment, *Prosecutor v. Stanislav Galic*, December 5, 2003.
44. Ibid.
45. Ibid.
46. Summary of Judgment, *Prosecutor v. Dr. Milomir Stakic*, July 31, 2003.
47. Summary of Judgment, *Prosecutor v. Blagoje Simic, Miroslav Tadic and Simo Zaric, and others*, October 17, 2003.
48. Summary of Judgment, *Prosecutor v. Radislav Krstic*, April 19, 2004.
49. Ibid.
50. Summary of Judgment, *Prosecutor v. Milorad Krnojelac*, September 17, 2004.
51. Summary of Judgment, *Prosecutor v. Mitar Vasiljevic*, February 25, 2004.
52. Ibid, 32.
53. Annex A to the Joint Motion for Consideration of Plea Agreement between Milan Babic and the Office of the Prosecutor, *Prosecutor v. Milan Babic*, January 22, 2004.
54. ICTY Press Release, May 30, 2003. / ICTY Press Release, June 11, 2003 ("Jovia Stanisic Transferred to the ICTY Detention Unit"). / ICTY Press Release, June 11, 2003 ("Franko Simatovic Transferred to the ICTY Detention Unit").
55. Indictment, *Prosecutor v. Pavkovic et al.*
56. Indictment, *Prosecutor v. Strugar.*
57. ICTY Press Release, December 12, 2003 ("Registry Imposes Communication Restrictions on Detainees with Regard to Political Campaigning in the Media from the Tribunal's Detention Unit").
58. S/RES/955 (1994).
59. *ICTR website.*
60. ICTR Press Release, October 9, 2003 ("The President of the ICTR Calls for Additional *Ad Litem* Judges").
61. ICTR Press Release, September 4, 2003 ("The Security Council Appoints Separate Prosecutors for the Two *Ad Hoc* U.N. Tribunals").
62. Ibid.
63. Judgment and Sentence, *Prosecutor v. Eliézer Niyitegaka*, May 16, 2003.
64. ICTR Press Release, June 19, 2002 ("Closing Arguments Presented in Laurent Semanza Case").
65. ICTY Press Release, May 15, 2003 ("Rwanda Tribunal Delivers Two Judgments Today").
66. ICTR Press Release, May 26, 2003 ("ICTR Hands Down First War Crimes Conviction").
67. Ibid.
68. ICTR Press Release, December 1, 2003 ("The Former *Bourgmestre* of Mukingo Convicted of Genocide").
69. "Radio Hate," *Legal Affairs*, September/October 2002.
70. "Reading Between Blurred Lines: Background and Issues in 'The Media Trial' at the ICTR," *Internews*, April 16, 2001.
71. ICTR Press Release, December 3, 2003 ("Three Media Leaders Convicted for Genocide").
72. Judgment and Sentence, *Prosecutor v. Jean de Dieu Kamuhanda*, January 22, 2004.
73. Judgment and Sentence, *Prosecutor v. André Ntagerura, Emmanuel Bagambiki and Samuel Imanishimwe*, February 25, 2004.
74. *SCSL website*, May 2004.
75. SCSL Press Release, June 2, 2004 ("Statement by Prosecutor David M. Crane: The Prosecution is Ready for the Trial of Charles Taylor").
76. SCSL Press Release, June 2, 2004 ("Statement by Justice Emmanuel Olayinka Ayoola").

Chapter 7

Furthering Trade in a Developing World

David Lynch

Now is the time for all World Trade Organization members to show realism, flexibility and a determination to make progress.
—World Trade Organization Director-General Supachai Panitchpakdi, *Address to the Third LDC Trade Minister's Meeting,* May 2004.

The United Nations and its related agencies have long been active in trade policy. And World Trade Organization Director–General Supachai Panitchpakdi's call to action is poignant now more than ever as the January 2005 deadline for the U.N. body's Doha Development Agenda (DDA) draws near. This chapter reviews the challenges and ideals related to DDA and other trade issues that have been discussed, debated and, in certain cases, drawn out among U.N. member states and trade-related agencies over the course of 2003 and early 2004. However, before delving into the current topics at hand, a bit of background is required.

Background: The United Nations Trade Machinery

Within the U.N. system, there are six core trade and development agencies that, through the Integrated Framework, work together to improve coordination, effectiveness and development of the international trading system. The most well-known of these agencies are the World Trade Organization (WTO) and the U.N. Conference on Trade and Development (UNCTAD). The former lowers trade barriers by facilitating multilateral trade negotiations such as the ongoing DDA negotiations, and uses its dispute-resolution mechanism to enforce the trade rules that its members make. UNCTAD provides research, analysis and training for government officials to build developing nations' trade capacity.

In June 2004, UNCTAD celebrated its 40th anniversary as it held its 11th quadrennial conference, UNCTAD XI, in São Paulo, Brazil. The conference focused on measures to ensure that global economic integration leads to development for developing nations because, as UNCTAD Secretary-General Rubens Ricupero said, "Open trade regimes and financial markets alone are not enough." [1]

In addition to WTO and UNCTAD, other U.N. trade-related bodies include the International Trade Center, the International Monetary Fund (IMF), the U.N. Development Programme (UNDP) and the World Bank. These last three agencies assist developing and least-developed countries to take better advantage of the world trading system by helping to increase their capacity to produce goods for export.

Other U.N. agencies play a role in trade issues in a less direct way. The Food and Agriculture Organization/World Health Organization Codex Alimentarius Commission, for example, establishes food safety standards. Also, the World International Property Organization (WIPO) creates standards for the protection of intellectual property rights, some of which are used in WTO's Agreement on Trade-Related Aspects of Intellectual Property Rights (TRIPS Agreement).

The Doha Development Agenda Negotiations

Today, World Trade Organization members are in the midst of complex and contentious trade negotiations known as the Doha Development Agenda. The negotiations have not kept to their ambitious timetable and it is unlikely they will be finished by the self-imposed January 2005 deadline. The September 2003 Cancún Ministerial Conference was supposed to demonstrate how close WTO members had come to putting the *Doha Declaration*—a ministerial declaration that sets broad outcomes for the DDA and serves as a roadmap to completing the DDA—into action with specifics. Instead, it demonstrated how far WTO members had to go to reach consensus. The primary division at Cancún was the ongoing split between developed and developing nations over a number of issues, but most importantly over agriculture. The following section outlines the key remaining divisions in the talks.

Agricultural Goods, Textiles and Apparel

In the DDA, developing nations have voiced their displeasure more strongly with the world trading system. They have long argued that trade rules tend to be most open in those economic sectors in which developed nations dominate, such as manufacturing, and tend to be the least open in those economic sectors in which developing nations have a comparative advantage: agriculture, textiles and apparel. In fact, these two sectors were excluded in WTO's forerunner, the General Agreement on Tariffs and Trade (GATT). To remedy these longstanding complaints, the Uruguay Round of negotiations, which began to be phased-in in 1995, brought these sectors into the multilateral trading system. Their inclusion in the WTO also made other changes in trade rules, such as freer trade in services, more palatable to developing nations. But developing nations have been disappointed by how slowly agricultural, textile and apparel provisions have been phased-in and how expensive it has been to administer numerous other provisions of the Uruguay Round.

Farm Subsidies

Developing nations have been increasingly upset about subsidies paid to farmers in the European Union, U.S. and other developed nations. According to the Organization for Economic Co-operation and Development (OECD), its members paid $311 billion in total supports to agriculture in 2001. There are different types of agricultural supports, with export subsidies widely viewed as the most trade-distorting. Critics charge that these supports depress world agricultural prices and therefore put many developing-nation farmers out of work. This issue is critical to developing nations because they are so dependent upon agriculture for jobs and export earnings. For instance, Burkina Faso and Mali receive about one-third of their export earnings from cotton and Chad receives about one-fourth. According to UNCTAD, cotton contributed 5 to 10 percent of the gross domestic product (GDP) in 2000-2001 in these countries and in Benin. Therefore, Benin, Burkina Faso, Chad and Mali called for the elimination of cotton subsidies and for compensation from developed nations until such subsidies are fully phased-out.[2]

Developing nations demanded greater movement in agriculture from developed nations in Cancún but offered less movement on issues of concern to developed nations. Developing nations were more prepared and determined for these negotiations than they have been in the past. Brazil and India, always among the most important developing nations in multilateral trade negotiations, were joined by China to play a lead role in the G-22, an informal grouping of developing nations. Developing nations were quite united and more mobilized than in many previous negotiations. The U.S. criticized those G-22 nations that were also negotiating bilateral free trade agreements with the U.S. and some, therefore, backed away from membership in the group, now known as the G-20, despite its fluctuating membership.[3]

Overall, developed nations did offer some changes in their negotiating positions. The European Union, Japan and the U.S. were very hesitant to give up support for their farmers. The E.U. remained committed to the Singapore issues as a focus for the DDA. The Singapore issues, so named because they were proposed at WTO's 1996 Ministerial Meeting in Singapore, are investment, competition policy, government procurement and trade facilitation. In the end, the U.S. and E.U. were not willing to forgo all subsidies to their farmers, nor was the E.U. prepared to abandon all of the Singapore issues. Others, like the Africa group, a group of 41 African nations, insisted that none of the Singapore issues be part of the negotiations. Thus the talks ended in deadlock.[4]

Cancún ended without a broad agreement on agriculture and therefore without a clear path to a successful DDA.

Many anti-globalization activists protesting the talks were clearly pleased to see developing nations stand up to developed nations. But this was not a victory for anti-globalization nor for developing nations. As President of Oxfam America Raymond C. Offenheiser said, "Oxfam takes no pleasure in the failure of the WTO talks in Cancún, which is a blow to poor nations that need immediate relief for their farmers." He clearly placed blame: "It appears the U.S. and E.U. were not prepared to listen and take the necessary steps." [5]

What's Next for Doha?

Since the Cancún Ministerial Conference, ongoing discussions have created some narrowing in the differences. Both the U.S. and the E.U. have made offers to cut some elements of their farm supports, but not all. For instance, the U.S. has called for an end to all farm subsidies, but is hesitant to give up its food-aid program. The U.S. government buys food from U.S. farmers and then donates the food as a form of foreign aid. This is widely viewed as an export subsidy. The most recent offer that came from the E.U. would eliminate export subsidies, but only if the U.S. gives up its food-aid program. The U.S. has agreed with the E.U.'s export subsidy reduction plan, which is more than one can say of E.U. member nations. France, the most vocal defender of farm supports, does not like the offer. Brazil, one of the leading G-20 countries, has signaled its agreement about export subsidies. Now the primary issue is access to agricultural markets, specifically tariff reduction. The DDA seems to have passed its largest roadblock, but the road continues to be bumpy.[6]

The DDA is the latest in a series of negotiating rounds that have brought down trade barriers during the post-World War II period. The difficulty of successfully reaching agreement in these multilateral agreements has increased because there are more countries negotiating more issues and many of the issues include "behind the border" problems such as subsidies to industries that were once considered to have been matters primarily of domestic concern. When GATT went into effect in 1948, there were only 23 signatories. There were 84 by the end of the Tokyo Round in 1979, 110 by the signing of the Uruguay Round in 1994 and there are currently 147 members of the now-named World Trade Organization.[7] Most trade negotiations are behind schedule. The real question is whether the WTO's diverse members can find sufficient consensus.

Other World Trade Organization Updates

Accessions and Applications

World Trade Organization members now account for more than 90 percent of world trade. The most significant traders that remain outside WTO are Saudi Arabia and Russia. Both have long sought WTO membership, but questions remain about their willingness to reform their economies enough to meet WTO requirements and satisfy WTO members. The European Union was the primary holdout, seeking greater openness in Russia's natural gas markets, but appears ready to sign an accord with the Russian Federation.

The U.S. therefore remains the primary hurdle to Russian membership. The U.S. is also the primary WTO member still requiring greater Saudi reforms before WTO entry.[8]

Nepal became WTO's 147th member on April 23, 2004. It is the first least-developed country (LDC) to join through the full accession negotiation process since WTO's founding in 1995. Nepal is the 30th LDC in WTO, with nine additional LDCs seeking accession: Bhutan, Cambodia, Cape Verde, Ethiopia, Laos, Samoa, Sudan, Vanuatu and Yemen. Cambodia is next on the list to join, having been approved for membership at WTO's September 2003 Cancún Ministerial Conference. Since then, however, Cambodia was granted an additional six months to ratify the accession agreement.[9]

Other nations seeking accession that have established working parties (*see below for details*) include Algeria, Andorra, Azerbaijan, Bahamas, Belarus, Bosnia-Herzegovina, Kazakhstan, Lebanon, Seychelles, Tajikistan, Tonga, Ukraine, Uzbekistan, Vietnam and the former Yugoslavia (Serbia and Montenegro).

Joining WTO is not easy, especially for poorer nations and those with less open economies. After formally applying, the process includes the following steps:

1) Establish a working party: Interested WTO members must form a working party. Typically, a working party includes the world's major traders and any nation with a particular trade concern with the acceding nation. For instance, because China was such a major trader, many nations were concerned about the precise level of openness to Chinese imports they would have to give in particular economic sectors. Similarly, many members also wanted to ensure access to China's markets during the phase-in period. All WTO members will trade with the acceding nation, but for some, joining a working party is not worth the expense.
2) Evaluate the economy: The working party, with input from the acceding nation, evaluates the acceding nation's economy.
3) Establish conditions for entry: Those WTO members that request a bilateral agreement with the acceding nation must negotiate a bilateral agreement that governs the phase-in period. As of April 2004, Saudi Arabia, for example, had reached agreement with 31 WTO members and had four more bilateral agreements left to complete.[10]
4) Vote: The entire WTO body, not just the working party, must then vote for accession of the interested nation.
5) Ratify: The acceding nation ratifies its accession and officially becomes a WTO member.

The most difficult step along the way is unlisted, but permeates the accession process, and that is the willingness and ability of the acceding nation to open its markets. Typically, subsidies to industry, greater governmental transparency and the protection of intellectual property rights, such as patents, are required reforms. These steps are politically painful and are sometimes technically difficult for poorer nations. Therefore, the *Doha Declaration* in paragraph nine calls for WTO members to be "committed to accelerating the accession of LDCs." For instance, if LDCs are given more time to phase-in WTO requirements, they would have more time to adjust their economies and develop needed administrative capacity. In reality, however, developed WTO member nations drive a hard bargain that sometimes requires acceding nations to meet new WTO requirements before they are phased-in. Cambodian Commerce Minister Cham Prasidh complained that the "package of concessions and commitments that we have to accept certainly goes far beyond what is commensurate with the level of development of a least developed country." [11]

Dispute Settlements

The WTO's dispute-resolution mechanism continues to be well-used and controversial at the same time. As of September 2003, the WTO's Dispute Settlement Body (DSB) has had just over 300 cases in less than nine years. That is roughly as many as its predecessor, GATT, handled in nearly 50 years. [12]

It is no surprise that the DSB is one of the primary differences between WTO and GATT. Since the GATT's dispute-resolution mechanism was easy to derail, the primary way that countries resolved their differences was through bilateral negotiations where power was the primary determinant of success. Power is, of course, still important in settling trade disputes, but WTO's DSB helps small- and medium-size countries negotiate with the world's more powerful countries. While poorer nations have won cases against larger nations, they lack the capacity to fully benefit from the DSB process. Cases take years and teams of lawyers—not to mention hefty financial resources. The WTO does offer training for developing nations' officials and WTO members have donated expertise and money to help developing nations more fully and effectively participate in the DSB process. Developing nations have been increasingly using the DSB, as a result, bringing 40 percent of all the DSB's cases since its inception. Sixty percent of DSB cases since 2000 have been brought by developing nations, most of which involve the world's largest traders. This is not surprising, given their disproportionate weight in world trade, economic size and level of legal expertise. [13]

The DSB's processes are complex and often, the WTO authorizes retaliation that leads the offending nation to change its ways. For instance, the U.S. imposed duties on imported steel from many nations and persisted with those duties even after losing WTO panel rulings. Predictably, the WTO authorized the E.U. to retaliate with tariffs. In the face of tariffs on $2.2 billion worth of U.S. exports to the European Union, U.S. President George W. Bush removed the steel duties before E.U. retaliation could begin. [14]

On the other hand, the U.S. has retaliated against the E.U. over bananas and hormone-fed beef. The latter retaliation continues as the E.U. still denies entry to U.S. hormone-fed beef. In the case involving the most money—the

Foreign Sales Corporation and ExtraTerritoriality Income (FSC-ETI) case—the E.U. has fought back against U.S. corporate tax breaks on profits earned from overseas production. A WTO appellate panel ruled that the tax breaks were an illegal export subsidy. The WTO subsequently authorized the E.U. to retaliate with trade sanctions of more than $4 billion for inadequate implementation. On March 1, 2004, the E.U. began a 5 percent tariff on $4 billion of U.S. exports to the Union. The tariffs will increase by 1 percent each month for a year.[15] The U.S. Congress is working on a plan that also meets WTO requirements, but progress has been slow.

Besides the U.S.-E.U. tango, there are other ongoing trans-Atlantic trade fights. In January 2004, the European Union, Canada, Japan, India, Brazil, Mexico, Chile and South Korea requested authorization from WTO to retaliate against the U.S. in a case involving U.S. anti-dumping rules, called the Byrd Amendment. The Byrd Amendment gave revenue from U.S. anti-dumping duties levied against foreign companies to the U.S. companies that initiated the dumping cases. In January 2003, a WTO appeals panel ruled that the Byrd Amendment was an illegal subsidy. The U.S. did not implement this ruling by the December 27, 2003 deadline.[16]

A recent WTO ruling is of particular interest to many developing nations. Brazil won a panel ruling against U.S. subsidies to its cotton farmers. Agricultural subsidies in general and, specifically, cotton subsidies hurt developing nation farmers, many argue, and now there is a WTO panel ruling to support their case. The dispute is far from over, but it will most likely have ramifications in the ongoing DDA negotiations.[17]

Getting Affordable Medicines to Developing Countries

To many, the lack of access to affordable medicines in developing countries, especially for HIV/AIDS, is an example of globalization gone wrong. As pointed out in Chapter 1, for instance, the vast majority of HIV-positive patients in Africa are lucky to get any medicine at all to diminish the ravages of the disease. This inability shortens their lives dramatically and helps the disease spread more rapidly.

Protesters, activist groups and developing nations have pressured—and continue to pressure—drug companies and their governments to do more to help. Specifically, they have called for drug companies to donate or sell HIV/AIDs medicines at steep discounts and have called for broader exceptions to patent and trade laws. Patents, many argue, make medicines more expensive for patients and governments to buy. Activists have long wanted easier authorization for countries to generically produce drugs still under patent. Developed countries, especially the United States, however, have feared that this would weaken the Agreement on Trade-Related Aspects of Intellectual Property Rights, adopted in the WTO's Uruguay Round. The U.S.

and other defenders of intellectual property rights argue that patents provide the economic incentive to invest in research and development in pharmaceuticals. Without patents, many of the HIV/AIDS medicines that are sought after would not have been invented.[18]

As the debate and AIDS pandemic continued in the late 1990s, developing nations came under pressure to convince skeptical developing nations to agree to a new round of WTO talks. As a result, drug companies and their governments conceded on drug patent rules for medical emergencies at the 2001 Ministerial Conference in Doha, Qatar, or so it was thought.

In Doha, developed nations agreed to allow poor countries to domestically produce medicines still under patent without violating trade and patent law, provided they face a medical emergency. This certainly helped some countries with sizable pharmaceutical capacity, but it offered no help to the majority of least-developed countries without the ability to produce the medicines. Developing nations and activists wanted to import generically produced medicines under patent law without running afoul of trade and patent law. Countries like India and Brazil have sizable generic industries and could export generic drugs to developing countries facing medical emergencies. The U.S. was the lone holdout on the issue. It feared the generic drugs could be easily diverted to developed countries in a violation of patent law and a reduction of pharmaceutical industry profits. The U.S. was concerned about which countries would qualify for patent waivers for traded medicines and for which diseases and medicines. The issue was supposed to be resolved by a December 2002 deadline that came and went. Finally, as the September 2003 Cancún meeting drew near, negotiators found a compromise palatable to the U.S. and its pharmaceutical industry. The compromise allows patent waivers for traded medicines for any disease. It applies only to medicines used for noncommercial reasons and importation must be under government control.[19]

This was a victory for developing nations in their efforts to gain access to affordable medicines. But as the E.U.'s top trade negotiator, Pascal Lamy noted, "We have solved about 10 percent of the problem of access to medicines by developing countries." The agreement does not guarantee that generic drugs will be produced and exported cheaply to those poor countries with medical emergencies. Activist groups such as Doctors Without Borders argue that the agreement requires too much red tape and its provisions are too ambiguous, opening the door for restrictive interpretation. Half a year after the WTO medicines agreement, WHO spokeswoman Daniela Bagozzi said, "From what we know and what we've heard, no country has issued a demand for a compulsory license [to import medicines] as authorized within the agreement." This has led activist groups to call for a renegotiation of the WTO medicines agreement.[20]

On the positive side, some countries are getting more aggressive in negotiations with drug companies to supply low-cost medicines. The Brazilian government, for instance, is giving AIDS medicines to all Brazilians who need them and has threatened to produce generic versions of those AIDS drugs that it does not already produce generically. But this is not a viable option for most developing nations.[21]

Even if the patent barrier to drug access is resolved, there are other outstanding nonpatent issues. As WIPO notes, 95 percent of the medicines on the WHO's Essential Drug List are off patent, yet many remain unavailable in poor countries. The reason: even at a $1 a day or less, medicines remain too expensive in countries where annual incomes average $1 a day per person. Moreover, there is often a lack of physical and medical infrastructure to effectively distribute and administer the medicines. Clearly there is much to be done on all fronts if developing nations are to get affordable access to medicines.[22]

Regional Trade Agreements

Regional trade agreements (RTAs), consisting of both bilateral and regional free trade agreements (FTAs), have always been controversial to both free traders and free-trade skeptics. To free traders, RTAs, by definition, deviate from the WTO norm of Most Favored Nation (MFN) status that requires treating all WTO members equally. Under WTO rules, RTAs are an allowed exception to MFN if the RTA lowers barriers internally and does not raise them externally. Furthermore, free traders note, RTAs may lead to trade diversion, where trade patterns are distorted to reflect trade laws instead of economic efficiency. At the very least, RTAs are confusing to keep straight, especially when there is overlapping membership. Free traders are also disturbed that RTAs too often marginalize poor nations by excluding them from larger agreements.

To critics of free trade, RTAs are damaging because they promote corporate-led globalization. They also argue that poor nations, to the extent that they are involved in RTAs, are exposed prematurely to more efficient industries from developed nations.

No matter the merits of RTAs, they are here to stay and they continue to increase in number. As of June 2000, there were 250 RTAs notified to the GATT/WTO, with more than half coming since the WTO's establishment in 1995.[23]

A large number of new RTAs continue to come from the change of opinion that Asia's major traders had about the wisdom of RTAs and, more specifically, bilateral trade agreements. China, Japan, Singapore and South Korea have been busy negotiating with individual countries and with already established RTAs. India has also begun to embrace RTAs, thereby spurring regional integration in South Asia.

The United States, which has traditionally focused more attention on

WTO negotiations and larger RTAs, has moved aggressively to form numerous bilateral free trade agreements. In recent years, it has completed and entered into bilateral RTAs with Chile, Jordan and Singapore. It completed RTAs with six Central American nations and is negotiating with another in the region. The U.S. completed a bilateral RTA with Australia in February 2004 and with Morocco in March 2004. The Bush Administration is now negotiating a bilateral RTA with Bahrain and has announced its intent to negotiate a bilateral RTA with Thailand.[24]

The E.U. has not gone along with this trend only because it already has numerous bilateral RTAs and requires regional economies to integrate with one another before or during economic integration with the Union.

Following is a look at RTAs in the region.

Africa

Economic development in Africa is more important than elsewhere simply because so many African countries are desperately poor. Home to 32 of the 38 countries identified by the World Bank and International Monetary Fund as Highly Indebted Poor Countries (HIPC), many African countries are considered too poor and indebted to ever develop without debt relief.[25] If the Millennium Development Goals' aim to halve extreme poverty is to be met by 2015, there is no time to waste. African regional integration could play a role in this development, especially since African trade barriers with one another remain high and domestic markets in most African countries are small.[26]

Africa has numerous RTAs. In fact, it has too many, according to some.

Enhanced HIPC Initiative: Status as of September 2003

COUNTRIES THAT HAVE REACHED DECISION AND COMPLETION POINTS	COUNTRIES BETWEEN DECISION AND COMPLETION POINTS		COUNTRIES STILL TO BE CONSIDERED FOR DECISION POINTS
Benin	Cameroon	Madagascar	Burundi
Bolivia	Chad	Malawi	Central African Rep.
Burkina Faso	Congo, Dem. Rep. of	Nicaragua	Comoros
Mali	Ethiopia	Niger	Congo, Rep. of
Mauritania	Gambia	Rwanda	Côte d'Ivoire*
Mozambique	Ghana	Sao Tome &	Lao PDR
Tanzania	Guinea	Principe	Liberia
Uganda	Guinea-Bissau	Senegal	Myanmar
	Guyana	Sierra Leone	Somalia
	Honduras	Zambia	Sudan
		Togo	

* Côte d'Ivoire reached the decision point under the original HIPC Initiative, but has not yet reached the decision point under the enhanced HIPC Initiative.

Source: United Nations Statistics Division, "World and regional trends," Millennium Indicators Database, http://millenniumindicators.un.org (accessed December 2003); based on data provided by IMF and World Bank.

Worse, cross-membership creates overlapping RTAs which is confusing and hinders integration. The establishment of the African Union (A.U.), and the related African Economic Community (AEC), are supposed to lower trade barriers and remove the confusion caused by overlapping RTAs. The AEC, if effective, would unify the many African RTAs toward continental-wide economic integration. While ambitious and modeled after the European Union, the A.U. is chronically short of financing, compounded by the burden of high poverty and instability in the region.

Among the RTAs that the AEC hopes to integrate are the East African Community (EAC), the Economic Community of Western African States (ECOWAS), the Common Market for Eastern and Southern Africa (COMESA), the Economic Community of Central African States (CEEAC), the Southern African Development Community (SADC) and the South African Customs Union (SACU).

Americas

Home to some of the world's largest RTAs, there have been numerous developments in the Americas. The United States, already the dominant member of the North American Free Trade Agreement (NAFTA), has long sought to fully develop the Free Trade Area of the Americas (FTAA) which would include 34 Western Hemisphere countries (all except Cuba). In December 2003, the U.S. signed the Central America Free Trade Agreement (CAFTA) with El Salvador, Guatemala, Honduras and Nicaragua. Costa Rica had also negotiated with the U.S. and initially declined to sign, but joined one month later. The Dominican Republic was included in March 2004, and negotiations between the U.S. and Panama began in April 2004. CAFTA now has seven members (Panama would make eight), but the entire agreement still requires ratification. The U.S. has also announced negotiations for an RTA with the Andean countries: Colombia, Peru, Ecuador and Bolivia, but the talks will begin without Bolivia.[28]

Will these actions reinvigorate FTAA? Not likely. Most FTAA opposition comes from Brazil and Venezuela. Venezuela's opposition stems from President Hugo Chávez, who has been the most strident FTAA opponent. Brazil's opposition has been more nuanced and remains more consequential for the fate of the FTAA. Brazil would prefer to first integrate more deeply with other South American nations in its RTA, the Common Market of the South, known as Mercosur, and then negotiate with the U.S. from a stronger position.[29]

Thus, Brazil has been slow to commit fully to FTAA. For its part, the U.S. does not want to open its markets in sugar and oranges, two areas of interest to Brazil. This hesitation prevented progress toward a deeply integrating FTAA at the ministerial meeting held in Miami in November 2003, but the Miami FTAA did reach an agreement to compartmentalize the disagreement. Brazil and the U.S. convinced other FTAA nations to allow nations to opt out of additional FTAA provisions that would go beyond basic FTAA ones. The additional provisions would be more controversial, thus allowing disagreement to exist in a separate compartment from the areas of wider agreement. Some called this "FTAA à la carte" or "FTAA lite." The FTAA à la carte design allows for greater political flexibility and ensured that the Miami talks ended more successfully than WTO's Cancún talks. Despite the momentum from Miami, American leaders expressed considerable doubts about free trade and FTAA at the Summit of the Americas in Monterrey, Mexico in January 2004, and have not been able to agree on what should be included in the basic FTAA accord. Continued disagreement led FTAA to postpone a scheduled meeting a number of times in early 2004. The fate of FTAA, facing a January 1, 2005 deadline, remains uncertain.

In other developments in the Americas, Peru joined Mercosur in August 2003 as an associate member. Mercosur now includes Argentina, Brazil, Paraguay and Uruguay as full members and Bolivia, Chile and Peru as associate members. Peru and Bolivia are members of the Andean Community and Brazil's hopes to include the other three Andean Community members in Mercosur—Colombia, Ecuador and Venezuela—finally met with success. In April 2004, these Andean Community nations agreed to enter into an RTA with Mercosur, thus linking all of South America in an RTA. Mercosur continues to recover from the financial crises in its two largest members, Argentina and Brazil; it also hopes to reach an RTA with the Union. These negotiations have long been stuck on the E.U.'s reluctance to open its agricultural markets, but Mercosur has recently backed away from that demand and the E.U. is proposing lower agricultural export subsidies in WTO talks. Other contentious issues remain, but this increases the chances of an E.U.-Mercosur FTA.[30]

NAFTA: 10 Years Later

The "patient"—the Mexican economy—was not thriving as many thought it should, so its own leaders and those from the world's strongest economy, the United States, prescribed an exercise regimen of economic openness. For a time, the exercise seemed to be working. The patient's vigor increased (substantial economic growth) and many signs suggested full recovery was possible (high foreign investment). The patient then committed to the exercise regimen more fully by joining the North American Free Trade Agreement, thus locking in many of the reforms. Mexico then suffered the economic equivalent of a heart attack (the peso collapse, or so-called Tequila Crisis of 1994-1995). The patient seems to have recovered from the heart attack, but it has been a difficult and painful recovery. Did the patient have the heart attack because of the exercise regimen or did the exercise help it recover from the heart attack more easily?

Mexico had suffered two economic heart attacks in the 1980s—high debt inspired peso collapses—so to place blame on NAFTA for recent financial problems is unfair. Clearly, NAFTA has not helped Mexico, the U.S. or Canada as much as NAFTA's political supporters said it would. Nor has NAFTA been as damaging as critics feared it would be. In fact, this was inevitable because both its proponents and opponents oversold their cases in the debate to pass NAFTA. Nevertheless, the question of the NAFTA effect is important to other patients. Mexico's experiences in NAFTA gives those developing nations that are considering greater economic openness with developed nations reasons to think that the exercise of openness gives benefits, but also that exercise regimens need to be created with greater care to avoid injuries. In analyzing NAFTA, it is important to also note that Mexico has been faulted for not making many other reforms during the last 10 years. For instance, tax collection is very low, thus the government's ability to fund many basic services remains low. And corruption remains high even as Mexico becomes more democratic.

As history suggests, NAFTA's record is mixed and difficult to untangle from the economic crisis that hit Mexico in late 1994, the year that NAFTA went into effect. Exports to and from each of the NAFTA countries did go up, at least partly because of NAFTA. There were very few changes in the U.S-Canadian economic relationship from NAFTA simply because the two countries were already quite integrated through the Canada-United States FTA (CUSFTA). Foreign investment in Mexico did go up substantially after 1994 and economic growth in the NAFTA region as a whole has been strong during NAFTA's 10 years, despite the post-technology boom going bust in the United States.[31]

Some U.S. manufacturing jobs surely went to Mexico's maquiladora production—assembly production using U.S. inputs—along the U.S.-Mexican border and the U.S. did lose manufacturing jobs during this period, but NAFTA's impact on overall U.S. job loss is small, according to most economists. Why? First, the U.S. economy was already open to imports from Mexico before NAFTA. Second, the U.S. increased exports to Mexico, thus creating jobs, including manufacturing jobs, to compensate in the aggregate for many lost jobs. Third, the U.S. economy is losing manufacturing jobs more broadly. In fact, in recent years, Mexico has lost many maquiladora jobs to Chinese production. According to the Mexican government, 325 of 1,122 maquiladoras that make clothing have closed since January 2001. To blame NAFTA for many lost manufacturing jobs in the U.S. is misplaced.[32]

NAFTA's influence on agricultural sectors, especially in Mexico, is a more straightforward case. Some segments of Mexican agriculture, like avocados, have done quite well exporting to the United States. But in Mexico's most socially important agricultural sector, NAFTA has been terrible. U.S. corn producers have increased their exports to Mexico considerably since NAFTA's inception, and this has hurt many poor and already struggling Mexican corn farmers. The Mexican government has also been faulted for not doing enough to either help them continue farming through better infrastructure and more cred-it, or to ease their transition into some other crop or industry.

One lesson for other developing nations is clear, according to the much cited study of NAFTA by the Carnegie Endowment for Interna-tional Peace: Developing nations cannot compete directly with highly mechanized and massively subsidized agriculture. The study calls for slower tariff reductions and special safeguards to slow and mitigate the effects of subsidized agriculture.[33]

Asia

There have long been RTAs in Asia, although Asian countries have not been known for accomplishing very deep integration of their RTAs or for going after bilateral agreements. But these days, Asian countries are com-peting to form bilateral RTAs, either between two countries or between one country and an established RTA. Singapore, which has an open economy with few farmers, has long led others in forming bilateral free trade agree-ments in the region. In the past two years, it has signed bilateral RTAs with Japan, Australia and the United States. It is now pursuing bilateral RTAs with Canada, India, Mexico and South Korea. The region's largest economies are now following Singapore's lead. Much of the competition for RTAs stems from the growing rivalry for influence between China and Japan, the former of which has been courting the Association of South East Asian Nations (ASEAN) in recent years. Japan has taken notice and negotiated a bilateral RTA with Mexico; the country is also working toward bilateral agreements with some ASEAN nations and hopes for an RTA with South Korea. India and South Korea are also involved in this competition. South Korea has signed a bilateral RTA with Chile and hopes for bilateral agreements with China and Japan. India is working toward agreements with Chile, Singapore, Thailand and ASEAN.[34]

Association of South East Asian Nations In October 2003, ASEAN members gathered in Bali, Indonesia agreed to a plan to create an E.U.-style ASEAN Economic Community by 2020. The six original ASEAN mem-bers—Brunei, Indonesia, Malaysia, the Philippines, Singapore and Thai-land—have already created the ASEAN Free Trade Agreement (AFTA). The newer ASEAN members will join AFTA as follows: Vietnam in 2006, Laos and Myanmar in 2008, and Cambodia in 2010. If the more ambitious ASEAN Economic Community plans are to be successful, repressive Myan-mar will have to reform. ASEAN nations are also planning freer trade with other Asian nations such as China, Japan and South Korea. China and ASEAN had already agreed to create the China-ASEAN Free Trade Area by 2010, but at Bali, they pledged to move faster toward realizing this goal. ASEAN members also agreed to form an RTA with India by 2011. Japan announced that negotiations with three ASEAN nations, Malaysia, the Philippines and Thailand, will begin this year.[35]

The Asia-Pacific Economic Cooperation The Asia-Pacific Economic

Cooperation forum (APEC) is an RTA of 21 countries, including the U.S., Canada, Mexico and other non-Asian nations. It has long had the goal of freer trade for its developed members by 2010 and by its developing members by 2020, but has done little substantively to move toward this goal. During its most recent summit in Bangkok in October 2003, APEC focused on security issues.[36]

South Asian Association for Regional Cooperation   The seven nations of the South Asian Association for Regional Cooperation (SAARC) agreed to create the South Asian Free Trade Area (SAFTA), scheduled to take effect on January 1, 2006. The region's developing countries, India, Pakistan and Sri Lanka, would cut their tariffs to between 0 and 5 percent on nonsensitive items within seven years of SAFTA's start, while SAFTA's LDCs—Bangladesh, Nepal, Bhutan and the Maldives—will have 10 years.[37] India and Pakistan's difficult relationship will certainly be a more important factor in determining SAFTA's success than tariff reduction proposals. Only a few years ago, India and Pakistan's talking about lower tariffs would have seemed trivial and unthinkable; both nuclear-armed nations were more concerned about the possibility that clashes between troops massed along their border might escalate into yet another war between the two adversaries.

BIMST-EC   The Bangladesh, India, Myanmar, Sri Lanka and Thailand–Economic Cooperation known as BIMST-EC will expand to include Bhutan and Nepal and form a free trade agreement. Bangladesh, however, has decided not to join the FTA; the country will remain a BIMST-EC member. India, Sri Lanka and Thailand plan to eliminate tariffs by 2012, with Bhutan, Myanmar and Nepal lowering tariffs in 2017.[38]

Europe

The European Union's membership jumped from 15 to 25 members on May 1, 2004. This is the most significant widening in E.U. history in terms of the number of countries and people that have joined, and in terms of the disparity in wealth between the new E.U. entrants and established members. As Irish Prime Minister Bertie Ahern said: "The E.U. has grown in size before. But this enlargement is different—in scale, in potential and in historical significance."

The new countries include eight former communist nations, the Czech Republic, Estonia, Hungary, Latvia, Lithuania, Slovakia and Slovenia and two noncommunist countries, Cyprus and Malta. In area, the E.U. increased by 25 percent. In population, it increased by 70 million—about 20 percent more. This makes the E.U. the largest single market in population and the second largest to NAFTA in economic size. The expansion will change voting in various E.U. institutions and will most likely require extensive changes to E.U. farm- and poverty-alleviation programs. The newcomers are not yet eligible to join the E.U. single currency, the euro, but could in the future. Of the older 15 E.U. nations, all but Denmark, the U.K. and Sweden have adopted the euro. Most of all, E.U. enlargement proponents hope it will spur economic investment and growth in the newcomers and help further institutionalize democracy.[39]

Expansion does not stop there. Bulgaria and Romania could join the Union as early as January 2007. Turkey has long sought membership, and the E.U. will vote in December 2004 on whether to open accession negotiations with that country. Croatia and Macedonia have formally applied for membership and await votes in E.U. institutions before negotiations can begin.[40]

The E.U.'s expansion also expands the European Economic Area (EEA). The EEA consists of the E.U. and three of the four European Free Trade Association (EFTA) nations: Iceland, Liechtenstein and Norway. Switzerland, which is not in the EEA, is also an EFTA member.[41]

Middle East

The economies of the Middle East are not known for their economic openness and, thus, the Middle East has met with limited success in integrating its economies. A number of subregional and regional RTAs have been proposed and some have been established, but they have not brought trade barriers down significantly.

Mediterranean Arab Free Trade Area Some recent movement toward RTAs include the Mediterranean Arab Free Trade Area (MAFTA), consisting of Jordan, Egypt, Morocco and Tunisia and the Greater Arab Free Trade Area (GAFTA) which includes 14 Arab League countries, approximately two-thirds of the Arab League Members. Most ambitious of all is the effort by the European Union, MAFTA, EFTA nations and a number of Central and Eastern European E.U.-candidate countries to form the Mediterranean Free Trade Area by 2010. This could include up to 41 countries with 600-800 million people. As a step toward that goal, the E.U. has been pressing the Euro-Mediterranean Partnership, in which the E.U. enters into Euro-Mediterranean Association Agreements (Euro-Med Agreements) with Middle Eastern and North African countries. These Euro-Med Agreements increase economic ties and promote economic openness in the regions' economies. This includes opening to more efficient E.U. industrial production, a step not universally welcomed in the region. To help implement these reforms, the E.U. has established technical and financial support through its MEDA program.[42]

The Gulf Cooperation Council The Gulf Cooperation Council (GCC), consisting of Bahrain, Kuwait, Oman, Qatar, Saudi Arabia and the United Arab Emirates, has negotiated on and off with the E.U. about forming an RTA. The E.U. required that the GCC integrate internally first, which the GCC did in establishing the GCC Customs Union in 2003. Negotiations for an E.U.-GCC FTA continue.[43]

The U.S. has also called for an RTA in the Middle East and North Africa as well as established bilateral RTAs with Israel and Jordan, finished negotiations with Morocco on an RTA and is currently negotiating an RTA with

Bahrain. The U.S. has also entered into a number of investment agreements with countries in the region, part of U.S. plans for deeper trade ties. Instability coupled with anger at U.S. policy toward Iraq and the Israeli-Palestinian conflict certainly makes any U.S.-sponsored RTA in the region more politically difficult for possible participants.

Looking Forward

The World Trade Organization predicts global economic growth of 3.7 percent in 2004 and world trade growth of 7.5 percent. This would be a better performance than 2003 when the world economy grew at 2.5 percent and trade grew at 4.5 percent. These figures amount to a modest recovery in 2003, but remain lower than the average growth since WTO's founding in 1995. Most of the improved performance stemmed from recovery in the U.S. and strong growth in Asia.[44]

The General Assembly's 59th Session will examine a number of trade-related items, including the New Partnership for Africa's Development (NEPAD) and issues related to African development. The Assembly will also examine the eradication of poverty—and there are host of trade-related items relevant here. For instance, the 58th General Assembly called upon WTO to redouble its efforts to successfully conclude the DDA negotiations. It is likely that the Assembly will address this again in its 59th Session with a specific call to ensure that developing nations and least-developed countries receive sufficient access to developed nation markets through tariff reduction, through appropriate, not abusive, use of anti-dumping measures and safety standards, and through the reduction of export subsidies.[45]

Commentary:
The China Issue
David Lynch

The college student's voice broke with emotion as she told of her mother's economic predicament. Her mom's job evaporated when the textile and apparel company she worked for closed because of competition from producers along the booming coast. Her mother was old, making retraining and finding a new job difficult. As production continues to go global, the student's story could have been from the Carolinas or indeed any developed or developing nation. But the student was from China—the same China that has been growing at a rate unprecedented anywhere else in the world and that has pulled millions of its own citizens out of poverty since it began economic reforms in the late 1970s. Yet while China is booming, it is also struggling to find jobs for its unemployed. China's Minister of Labor and Social Security, Zheng Silin, predicts that 24 million urban dwellers will search for jobs in 2004 and less than half will find them.

China serves as a metaphor for today's world: globalization has the immense capacity for bringing millions out of poverty, yet by itself, globalization does not guarantee development. Even where there has been success with globalization in China, a host of other problems emerge: wrenching social change, inequality and environmental degradation.

To some, China's integration into the global economy is a bit like Wal-Mart's entry into a local market. Local businesses fear being put out of business by the chain, but also hope to be suppliers to such a fast-growing economic entity. At first glance, Wal-Mart's primary advantage is low prices, offered because of wages and massive-scale economies. However, Wal-Mart, like China, does not do well simply because of lower wages. While Wal-Mart has been at the forefront of inventory management, for instance, China has nurtured higher technology production and removed many wasteful regulations.

One shouldn't take this analogy too far, however. China's problems are many. In winter 2003 and spring 2004, the country's economy grew at a rate that is clearly unsustainable. According to the WTO, China's imports expanded by 40 percent in dollar terms in 2003 and its exports increased by 35 percent. This is amazing considering that China was already a major trader. Yet the country's financial system has long made lending decisions based on personal contacts, not merit, and Chinese banks are so saddled with bad loans that they are at risk of bankruptcy if the economy slows.

Those that view Chinese economic growth as unsustainable and fear a hard landing are reminded of the Asian miracle and subsequent Asian financial crisis of the 1990s. Others think that China can, like Wal-Mart, sustain growth for a surprisingly long time. For the sake of Chinese workers, one hopes, the growth is sustainable. Even so, growth, much like globalization itself helps some while hurting others; it creates both excitement and anxiety.

Endnotes

1. "Secretary-General's Message," *UNCTAD XI website*.
2. "Economic Development in Africa, Trade Performance and Commodity Dependence," *UNCTAD website*. / WTO 2003 Annual Report. / "Trade Stitched Up," *Economist*, July 26, 2003.
3. "Cancún Briefing Notes," *WTO website*. / "Rich-Poor Rift Triggers Collapse of Trade Talks," *Washington Post*, September 15, 2003. / "Delegates From Poorer Nations Walk Out of World Trade Talks, *New York Times*, September 15, 2003, among others.
4. Ibid.
5. "A Disaster for Poor Farmers in Third World," Letter to the Editor, *Wall Street Journal*, September 18, 2003.
6. "E.U. Proposes Eliminating Subsidies, *Wall Street Journal*, May 11, 2004. / "France Splits With Europe Over Farm Subsidy Plan, *New York Times*, May 11, 2004, among others.
7. WTO 2003 Annual Report.
8. WTO 2003 Annual Report. / "E.U. Nears Accord to Back Russia in Bid for WTO," *Wall Street Journal*, May 14, 2004.
9. "Accessions, Nepal" and "Least Developed Countries," *WTO website*. / "Nepal to Join WTO as 147th Member," *U.N. Wire*, March 26, 2004.
10. "China Signs WTO Deal With Saudi Arabia," *Financial Times Information*, April 4, 2004. / "Saudi Arabia to Join WTO," *Financial Times Information*, March 27, 2004.
11. "Cambodia and Nepal Win WTO Entry," *BBC News*. / "LDC Accession to the WTO – Learning from Nepal, Cambodia and Vanuatu," 4, March 2004. / WT/MIN(01)/DEC/1 (WTO Ministerial Declaration, also known as the *Doha Declaration*).
12. WTO Press Release 353, 2003.
13. Ibid.
14. "Bush Ditches Steel Import Duties," *BBC News*, December 4, 2003.
15. "Transatlantic Tiff," *Economist*, March 6, 2004.
16. "Europe Seeks Permission to Punish U.S., Citing Trade Ruling," *New York Times*, January 16, 2004. / "WTO Sends U.S. Sanctions Dispute to Arbitration," *Reuters*, January 26, 2004. / "U.S.: Will Fight Sanctions Effort at WTO," *Reuters*, January 15, 2004.
17. "WTO Rules Against Cotton Subsidies," *Washington Post*, April 27, 2004. / "WTO Rules Against U.S. on Cotton Subsidies," *New York Times*, April 27, 2004.
18. "Striking a Balance: Patents and Access to Drugs and Health Care," *WIPO website*, 2004.
19. "U.S. Reaches Patent Compromise to Provide Drugs to Poor Nations," *Wall Street Journal*, August 28, 2003.
20. "WTO Drug Pact Lifts Trade Talks," *Wall Street Journal*, September 3, 2003. / "Joint NGO Statement on TRIPS and Public Health WTO Deal on Medicines: A 'Gift' Bound in Red Tape," *Oxfam website*. / "Poor Countries Fail to Take Advantage of WTO Accord on AIDS Drugs," *Agence France-Presse*, March 7, 2004.
21. "Brazil to Stir Up AIDS-Drug Battle," *Wall Street Journal*, September 5, 2003.
22. "Poor Countries Fail to Take Advantage of WTO Accord on AIDS Drugs," *Agence France-Presse*, March 7, 2004.
23. WTO 2003 Annual Report.
24. "U.S., Morocco Sign Free Trade Agreement," *Washington Post*, March 3, 2004. / U.S. Office of the Trade Representative Press Releases: January 26, 2004, 04-08, 04-15, 2004-10, 2004-34. / "Middle East Free Trade Initiative," *U.S. Office of the Trade Representative website*.

25. "About HIPC," *World Bank website.*
26. "Africa Making Strides But Still Suffers From Disadvantages, U.N. Official Says," *U.N. News Service*, October 14, 2003. / "Trade and Regional Integration Division Objective," *U.N. Economic Commission for Africa website.* / "Economic Development in Africa, Trade Performance and Commodity Dependence," *UNCTAD website.*
27. "Afrabet Soup," *Economist*, February 8, 2001. / "Experts Discuss Funding of African Integration," *Panafrican News Agency Daily Newswire*, April 3, 2004. / "Consolidating the African Union," Addis Tribune, March 26, 2004.
28. "A Pact on Central America Trade Zone, Minus One," *New York Times*, December 18, 2003. / "Costa Rica to Be 5th Country in New Trade Pact With U.S.," *New York Times*, January 26, 2004. / U.S. Office of the Trade Representative Press Releases 2003-74, 04-19, 2004, 2004-25, 2004-26 and 2004-35.
29. "Trade Wind: Brazilian Diplomacy," *Economist*, June 28, 2003. / "Call Made for South American Trade Bloc," *Washington Post*, August 26, 2003, among others.
30. "Recruitment Drive: Trade in South America," *Economist*, August 30, 2003. / "Peru Signs Free Trade Pact With Mercosur," *Wall Street Journal* August 26, 2004. / "Uruguay: Little Kid on the Bloc," *Christian Science Monitor*, August 29, 2003, among others.
31. "Free Trade on Trial," Economist, December 30, 2003. / "10 Years Later, NAFTA Harvests a Stunted Crop," *Chicago Tribune*, December 14, 2003.
32. "As China Gallops, Mexico Sees Factory Jobs Slip Away," *New York Times*, September 3, 2003.
33. "NAFTA's Promise and Reality, Lessons From Mexico for the Hemisphere," *Carnegie Endowment for International Peace website*, 2003.
34. "Everybody's Doing It," *Economist*, February 26, 2004. / "Singapore Leads India Charge," *Wall Street Journal*, April 5, 2004. / "Chile to Begin Trade Negotiations With India," *Wall Street Journal*, April 22, 2004.
35. "Asean Leaders Agree On Trade Plan," *BBC News*, October 7, 2003. / "Southeast Asian Bloc Drafts Free Trade Plan," *Wall Street Journal*, October 7, 2003. / "Asian Leaders Sign Trade and Security Pacts," *Wall Street Journal*, October 9, 2003, among others.
36. "APEC to Support WTO Efforts to Resume Trade Talks," U.N. Wire, October 20, 2003. / "Bush in Asia: All About Security," *Christian Science Monitor*, October 20, 2003 . / "APEC Outcomes and Outlook, 2003-2004," *APEC website.*
37. "South Asia Ministers Sign Agreement on Free Trade," *Reuters*, January 6, 2004. / "South Asia Trade Deal to Improve India-Pakistan Ties," *Reuters*, January 2, 2004.
38. "Bangladesh Opts Out of Trade Deal," *BBC News*, February 9, 2004. / "BIMSTEC Welcomes Nepal, Bhutan into Grouping," *Indian Express*, January 24, 2004.
39. "State of the Union," *Wall Street Journal*, April 30, 2004. "Q&A: E.U. Enlargement," *BBC News*, May 1, 2004.
40. "1st May Enlargement Day," E.U. website. / "E.U. Could Hold Talks With Turkey Next Year," *New York Times*, March 16, 2004.
41. "E.U./European Economic Area: Simultaneous Enlargement on May 1," *European Report*, April 28, 2004. / EFTA Press Release, March 30, 2004.
42. WTO 2003 Annual Report, "The Euro-Mediterranean Partnership," *E.U. website.* / "The Euro-Mediterranean Agreements, Partnership or Penury?" *Oxfam website.*
43. "Bilateral Trade Relations: Gulf Region," *E.U. website.*
44. WTO Press Release 373, April 5, 2004.
45. U.N. Press Release GA/10224. / A/59/50. / A/58/481/Add.1.

Chapter 8

Managing and Budgeting for a Global Forum

Simon Chesterman, Anthony Mango
and Lawrence Woocher

As the Secretary-General has emphasized recently, this is not a panel on U.N. reform. It is a panel on building collective security for the 21st century. Of course, the panel may tackle the reform of institutions, including the Security Council, the Economic and Social Council, the General Assembly and the Trusteeship Council. But it will do so only if it deems it necessary for meeting the new challenges of international security. The Panel recognizes the scope of its challenge, the short time frame, and the high expectations from U.N. members and from public opinion.

—High-Level Panel Chairman Anand Panyarachun,
   Asia High-Level Symposium on Threats, Challenges and Change, April 2004.

As the United Nations heads into its 60th anniversary year, 2005, another round of discussions on budgeting, management and, of course, reform, will come into play among member states. As demonstrated in the first seven chapters of this book, the U.N. is constantly acting around the world to fight disease and protect water resources and human rights as well as to make peace and open both trade and legal barriers. This chapter delves into the crux of each of these U.N. endeavors—the financial and staff resources that make it all happen. As with any international policy-making body, ideas for change and improvement emerge, requests for increasing or lowering budgets are made, and building and staffing issues arise. Over the course of 2003 and early 2004, the U.N. dealt with these matters while also planning for its anniversary year and implementation of the capital master plan. The following pages outline the specifics, beginning with a look at U.N. reform.

United Nations Reform: Where it Stands Now

Simon Chesterman

Reform of the United Nations is sometimes said to be like the weather: everyone talks about it; nobody can do anything about it. Speaking to the General Assembly on September 23, 2003, U.N. Secretary-General Kofi Annan noted that, three years earlier, "we shared a vision, a vision of global solidarity and collective security, expressed in the Millennium Declaration." In the wake of the Iraq invasion, he said, that consensus was called into question. Without referring to any country, the S.G. warned that a policy of pre-emptive intervention—such as that adopted in the U.S. National Security Strategy published one year after the September 11, 2001 attacks[1]—represented a "fundamental challenge to the principles on which, however imperfectly, world peace and stability have rested for the last 58 years." Nevertheless, he warned, it was not enough to denounce unilateralism without also addressing the security concerns "that make some states feel uniquely vulnerable."[2]

The High-Level Panel on Threats, Challenges and Change that was named soon after that speech is now the most prominent effort to reform the United Nations. But it is only one of many such efforts.

Previous Reform Efforts

The U.N. Charter is much like a constitution. And, like most constitutions, it is designed to be difficult to amend. Article 108 of the Charter, for example, requires an amendment to be ratified by two-thirds of the U.N. member states, including all permanent members of the Security Council (P-5).[3] The Charter has been amended three times, all in the period 1963-1973. The first amendment expanded the membership of the S.C. from 11 to 15 and increased the number of votes necessary to pass a resolution from seven to nine; it also expanded the membership of the Economic and Social Council (ECOSOC) from 18 to 27. The second amendment corrected the amendment procedures themselves, while the third further increased the membership of ECOSOC from 27 to 54.[4]

Since the Council is widely seen as the most influential part of the U.N. system, much discussion of reform focuses on its membership. In 1993, the General Assembly established an open-ended working group to consider, among other things, the question of increasing Council membership.[5] Now more than a decade into its deliberations, there is still no agreement on an appropriate formula for Council representation and the body is jokingly referred to as the "never-ending working group." Issues of general consensus are that the Council should be expanded, and should probably include new permanent members but perhaps without granting newcomers the coveted veto, currently held by only the P-5.[6] Efforts to abolish the veto itself are not currently taken seriously. Even proposals to limit it—such as that discussed in the report of the International Commission on Intervention and State Sovereignty titled The Responsibility to Protect, which outlined a possible "code of conduct" whereby permanent members without vital national interest at stake would agree not to use their veto to block a resolution responding to a humanitarian crisis[7]—appear to be off the table.

There is, however, much that can be done to improve the effectiveness of the world body without amending the Charter. Indeed, in the case of the Council, there is a tendency to conflate the question of the S.C.'s "representativeness" with that of its effectiveness. Would expanding the Council's membership make it more capable of responding to threats to international peace and security? It is arguable that other areas of reform, such as transparency of Council decision-making practices, the analytical role of the U.N. Secretariat, the availability of forces under U.N. command and financial and human resources devoted to peacekeeping would better address the problems the S.C. currently faces. For this reason, the position of some governments is to support Council expansion in theory while opposing any specific reforms to membership in practice.

Beyond the Council, other notable reform processes that remain ongoing include the possibility of ECOSOC reform. Following the adoption of General Assembly Resolution 270B, there has been increased discussion of strengthening the role of ECOSOC. In his September 2003 report on the implementation of the *Millennium Declaration*, the S.G. emphasized that ECOSOC's role—"indeed the role of the United Nations as a whole in economic and social affairs, and its relationship to the Bretton Woods institutions—needs to be re-thought and reinvigorated."[8]

Uncontroversial areas of reform include strengthening ECOSOC's coordination capacity (perhaps including its relations with the S.C.), elaborating a multiyear program of work for ECOSOC based on "cross-cutting themes," and a review of the working methods of the functional commissions with a view to better implementing the outcomes of major U.N. conferences and summits.[9] More ambitious proposals concern the relationship between ECOSOC and the Bretton Woods institutions. The introduction of annual discussions between ECOSOC and the boards of the World Bank and the International Monetary Fund are the most significant development in this relationship, but it seems highly unlikely that countries that resist dilution of their direct control of these institutions would allow them to be constrained through external governance.[10] *(See Commentary for more details on ECOSOC reform.)*

The High-Level Panel

As indicated earlier, the High-Level Panel on Threats, Challenges, and Change was set up in response to the political crisis that followed the U.S.-led invasion of Iraq in March 2003. Specifically, the Panel's terms of reference ask it to:

1) Examine today's global threats and provide an analysis of future challenges to international peace and security;
2) Identify clearly the contribution that collective action can make in addressing these challenges; and
3) Recommend the changes necessary to ensure effective collective action, including but not limited to a review of the principal organs of the United Nations.[11]

On November 3, 2003, the S.G. announced the 16 members of the Panel in a letter to the president of the General Assembly.[12] Chaired by Anand Panyarachun, a former prime minister of Thailand, the panelists include Robert Badinter of France, João Clemente Baena Soares of Brazil, Gro Harlem

Brundtland of Norway, Mary Chinery-Hesse of Ghana, Gareth Evans of Australia, David Hannay of the United Kingdom, Enrique Iglesias of Uruguay, Amre Moussa of Egypt, Satish Nambiar of India, Sadako Ogata of Japan, Yevgeny Primakov of Russia, Qian Qichen of China, Nafis Sadik of Pakistan, Salim Ahmed Salim of Tanzania and Brent Scowcroft of the United States.

The Panel met for the first time in Princeton, N.J., on December 5-6, 2003. It was originally asked to report back to the S.G. by August 15, 2004—a deadline that was later pushed back to December 2004. Subsequent formal meetings were held in Geneva in February 2004 and Addis Ababa in April 2004; others are scheduled to occur in July in Vienna and over the fall in New York. Panel members also took part in a variety of side meetings and consultations around the world.

A key question circling the Panel is how broadly it should interpret its mandate: in particular, the "threats" to which its title refers. In his September 2003 speech, the S.G. referred to "hard" and "soft" threats—with the latter denoting "the persistence of extreme poverty, the disparity of income between and within societies, and the spread of infectious diseases, or climate change and environmental degradation."[13] The final sentences of the terms of reference state that "the Panel's work is confined to the field of peace and security."[14]

In place of "hard" and "soft" threats, consideration has turned to six "baskets" of threats: 1) intrastate violence; 2) interstate rivalry and war; 3) economic and social issues, including infectious diseases; 4) weapons of mass destruction; 5) terrorism; and 6) organized crime. A point of continuous discussion for the Panel is whether these threats should be prioritized, and how the "soft" threats figure in discussions of peace and security.

Since the S.C. passed a resolution in 2000 stressing that HIV/AIDS "if unchecked, may pose a risk to stability and security,"[15] it has been accepted that "soft" threats such as disease may have an impact on traditional security questions—most obviously through the impact of the HIV/AIDS pandemic on the armed forces of various African countries. But some argue that defining poverty, for example, as a threat on par with terrorism or interstate violence does little more than render the word "threat" vague. Poverty may be a partial cause—or, in some cases, an effect—of conflict, but there are other policy frameworks in place to deal with this and related issues, most prominently the Millennium Development Goals.

One way of resolving this question might be through explicitly recognizing the disparate ways in which different stakeholders perceive threats. While the combination of terrorism and weapons of mass destruction is the primary fear of many countries in the industrialized North, economic concerns dominate in the South. It might be possible, therefore, to link these issues and secure greater support and cooperation by countries in the South for counter-terrorism and counter-proliferation activities in exchange for greater development assistance and reform of agricultural subsidies by countries in the North.

Much speculation on the Panel's deliberations has focused on the question of reforming the Security Council. In his September 2003 speech, S.G. Annan drew attention "to the urgent need for the Council to regain the confidence of States, and of world public opinion—both by demonstrating its ability to deal effectively with the most difficult issues, and by becoming more broadly representative of the international community as a whole, as well as the geopolitical realities of today." Noting that the composition of the Council had been on the agenda of the General Assembly for over a decade, he stressed the need to address the issue with greater urgency.[16] The terms of reference for the Panel, however, emphasized the need for effectiveness, calling on it to "recommend the changes necessary to ensure effective collective action, including but not limited to a review of the principal organs of the United Nations."[17]

A danger for the Panel is that if it makes concrete recommendations on the membership of the Council, this may be the only part of its report to which serious attention is paid—and according to the success or failure of which the Panel's legacy is determined. Given the difficulties of securing agreement among the various member states, the chances of being successful in this area appear slim. Nevertheless, failing to address Council reform at all would be seen by many as an abdication of responsibility. As a result, it seems probable that the Panel will embrace Council expansion in principle, perhaps elaborating on factors that should determine how the models of expansion should be generated, but refrain from committing itself to any particular model at this time.

Each of these issues, of course, remains at some distance from the driving force of this reform process: the troubled relationship between the U.N. and the United States. The dilemma is that the impetus for change and the desire of many member states to see the Panel succeed arises primarily from those who are worried about future Iraq-style divisions. This does not, at present, include the United States. There is a risk, therefore, that the U.S. will reject anything that does not increase its influence in the U.N. and protect its freedom of action, when it is precisely the exercise of such influence and freedom that led to divisions in the first place. These political divisions lie at the heart of the present impetus to reform the United Nations, but the transformations that are necessary to ensure that the U.N. is both effective and legitimate cannot take place within the organization alone.

Looking Forward

The Secretary-General will refer to the work of the High-Level Panel in his address to the General Assembly, but this work will be far from over. The Panel is scheduled to meet twice in New York in September and November to finalize its report, for release in December 2004. In many ways, that is when the work of the panelists will really begin. For the Panel's recommendations to have any purchase, it will be essential to obtain support in key capitals—and to have strong advocates who are above the political fray in their domestic constituencies. It is hoped that the panelists will fulfil this function and become salesmen and saleswomen for the report. In addition, it is most likely that some form of "Friends' Group" will be constituted to advocate in favor of the report's recommendations.

Deliberations on responding to the Panel's report in 2005 will coincide with the High-Level Meeting to review the *Millennium Declaration* and to evaluate progress toward the MDGs. Depending on the linkage that the Panel establishes between peace and security on the one hand and development on the other, there is a slim possibility that the same high-level meeting might embrace consideration of both the MDGs and the Panel's report.[18]

United Nations Personnel and Administration: The Issues at Stake

Anthony Mango

At its 58th session in 2003-2004, the United Nations General Assembly dealt mainly with budgetary issues, including the adoption of the program budget for 2004-2005. It will focus more intently on personnel and management at its 59th session in fall 2004. However, a few personnel-related issues were discussed at the 58th session and are outlined below.

Hazard Pay

In discussing the U.N. common system, the Chairman of the International Civil Service Commission, Mohsen Bel Hadj Amor, reported that the new master standard for the classification of posts in the professional and higher categories was ready for promulgation. He also reported that the Commission had made progress in its study of "broad-banding"—an approach that would assign a range of two or three grades depending on qualification and performance level to each post rather than one particular grade to each post. A pilot study introducing a link between broad-banding and pay-for-performance will be undertaken in 2004. Responding to a request by the General Assembly, the Commission also re-examined its decision to raise the hazard pay of locally recruited general service staff from 20 percent to 30 percent of the midpoint of the local salary scale.[1]

Even though the Commission chairman pointed out that setting the amount of hazard pay was within the authority of the Commission, the Assembly, for the second time, requested the Commission to reconsider and decide on a smaller increase; it is to report on the implementation of this request at the Assembly's 59th session.

The representative of Canada, speaking also on behalf of Australia and New Zealand, said that linking pay with performance was a very high priority and should be tested, perhaps starting with managers, before a decision was taken on broad-banding. The representative of Japan added that, generally speaking, he could support the introduction of broad-banding and pay-for-performance, provided there was a fair and reliable performance appraisal system. The United States representative was concerned about broad-banding because, as he pointed out, the system did not distinguish between degrees of difficulty and responsibility within the band; a credible, reliable and acceptable performance appraisal system would have to come first—a point that was also made by the Canadian representative. The representatives of China and the Russian Federation requested that the introduction of pay-for-performance not lead to extra costs.[2]

As for the two staff associations, representatives said they were opposed to the pay-for-performance approach because it would be difficult to maintain systemwide consistency and might lead to cronyism and favoritism; they had no confidence in the existing performance-appraisal system.

Administration of Justice

The Assembly amended the Statute of the U.N. Administrative Tribunal to state that Tribunal "members must possess judicial or other relevant legal experience in the field of administrative law or its equivalent within the member's national jurisdiction."[3] The Statute of the Administrative Tribunal of the International Labour Organization already contained such a provision. Moreover, the Secretary-General was asked to ensure the independence of the U.N. Administrative Tribunal and the separation of its secretariat from the U.N. Office of Legal Affairs. A report on the financial independence of the Tribunal is to be submitted at the Assembly's 59th session.

Staff Partner Entitlements

At its first resumed 58th session in March 2004, the Fifth Committee of the Assembly devoted nearly four meetings to a highly repetitive and at times acrimonious debate on paragraph four of the Secretary-General's Bulletin titled "Family Status for Purposes of United Nations Entitlements." The bulletin stated that "a legally recognized domestic partnership contracted by a staff member under the law of the country of his or her nationality will also qualify the staff member to receive the entitlements provided for eligible family members." In other words, partners of gay and lesbian staff entitled to benefits in their home nations would also be entitled to benefits under the U.N. system.

The validity of the S.G.'s decision to extend family benefits to members of domestic partnerships was questioned by the representative of Iran, speaking on behalf of the Organization of the Islamic Conference. He was supported by the representatives of Indonesia, Syria, Pakistan, Kuwait, Egypt, Saudi Arabia, Sudan, Tunisia, Bangladesh, Malaysia, Bahrain, Yemen, Kenya and Cameroon. They argued that there was no consensus among the member states on the question of domestic partnerships and same-sex marriages—as had been made abundantly clear during the debate on the Regulations of the U.N. Joint Staff Pension Fund in 2000. They also argued that the S.G.'s bulletin was inconsistent with staff regulations and rules because the term "domestic partnership" was not used in these instruments, and an amendment of the regulations and rules required action by the Assembly. Lastly, they pointed out that an extension of family benefits to members of domestic partnerships would have financial implications. For these reasons, they asked that the bulletin be withdrawn.[4]

In response, the S.G.'s representatives said that the bulletin was neutral on the substance of the question and did not imply recognition in principle of the validity of same-sex marriages or domestic partnerships. The staff regulations and rules did not contain a definition of "marriage" or "spouse." Regarding procedure, the bulletin followed the long-established practice of recognizing the law of the country of which the staff member is a national (as witness the recognition of polygamy in the case of staff members who are nationals of countries where polygamy is legal), and the bulletin simply reflected changes that had occurred in the laws of several member states. They also said that there would be no measurable financial implications.

The S.G.'s approach was endorsed by the representative of Ireland, speaking on behalf of the European Union and associated States, and the representatives of Canada, Costa Rica, Brazil, Norway, Peru, Australia and New Zealand.[5]

In a compromise text, Resolution 58/285, the G.A. decided that the U.N.'s practice of determining personal status for the purpose of the entitlements could be referenced to the law of nationality of the staff member concerned.[6]

Composition of the Secretariat

The composition of the U.N. Secretariat comes up for discussion at each session of the Assembly, with particular attention paid by member states to the geographical distribution of staff and, to a lesser degree, the gender makeup. At the 58th session, the Assembly considered the report by the S.G. covering the period July 1, 2002, to June 30, 2003.[7] According to this report, the total number of staff members holding appointments of one year or more, funded from assessed or voluntary contributions, was 37,705 as of June 30, 2003, 15,082 of whom were serving in the Secretariat. The number of staff in posts subject to geographical distribution (i.e., senior and non-linguist professional staff funded from the regular budget) was 2,491. These posts are divided among member states on the basis of "desirable ranges" that are calculated using a formula reflecting the country's membership, the rate at which it is assessed for the regular budget, and the size of its population.[8] As of June 30, 2003, 17 member states were unrepresented (i.e., they had no nationals in posts subject to geographical distribution), one more than the previous year. Ten member states were under-represented—one fewer than the previous year, and 19 were over-represented, also one fewer than the previous year. The geographical distribution of posts at the senior and policy-making levels is the subject of particularly close scrutiny in the Fifth Committee. The S.G.'s report indicates that the proportion of such staff from both developed and developing countries declined during the year under review, while the proportion of such staff from countries with economies in transition (i.e., former Communist countries) increased.

As of June 30, 2003, 111 posts graded D-1 and above were held by female staff members. Of all posts subject to geographical distribution, 41.8 percent were held by women.

In the year under review, 168 appointments were made to posts subject to geographical distribution, of which 34 were of nationals of under-represented member states and 26 of nationals from over-represented states.

During discussion of the report, Japan's representative said that more attention should be paid to the degree of under-representation, while the U.S. representative expressed concern over the trends indicated in the report; if such trends continued, the U.S. would also become under-represented.

Joint Inspection Unit

The Joint Inspection Unit (JIU), an organ consisting of not more than 11 inspectors appointed by the U.N. General Assembly with due regard to the principle of equitable geographical representation, has been in existence since 1968. Its remit extends not only to the U.N. itself but also to the specialized agencies that have accepted its statute. Informally, the relevance and usefulness of JIU has been questioned; this has been particularly true of specialized agencies in some of which the question of withdrawing from the unit's activities has been mooted.[9] In recent years, however, the question resurfaced in the context of U.N. reform.

In 2003, JIU undertook an in-depth review of its statute and working methods and adopted a strategic framework addressing the selection of topics for—and quality of—its reports. The results were reported to the 58th Assembly. While the steps taken by JIU were generally welcomed, opinions differed on whether they went far enough. The representative of Ireland, speaking on behalf of the E.U. and associated states, as well as the representatives of Canada and the United States, were in favor of action that might require amending the unit's statute. Such amendments might include reducing the number of inspectors, strengthening the role of the unit's Chairman and establishing collective responsibility for the unit's work instead of allowing inspectors to be responsible only for their own reports. By contrast, the representatives of Senegal, Tanzania, the Russian Federation, Pakistan and China were of the opinion that the work of the unit could be improved without amending its statute at this stage.[10]

In Resolution 58/286, the Assembly welcomed the internal reform process undertaken by JIU and decided to revert to the issue of reforming the unit at its 59th session.

The Capital Master Plan

On December 20, 2002, the General Assembly adopted Resolution 57/292 in which it approved a "capital master plan" for refurbishing and expanding the U.N. Headquarters complex in New York. Since the main buildings of the complex were built in the early 1950s, the passage of time has led to the need for major repairs and because resources for these repairs were not available in the 1990s, the buildings are continuing to deteriorate. The plan envisions the complete overhaul of seven structures located on the 17-acre site as well as construction of a new "swing building" across the street to house the U.N. Secretariat during work on the complex. Some proposed upgrades include: replacement of heating and air-conditioning systems; upgrading of electrical wiring and technology infrastructure; replacement of ceilings and removal of asbestos; and installation of a comprehensive automatic building management system.

In a progress report submitted to the Assembly's 58th session, the S.G. indicated that it had not proved possible to finalize the construction funding arrangements in 2003, as had been hoped. In the meantime, progress was made in selecting the architect for the proposed new building (to be known as DC-5) and New York City authorities had been working with the local community on how to mitigate the loss of the playground site in which the swing building will be erected. Contracts for a total of $12.3 million had been entered into with 21 vendors. Although 19 of them are from the United States, the largest contract (for $8.5 million) went to an Italian company. Out of the $25.5 million appropriated by the Assembly for the plan for 2002-2003, $16.9 million had been committed. In a separate report, the S.G. provided details of possible alternatives for the construction of three additional conference rooms, one of which would accommodate 100 delegates, and two for 60 delegates each; the two smaller rooms could be combined to form a larger room as necessary. The cost of construction, estimated at $6 million, is already included in the overall projected budget for the plan (around $1 billion).[11]

The FY2005 budget request released by the Bush Administration in February 2004 includes $1.2 billion for a loan to the U.N. for the headquarters' renovation. Although discussions in 2002 expressed hope in U.N. circles that the loan might be interest-free, the U.S. budget request provides for the payment of interest at the current U.S. Treasury rate of 5.54 percent. The loan would be paid at the annual rate of $400 million over three years, and would be repayable over 30 years. The S.G. estimated that the total amount of the interest payable over the 30-year period would be $1,311 million.[12] Before going into effect, the loan is subject to approval by the U.S. Congress and the U.N. General Assembly. As the U.S. is assessed at the rate of 22 percent for the U.N. regular budget (see below for more details), $288.4 million of the interest charged for the loan would be paid by the U.S. itself.

When the S.G.'s report in document A/58/729 was considered in the Fifth Committee at its first resumed session in March 2004, there was widespread disappointment over the interest-attached loan. The representative of Ireland, speaking on behalf of the European Union, expressed strong concern that the result of the U.S. proposal would be to more than double the cost of the project, and recalled that during the negotiations in December 2003, it had been understood by the Fifth Committee that the U.S. offer would be in the form of an interest-free loan. The E.U. continued to believe that the host country of the U.N. complex (i.e., the United States) should provide a substantial portion of the funding. Japan's representative said that the U.S. proposal fell short of what her delegation had expected. India's representative expressed the hope that the S.G. would consult with U.S. authorities so that the terms and conditions of the potential loan would be acceptable to all member states.[13] Overall, it was clear that most member states wanted the S.G. to continue to explore all financing options, including seeking private contributions and setting up a financial advisory board.

For its part, the U.S. representative pointed out that the discussions in Congress were expected to be finalized by the end of September 2004. Any loan offer approved by Congress would be valid until September 30, 2005, and the actual loan agreement would have to be signed by that date.[14]

On May 5, 2004, U.N. Under-Secretary-General for Management Catherine Bertini informed the Fifth Committee that, if all went well, the construction of the DC-5 building (the "swing building") might begin in late 2005. She said that in the meantime the Secretariat was looking into various alternatives of financing the construction, including a shorter repayment period of the loan, earlier payment by member states of their assessments and voluntary financing. She pointed out that the proposed $1.2 billion loan related solely to the construction of the DC-5 building. The refurbishment of the existing Headquarters complex would be paid for through assessments on member states.

The E.U. had informally suggested that a U.N. financial facility be set up for the repayment of the principal and interest on the loan, to be fed by national contributions based on a special scale of assessments without a "ceiling" rate. (Under such a scale, the U.S. rate would be about 31 percent, instead of 22 percent.) While the suggestion was favorably received by the vast majority of member states, it was unacceptable to the United States. In the absence of consensus on a resolution, further consideration of the question was deferred to the 59th session.

United Nations Budgets: Past, Present and Future
Anthony Mango

Regular Program Budgets

The final General Assembly-approved appropriations for 2002-2003 amounted to $2.97 billion in expenditures, $76.7 million more than had been approved in 2002, and $428.1 million in income.[15] Much of the increase was attributable to differences between projected and actual currency exchange rates and inflation indices, particularly to the weakening of the U.S. dollar in 2003 against the Swiss franc and the euro, in which the U.N.'s expenses in Geneva and Vienna are defrayed. The breakdown of the final appropriations for 2002-2003 can be found in Table A.

The Fifth Committee

Consideration of the Secretary-General's estimates for 2004-2005 was the principal business of the Fifth Committee at the Assembly's 58th session. The S.G. requested $3.058 billion, estimating that his request provided for "real growth" of 0.5 percent. In its related report, the Advisory Committee on Administrative and Budgetary Questions (ACABQ) recommended that the S.G.'s estimates be reduced by $41 million to $3.017 billion, resulting in a decrease in resources, in real terms, by 0.4 percent.[16] Activities approved by the Economic and Social Council in 2003 and by the Assembly itself at its 58th session involved additional requirements totaling $18.1 million. The recosting exercise *(see below)* to reflect changes in currency exchange rates and inflation assumptions from the beginning of 2003—when the S.G.'s estimates were drawn up—to October 2003, added a further $150.5 million; once again, the further weakening of the U.S. dollar greatly contributed to the need for these additional resources.

In a departure from past practice, discussion of the program budget proposals at formal meetings of the Fifth Committee was limited to a general debate on the budget as a whole, while the discussion of individual sections took place at informal meetings. The general debate revealed the traditional split between the developing countries, which insisted on the need for adequate resources for economic and social development, and the major contributors, several of whom advocated zero-nominal growth. Twenty-six delegations put forward the developing countries' position. Their statements betrayed their continuing concern that budgetary "reform" not become a pretext for budget "cutting." They stressed that results-based budgeting was not an end in itself and that it should be implemented in a gradual and incremental manner; their interest in inputs would remain until member states were confident that the objectives of programs and activities were indeed being met. Given the ever-increasing mandates that the U.N. must carry out, the developing countries were opposed to the zero-nominal-growth approach. Specifically, they were concerned about using extra-budgetary resources for priority areas, and pointed out that most extra-budgetary resources were tied to the implementation of the wishes of the donors. The representatives of Norway and Switzerland likewise said that increased reliance on extra-budgetary funding was unfortunate. The former agreed with the developing countries that a zero-growth budget was no longer an option.[17]

On the other hand, the U.S. representative argued that, despite the termination of 912 outputs (e.g., a press release or report, mission or meeting), more could be done. Obsolete and ineffective activities could be terminated, for example. The representative favored the elimination of posts that had remained vacant for more than two years, the closing of the U.N. Information Center in Washington, D.C., (which—by itself—would save about $1 million) and a reduction in the number of meetings. Canada's representative also said that the number of terminated outputs was too low. The representative of Italy, speaking on behalf of the members of the European Union, said there was a need to take a hard look at the staffing table. The representative of the Russian Federation voiced concern over the absence of close, concrete linkages between resources and activities. The representative of Japan said that it was important that the level of the budget not exceed $3 billion.[18]

Recosting The U.N.'s budgetary practice provides for three adjustments of foreign exchange rates and inflation assumptions during a budgetary cycle; this exercise is known as "recosting." The first involves updating the rates and assumptions used in the preparation of the S.G.'s initial estimates to reflect the situation some 10 months later, when those estimates are considered by the Assembly. At the end of the first year of the biennium, such as December 2002 for the 2002-2003 biennium, the appropriations are again adjusted based on the first budget performance report to reflect the latest available data. The exercise is repeated a third time at the end of the second year of the biennium, based on the second performance report. Final appropriations are then approved.

Several speakers at the 58th Assembly session addressed the suggestion of ACABQ that the recosting exercise that traditionally precedes the adoption of the program budget be deferred for a year and combined with the recosting at the end of the first year of a biennium.[19] The consensus was to include the provisions for recosting for all program-budget sections—except for section 23, which refers to the regular program of technical cooperation. The Assembly also decided to revert to the question of recosting at its 59th session in the context of the first performance report, at which time it would have an updated S.G. report regarding the first nine months of 2004 as well as a report from the Board of Auditors. Considering that currencies both depreciate and appreciate over the years, the Assembly requested the S.G. to submit a report at its 60th session on the possibility of establishing a reserve fund to utilize currency gains.[20]

Other decisions by the Fifth Committee resulted in reductions totaling nearly $25 million over and above the $41 million cut recommended by ACABQ. Nearly half the additional reductions related to general service and other support staff. ACABQ had informed the Fifth Committee that it was of the opinion that the number of staff members in these categories (approximately 57 percent) should be reduced through attrition, taking into account investment in communication and information technology; and bearing in mind that 268 such staff were expected to retire by the end of 2005.[21]

In the general debate, ACABQ's comments were endorsed by representatives from Canada and the United States.[22] The Fifth Committee decided to impose a freeze on recruitment to the general service and related categories, with a consequential reduction of the budget by $11.9 million, and to abolish six general service posts, thereby saving $900,000. Reductions were also made in the provisions for common services ($3.2 million), publications ($400,000), general temporary assistance ($2.5 million), overtime and night differential ($2 million) and U.N. information centers ($2 mil-

Table A: Final 2002-2003 Appropriations / Initial 2004-2005 Appropriations (in $US millions).

PART/SECTION	2002-2003	INCREASE/(DECREASE)	2004-2005
PART I: Overall Policy-Making, Direction & Coordination	**$540.7**	**$53.2**	**$593.9**
1. Overall policy-making, direction & coordination	51.8	6.7	58.5
2. General Assembly affairs & conference services	488.9	46.5	535.4
PART II: Political Affairs	**$360.4**	**$(11.2)**	**$349.2**
3. Political affairs	263.6	(24.0)	239.6
4. Disarmament	16.2	1.8	18.0
5. Peacekeeping operations	76.5	9.6	86.1
6. Peaceful uses of outer space	4.1	1.4	5.5
PART III: International Justice & Law	**$63.7**	**$6.5**	**$70.2**
7. International Court of Justice	28.3	3.2	31.5
8. Legal affairs	35.4	3.3	38.7
PART IV: International Cooperation for Development	**$296.4**	**$40.1**	**$336.5**
9. Economic & social affairs	126.9	10.8	137.7
10. Least-developed countries, land-locked developing countries & small-island developing states	2.2	2.0	4.2
11. U.N. support for the New Partnership for Africa's Development	6.1	3.3	9.4
12. Trade and development	93.1	13.2	106.3
13. International Trade Centre, UNCTAD & WTO	20.4	3.1	23.5
14. Environment	8.9	1.6	10.5
15. Human settlements	13.6	1.9	15.5
16. Crime prevention & criminal justice	7.4	2.0	9.4
17. International drug control	17.8	2.2	20.0
PART V: Regional Cooperation for Development	**$351.5**	**$37.1**	**$388.6**
18. Economic & social development in Africa	78.9	16.7	95.6
19. Economic & social development in Asia and the Pacific	58.6	8.0	66.6
20. Economic development in Europe	47.3	2.9	50.2

Part/Section	2002-2003	Increase/(Decrease)	2004-2005
21. Economic & social development in Latin America & the Caribbean	73.4	7.4	80.8
22. Economic & social development in Western Asia	49.4	3.1	52.5
23. Regular program of technical cooperation	43.9	(1.0)	42.9
Part VI: Human Rights & Humanitarian Affairs	**$147.6**	**$23.1**	**$170.7**
24. Human rights	48.1	8.7	56.8
25. Protection of & assistance to refugees	49.3	7.4	56.7
26. Palestine refugees	29.5	4.4	33.9
27. Humanitarian assistance	20.7	2.6	23.3
Part VII: Public Information	**$147.4**	**$8.5**	**$155.9**
28. Public information	147.4	8.5	155.9
Part VIII : Common Support Services	**$458.1**	**$58.1**	**$516.2**
29. Management & central support services	458.1	58.1	516.2
Part IX: Internal Oversight	**$21.0**	**$2.2**	**$23.2**
30. Internal oversight	21.0	2.2	23.2
Part X: Jointly Financed Administrative Activities & Special Expenses	**$90.0**	**$12.4**	**$102.4**
31. Jointly financed administrative activities	8.1	14.9	23.0
32. Special expenses	81.9	(2.5)	79.4
Part XI: Capital Expenditures	**$88.9**	**$(30.2)**	**$58.7**
33. Construction, alteration, improvement & major maintenance	88.9	(30.2)	58.7
Part XII: Staff Assessment	**$388.9**	**$(6.6)**	**$382.3**
34. Staff assessment	388.9	(6.6)	382.3
Part XIII: Development Account	**$13.1**	**-**	**$13.1**
35. Development account	13.1	-	13.1
Grand Total, Expenditures	**$2,967.7**	**$193.2**	**$3,160.9**

Source: A/Res/58/267 and A/Res/58/271.

lion). The 2005 funds for JIU were deleted, pending completion of the aforementioned survey of the unit. Responding to criticism by ACABQ that, in recent years, the Fifth Committee had applied across-the-board lump-sum reductions to the budgetary appropriations, the Committee provided a detailed expenditure breakdown of the reductions.[23]

Security Measures Marked

Three months after the adoption of the regular program budget for 2004-2005, the Secretary-General submitted a request for additional resources to strengthen the security and safety of U.N. operations, staff and premises for a total amount of $92.4 million, of which $71.9 million relates to the U.N. regular budget, $13.5 million is for peacekeeping operations, and $0.6 million for the International Criminal Court for Rwanda. The balance of about $6.4 million is to be funded by other organizations in Vienna through cost-sharing. This request comes on top of $57.8 million for security measures which was appropriated by the G.A. two years ago, but only $27.4 million was spent during 2002 and 2003.[24]

Under the regular budget, the new request includes nearly $40 million for construction and alteration of premises at U.N. Headquarters in New York and the U.N. offices in Geneva, Vienna, Nairobi, Addis Ababa, Bangkok and Santiago (Chile) to improve their security. The S.G. also requested 123 new posts for field security officers and security guards, of which 58 already exist, but are funded through extra-budgetary resources, and $6.2 million for the six-month period from July 1 to December 31, 2004, for temporary assistance for a further 164 posts.[25]

Of the $13.5 million requested under the peacekeeping operations budgets, $12 million relates to construction and alteration of U.N. premises to improve their security.

The S.G. indicated in his report that a further report would be submitted to the Assembly at its 59th session focusing on longer-term measures that he would be proposing in light of an ongoing study of security arrangements. In its related report, ACABQ, citing existing uncertainties and ongoing studies, and the absence of a comprehensive review of security arrangements, recommended that, at this stage, the Assembly appropriate $40 million (gross) under the regular budget to enhance the security and safety of U.N. operations, staff and premises, as compared to $71.9 million requested by the Secretary-General. While recommending approval of the request for $13.5 million for peacekeeping operations, the Committee recommended that $4.3 million of this amount not be appropriated at this stage but be accommodated within existing budgets.[26]

Introducing the S.G.'s report in the Fifth Committee, Under-Secretary-General for Management Catherine Bertini said that the attack on U.N. premises in Baghdad in August 2003 had radically changed the security environment in which the organization operates. In the past, the U.N. flag had provided protection to U.N. staff, but that was no longer the case. If the budget request was reduced, the S.G. would be faced with almost impossible choices as to which high-risk field offices should not be accorded the required level of security protection.

In the ensuing debate, member states generally agreed that urgent steps to improve security arrangements needed to be taken, but opinions differed on whether to follow ACABQ's recommendations.[27]

After difficult informal negotiations, the Fifth Committee approved a resolution by which the S.G. is authorized to enter into commitments for up to $38 million for security-related infrastructure projects. An amount of $18.3 million is appropriated under the regular budget for security-related temporary assistance requirements. Of the posts requested by the Secretary-General, 58 new field security posts for the Office of the U.N. Security Coordinator are approved, and $2.8 million is appropriated toward their cost. The S.G. is requested to submit a comprehensive report on the question of strengthening security and safety to the G.A. at its 59th session, in light of which the Assembly will consider, among other things, the question of transferring the cost of field security posts to the regular budget; they are currently financed from extra-budgetary resources.

In statements made in connection with the adoption of the resolution, the representatives of Ireland, Canada and Norway said that while they joined in the consensus, they regretted that more funding had not been approved. By contrast, the Indian representative said that while his delegation attached great importance to the question of security and safety, just "throwing money at it" was clearly not enough; the Egyptian representative agreed.

Staffing

In his program budget proposals for 2004-2005, the S.G. also proposed a staffing table of 9,179 posts, 117 more than the 9,062 posts approved for 2002-2003.[27] The Assembly approved a regular-budget staffing table for 2004 totaling 9,118 posts, comprising 3,910 posts in the professional and higher categories and 5,208 posts in the general service and other categories; one additional professional post will be added in 2005. These totals include 62 new posts (50 in the professional and higher categories) and 52 posts previously charged to temporary resources (38 in the professional and higher categories). The staffing table for 2004-2005 includes one Deputy Secretary-General, 27 Under-Secretaries-General and 21 Assistant Secretaries-General.[29]

The program budget proposals for 2004-2005 included 44 reclassifications as well. The upward reclassification of posts and the resulting "grade creep" has been a matter of continuing concern to member states. In its report on the proposed program budget for 2004-2005, ACABQ advocated an approach designed to maintain the existing relationship between grades and to minimize, if not end, "grade creep." To that end, ACABQ recommended that the S.G. be given the authority to reclassify posts in grades G-1 to G-6 in the general service category, and in grades P-1 to P-5 in the professional category, provided that the overall number of posts in each grade did not change. To implement such a system, the Secretariat staffing would be managed as a whole.[30] In the general debate in the Fifth Committee, views differed on whether the S.G. should have such authority.[31]

In Resolution 58/270 the G.A. requested the S.G. to begin, on an experimental basis, with the redeployment of posts as necessary to meet the evolving needs of the Organization.[32] A comprehensive report on the experiment is to be submitted to the G.A. at its 60th session.

At the Assembly's 57th session, no consensus had emerged on whether to accept the S.G.'s proposal that the technical secretariats of the Fifth and Sixth Committees (which had traditionally been provided by the Office of Program Planning, Budget and Accounts and the Office of Legal Affairs, respectively) be transferred to the Department of General Assembly and Conference Management. The impasse continued at the 58th session, and in Resolution 58/270, the Assembly decided to defer the matter to the 59th session, with a view to taking a decision in the context of the proposed program budget for 2006-2007.

Reform

In September 2002, S.G. Kofi Annan submitted his report *Strengthening of the United Nations: An Agenda for Further Change*, which contained several proposals relating to programming and budgeting. No consensus on those proposals could be reached at the Assembly's 57th session, and it was decided that they would be considered again at the 58th session.

Introducing his program budget proposals for 2004-2005, S.G. Annan pointed out that, in line with the *Agenda for Further Change*, the budget document was shorter and better aligned with approved priorities. Some $100 million had been shifted among subprograms, 810 posts had been redeployed and more than 900 outputs had been discontinued.[33] ACABQ welcomed the changes and improvements in the proposed program budget document, including the introduction of performance targets, while pointing out that much more needed to be done to successfully shift the current emphasis on inputs to results achieved and accountability.[34] In the Fifth Committee discussion, several speakers welcomed the fact that the document was shorter than before, but others pointed out that the proposed program budget must continue to contain all the information that member states need to make an informed decision.

The Committee also reviewed a report by the S.G. on improvements in the U.N.'s current process of planning and budgeting, in which S.G. Annan proposed that the medium-term plan be replaced by a strategic framework document that would comprise a plan outline; this would reflect the longer-term objectives of the United Nations. The strategic framework document would also include an expanded budget outline that would provide a strategic connection between programs and resource allocations.[35] Also before the Committee was a report on the intergovernmental review of the program budget and the medium-term plan, in which the S.G. recommended that the role of the Committee for Program and Coordination (CPC) be redefined: the Committee would no longer review the medium-term plan, the budget outline and the program budget, but instead would play a stronger role in the assessment of the results achieved at the end of the budget or plan period.[36]

In the ensuing discussion, the S.G.'s proposals were, on the whole, welcomed. At the same time, several delegations were still concerned that the role of member states in the programming and budgeting process not be diminished.[37] In Resolution 58/269, the Assembly took a step toward accepting the strategic framework approach, but decided that the budget outline would continue to be a separate document. It requested the S.G. to prepare, on a trial basis, for submission at the G.A.'s 59th session, a strategic framework to replace the current four-year medium-term plan, which would comprise in one document a plan outline, reflecting the longer-term objectives of the organization, and a two-year program plan. The Assembly also decided to review the format, content and duration of the strategic framework at its 62nd session, when a final decision would be taken.

In the same resolution, the Assembly decided that CPC would no longer consider the budget outline. It invited the Committee instead to submit proposals on how its role in monitoring and evaluation could be enhanced and its effectiveness improved. It also requested that the Committee provide comments on the new programming and budgeting process outlined in the resolution.

Peacekeeping Operations Budgets

The financial year for peacekeeping operations runs from July 1 to June 30. For the year 2003-2004, which ends on June 30, 2004, apportionments for peacekeeping operations total $2.82 billion. For 2002-2003, apportionments totaled $2.61 billion, and actual expenditure was $2.39 billion.[38]

The Secretary-General's budget estimates for the financial year 2004-2005 for the 11 continuing operations total $2.68 billion, $136.6 million less than for 2003-2004. The decrease is attributable to expected lower requirements for the missions in Sierra Leone (UNAMSIL), Kosovo (UNMIK) and Timor-Leste (UNMISET), totaling $563 million. The largest increase ($308.1 million) is for Liberia (UNMIL). However, the representative of Serbia and Montenegro told the Fifth Committee that the reduction in UNMIK's budget should be reconsidered in light of recent outbreaks of violence. (The UNMIL amount in Table B reflects projected requirements pending the finalization of the budget.) In its related report, ACABQ recommended reductions totaling $22.5 million.

Introducing the Secretary-General's report, Jean-Pierre Halbwachs, the U.N. Controller, put the Fifth Committee on notice that peacekeeping requirements in 2004-2005 were most likely to be greater than the total of some $2.7 billion that would be needed for the 11 continuing operations.[39] The additional requirements would relate to the newly established missions in Burundi, Côte d'Ivoire and Haiti, to the UNMIL mission in Liberia, the budget for which was being finalized, and to the UNMISET mission in Timor-Leste, which was likely to be extended. Further requirements might arise depending on decisions to be taken by the Security Council regarding oper-

Table B: Peacekeeping Operations Budget Estimates for 2004-2005 ($US millions).

U.N. Peacekeeping Force in Cyprus (UNFICYP)	47.4
U.N. Organization Mission in the Democratic Republic of Congo (MONUC)	718.3
U.N. Disengagement Observer Force (UNDOF)	40.9
U.N. Mission of Support in East Timor (UNMISET)	9.4
U.N. Mission in Ethiopia and Eritrea (UNMEE)	201.5
U.N. Observer Mission in Georgia (UNOMIG)	32.4
U.N. Interim Administration Mission in Kosovo (UNMIK)	272.2
U.N. Interim Force in Lebanon (UNIFIL)	94.7
U.N. Mission in Liberia (UNMIL)	872.6
U.N. Mission in Sierra Leone (UNAMSIL)	199.8
U.N. Mission for the Referendum in Western Sahara (MINURSO)	42.0
Subtotal for Missions Alone	**2,531.2**
U.N. Logistics Base at Brindisi*	28.8
Support account*	122.1
Grand Total	**2,682.1**

* These costs are apportioned pro rata to the missions.   Source: A/58/705.

ations in Sudan. *(See Chapter 4 for more details about these missions.)* Therefore, requirements for peacekeeping operations might exceed $4 billion, the highest in 10 years. The 2004-2005 budget estimates for the continuing operations provided for 10,652 posts for international and national staff in the peacekeeping missions, and 913 posts for the Brindisi base and the Support Account, for a total of 11,565 posts. According to Mr. Halbwachs, the number of military personnel would increase by 60 percent by the time all envisioned missions were fully deployed; their civilian staff would also increase. If this should occur, it may be necessary, at least temporarily, to increase the staffing of the U.N. Department for Peacekeeping Operations.[40]

In the ensuing debate, the representative of Ireland said that she expected that savings, over and above those recommended by ACABQ, would be possible. The representative of Japan voiced concern at the growing cost of peacekeeping operations. Member States' resources were not unlimited, he said. Increasing peacekeeping budgets consumed resources that might otherwise flow into development and poverty alleviation activities. He suggested that when deciding to establish a peacekeeping mission, the S.C. also formulate its exit strategy.[41]

In a series of resolutions approved on May 28, the Fifth Committee recommended to the Assembly that it appropriate $2,613.4 million for the year starting on July 1, 2004, for the 11 continuing peacekeeping operations.

Decisions were also made on the financing of the three new peacekeeping missions: the U.N. Operation in Côte d'Ivoire (UNOCI), the U.N. Stabilization

Mission in Haiti (MINUSTAH) and the U.N. Operation in Burundi (ONUB). UNOCI took over from the U.N. Mission in Côte d'Ivoire (MINUCI), which was financed from the regular budget. It was established by S.C. Resolution 1528 of February 27, 2004, initially for a 12-month period as from April 4. The S.G. estimated requirements through June 30, 2005 at $502.4 million. In its related report, ACABQ recommended an amount of $297 million for requirements through the end of 2004; it also recommended that the S.G. submit revised estimates in the fall. The Fifth Committee accepted the ACABQ recommendation, and recommended that the G.A. appropriate $307.5 million (including $10.4 million for the operation's pro rata share of the costs of the Brindisi base and the support account through June 30, 2005).

For UNSMIH, the Fifth Committee authorized the S.G. to enter into commitments and apportioned $221.7 million for the period May 1 - October 31, 2004. ONUB was established by S.C. Resolution 1545 of May 21, 2004. The S.G. submitted an interim budget in the amount of $200.7 million for the period through December 31, 2004, and ACABQ recommended that the amount be reduced to $156 million for the period through October 31, 2004. The Fifth Committee accepted the ACABQ recommendation.[42]

As for the S.G.'s proposal that the appointments of about 1,600 professional and 5,000 national (i.e., local) staff be converted from short-term to regular-term, ACABQ was critical on the grounds that it had never been intended to create long-term career opportunities for the staff in question, and that the financial impact of the proposal had not undergone reliable analysis. ACABQ suggested that the matter be referred to the G.A. for decision, pending which there should be no further conversions.[43]

The Fifth Committee endorsed the ACABQ recommendations. It requested the S.G. to submit a comprehensive report at the 59th session on the U.N.'s strategy for meeting current and future human resource requirements for peacekeeping missions. The Committee also decided to suspend until December 31, 2004, the application of the four-year maximum limit for appointments of limited duration under the 300 series of the staff rules in peacekeeping operations (which limit had been set pursuant to G.A. resolution 52/216). In the meantime, no further conversions should take place.[44]

International War Crimes Tribunals Budgets

In 2003, member states were assessed $119.15 million for the International Criminal Tribunal for Former Yugoslavia and $98.1 million for the International Criminal Tribunal for Rwanda.[45] In light of its consideration of the second performance reports on the budgets of the two tribunals for the biennium 2002-2003, the General Assembly, through Resolution 58/252, increased the Rwanda Tribunal budget to $208.5 million gross ($187.3 million net), and in Resolution 58/254, increased the Former Yugoslavia Tribunal budget to $288.3 million gross (254.6 million net).

Turning to the tribunals' budgets for 2004-2005, the Assembly, in Resolution 58/253, approved a budget of $235.3 million gross for the Rwanda

Tribunal. In Resolution 58/255, it appropriated $298.2 million gross for the Former Yugoslavia Tribunal for 2004-2005. In both cases, the approved budgets include requirements for the tribunals' Investigation Divisions for 2004, but not for 2005, as that year's budget will be considered in the Assembly's 59th session. In the same resolutions, the Assembly decided that total assessments for 2004 would amount to $174.7 million for the Former Yugoslavia Tribunal and to $122.2 for the Rwanda Tribunal.

Assessments, Arrears and the Financial Situation of the United Nations

Anthony Mango

The financial situation of the United Nations at the end of 2003 was marginally better than it was a year earlier. Total unpaid assessments in respect to the regular budget, peacekeeping operations, the two international tribunals and the capital master plan account declined from $1.68 billion on December 31, 2002, to $1.6 billion on December 31, 2003. On the latter date, member states owed the organization $441.7 million for the regular budget, $87.9 million for the international tribunals, $1.07 billion for peacekeeping operations and $7 million to the capital master plan account.

Twenty-seven countries, including permanent Security Council member the United Kingdom, had either paid their assessments in their entirety or owed less than $100. On the other hand, the U.S. owed $762.1 million as of December 31, 2003—just under 50 percent of the total. Other major debtors included Japan at $219 million, Ukraine at $154 million, Brazil at $92.1 million and Argentina at $92.1 million.[46]

On May 4, 2004, Management Under-Secretary-General Catherine Bertini informed the Fifth Committee that some $661 million of regular-budget contributions had been received by the end of April. Because of the need for some cross-borrowing between accounts later in the year, she expected that there would be a year-end cash deficit of some $7 million for the regular budget and related reserve accounts. As for peacekeeping cash, she expected to end the year with a positive balance of about $931 million. The financial prospects for the two war crimes tribunals were very bleak, however. She expected that, at year-end, they would have a cash deficit of $100 million; in fact, a freeze on recruitment had been imposed for the Rwanda Tribunal.[47]

In the ensuing debate, speakers voiced alarm at the financial situation of the two international war crimes tribunals. Japan's representative said his country was dissatisfied with their management and that it was essential to rationalize their budgets. The representative of South Korea, while emphasizing the importance of bringing perpetrators to justice, wondered to what extent and for how long the U.N. could commit financial resources equivalent to 7 percent of Rwanda's gross national product to run the tribunal at the expense of other, more pressing priorities.

As for arrears, or unpaid dues, to peacekeeping budgets, India's representative expressed concern at the prospect that the amounts owed by the U.N. to countries contributing troops and equipment would go up substantially. More than $100 million was already owed in respect to six closed missions that were in net cash deficit, and he feared that troop and equipment contributors to the U.N. missions in Kosovo and Western Sahara would meet the same fate. The representative of South Korea stressed the importance of consultations with major contributors to the budget before the S.C. made decisions on peacekeeping operations or missions with significant financial implications.

Responding to a suggestion by the representative of Algeria that the Secretariat should send reminder letters to member states in arrears, Ms. Bertini said that the Secretariat could send out quarterly reminders.[48]

On a positive note, on December 31, 2003, the U.N. reported that it owed troop- and equipment-contributing states $442.7 million, considerably less than the $705.1 million owed on January 1, 2003.[49]

Regular Budget Assessments

Article 17 of the U.N. Charter states that "the expenses of the Organization shall be borne by the Members as apportioned by the General Assembly." From the outset, the Assembly decided that this apportionment should be based "broadly" on each member state's capacity to pay. While it has been agreed that a country's capacity to pay is linked to the size of its economy, measured by the country's gross national income (GNI-formerly referred to as gross national product), it has also been recognized that other factors (i.e. a country's population, natural disasters or civil strife) affected capacity to pay over a short- or medium-term. The relative importance of these factors has been the subject of endless debates in the G.A.'s Committee on Contributions and its Fifth Committee. To avoid excessive fluctuations, it has also been agreed that the GNI figures would be averaged over a multi-year base period. The shape of the scale is also affected by the political decision that no country should be assessed at a rate higher than an agreed "ceiling" (justified by the argument that the organization should not be excessively beholden to any one member for its financial health) and an agreed "floor" that may be likened to a basic "membership fee." Both the ceiling and the floor rates have been repeatedly lowered over the years.

The scale of assessments for 2004-2006 that the Committee on Contributions submitted to the G.A. for approval in 2003 was constructed on the elements and criteria approved by the Assembly in 2000 in accordance with Resolution 55/5B. The differences between the two scales reflected the fact that the scale for 2004-2006 was based on more recent GNI data (for the years 1996-2001). In Resolution 55/5C, the Assembly had decided to "review the position at the end of 2003 and, depending on the status of contributions and arrears, to determine all appropriate measures to remedy the situation, including adjustments of the ceiling." This provision was included

Table C: Top 10 Member States' Assessments in 2004-2006.

United States	22%	Italy	4.89%
Japan	19.47%	Canada	2.81%
Germany	8.66%	Spain	2.52%
United Kingdom	6.13%	China	2.05%
France	6.03%	Mexico	1.88%

Source: A/Res/58/1B.

to meet the concerns of some countries that the U.S. might renege on the bargain, whereby the ceiling rate was lowered from 25 to 22 percent in exchange for a promise by the U.S. to substantially reduce its unpaid arrears of contributions. No member state requested such a review in 2003.

In the discussion in the Fifth Committee, Japan's representative reiterated his country's view that its assessment rate of nearly 20 percent was unfair. He referred to the fact that the S.C. reform process was at a standstill, and that the U.N. Charter still contained the so-called "enemy clauses." He said that the scale needed to be more balanced, in conformity with each member state's actual economic performance and its status and responsibilities in the United Nations, but he did not request that Japan's rate of assessment be reduced. The representatives of several developing countries, including China, drew attention to the very steep increases in their assessment rates. Others stated that the scale still had some technical flaws and did not fully reflect countries' capacity to pay. Despite these reservations, the scale was approved by consensus.[50]

China (in 9th place) and Mexico (in 10th place) are newcomers to the "Top 10," replacing Brazil and South Korea, respectively, and the U.K. (in 4th place) switched rankings with France. Taken together, the 10 member states in Table C contribute more than three-quarters of the U.N.'s regular budget. At the other end of the scale, the number of countries assessed at the "floor" rate of 0.001 percent increased to 48, two more than under the 2003 scale.

In Resolution 58/1A, the 58th General Assembly permitted 10 other countries to retain their votes until June 30, 2004, despite the fact that the amount of their arrears exceeded the amounts of the contributions due from them for the preceding two full years. The reason given was that their failure to pay reflected conditions beyond their control. The 10 countries in question are: Burundi, Central African Republic, the Comoros, Georgia, Guinea-Bissau, Moldova, Niger, Sao Tome and Principe, Somalia and Tajikistan. Except for Georgia, all these countries are assessed at the "floor" rate of 0.001 percent. Georgia, Moldova, Sao Tome and Principe, and Tajikistan agreed to pay off their arrears over a period of years, while also paying their annual assessments, but implementation of these voluntary multi-year payment plans has been spotty.

As of December 31, 2003, outstanding contributions to the regular budget totaled $441.7 million, as compared to $305 million a year earlier.

Table D: Top Amounts Owed to the United Nations as of December 31, 2003.

United States	$268 million*	Japan	$ 19.1 million
Brazil	$ 53.9 million	Iraq	$ 12.8 million
Argentina	$ 41 million	Venezuela	$ 8 million

The Bush Administration's FY2005 budget request includes nearly $362.2 million for its assessed contribution to the U.N. regular budget for the calendar year 2004.

According to U.N. figures, the U.S. owed $268 million in unpaid regular-budget assessments, as against $190 million at the end of 2002. Six countries were responsible for more than 90 percent of the total amount owed for the regular budget, as shown in Table D.

Nine other countries owed more than $1 million each, and 45 countries owed between $1,000 and $1 million each. Only two-thirds of the membership (131 out of 191 member states) had paid their regular-budget assessments for 2003 and for previous years in full by December 31; a year earlier, the corresponding number was even smaller—117.[51]

Peacekeeping Operations Assessments

The scale of assessments for peacekeeping operations is derived from the scale for the regular budget. It differs from the latter in that poorer countries are assessed at lower rates than they are for the regular budget. The difference is then added to the assessments of the P-5 countries in recognition of their special responsibilities for the maintenance of international peace and security. In Resolution 55/235 of December 23, 2000, the Assembly decided that, for the purpose of peacekeeping operation assessments, each member state would be assigned to 1 of 10 levels (A through J) with various accompanying rates.

Countries can volunteer to be placed at a higher level, and several have done so; the higher assessment is phased-in over a period of years. For the purposes of the 2004-2006 scale of assessments for peacekeeping operations, the average per capita GNI is $5,094 (calculated over the base period 1996-2001).

In the peacekeeping scale for 2004-2006, 29 countries are assigned to level B (regular budget rate), 27 countries to levels C-H (7.5 to 70 percent discounted rate), 81 countries to level I (80 percent discounted rate) and 49 countries to level J (90 percent discounted rate). As a result of the discounts granted to member states in levels C through J, the P-5 were assessed, as of January 1, 2004, at a total rate of 45.26 percent, compared to 37.31 percent under the regular-budget scale.[52] Table E demonstrates these figures.

Cross-Borrowing

Addressing the Fifth Committee on October 21, 2003, Ms. Bertini reported that because of the slow payment of regular-budget assessments, it had become necessary for the S.G. to borrow funds from peacekeeping accounts to meet regular-budget requirements. She said she expected that as much as

Table E: Assessment Levels to the Permanent
Five Members, as of January 2004.

MEMBER STATE	REGULAR BUDGET SCALE	PEACEKEEPING OPERATIONS SCALE
China	2.05%	2.49%
France	6.03%	7.32%
Russian Federation	1.10%	1.33%
United Kingdom	6.13%	7.43%
United States	22.00%	26.69%
Grand Total	37.31%	45.26%

$125 million would have to be borrowed at the end of November. She warned that S.G. Annan's ability to cross-borrow would be severely limited in 2004.[53]

As of December 31, 2003, unpaid assessments for peacekeeping operations totaled $1.07 billion, as compared to $1.34 billion at the end of 2002. The U.S. owed $482.2 million (45 percent of the total), compared to $536 million in December 2002. Thirty-one countries, including the Russian Federation and United Kingdom, had no unpaid contributions to peacekeeping operations or owed only minimal amounts of under $100.[54]

In March 2004, S.G. Annan informed the Fifth Committee that, as of February 29, the net cash available for credit to member states amounted to some $57.4 million—nearly $27 million less than the $84 million he was required to pay. He explained that he had to borrow some $152 million to keep going the U.N. missions in Kosovo and Western Sahara and the tribunals for former Yugoslavia and Rwanda because of the nonpayment by member states of their assessments for these two missions and the tribunals. The S.G. also recalled that, in February 2004, the Council had established the U.N. Operation in Côte d'Ivoire and declared its readiness to establish a follow-up stabilization force in Haiti. Furthermore, discussions were underway regarding the extension of the U.N. Mission of Support in East Timor and the establishment of U.N. operations in Burundi and potentially Sudan. The only cash available to him was the $57.4 million remaining in the accounts of closed peacekeeping missions and $74 million in the Peacekeeping Reserve Fund. He therefore sought the Assembly's permission to postpone the payment of the amount of $84 million due in March 2004.[55]

In its related report, ACABQ stated that it had been informed by the S.G. that it was expecting that three missions—in Côte d'Ivoire, Haiti and Sudan—would start by June 2004, and that they would require pre-mandate commitment authority of $50 million each.[56]

The representative of Ireland pointed out that the member states that paid their assessed contributions on time and in full were effectively subsidizing those that did not, and that allowing the S.G. to retain member states' money from closed missions was simply another form of subsidy. She urged the U.S. to actively review and adjust its schedule of payments of its assessed contributions to the United Nations. (The Bush Administration's FY2005 budget request, released in February 2004, includes $650 million for assessed contributions for peacekeeping operations in 2004, $45 million less than the FY2004 level. The reduction is attributed to the projected closing of UNTAET, the U.N. Transitional Administration in East Timor and significant reductions in requirements for UNAMSIL, MONUC and UNMEE.)[57] She also requested a clear statement from the S.G. as to the causes of the cash-flow problem; this request was seconded by the representative of Australia, speaking also on behalf of Canada and New Zealand.

As there was no other way of dealing with the problem, there was broad support for the S.G.'s proposal that payment to member states of the amount of $84 million be deferred.[58] By Resolution 58/288 of April 8, 2004, the G.A. decided to postpone until June 30 the return to member states of the amount of some $84 million. The Assembly also decided that as of July 1, individual member states would have the choice of requesting either that the amounts due to them be paid or that these amounts be credited against their outstanding assessed contributions; they were encouraged to opt for the latter alternative.[59]

The Fifth Committee decided that further consideration of the funds of closed peacekeeping missions as of June 30, 2003 and the Peacekeeping Reserve Fund be deferred to the 59th session in the fall of 2004.[60]

International Tribunals Assessments

Assessments for the international war crime tribunals for the former Yugoslavia and Rwanda are based half on the regular-budget scale and half on the peacekeeping-operations scale. As of December 31, 2003, 107 member states owed a total amount of $87.9 million—more than twice the $43 million outstanding at the end of 2002. Japan owed $40.9 million, or 46.5 percent of the total. Other major debtors included the U.S. at $12 million, the Russian Federation at nearly $11 million and Brazil at $9.7 million. Eighty-four member states had paid their assessments in full.[61] The Bush Administration's FY2005 budget request includes almost $31 million for the U.S.-assessed share of the expenses for the two tribunals.

Unlike the international war crime tribunals for the former Yugoslavia and Rwanda, the Special Court for Sierra Leone, which began operations in Freetown in July 2002, has been financed from voluntary contributions—despite the S.G.'s initial proposal that funding be derived from assessments. In a report to the Assembly, S.G. Annan stated that while voluntary contributions would be sufficient to fund the first two years of the Court's operations, through June 30, 2004, a subvention from the regular budget would be needed thereafter.[62] In April 2004, the Assembly authorized the Secretary-General, as an exceptional measure, to enter into commitments of up to $16.7 million to supplement the Court's financial resources for the period of July 1 to December 31, 2004, on the understanding that any regular budget funds appropriated for the Court would be refunded upon its liquidation. The Assembly noted that the Court is expected to complete its work by the end of 2005 and it appealed to member states to not only contribute voluntary funds to the Court but also to honor existing pledges.

Capital Master Plan Assessments

Of the $25.5 million assessed on member states for the capital master plan account, $7 million was unpaid as of December 31, 2003; Japan owed $4.9 million (or 70 percent) of the outstanding amount.[63]

Looking Forward

The 59th General Assembly will focus less on budgeting and more on personnel and management. It will consider, among other things, the operation and management of U.N. libraries, the availability of local capacity to replace internationally-recruited general service staff, the efficiency and cost-effectiveness of all the activities of the Department of Public Information, equitable geographical distribution of posts in the U.N. Secretariat, outsourcing, and the common and joint services of the U.N. system organizations in Geneva and Vienna. Several budgeting and financial questions will also be considered, among them the first program budget performance report for the current biennium, the capital master plan, and security and safety arrangements.[64]

In addition to reporting on hazard pay for locally recruited staff, the International Civil Service Commission will report on its review of the mobility and hardship scheme, on the linkage between the mobility and hardship allowance, and on the base/floor salary scale for the professional and higher categories.

With regard to the Joint Inspection Unit, the G.A. may agree to strengthen the position of its Chairman by extending its term of office (replacing the current system of rotation). However, it is unlikely that the size of the unit will be reduced or that stringent qualification requirements will be introduced—too many member states appear to be more interested in securing inspector posts for their nationals than in the quality of the reports issued by the unit.

Since the Assembly has already approved an assessment scale for 2004-2006, it will not have any major items to discuss in this area. The Assembly did, however, ask the Committee on Contributions last year to continue its consideration of 1) possible systematic criteria for deciding when market-exchange rates should be replaced by price-adjusted rates of exchange or other conversion rates; 2) measures to encourage the payment of arrears; and 3) the criteria for *ad hoc* adjustments of assessment rates. Last but not least, the Assembly will face the question of the outstanding assessed contributions of the former Yugoslavia amounting to $16.17 million, consideration of which has been deferred for the second year running.

Overall, the decisions made by the Assembly at its 58th session constitute substantial progress in the programming and budgeting reform process outlined in the Secretary-General's *Agenda for Further Change*. But the concern of the developing countries that reform might be used as a pretext for downgrading economic and social development has not been dissipated. Much will depend on member state reception at the 59th session to the first strategic framework document and particularly its biennial program plan. On the whole, it looks as though the hard decisions are being postponed to the 62nd session of the Assembly in 2007.

Commentary:
Reforming the Economic and Social Council
Lawrence Woocher

The United Nations' Economic and Social Council, known as ECOSOC, was envisaged in the U.N. Charter as the principal body for promoting economic and social development. But during its six-decade history, it has been overshadowed by other economic and development bodies—the World Bank, the International Monetary Fund and the U.N. Development Programme, to name a few—and even more so by the U.N. Security Council. As security issues have taken on renewed urgency since September 11, 2001, the gap in public attention and perceived relevance between the Security Council and ECOSOC has grown to new lengths.

While development bodies that disburse significant funds and that have large on-the-ground operations can be secure in their continued relevance, ECOSOC does not seem as stable. Its main activities are overseeing, coordinating, consulting and passing resolutions. It is difficult to discern the unique contributions these activities make toward addressing the most pressing global economic and social issues. Unless its structure, goals and operations are rethought and altered according to new challenges, ECOSOC risks its own slow ebb into irrelevance.

There are significant institutional and political obstacles to reforming ECOSOC. For example, its large but far-from-universal membership hampers its efficiency without imbuing it with the legitimacy of an inclusive body like the General Assembly. Its oversight responsibility for more than two-dozen specialized agencies and commissions overfills ECOSOC's agenda, overstretching its analytic capacity. Yet, the U.N. body lacks effective levers to influence these subsidiary bodies. And ECOSOC's lack of major financial resources to promote development means it does not have the power of the World Bank or other donors to affect policy in developing nations.

Recognizing these and other factors impeding ECOSOC's effectiveness, governments, civil-society groups and analysts have formulated dozens of reform proposals over the years. But none has gained sufficient attention or support.

There is, however, some basis for cautious optimism today. The Millennium Development Goals (MDGs) offer an orienting mechanism for reconceptualizing ECOSOC's focus and operations. As the agreed framework for measuring progress in the world's efforts to reduce poverty and advance human development, the MDGs reflect the same aims that ECOSOC was mandated to promote under the U.N. Charter. This congruence suggests ECOSOC should measure its success in large part by the extent that it promotes the realization of the MDGs.

Governments should devise creative strategies and mobilize all relevant capabilities within and outside the U.N. system, including a critical review of ECOSOC's current capacity and untapped potential. The global commitment to the MDGs presents an opportunity to invigorate ECOSOC that should not be missed.

Endnotes

Reform

1. *The National Security Strategy of the United States of America*, The White House, September 2002.
2. Secretary-General's Address to the General Assembly, New York, September 23, 2003.
3. U.N. Charter, Article 108.
4. U.N. Charter, Introductory Note.
5. A/RES48/26 (1993).
6. In March 1997, Razali Ismail, chairman of the working group and in a bold attempt to move discussions in the group forward, presented a paper synthesizing the majority view regarding expansion of the Council. His proposal envisioned increasing Council membership from 15 to 24 by adding five permanent members and four non-permanent members.
7. *The Responsibility to Protect,* International Commission on Intervention and State Sovereignty, International Development Research Centre, December 2001.
8. A/58/323 (Report of the Secretary-General on the Implementation of the U.N. *Millennium Declaration,* 2003).
9. Statement by H.E. Ambassador Marcello Spatafora, permanent representative of Italy, to the General Assembly, October 27, 2003. / *Permanent Mission of Italy to the United Nations website.*
10. *The International Aid System 2005–2010: Forces For and Against Change*, Overseas Development Institute Working Paper, March 2004. / Special High-Level Meeting of ECOSOC With the Bretton Woods Institutions, April 22, 2002.
11. SG/A/857 (2003).
12. Letter from the Secretary-General to the President, November 2003.
13. Ibid, 2.
14. Ibid, 11.
15. S/RES/1308 (2000).
16. Ibid, 2.
17. Ibid, 11.
18. *A Fork in the Road? Conversations on the Work of the High-Level Panel On Threats, Challenges and Change*, International Peace Academy, 2004.

Personnel, Budgets and Arrears

1. U.N. Press Release GA/AB/3587 (March 11, 2003).
2. GA/AB/3558. / GA/AB/3589.
3. A/Res/58/87.
4. U.N. Press Releases GA/AB/3605 (March 15, 2004), 3608 (March 19, 2004), 3611 (March 25, 2004).
5. Ibid.
6. A/58/750.
7. A/58/666.
8. A/Res/58/268 and 270.
9. U.N. Press Release GA/AB/3604 (March 10, 2004). / A/Res/55/230.
10. Ibid. / GA/AB/3598.
11. A/58/599 and 556.
12. A/58/729.
13. U.N. Press Release GA/AB/3606 (March 16, 2004).
14. Ibid.
15. A/Res/58/267. / A/58/572/Add.1.

16. A/58/7.
17. U.N. Press Releases GA/AB/3582-3586 (March 28-March 31, 2003).
18. Ibid.
19. Ibid, 16.
20. A/Res/58/270. / A/58/573.
21. Ibid, 16.
22. U.N. Press Release GA/AB/3582 (October 28, 2003).
23. A/58/573. / GA/AB3603.
24. A/58/756. / A/58/558/Add.1.
25. A/58/758.
26. A/58/758.
27. GA/AB/3615.
28. A/58/6.
29. A/58/73.
30. Ibid, 16.
31. U.N. Press Releases GA/AB/3584 and 3585 (March 29 and March 30, 2003).
32. A/Res/58/270.
33. Ibid, 22.
34. Ibid, 19.
35. A/58/395 and Corr.1.
36. A/57/786.
37. U.N. Press Release GA/AB/3591 (November 10, 2003).
38. A/58/705.
39. The U.N. Military Observer Group in India and Pakistan (UNMOGIP), the oldest U.N. peacekeeping operation in Asia, also continues to monitor the disputed state of Jammu and Kashmir. In addition, the U.N. Truce Supervision Organization (UNTSO) continues to monitor and assist peacekeeping missions in the Middle East.
40. U.N. Press Release GA/AB/3613.
41. Ibid. / U.N. Press Releases GA/AB/3614.
42. A/AB/3621 and 3624.
43. Ibid.
44. A/AB/3624 (as of June 3, 2004).
45. ST/ADM/SER.B/619.
46. Ibid.
47. GA/AB/3614.
48. GA/AB/3615.
49. A/58/705.
50. U.N. Press Releases GA/AB/58/3576, 3577 and 3602 (October 15 and October 16, 2003 and December 18, 2003).
51. Ibid, 39.
52. A/58/157/Add.1.
53. U.N. Press Release GA/AB/3578 (October 21, 2003).
54. Ibid, 29.
55. A/58/723.
56. A/58/732.
57. U.N. Press Release GA/AB/3607 (March 17, 2004).
58. A/58/582/Add.1.
59. A/AB/3624 (June 3, 2004).
60. UNA-USA Press Release (February 4, 2004).
61. Ibid, 39.
62. A/58/733.
63. Ibid, 39.
64. A/Res/58/270.

Essays

The Challenges to Fighting HIV/AIDS: Local Solutions for a Global Partnership

Yanzhong Huang

In combating HIV/AIDS, strongly affected countries are obliged to reinvigorate health-related state apparatuses, revamp public health financing systems and effectively engage the civil society to promote better health outcomes. But beefing up state capacity also means building more effective partnerships and institutions internationally. Given that the HIV/AIDS crisis reduces state capacity just when ever-increasing capacity is needed to tackle the challenges, purely endogenous solutions are unlikely to be successful. As a result, system capabilities have to be imported (i.e., foreign aid). Foreign aid not only helps finance medicine and care for those with the disease, but it also helps provide personnel training, among other things. Equally important, by subjecting recipient governments' agendas to the donor's organizational goals, involvement of global actors helps galvanize the high-level leadership that is needed in addressing the crisis.

Until the creation of the Joint United Nations Programme on HIV/AIDS (UNAIDS) in 1996, the World Health Organization (WHO) had the lead responsibility on AIDS at the United Nations. By the mid-1990s, it was becoming clear that the HIV/AIDS epidemic was not just a public health crisis, and that its advance would not be halted by one-dimensional interventions. The disease's unique patterns of transmission and impact on development made—and continue to make—it necessary to consider additional factors such as poverty, deprivation, disempowerment, gender inequality and access to health services. These multifaceted challenges demanded a multifaceted approach, including a global response that involved U.N. organizations beyond WHO.

With the establishment of UNAIDS, the global campaign against the disease received additional impetus. As the leading advocate for a comprehensive response to the epidemic, UNAIDS has helped strengthen a shared understanding of respective U.N. agencies' comparative advantages while developing an appropriate division of responsibilities on HIV/AIDS issues. Among its co-sponsors, WHO provides technical support and builds health-sector capacity in affected countries; the U.N. Children's Fund (UNICEF) and U.N. Population Fund (UNFPA) focus on the disproportionate impact of HIV/AIDS on young people and mothers; while the U.N. Development Programme (UNDP) and World Bank emphasize action-oriented advocacy and the integration of HIV/AIDS into the development framework.

In addition to these U.N. bodies, government agencies, not-for-profit groups and the private sector are also actively involved in initiating and implementing a series of bilateral and multilateral assistance programs to fight HIV/AIDS. These programs are funded by national governments, the World Bank, foundations, corporations, bilateral donors and the recently created Global Fund to Fight AIDS, Tuberculosis and Malaria (the Global Fund). The engagement of such global actors has certainly transformed the opportunities for developing and implementing effective responses to the pandemic. Their effectiveness, however, can be weakened by potential financing and coordination problems.

Because of financial constraints, many programs can last only for a short while. Programs underwritten by the Global Fund, for example, have a five-year mandate. Yet, according to UNAIDS, an effective global campaign against the epidemic requires not only $7 billion to $10 billion annually in low- and middle-income countries, but it also requires that such a campaign be maintained for at least a decade.

To make matters worse, financing problems are starting to cripple existing initiatives, including WHO's 3 by 5 initiative (*see Chapter 1 for details*). This leads to a key question: how will critical services be maintained after donor funds are used up?

Creating additional funding organizations may help mobilize more resources to fight the disease. However, unless programs and organizations can leverage substantial new commitments and contributions, these new funds would potentially compete with existing funds and programs for the limited pool of resources, generating a suboptimal outcome.

Indeed, donations to the Global Fund are now about $1.6 billion a year, barely 20 percent of the amount that Secretary-General Kofi Annan said was needed when the fund was created. Financing problems can also be found in the implementation stage of new HIV/AIDS programs, when resources generated by new funds are used to replace or reduce other sources of financing. Since many bilateral and multilateral assistance programs do not require matching funds from host governments, the latter can become so dependent on external funding that their incentives to attract additional investments to support program implementation can be reduced. China's recent decision to spend $24 million yearly on a special fund for HIV/AIDS prevention, care and treatment was hailed as a breakthrough, yet almost all the money came from a Global Fund donation, and the government was estimated to have spent only $2 million a year to address the epidemic.

Moreover, proliferation of individual initiatives can lead to duplication of research, training and treatment efforts. In Zimbabwe, Doctors Without Borders plans to treat 1,000 patients with three antiretroviral drugs combined by two approved Indian generic makers, costing $244 to $292 per patient per year. Yet the U.S. Centers for Disease Control and Prevention (CDC) plans to treat the same number of patients by buying the same drugs from three separate U.S. pharmaceutical companies, allegedly costing $562 a year. To ensure that resources are better utilized, there should not only be more information sharing among donor agencies, but interested parties should also plan jointly to build consensus in fighting HIV/AIDS.

Some donors, notably the Bill & Melinda Gates Foundation, have focused on extremely high-risk interventions (e.g., sex workers, truckers along major national highway routes and intravenous drug users). This approach has strong epidemiological justification, yet the chain of risk extends to the truckers' home communities and to the clients of sex workers, etc. Reaching these audiences requires other operators–national and international–to provide the kind of people-intensive interventions that raise awareness of the general population, provide direct care and empower women in the fight against HIV/AIDS. Moreover, such large-scale projects, while ideal on the surface, may not be able to keep up with the need. Scaling up may not be possible or even desirable in a large and diverse country like India or China, for instance.

These problems can be further complicated as the involvement of multiple actors with different priorities could politicize and/or limit the effectiveness of anti-AIDS programs. For example, ideological differences among constituencies within a donor country, if left unchecked, may place divergent demands on host governments and their international partners. While liberal groups and the broader medical establishment may push for prevention strategies such as comprehensive sex education and condom distribution, their conservative counterparts may be much more enthusiastic than others about policies such as the promotion of abstinence.

Unlike this donor-driven approach, an alternative strategy focuses on country-based coordinating mechanisms to link government officials with nongovernmental organizations (NGOs), bilateral donors and international organizations in policy-making and program implementation. Still, a single-minded emphasis on country-led processes can be problematic, for many affected countries lack the health system capacity to deliver services, generate accurate national surveillance data or ensure effective policy coordination. While donor governments, NGOs and private foundations can play an instrumental role in training health personnel and providing the necessary equipment, state capacity cannot be strengthened across the board overnight.

Given the problems and concerns inherent in the donor-driven approach and the country-led process, a more pragmatic approach would minimize reliance on existing national systems to address the urgency of the crisis on the one hand, and seek international partnerships in building national capacities to make the current programs sustainable on the other hand. In Haiti, for example, a Boston-based not-for-profit group called Partners in Health created a successful program in which hundreds of the country's vast pool of unemployed and underemployed workers have been trained to dispense medicines and spread the word about condoms preventing HIV infection. The program received a grant from the Global Fund to build clinics, laboratories and pharmacies and install generators and satellite dishes in a region characterized by a dearth of electricity and phones.

The community-based Haitian model also pinpoints the need to build global partnerships at the local level. Mounting evidence suggests that intervention programs work better when they seek the participation of potential users and when they tap into the community's reservoir of social capital rather than work against it. By empowering communities to design and carry out their own programs, based on locally determined needs, state capacity can not only be enhanced, but the highest coverage can also be achieved. This is especially true in the case of societies that derive their vitality and resilience from the solidarity of small communities. Kinship or clan groups, or traditional self-help community arrangements, for example, can be adapted and mobilized to meet prevention, treatment and service goals. What is needed is the transcendence of state ownership and "standard" programmatic approach to local ownership of the planning and implementation process. Of course, as the Haitian case suggests, successful and sustainable local solutions also require commitment of financial, technological and institutional support from external actors. These can only materialize with partnerships between public and private actors, between local and national governments and between national and international actors.

Arab Human Development: Another Name for Survival

Samir Sanbar

After the fall of the Soviet Union, a United Nations team exploring a unified presence in the Commonwealth of Independent States heard several buzzwords from leaders as they discussed future human development of the new states. Words and phrases such as "culture of openness," "market forces," "civil society" and, of course, "freedom" and "democratic values" were presented and sprinkled around with eloquent assertiveness. Then serving as Assistant-Secretary-General for the U.N. Department of Public Information, I raised the need for working together to strengthen a varied free press with one of these leaders. He quickly responded, "Of course we shall cooperate, and the press will do whatever we tell them."

Clearly, to an internationalist, development was—and is—another word for peace; to a politician, it meant—and in some cases still means—another vehicle for survival. This general impression among developing states and their leaders that human development efforts are mainly verbal—that is, politically correct rather than targeted to a specific focus or a practical outcome—applies directly to the changing nature of today's Arab world.

What many do not realize is that human development requires an international response—a joint effort, so to speak—as well as a cautious step. Practical proposals by credible sources responding to ascertained needs could inch their way to success in the Arab region despite—or sometimes with the help of—Arab governments. However, in doing so, several points of weariness and skepticism will have to be considered. The strategically located and naturally rich Arab region has become suspicious of strangers bearing gifts of change. And the past, no doubt, provides justification for such thinking: Napoleon invaded Egypt to civilize it; General Charles Gordon occupied Sudan in the name of enlightenment; Churchill invoked freedom and better life; and most recently, American-led forces have seized Iraq in the name of freeing people—and the world—from Saddam Hussein's wrath. This history, along with the swiftly changing world in which grassroots forces are gradually gaining ground, has led some of today's Arab governments to apply a pre-emptive sort of reform when it comes to development. As Yemen President Ali Abdullah Saleh advised his counterparts: "If we don't shave, they will do it for us."

Clearly, rhetoric from outside the region often plays into the hands of the forces most adamant against any reform. As another visiting official to New York recently confided, "Democracy is a foreign conspiracy"—and he had press statements to prove it. It is important, therefore, as states move forward that the homegrown proposals to assist in human development are more likely to be accepted and implemented.

Credibility is equally crucial. So many experts on the Arab region have mushroomed recently, for obvious reasons. Their self-assured pronouncements, or attempts to network with anyone regardless of valid worth, only add to the confusion. An overlooked credible source is an intellectual one: the often disdained academics. Like thousands of others, I remember with fond respect my professors at the American University of Beirut. Similar experiences are shared by Arab students within the United States, United Kingdom, France and elsewhere. A wide group of former and current academics could contribute to development needs not only with a perceptive framework, but also with a real human dimension.

When it comes to most non-state actors, oil-rich Gulf states have been overlooked in serious developmental planning. Except as a source of funding, there seems to be very little concerted international consideration for 18 million people, about 70 percent of whom are under 30 years old; there are absolutely no statistics on women. Some argue that official U.N. Development Programme (UNDP) presence there is more profitable to the employed experts than to the host countries.

Strengthening interested associations is therefore another potential area of value. Several U.N. Information Centers maintain regular contact with enthusiastic supporters in various fields of development. But there needs to be a stronger grassroots umbrella organization for development issues—one that can work directly with the UNDP. It is time for an initiative to effectively coordinate and mobilize such nongovernment interest.

Fortunately, there is a previously unnoticed publication on Arab Human Development headed up by UNDP's Rima Khalaf Hunaidi, which has caught unprecedented public attention and is beginning to motivate such a mobilization. Part of the report's unusual impact is based on the fact that it was drafted in the Arab region by credible, enlightened thinkers in touch with its realities. The report was also successful thanks to a welcome approach by UNDP Administrator Mark Malloch Brown to place communications in the mainstream of the agency's operations. The report has already moved governments to take some action and offer civil societies in the region a mission. It also has pushed for urgent work in three main areas: freedom, education and better prospects for women. The proof of movement in at least one area was in the actual production of the report itself—it took one woman, Ms. Hunaidi, to do what several men could not in producing this essential Arab Human Development report.

Looking ahead, this annual report, accompanied by increased interaction between grassroots, civil society, U.N. agencies such as UNDP and governments may prove to be the ultimate jump start to effective Arab human development. Such progress would lead not only to survival in the region, but also potentially peace.

The U.S. Election Campaign: Will a Divided Electorate Impact the United Nations?

Edward C. Luck

The good news is that the United Nations, for once, is not being ignored in this year's United States presidential election campaign. The bad news is that the world body, for once, is not being ignored in the campaign. Will this increased attention augur a fundamental shift in the U.S. approach to the organization? Experience counsels modest expectations.

On the one hand, the number of references to the U.N. by both sides belies the often repeated claim by U.S. President George W. Bush and his supporters that the organization is on the brink of irrelevancy. Both the President and his presumptive Democratic rival, Senator John Kerry, have called for paying U.N. dues, exercising global leadership and reforming the U.N. to enhance its effectiveness. Both claim to be friends of the world body and proponents of its purposes and principles. To no one's surprise, neither candidate has been inclined so far to offer much in the way of details or strategies for accomplishing these goals. What is unusual is how often each side has invoked the name and image of the U.N. to stir core constituencies and to highlight the differences between themselves.

On the other hand, one should not mistake frequent references to the U.N. for a debate about the world body. As of this writing, there is little reason to expect its name to emerge over the campaign. The United Nations, quite simply, is unlikely to be a campaign issue when the debates get going this fall. Controversies over the twin wars on terrorism and Iraq have already assured that the stewardship of American foreign policy will be on the minds of the electorate and the candidates far more acutely than in years past. So there will be instrumental and symbolic references to the United Nations—instrumental because so much of the visible drama of U.S. diplomacy is played out on the U.N. stage, and symbolic because its place in the conduct of U.S. foreign policy remains a polarizing issue in domestic politics. The key questions, however, will not be about the forum, but about the ends the Bush Administration sought to achieve in Iraq and the tactics it employed there in the run-up to and aftermath of the U.S.-led intervention.

Many in the U.N. community are no doubt pleased to see the growing debate in the U.S. over the allegedly unilateralist instincts of the Bush Administration. Those calling on Washington to adopt a more U.N.-centric foreign policy may well feel a dual sense of vindication and optimism. But caution is in order. Bad news for President Bush or for neoconservative strategists may not translate into good news for the United Nations. Public doubts about the war in Iraq have not led to enthusiasm for the organization. In late August 2003, when asked by the Gallup Organization how the Security Council's lack of support for the invasion affected their "view of the United Nations," 55 percent of Americans polled said "less favorably" compared with 15 percent who said "more favorably." That survey, strikingly, found the highest "poor performance" response–60 percent–in the more than 50 years that Gallup has been asking Americans, "Do you think the United Nations is doing a good job or a poor job in trying to solve the problems it has had to face?" In just 18 months, public ratings of the U.N.'s performance went from their highest levels to lowest levels in history. When Gallup again posed that question in February 2004, the news was no better, with 60 percent still rating the U.N.'s performance "poor." Likewise, a Pew survey in late February-early March 2004 recorded the lowest favorable numbers for the U.N. in its 14 years of polling. These findings persisted long after the Democratic presidential candidates escalated their attacks on the President's unwillingness to delay the war until he could garner broader international support through the Security Council

The demographic breakdown of the February 2004 Gallup survey confirms that conservatives (at 71 percent), as always, are more likely than liberals (at 44 percent) to give the U.N. a poor rating. This helps explain why the President and his Democratic rivals simultaneously delivered sharply divergent messages about the U.N. to their core supporters during the primary season. But the results also suggest that the chances of a pro-U.N. bandwagon appearing during the general election campaign are slim. In the two Gallup surveys, as has been the norm, more educated and more affluent Americans tended to be more critical of the U.N.'s performance (suggesting that ignorance is not the chief source of American complaints about it). The sharpest drop in "good job" responses between January and August 2003, moreover, came from those with a post-graduate education (-22 percent) and from liberals (-19 percent), two seemingly natural constituencies. Though not as hard on the U.N. as Republicans or conservatives were, 57 percent of independents and 58 percent of moderates gave the U.N. a "poor" rating. These are the voters most likely to decide the election.

There are powerful substantive, as well as political, reasons why the terms of the foreign-affairs debate within the U.S. differ so markedly from those employed in the verbal jousting within the Security Council last year. Neither President Bush nor Sen. Kerry would delegate ultimate decisions on the use of American forces to votes within the Council. The "permission slip" analogy employed by the President in his January 2004 State of the Union address has apparently been received warmly on the hustings as well. For his part, Sen. Kerry, in the weeks before the Iowa caucuses, chastised Democratic presidential hopeful Howard Dean for asserting that the U.S. should not have intervened in Iraq without Security Council authorization. In Sen. Kerry's words, "to permit a veto over when America can or cannot act not only becomes little more than a pretext for doing nothing–it cedes our security and presidential responsibility to defend America to someone else–a profound danger for both our national security and global stability." He has criticized the President for rushing to war, for failing to get more allies on board first and for not making the U.N. a full partner in the post-conflict reshaping and rebuilding of Iraq. But his position remains far from the claim voiced by France, Germany, Russia, China and the Secretary-General, among others, that only the Council can legally authorize the use of force.

On two other issues considered litmus tests of America's commitment to multilateralism by many of the President's foreign critics–the *Kyoto Protocol* on global warming and the International Criminal Court (ICC)–Sen. Kerry has not offered a radical departure from past U.S. policies. On Kyoto, he joined 94 Senate colleagues in voting for the resolution insisting that major developing countries be included in the provisions of any future accord. He has repeatedly stressed, however, the importance of moving forward on a revised global convention on curbing greenhouse gases. He has been more circumspect about the ICC, voting for the American Servicemembers' Protection Act, as well as for an amendment that would permit limited U.S. cooperation with the ICC on some egregious cases. On both issues, Sen. Kerry appears to be in the Senate mainstream.

Certainly there are important differences between the world views of President Bush and Sen. Kerry, including their attitudes toward international law and organization. Many of these surfaced in the early months of the campaign, but as President Wilson learned in 1919, President Truman in 1947 and President Clinton in 1995, the conduct of foreign policy by a Democratic president, especially concerning multilateral institutions, is seriously constrained when Republicans hold a majority in Congress. Given his dozen years on the Senate Foreign Relations Committee, Sen. Kerry must be acutely aware of how the separation of powers affects the development and implementation of American policy, particularly on questions as partisan as those involving global norms and institutions.

Presidents set the tone, style and priorities of U.S. foreign policy. Effective and sustainable presidential leadership, however, also requires taking public and Congressional sentiments into account, even as it seeks to shape them. And, as of this writing, there seems to be more domestic support for a change in the style of American diplomacy than in the substance of U.S. goals and policies. Perhaps this is good news for the United Nations, after all, since nowhere do style points matter more than at the world body.

Appendices

Appendix A: United Nations System Chart

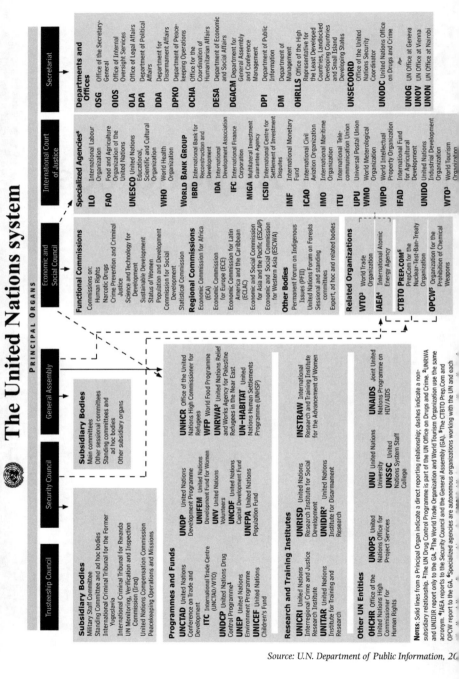

Source: U.N. Department of Public Information, 20

Appendix B: Acronyms

ABM Anti-Ballistic Missile Treaty

ACABQ Advisory Committee on Administrative and Budgetary Questions

ASEAN Association of Southeast Asian Nations

ASP Assembly of States Parties, referring to the International Criminal Court

ATA Afghan Transitional Authority

A.U. African Union

BPOA Barbados Programme of Action

CAP Consolidated Appeals Process, for Humanitarian Assistance

CAR Central African Republic

CBD Convention on Biological Diversity

CBM Confidence Building Measure

CD Conference on Disarmament

CEDAW Convention on the Elimination of All Forms of Discrimination Against Women

CND Commission on Narcotic Drugs

CPC Committee for Program and Coordination

CSD Commission on Sustainable Development

CSW Commission on the Status of Women

CTBT Comprehensive Nuclear Test-Ban Treaty

CTC Counter-Terrorism Committee

DDA Doha Development Agenda

D.G. Director-General

DMZ Demilitarized Zone

DOTS Directly Observed Therapy Short-Course Strategy

DPA United Nations Department of Political Affairs

DPI United Nations Department of Public Information

DPKO United Nations Department of Peacekeeping Operations

DPRK Democratic People's Republic of Korea (North Korea)

DRC Democratic Republic of Congo

DSB Dispute Settlement Body of the World Trade Organization

ECOSOC United Nations Economic and Social Council

ECOWAS Economic Community of West African States

EEZ Exclusive Economic Zone

E.U. European Union

FAO Food and Agriculture Organization

FRY Federal Republic of Yugoslavia

FTAs Free Trade Agreements

G.A. General Assembly

G7 Group of Seven

G8 Group of Eight

GATT General Agreement on Tariffs and Trade

GDP Gross Domestic Product

GNP Gross National Product

GNI Gross National Income

GOARN Global Outbreak Alert and Response Network of the World Health Organization

GPHIN Global Public Health Intelligence Network of the World Health Organization

HIPC Heavily Indebted Poor Countries

HRW Human Rights Watch

IAEA International Atomic Energy Agency

ICC International Criminal Court

ICJ International Court of Justice

ICMP Illicit Crop Monitoring Program

ICRC International Committee of the Red Cross

ICTR International Criminal Tribunal for Rwanda

ICTs Information and Communications Technologies

ICTY International Criminal Tribunal for the Former Yugoslavia

IDF Israel Defense Forces

IDPs Internally Displaced Persons

IEMF European Union-led Interim Emergency Multinational Force in the Congo

ILC International Law Commission

ILO International Labour Organization

IMF International Monetary Fund

IMO International Maritime Organization

INCB International Narcotics Control Board

INTERPOL International Criminal Police Organization

IOM International Organization for Migration

ISAF International Security Assistance Force, Afghanistan

ITLOS International Tribunal for the Law of the Sea

ITU International Telecommunications Union

JIU Joint Inspection Unit

LDC Least-Developed Country

LLDC Landlocked Developing Country

MDGs Millennium Development Goals

MINUCI United Nations Mission in Côte d'Ivoire

MINURSO United Nations Mission for the Referendum in Western Sahara

MINUSTAH United Nations Stabilization Mission in Haiti

MONUC United Nations Organization Mission in the Democratic Republic of Congo

NAFTA North American Free Trade Agreement

NAM Non-Aligned Movement

NATO North Atlantic Treaty Organization

NEPAD The New Partnership for Africa's Development

NGO Nongovernmental Organization

NPT Nuclear Nonproliferation Treaty

NSS National Security Strategy

OAU Organization of African Unity

OCHA Office for the Coordination of Humanitarian Affairs

ODA Official Development Assistance

OECD Organization for Economic Cooperation and Development

OFFP Oil-for-Food Programme

OHCHR Office of the United Nations High Commissioner for Human Rights

ONUB United Nations Operation in Burundi

OSCE Organization for Security and Cooperation in Europe

P-5 Permanent Five Members of the Security Council: the United States, United Kingdom, Russian Federation, France and China

PISG Provisional Institutions of Self-Government

PTBT Partial Test-Ban Treaty

RTAs Regional Trade Agreements

RUF Revolutionary United Front, Sierra Leone

SARS Severe Acute Respiratory Syndrome

S.C. Security Council

SCSL Special Court for Sierra Leone

S.G. Secretary-General

SIDS Small Island Developing States

SFRY Socialist Federal Republic of Yugoslavia

SRSG Special Representative of the Secretary-General

U.K. United Kingdom

U.N. United Nations

UNAIDS United Nations Joint Programme on HIV/AIDS

UNAMA United Nations Assistance Mission in Afghanistan

UNAMSIL United Nations Mission in Sierra Leone

UNCITRAL United Nations Commission on International Trade Law

UNCLOS United Nations Convention of the Law of the Sea

UNCND United Nations Commission on Narcotic Drugs

UNCTAD United Nations Conference on Trade and Development

UNDAF United Nations Development Assistance Framework

UNDC United Nations Disarmament Commission

UNDCP United Nations International Drug Control Programme

UNDG United Nations Development Group

UNDOF United Nations Disengagement Observer Force

UNDP United Nations Development Programme

UNEP United Nations Environment Programme

UNESCO United Nations Educational, Scientific and Cultural Organization

UNFDAC United Nations Fund for Drug Abuse Control

UNFICYP United Nations Peacekeeping Force in Cyprus

UNFIP United Nations Fund for International Partnerships

UNFPA United Nations Population Fund

UNHCHR United Nations High Commissioner for Human Rights

UNHCR United Nations High Commissioner for Refugees

UNICEF United Nations Children's Fund

UNIFEM United Nations Development Fund for Women

UNIFIL United Nations Interim Force in Lebanon

UNIKOM United Nations Iraq-Kuwait Observation Mission

UNMEE United Nations Mission in Ethiopia and Eritrea

UNMIBH United Nations Mission in Bosnia and Herzegovina

UNMIK United Nations Mission in Kosovo
UNMIL United Nations Mission in Liberia
UNMISET United Nations Mission of Support in East Timor
UNMOGIP United Nations Military Observer Group in India and Pakistan
UNMOP United Nations Mission of Observers in Prevlaka
UNMOT United Nations Mission of Observers in Tajikistan
UNMOVIC United Nations Monitoring, Verification and Inspection Commission, Iraq
UNOB United Nations Office in Burundi
UNOCHA United Nations Office for the Coordination of Humanitarian Affairs
UNOCI United Nations Operation in Côte d'Ivoire
UNODC United Nations Office on Drugs and Crime
UNOMIG United Nations Observer Mission in Georgia
UNOMIL United Nations Observer Mission in Liberia
UNOMSIL United Nations Observer Mission in Sierra Leone
UNOPS United Nations Office for Project Services

UNPOB United Nations Political Office in Bougainville
UNPROFOR United Nations Protection Force
UNSCOM United Nations Special Commission for Iraq
UNSIMIC United Nations Settlement Implementation Mission in Cyprus
UNTAET United Nations Transitional Authority in East Timor
UNTOP United Nations Tajikistan Office of Peace-Building
UNTSO United Nations Truce Supervision Organization
U.S. United States
WEHAB Water, Energy, Health, Agriculture and Biodiversity
WFP World Food Programme
WFUNA World Federation of United Nations Associations
WHO World Health Organization
WIPO World Intellectual Property Organization
WMD Weapons of Mass Destruction
WMO World Meteorological Organization
WSSD World Summit on Sustainable Development
WTO World Trade Organization

Appendix C: Glossary

ad hoc For a specific or temporary purpose.

ad litem Latin phrase meaning "for the litigation."

ambassador The highest rank of a diplomatic representative sent by one government to another or to an international organization.

amicus, amici curiae Latin for "third party."

arrears The unpaid portion of a member state's **assessment** for a given financial period.

assessment The amount that a member state must pay as its contribution toward the expenses of the U.N. in the financial period as set out in the relevant budget adopted by the General Assembly.

atrocities Acts of unusual cruelty or brutality, usually perpetrated on large groups of defenseless persons.

autonomy Self-governance.

bilateral An agreement or exchange involving two parties.

Bonn Agreement This December 5, 2001 agreement created an interim administration to lead Afghanistan for two years until a "fully representative government can be elected through free and fair elections."

Bretton Woods Institutions Including the World Bank and International Monetary Fund, the Institutions were set up at a meeting of 43 countries in Bretton Woods, New Hampshire, in July 1944 to help rebuild the shattered postwar economy and to promote international economic cooperation.

Bush Doctrine Also known as the new National Security Strategy (NSS) of the United States, as of September 2002, providing for the preemptive use of force.

coalition Temporary alliance between two or more political units, not necessarily including the United Nations, for the purposes of joint action. In the case of the Spring 2003 Iraq war, the "coalition of the willing" involved primarily the United States, the United Kingdom, Australia and Poland.

collective security A concept that seeks to ensure peace through enforcement by the community of nations.

commission A body created to perform a particular function, whether administrative, legislative or judicial.

Commonwealth of Independent States (CIS) A union of 12 of the 15 former Soviet Republics, created in December 1991 to promote a common economic space and humanitarian policy.

complementarity In legal terms, the principle that states should have the right and duty to investigate and prosecute cases.

Comprehensive Nuclear Test-Ban Treaty (CTBT) Opened for signature on September 10, 1996, it established a global verification regime.

consolidated appeals process (CAP) A mechanism used by aid organizations to plan, implement and monitor their activities; they use this data to produce a Common Humanitarian Action Plan and appeal and then present it to the international community every year.

convention A practice or custom followed by **states parties**. Some international laws are called conventions, such as the *Convention on the Rights of the Child*.

coup d'état A sudden, forceful stroke in politics, especially the violent overthrow or alteration of an existing government.

cross-borrowing Borrowing from one account to meet the needs of another

Dayton Peace Accords An agreement among Bosnia, Herzegovina, Croatia, and the Federal Republic of Yugoslavia in 1995 to respect the sovereignty of each nation and to settle future disputes.

delegate A representative.

delegation A group of delegates.

demilitarized zone (DMZ) The area between the forward line of the parties, into which they have agreed not to deploy military forces and which may be placed under the control of a **peacekeeping operation**.

democracy A form of government in which the right to make political decisions is exercised directly by the whole body of citizens. In direct democracy, citizens rule directly through procedures of majority rule. In representative democracy, citizens exercise the same right not in person but through representatives chosen by them.

developed countries Those with more fully industrialized economies, more productive agriculture and a high standard of living.

developing countries Those not yet fully industrialized and that have limited specialization, not enough financial savings, a population that is outgrowing its resources and a low standard of living.

diplomacy The conduct of relations between nations—often through diplomats, as in making agreements.

diplomatic immunity Special rights given to diplomats, including immunity from the laws that operate in the country to which they are assigned.

disarmament The reduction or removal of armed forces and armaments.

displaced person Someone rendered homeless as a result of war or disaster. An individual fleeing such conditions who crosses a border is considered a **refugee**. Anyone who takes flight but never leaves his/her country is an **internally displaced person**.

draft resolution A document that has been approved by the chairperson for discussion in formal debate; it is written in the form of a U.N. **resolution** but has not been passed by the committee.

dumping In relation to trade, the selling of goods in a foreign market at below the cost of production or at lower than they are sold in the home market.

Economic and Social Council (ECOSOC) A 54-member body elected by the General Assembly to three-year terms; ECOSOC is responsible for coordinating and overseeing the United Nations' economic and social work.

ethnic cleansing The expulsion, imprisonment or killing of ethnic minorities by a dominant majority group.

European Union (E.U.) Headquartered in Brussels, Belgium, this group of 25 countries aims to promote economic and social progress for a strong European presence in the world, as well as to ensure a free, secure and just European citizenship.

free trade Trade carried on without governmental regulations.

G7 Group of Seven First made up of the seven most industrialized nations—Canada, France, Germany, Italy, Japan, the United Kingdom and United States—the group now includes the Russian Federation and is more often referred to as the **Group of Eight**.

G8 Group of Eight *See above.*

G-22 An informal group of developing nations, now known as the **G-20**.

G-77 Group of 77 was established on June 15, 1964 by 77 developing countries and now has 133 members. As the largest developing coalition in the United Nations, the Group of 77 provides the means for the developing world to promote its collective economic interests and enhance its joint negotiating capacity.

General Agreement on Tariffs and Trade (GATT) This 1947 agreement was incorporated into and superseded by the World Trade Organization in January 1995. The 100-plus members of GATT established the norms and rules of international trade, with the aim of reducing trade barriers. WTO offers a dispute-settlement system for enforcing those rules.

General Assembly (G.A.) The central deliberative organ of the United Nations. Each of the 191 **member states** is represented equally and has a vote.

genocide The systematic killing or extermination of a whole people or nation.

Global Fund The Global Fund for HIV/AIDS, Tuberculosis and Malaria is a non-U.N. body but was initiated by Secretary-General Kofi Annan.

grassroots Originating among or carried on by the common people.

gross domestic product (GDP) An economic measure defining the total value of all products manufactured and goods provided within that territory during a specified period (most often, per year). GDP, like **GNP** *(see below)* is used as a means of assessing the condition of a nation's economy.

gross national product (GNP) The value of all the goods and services produced by a country's nationals in a one-year period.

guerrilla A member of a small force of irregular or "rebel" soldiers, usually volunteers, who make surprise raids, etc.

habeas corpus Latin for "you should have the body," requiring the government to produce a prisoner before a court and justify his or her imprisonment.

The Hague Home to numerous international courts and tribunals, located in The Netherlands.

human rights law The set of obligations that regulate state behavior toward groups and individuals in the spheres of political, civil, economic, social and cultural rights.

immunity Exemption from the application of a rule or jurisdiction.

indictment A formal written statement by a court or other authority authorizing a prosecutor to initiate trial on the basis of specified charges.

indigenous Native.

inter alia Latin term for "among other things."

interstate Actions between two or more states or countries.

International Atomic Energy Agency (IAEA) Established in 1957 and headquartered in Vienna, the Agency serves as the world's foremost center for nuclear information and cooperation. IAEA is also the chief inspector of the world's nuclear facilities.

International Court of Justice (ICJ) Also known as the World Court, it is the main judicial organ of the U.N. for settling civil disputes between member states and giving advisory opinions to the U.N. and its agencies; it does not hear cases brought by or against individuals or private organizations nor does it hear criminal cases.

International Criminal Court (ICC) A permanent court with jurisdiction over individuals accused of committing serious war crimes, crimes against humanity or genocide after July 1, 2002.

international criminal law Pertaining to those violations of international law that give rise to individual criminal accountability (e.g., very serious war crimes, crimes against humanity and the crime of aggression).

International Criminal Tribunal for the Former Yugoslavia (ICTY) Established by the Security Council on May 25, 1993, the ICTY is mandated to prosecute persons responsible for serious violations of international humanitarian law committed in the territory of the former Yugoslavia since 1991.

International Criminal Tribunal for Rwanda (ICTR) Established by the Security Council on November 8, 1994, the ICTR is mandated to prosecute persons responsible for genocide and other serious violations of international humanitarian law committed in the territory of Rwanda, or by Rwandan citizens in the territory of neighbor states, between January 1 and December 31, 1994.

international humanitarian law Also called the law of war or armed conflict law, aims to protect persons who are not taking part in hostilities, and restricts the means and methods of fighting.

international law Traditionally defined as the body of agreements and principles governing relations between states, it increasingly regulates state behavior toward non-state actors.

International Law Commission (ILC) Established in 1947 with a membership of 15 persons of recognized competence in international law, it encourages the progressive development of international law and its codification.

internally displaced person (IDP) *See displaced person.*

intifada The word has come to symbolize the Palestinian uprising against the Israeli occupation.

intrastate Actions within a state or country.

Kyoto Protocol 1997 treaty resulting from the U.N. Framework Convention on Climate Change, this agreement outlines goals to limit greenhouse gas emissions and honor gas reduction commitments among the signatory nations.

League of Nations An international organization created after World War I to promote international cooperation and achieve international peace and security. However, when the League fell passive in the face of member states' aggressions, it ceased to exist.

least-developed country (LDC) A country characterized by a low standard of living, limited industrial capabilities and long-term impediments to economic growth.

Loya Jirga A Pashtun phrase meaning "grand council." For centuries, leaders in Afghanistan have convened *Loya Jirgas* to choose new kings, adopt constitutions and decide important political matters. The most recent *Loya Jirga* process was set in motion by the **Bonn Agreement** of December 5, 2001.

mandate An authoritative command given by the Security Council or General Assembly to a U.N. mission or representative.

maquiladora Assembly production in Mexico using U.S. resources.

member state One of the current 191 countries belonging to the United Nations.

Millennium Summit Conference that took place from September 6-8, 2000 at U.N. Headquarters in New York City, assembling 150 heads of state and government to tackle global challenges. At this Summit, the *Millennium Declaration* was created, which outlines the eight Millennium Development Goals.

Montreal Protocol Originally signed in 1987 and amended in 1990 and 1992, this international pact aims to protect the stratospheric ozone layer.

multilateral Involving or participated in by more than two nations or parties (as in multilateral agreements).

nation Individuals in a specific geographical area who share common customs, history, language, etc., under the rule of one government.

nation-state A state with a single predominant national identity.

national interest Interests specific to a nation-state, especially including survival and maintenance of power.

Non-aligned Countries An alliance of Third World states, it aims to promote the political and economic interests of developing countries. At the United Nations, it is referred to as the Non-aligned Movement.

nongovernmental organization (NGO) A not-for-profit organization that contributes to development through cooperative projects, financial and material aid, the dispatch of personnel and education. Some NGOs are accredited by the United Nations system and can represent their interests before ECOSOC.

North American Free Trade Agreement (NAFTA) An agreement that entered into force in January 1994 among Canada, the United States and Mexico.

North Atlantic Treaty Organization (NATO) Formed on April 4, 1949, when 12 independent nations signed the North Atlantic Treaty and committed to each other's defense, it grew by four more nations between 1952 and 1982 and now has 26 members.

Nuclear Nonproliferation Treaty (NPT) Taking effect in 1970, it was intended to limit the number of states with nuclear weapons to five: the United States, the Soviet Union, the United Kingdom, France and China. More than 140 states have pledged not to acquire nuclear weapons and to accept the safeguards of the International Atomic Energy Agency.

observer mission Unarmed officers to staff observation posts for monitoring ceasefires and armistices.

peace enforcement Also known as third-generation peacekeeping, peace-enforcing does not require consent from the conflicting parties and is undertaken to protect the populace from an aggressor or a civil war.

peacekeeper Person assigned the task of helping to maintain peace where conflict has just ended. Peacekeepers can include civilian staff whereas "peacekeeping soldiers" cannot.

peacekeeping operation An operation involving military personnel, but under the precepts of impartiality and neutrality, undertaken by the U.N. to help maintain or restore international peace and security in areas of conflict. Peacekeeping has evolved into second-generation peacekeeping (preventive diplomacy and post-conflict peace-building), which is often multidimensional, based on the consent of the parties involved and has a greater and riskier U.N. role. Third-generation peacekeeping refers to peace enforcement.

peace-building mission Aimed at development activities in post-conflict regions to ensure that the conflict does not reignite.

peacemaking Diplomatic process of brokering an end to conflict, principally through mediation and negotiation. Military activities contributing to peacemaking include military-to-military contacts, security assistance, shows of force and preventive deployments.

permanent five (P5) Refers to the five permanent members of the U.N. **Security Council**: the United States, Russian Federation, United Kingdom, China and France.

political office U.N. political offices work to support the peacekeeping and peacebuilding missions through reconciliation and negotiation between parties.

preventive deployment Interposition of a military force to deter violence in a zone of potential conflict where tension is rising among parties.

preventive diplomacy Also known as conflict prevention, this action prevents disputes from arising between parties and limits.

protocol A document that records the basic agreements reached in negotiations before the final form in which the agreement appears.

recosting This U.N. budgetary practice provides for adjustments of foreign exchange rates and inflation assumptions during a budgetary cycle.

referendum The principle or practice of submitting to popular vote a measure passed on or proposed by a legislative body or by popular initiative.

refugee *See displaced person.*

regular budget Includes expenditures of the U.N. Secretariat in New York, the U.N. offices in Geneva, Vienna and Nairobi, the regional commissions as well as the International Court of Justice and the Center for Human Rights in Geneva. More than 70 percent of the U.N. regular budget is earmarked for staff costs. The scale of assessment (how much each country owes) is based on the principle of capacity to pay.

repatriate To restore or return to the country of origin, allegiance or citizenship.

resolution A document passed by a committee or body that expresses the opinions and decisions of the United Nations

rule of law A term recently used to describe the activities during peacebuilding that re-establish the rule of law, in opposition to the rule of power. Activities include such things as rebuilding courts and rewriting constitutions.

sanction A coercive economic or military measure, usually adopted by several nations in concert, for forcing a nation violating international law to desist or yield to adjudication.

Security Council (S.C.) The organ of the United Nations with responsibility for maintaining peace and security is composed of five permanent members (France, China, the Russian Federation, the United Kingdom and United States) and 10 rotating members elected to two-year terms by the General Assembly so that they represent a geographical distribution.

Secretariat The U.N. organ responsible for running the daily affairs of the organization. The Secretariat is made up of international civil servants and led by the **Secretary-General**. *(See below.)*

Secretary-General The chief administrative officer of the U.N. and head of the **Secretariat**. *(See above.)*

self-determination Freedom of the people of a given area to determine their own political status or independence.

sovereign The highest or supreme political authority.

state-building (nation-building) The concept of rebuilding a post-conflict country, most often so that the sovereignty of the nation is recognized by the international community.

state party Countries that are party to— or have joined as a member—a particular group or have signed/ratified a particular protocol, convention or other docment.

sustainable development A newer, widely used international term for development that meets the needs of the present without compromising the ability of future generations to meet their own needs.

terrorism The systematic use of terror or unpredictable violence against governments, the public or individuals to attain a political objective.

treaty A formal, binding international agreement. In the U.S., treaties proposed by the executive branch and negotiated with a foreign country must be approved by a two-thirds majority in the Senate and ratified by the President.

Trusteeship Council The U.N. body originally given jurisdiction over 11 former colonies. The Council agenda shrank as one trust territory after another achieved independence or merged with a neighbor.

United Nations Charter The fundamental set of rules according to which the United Nations exists and operates. It was drawn up and signed by the representatives of 50 countries in 1945.

Universal Declaration of Human Rights **(UDHR)** A historic proclamation of the basic rights and freedoms to which all men and women are entitled adopted by the General Assembly on December 10, 1948, commemorated every year as Human Rights Day.

war crime A crime, such as genocide or maltreatment of prisoners, committed during or in connection with war.

World Bank A multilateral lending agency that aims to reduce poverty by promoting sustainable economic growth.

Index

A

Abaka, Charlotte, 74–75
Abbas, Mahmoud, 140–42
Abe, Nobuyasu, 169
Abizaid, John, 162
Abkhazia. *See* Georgia-Abkhazia
Abu Ghraib, 230, 231–32
ACABQ, 264, 265, 268–73
Administrative issues. *See* Personnel and administrative issues of U.N.
Adolescent health and rights, 93–94
Afghan Counter-Narcotics Directorate, 190
Afghan Donors Conference, 121
Afghan Independent Human Rights Commission, 65
Afghanistan, 186
    humanitarian assistance, 85–86
    human rights, 64–66, 78
    narcotics, 149, 190–91
    peacekeeping operations, 119–22
    U.N. offices, bombing of, 120
    women, rights of, 42, 65
Africa
    development, partnership for, 47–49
    food emergencies, 39–40
    humanitarian assistance, 81, 83
    peacekeeping operations, 108–18
    regional trade agreements (RTAs), 242–43
African Charter on Human and People's Rights, 74
African Mission in Burundi (AMIB), 87
African Union Summit, 17
Agenda for Further Change, 280
Ageing, 41–42
Agricultural goods, Doha Development Agenda, 234–36
AIDS. *See* HIV/AIDS
AKEL Party, 129
al-Sadr, Moktada, 159
Alexandre, Boniface, 70
Algiers Peace Accord, 113
Allawi, Ayad, 140
Alleyne, George, 10
All-Parties Hurriyat Conference, 124
Almaty Programme of Action, 43
Al Qaeda, 186, 191, 230
Al-Sistani, Ali, 138, 139
Al-Yawar, Ghazi, 140
American Physical Society, 180
American Servicemembers' Protection Act of 2002 (ASPA), 217, 294

American University of Beirut, 291
Americas
    peacekeeping operations, 118–19
    regional trade agreements (RTAs), 243–44
AMIB. *See* African Mission in Burundi
Amnesty International, 68, 70
Amor, Mohsen Bel Hadj, 258
Andean Community, 244
Angola, humanitarian assistance, 86–87
Annan, Kofi, 1, 107
    cross-borrowing, 277–79
    Darfur, 148
    donation by, 10
    environment, sustaining, 33
    genocide, prevention, 64
    Global Coalition on Women and AIDS, 11
    human rights, 58
    Afghanistan, 65
    India-Pakistan dialogue, 123
    international community, call to, 7
    Israel-Palestine, 142
    Millennium Development Goals, meeting, 50, 52, 53
    Myat, firing of, 166
    Nepal, 147
    official development assistance, on, 46
    reform of United Nations, 253–54, 256–57
    Special Envoys on HIV/AIDS, 10
    Task Force on HIV/AIDS, 6
    women in developing countries, 42
Antiretroviral drugs (ARVs), 2
    access to, 7–8
    generic, 8
Apparel, Doha Development Agenda, 234
Arab human development, 290–91
Arab nationalism, 193
Arafat, Yasser, 141–42
Arbour, Louise, 61, 78
Aristide, Jean-Bertrand, 70, 90–91, 118–19
Artemis, 69
Arusha Accords, 87
ARVs. *See* Antiretroviral drugs
ASEAN. *See* Association of South East Asian Nations
Asia
    peacekeeping operations, 119–26
    regional trade agreements (RTAs), 246

Asia-Pacific Economic Cooperation, 246–47
ASPA. *See* American Servicemembers' Protection Act of 2002
The Assembly, *See* General Assembly and/or specific General Assembly session number
Assembly of States Parties, 216
Assembly resolution. *See specific resolution*
Assessments. *See* Financial situation of United Nations
Association of South East Asian Nations (ASEAN), 246
ATS (amphetamine-type stimulants), 192
Avian influenza, 14
Axworthy, Lloyd, 113
Ayala-Lasso, José, 60
Aznar, José Maria, 161

B

Babic, Milan, 223
Badinter, Robert, 255
Baker, James, 165
Bananas, dispute over, 238–39
Bangladesh Rural Action Committee, 66
Banovic, Predrag, 223
Barak, Ehud, 142
Barayagwiza, Jean-Bosco, 227
Barbados Programme of Action (BPOA), 34
Bassiouni, Cherif, 66
Ba'th Party, 159–60
Beef, hormone-fed, 238–39
Beijing Platform for Action, 67
Beilin, Yossi, 142
Beirut, American University, 291
Bellagio Child Survival Study Group, 23
Bertini, Catherine, 263, 268, 274, 277–78
Bicamumpaka, Jerome, 228
Biological diversity, maintaining, 36–38
Biological weapons, 179
Biological Weapons Convention, 179
Biosafety, 36
Bizimungu, Casimir, 228
Blair, Tony, 34, 163–64, 167
Blaney, John W., 115
Blix, Hans, 164
Bolivia, conflict, 145–46
Bondevik, Kjell Magne, 183
Bonn Agreement (2001), 64, 65, 66
Bonomy, Iain, 219

Nikolic, Dragan, 223
Nikolic, Momir, 223
Niyitegeka, Eliézer, 226
Noncommunicable diseases, prevention of, 20–21
Nonproliferation Treaty (NPT), 169, 170–71
Review Conference, 176
Nonproliferation, United Nations' role, 169–71
North American Free Trade Agreement (NAFTA), 243, 244–47
North Atlantic Treaty Organization (NATO), 120, 121, 132–35
North Korea. See Democratic People's Republic of Korea
North-South ideological divide, 81–82
NPT. See Nonproliferation Treaty
Nunn-Lugar Cooperative Threat Reduction Program (CTR), 178, 180
Nzirorera, Joseph, 228

O

OAS. See Organization of American States
Obote, Milton, 148
Obrenovic, Dragan, 223
Ocean resources, preserving, 35–36
OCHA. See U.N. Office for the Coordination of Humanitarian Affairs
ODA. See Official Development Assistance
OECD. See Organization for Economic Co-operation and Development
Offenheiser, Raymond C., 236
Office of the High Commissioner for Human Rights (OHCHR), 60–62, 64
Afghanistan, 65
Consolidated Appeals Process (CAP), 81–82
Democratic Republic of Congo, 69
humanitarian assistance, 80, 81
indigenous rights, decade of, 77
Recommended Principles and Guidelines on Human Rights and Human Trafficking, 102
terrorism and, 186
Official Development Assistance (ODA), 46–48
OFFP. See Oil-for-Food Programme
Ogata, Sadako, 256
OHCHR. See Office of the High Commissioner for Human Rights

Oil-for-Food Programme (OFFP), 91
Okello, Tito, 148
ONUB. See U.N. Operation in Burundi
OPCW. See Organisation for the Prohibition of Chemical Weapons
Opium Poppy Survey, 149
Organisation for the Prohibition of Chemical Weapons (OPCW), 178–79
Organisation of Security and Cooperation in Europe (OSCE), 125
Organisation for Economic Co-operation and Development (OECD), 235
Organization of American States (OAS), 90, 185
Organization of the Islamic Conference, 17
OSCE. See Organisation of Security and Cooperation in Europe
Oxfam, 236

P

PAHO. See Pan American Health Organization
Pakistan. See also India-Pakistan weapons of mass destruction (WMD), 175–76
Palestine. See Israel-Palestine
Pan American Health Organization (PAHO), 24
Panitchpakdi, Supachai, 233
Panyarachun, Anand, 253
Papadopoulos, Tassos, 129
Parnohadiningrat, Sudjadnan, 170
Pavkovic, Nebojsa, 224
Peacekeeping operations, 107–56
Afghanistan, 119–22
Africa, 108–18
Americas, 118–19
Asia, 119–126
assessments, 277–79
Bolivia, 145–46
Bougainville, 122
budgets, 271–73
Côte d'Ivoire, 111–13, 271–73, 278
cross-borrowing, 277–79
Cyprus, 127–30, 272
Darfur, 147–48
Democratic Republic of Congo, 110–11, 272
Eritrea, 113–14, 272
Ethiopia, 113–14, 272
Europe, 127–36
forecasting, 118, 126, 135–36, 145

Georgia-Abkhazia, 130–32, 136
Haiti, 118–19, 271, 273
India-Pakistan, 122–24
Iraq, 136–40
Israel-Palestine, 140–44
Kosovo, 132–35, 271–72, 275, 278
Lebanon and Golan Heights, 144–45, 272
Liberia, 114–16, 271–72
looming conflicts, 145–48
Middle East, 136–45
Nepal, 146–47
Sierra Leone, 116, 271–72, 279
Sudan, 147–48, 259, 272, 278
Tajikistan, 124–25, 276
Timor-Leste, 125–26, 271
Uganda, 148
Western Sahara, 116–18, 272, 275, 278
Peace Plan for Self-Determination of the People of Western Sahara, 117–18
Peace Process Consultative Committee, 122
People of Taiwan, donations, 10
"Permission slip" analogy, 293
Personnel and administration issues of U.N., 258–63
administration of justice, 259
capital master plan, 261–63
hazard pay, 258–59
Joint Inspection Unit (JIU), 261
Secretariat, composition of, 260–61
staff partner entitlements, 259–60
Pharmaceuticals. See Drugs
Philippines, 52
Piot, Peter, 5
PISG. See Provisional Institutions of Self-Government
PNTL. See Policia Nacional de Timor-Leste
Policia Nacional de Timor-Leste (PNTL), 126
Polio, 16–18
POLISARIO. See Frente Popular de Liberación de Saguía el Hamra y Río de Oro
Population, poverty and, 41–42
Poverty, population and, 41–42
Powell, Colin, 157, 164, 166
Israel-Palestine, 143
North Korea, 171
Prachanda, Comrade, 146
Preparatory Committee (PrepCom), 169, 170–71
Primakov, Yevgeny, 256
Prison abuse, 230–31
Programme of Action, 43, 48, 51

MEMBERSHIP APPLICATION

Join UNA-USA today and become part of a nationwide movement for a more effective United Nations!

The United Nations Association of the United States of America (UNA-USA) is the nation's largest grassroots foreign policy organization and the leading center of policy research on the U.N. and global issues. UNA-USA offers Americans the opportunity to connect with issues confronted by the U.N. and encourages public support for strong U.S. leadership in the United Nations. UNA-USA is a member of the World Federation of United Nations Associations.

For more information, visit our website at **www.unausa.org**.

To join UNA-USA, please return this form, along with your payment to UNA-USA, to:

UNA-USA MEMBERSHIP SERVICES
801 Second Avenue, New York, NY 10017

___ $1,000 Lifetime (one-time dues payment)

___ $500 Patron

___ $100 Sponsor

___ $40 Member

___ $25 Introductory (first year only)

___ $25 Limited Income

___ $10 Student

___ Please send me information on UNA-Student Alliances.

___ Please send me information on making a Planned Gift through the Eleanor Roosevelt Society.

NAME

ADDRESS

CITY, STATE AND ZIP

HOME PHONE

BUSINESS PHONE

EMAIL

In addition to my membership dues, I would like to make a contribution to:

___ UNA-USA National Programs in the amount of $_____

___ My Local UNA-USA Chapter in the amount of $_____

(Contributions are tax deductible to the extent provided by law.)

NAME ON CREDIT CARD

BILLING ADDRESS

Check one:

___ AMEX ___ MasterCard ___ Visa

CREDIT CARD NUMBER

EXPIRATION DATE

SIGNATURE

Membership in UNA-USA is open to any citizen or resident of the United States of America who is committed to the purposes of UNA-USA, a 501(c)3 not-for-profit educational organization.

320